Eucharist
Through The
Centuries

A selection of Eucharistic texts beginning with the Bible and continuing through the patristic medieval and modern eras.

Roberto de la Vega, Archdiocese of Santa Fe

ISBN 0-9651601-2-2

Printed in the United States of America
First Printing, July 1998

Circle Press
Hamden, CT

Contents

Chapter VIII 173

THE EUCHARIST IN THE FIFTH CENTURY

THE EUCHARIST IN THE SIXTH CENTURY

Preface

The main purpose of this work is to trace elements of Eucharistic doctrine from the day our Lord Jesus Christ announced it for the first time in the synagogue in Capernaum (John, Chapter 6) down to our own day. The doctrine is tracked from the words themselves of those who were witnesses to the doctrine in their day and in their locality, as we find their testimony in the rich legacy of their writings.

Despite the ravages of time and the wanton destruction by Vandal and Moorish invaders, there is a surprisingly large amount of documentary evidence for the Catholic Church's teaching on the Eucharist. The evidence is both clear and constant, and is gathered from all parts of the world where Christianity had spread.

Although most aspects of the Church's Eucharistic doctrine are found in this work, special regard has been paid to what has come to be called simply "the Real Presence." This doctrine, defined especially by the Ecumenical Council of Trent in 1551, holds that, after the consecration of the bread and wine at Mass, "our Lord Jesus Christ, true God and true man, is contained truly, really and substantially" under what appears to be bread and wine. In tracing elements of Eucharistic doctrine throughout its history, emphasis was given to the Real Presence, because there can no longer be any doubt that many Catholics today are ignorant of this doctrine or simply deny it. This is seen not only from what they say and write about the Eucharist, but also from the way they conduct themselves in the presence of the Blessed Sacrament, and even from the manner in which they receive Holy Communion.

An effort has been made to present this work in a series of meditations on the Eucharist. The author hoped not only to instruct the mind with truth, but also to move the will to love the truth presented, so that the reader will be able better to know and love our blessed Savior in His Eucharistic presence. Therefore, where it appeared that the sequence would not be unduly disturbed, to the doctrinal content on most pages there has been added a thought to warm the reader's heart.

As we trace the doctrine of the Eucharist through the ages, we notice that the doctrine remained the same, as of course it must. However, the various witnesses to the doctrine present it from differrent aspects, as could be expected. One might compare their testimony to a cut diamond. The diamond is one and remains the same, as does the doctrine. And just as the various facets of the diamond give it a different appearance, so also the historical witnesses to the doctrine of the Eucharist present it from different angles.

To preserve wherever possible the format of a meditation on each page, and to avoid a sense of repitition, after the presentation of the doctrine by the historical witness there follows on most pages a gentle reminder of the apex of the Eucharistic sacrifice on Calvary. The three crosses are usually followed by a short quotation from Sacred Scripture, the Liturgy of the Hours, or an ancient hymn. Anyone desiring to read only the historical witness to the doctrine may, of course, omit everything following the three crosses without any loss.

Feast of Corpus Christi, 1996   Rev. Roberto de la Vega
Belen, New Mexico

✝ ✝ ✝

Author's Note of Appreciation

I am most grateful to two of my fellow workers in the Archdiocese of Santa Fe, Father Laurier A. Labreche of Albuquerque and Father Arthur Anstiss of Socorro, NM, as well as to Mrs. Rita Sonski of Somers, CT, and Miss Betty Tagney of Socorro, NM, and Mr.Carey Kangas of Albuquerque.

All of them were good enough to proofread my manuscript and offer suggestions, which I was glad to incorporate in this work.

Acknowledgment and Abbreviation of Authors and Authorities Quoted or Cited

A.F.   Latin Hymns, by Rev. Adrian Fortescue; 1913; Roman Catholic Books; Harrison, N.Y.

A. Flannery   VATICAN COUNCIL II, The Counciliar and Post-Counciliar Documents, edited by Austin Flannery, O.P.; The Liturgical Press; Collegeville, Minn.

Cayre   Manual of Patrology, by F. Cayre, A.A.; translated by H. Howitt, A.A., B.A.; Desclee & Co.; Tournai, Belgium; 1936; 2 Vols.

C.C.C.   CATECHISM OF THE CATHOLIC CHURCH

DS   ENCHIRIDION SYMBOLORUM, DEFINITIONUM ET DECLARATIONUM de rebus fidei et morum; edited by Henry Denzinger and Adolf Schoemetzer, S.J.; 36th. edition; 1976; B. Herder Book Co.; St. Louis, Mo.

De Journel   Enchiridion Patristicum, edited by M. J. De Journel, S. J.; Latin-Greek texts; 1953; B. Herder Book Co.; Friburg, Bris. Most quotations are my English translation of the Latin texts.

De la Taille   MYSTERIUM FIDEI de Augustissimo Corporis et Sanguinis Christi Sacrificio atque Sacramento, by Maurice de la Taille, S.J.; third edition; 1931; Gabriel Beauchesne; Paris, France. Most of my explanations of the Mass are based on this Latin work.

E   EUCARISTIA; a Eucharistic Encyclopedia, written by 28 French authors and published under the direction of Maurice Brillant by Dedebec, Ediciones Desclee, de Brouwer; the authorized Spanish translation was published in Buenos Aires in 1949. Quotations from Medieval and Modern authors are my translations from the Spanish text.

Abbreviations of Biblical Books:

Co-Corinthians; Gen-Genesis; Jn, John-Gospel of St.John; Lk-Gospel of St. Luke; Mal-Malachi; Mt, Math-Gospel of St. Matthew; Mk-Gospel of St. Mark; Rev-Book of Revelation

Jungmann   MISSARUM SOLEMNIA: THE MASS OF THE ROMAN RITE; Its origins and Development, by Rev. Joseph A. Jungmann, S.J.; translated from the German by Rev. Francis A.Brunner, C.SS.R; 1951; Benzinger Bros. Inc.; New York; 2 Vols. This work was used to verify quotations from other sources.

Kirch   ENCHIRIDION FONTIUM HISTORIAE ECCLESIASTICAE ANTIQUAE; edited by Conrad Kirch, S.J.; 6th edition; Latin-Greek; 1947; B. Herder Book Co.; Barcelona, Spain. Most of my quotations from this work are my English translation of the Latin text.

Laux   CHURCH HISTORY, by John J. Laux, M.A.; 1945 edition; Benzinger Bros.,Inc.; New York

Mourret-Thompson   HISTORY OF THE CATHOLIC CHURCH, by Rev. Fernand Mourret,S.S. & Rev. Newton Thompson,S.T.D.; 8 Vols.; 1946; B. Herder Book Co.; St. Louis, Mo.

Papal Documents   NCWC News Service; St. Paul Editions

Quasten   PATROLOGY, by Johannes Quasten; 2 Vols.; The Newman Press; Westminster, Md.

Sources   The Sources of Catholic Dogma; Roy J. Deferrari's English translation of Denzinger's Enchiridion Symbolorum (30th edition); 1955; B. Herder Book Co.; St. Louis, Mo.

TEP   TEXTOS EUCARISTICOS PRIMITIVOS; edited by Jesus Solano,S.J.; 2 Vols.; Biblioteca de Autores Cristianos; 1978; Madrid, Spain. Bilingual, with original Patristic texts and Fr. Solano's Spanish translation. My English translations were from his Spanish text.

Chapter I

THE EUCHARIST, PREFIGURED IN THE OLD TESTAMENT

The sacrifice of the Mass was prefigured in the Old Testament by the various sacrifices mentioned from the time of Adam and Eve until the time of our Lord. Indeed, since the Mass is the consummation and perfection of all those sacrifices, it contains every kind of good that the ancient sacrifices signified (Trent, DS 1742).

One of the outstanding milestones in the history of salvation was the calling of Abraham by God to become the father of the Jewish race. From the Jews salvation would be offered to all mankind by our Lord Jesus Christ, a descendant of Abraham by his birth as man. Abraham lived nearly twenty centuries before Christ, just as we live about twenty centuries after Christ.

Of all the types or figures of the Mass in the Old Testament the best known is the sacrifice of bread and wine that Melchisedek, King of Salem (Jerusalem), offered in thanksgiving for Abraham's victory in battle (Gen 14). Although not a Jew, Melchisedek believed in the one, true God: "He was a priest of God Most High." At that time God had not yet instituted the Jewish (levitical) priesthood. Psalm 110 presents Melchisedek as a figure of the future Messiah (Jesus Christ), who is also to be both king and priest. In Chapter 7 of his Letter to the Hebrews, St. Paul develops similarities between Melchisedek and our Lord. One similarity of particular interest is the fact that the Bible mentions no predecessor or successor of Melchisedek in his priesthood. So too with Christ. His priesthood is eternal; and he shares it with human priests, who do not succeed him but who exercise his priestly powers and authority in his name.

† † †

Help us, O Lord to learn
The truths thy Word imparts:
To study that thy laws may be
Inscribed upon our hearts.
W.W.Reid

Besides the various foreshadowings of the Eucharist found in the sacrifices mentioned in the Old Testament, especially that of Melchisedech, there is an explicit prophecy of the Mass made by the Prophet Malachi about 440 years before Christ (3). Disobeying specific liturgical instructions that God had given, the Jewish priests were offering defective animals in sacrifice to God. God had instituted the sacrifice of animals as the highest liturgical act of worship, but the priests were offering animals that were blind or lame or diseased. God told them to offer such animals to their leader and see if the man would be pleased with them! "I am not pleased with you, says Yahweh Sabaoth; from your hands I find no offerings acceptable."

Through the Prophet Malachi God then spoke of a pure sacrifice that would be acceptable to him and would be offered not only by the Jews but also by the Gentiles (non-Jews, "the nations"). It would be offered not only in the Temple in Jerusalem, but also throughout the world, "east and west." "From farthest east to farthest west my name is honored among the nations and everywhere a sacrifice of incense is offered to my name, and a pure offering too, since my name is honored among the nations, says Yahweh Sabaoth."

In the Ecumenical Council of Trent the Church identified the Mass with that "pure sacrifice" that Malachi mentions. "And this (the Mass) is surely that pure offering which cannot be contaminated by any unworthiness or any malice of those offering it. (The Mass) is that pure offering which the Lord, through Malachi, foretold to be offered everywhere to God's name, which would be great among the nations" (4).

Malachi was the last, or one of the last, of the Old Testament Prophets. It is worth noting that it was through him that God would make the prediction concerning the Mass, which makes present the "pure sacrifice" of Christ on our altars throughout the world until the end of time (5).

(3) Malachi 1: 1-11 (4) DS 1742 (5) S,1,6
Hidden God,devoutly I adore you. (St. Thomas A.)

.

Chapter II

CHRIST PROMISES THE EUCHARIST

After considering that the Eucharist was prefigured and prophesied in the Old Testament,we turn now to the New Testament. There we find Jesus promising to give the Eucharist not only to his listeners, but also to all those who would be properly disposed by faith in him. We find this great promise in St. John's Gospel, Chapter 6.

Reputable Bible scholars believe that John wrote his Gospel in his old age, some time between the years 90 and 100 a.d. This would have been 60 to 70 years after he had witnessed the events in Christ's public life. The other three Evangelists (Matthew, Mark and Luke) had written their Gospels some years earlier. John, therefore, does not narrate the miracles of Jesus that the other three had narrated. However, it is interesting to note that John makes an exception with the two miracles Jesus worked to facilitate faith in the Eucharist, namely the multiplication of the loaves and his walking on the water.

On one occasion the Apostles returned very tired from a missionary journey. Knowing they could get no rest in the city, Jesus took them by boat to an isolated place across the Sea of Galilee, some 6 to 8 miles from the city. But many people saw the direction in which the boat was headed, so they walked along the shore of the Sea and arrived before the boat. Jesus taught the people and healed their sick. Late in the afternoon the Apostles told him to dismiss the people, so they could find lodging and food in the nearby villages. There was a little boy in the crowd who was carrying five round barley loaves of bread, each about ten inches in diameter and about half an inch thick. He also carried two salted fish. Jesus made the people sit on the grass in companies of hundreds and fifties. With their multicolored clothing they looked like huge flower beds. Jesus took the bread and fish, looked up to heaven, blessed them, and gave them to the Apostles to distribute among the people as much as they wanted. The bread and the fish kept multiplying in the hands of the Apostles, until all five thousand men (not counting women and children) had had their fill. They even filled twelve hampers with scraps of bread that were left over. Jesus had wanted to prepare the

Apostles, the people and us to accept the great promise of the Eucharist he would announce the following day. But the people, overwhelmed by the tremendous miracle they had seen and partaken of, were about to take him by force and make him king.

Seeing the reaction of the crowd that wanted to make him king, Jesus ordered the Apostles to return by boat to the city (Capernaum). He dismissed the people and retired to the nearby hills to pray. Did he pray that all mankind would accept the doctrine of the Eucharist he would announce for the first time the following day? Did he pray that all members of his Church would treat the Eucharist with the proper respect?

While our Lord was spending the night in prayer, the Apostles were having a hard time rowing the six miles back to Capernaum. It was already "the fourth watch," that is, between three and six o'clock in the morning, and the Apostles were only half way to their destination due to a strong head wind. Jesus, after having shown that bread is but a creature in his hands, a creature with which he could do as he wished, now would show the Apostles that his human body also was likewise a creature subject to his divine power.

Jesus came walking on the water toward the Apostles struggling with their boat. Seeing him at some distance and not recognizing him, they were terrified and cried out, "It is a ghost!" (Unless noted otherwise all quotations are from John, Chapter 6.) Jesus shouted to them, "Courage! It is I. Do not be afraid."

The Apostle Peter, perhaps a little ecstatic over the multiplication of the loaves, dared to answer Jesus by saying, "Lord, if it is you, tell me to come to you across the water. Jesus wanted to teach Peter, the other Apostles and us the necessity of having faith and trust in God's words, especially when we deal with the Eucharist. So Jesus says to Peter, "Come." Peter gets out of the boat and starts walking across the water toward Jesus. But when he realizes how strong the wind is, he loses his confidence and begins to sink. "Lord, save me!" he cries out. Jesus puts out his hand immediately and holds Peter up, while he says to him, "Man of little faith, why did you doubt?" As Jesus and Peter get into the boat, the wind stops.

The Apostles show they finally understand the essential meaning of the two miracles by bowing down to Jesus and declaring, "Truly you are the Son of God."

† † †

Soul of Christ, sanctify me.
Body of Christ, save me.

Jesus had worked the miracle of the loaves on a Thursday, almost a year to the day when he would institute the Eucharist on the first Holy Thursday. The crowd that had remained all night knew that Jesus had not gone in the one and only boat belonging to one of the Apostles. The next day they looked for Jesus; but not finding him, they returned to Capernaum on foot or in the boats that had come for them. The day was Friday.

That evening at the first Sabbath service in the synagogue some who had witnessed the miracle of the loaves asked Jesus when and how he had returned to Capernaum. Their question gave Jesus an easy opportunity to start his great discourse on the Eucharist. He read their hearts. He could see that the spiritual content and meaning of the miracle of the previous day had not occurred to them, that their hearts were set only on the material blessing. The people had not recognized God working the miracle of multiplying the bread; they saw only the bread that had been miraculously multiplied. "You are not looking for me because you have seen miracles, but because you had all the bread you wanted to eat. That rebuke or correction by Jesus may seem harsh; but he saw that it was necessary for them, just as it is for us when we pray for material benefits only. Jesus corrects them: "Do not work for food that cannot last," that is, material food, food that perishes, material blessings. Rather, Jesus says, "Work for food that endures to eternal life," that is, supernatural food, the Eucharist, which gives us the life and strength to enter heaven, not like the miraculous bread they had eaten the day before and which sustains life only for a little while.

29

When Jesus was able to turn their minds away from material things to those spiritual, the people showed some good will by asking him what they must do to please God: "What must we do if we are to do the works that God wants?" What God the Father wanted them to do most at that time was to recognize Jesus as the Father's ambassador, as the Messiah, as the Christ, the Savior. If they did that, they would believe the words of Jesus about the Eucharist and about everything else. Jesus answers their question: "This is working for God: you must believe in the one he has sent." Again Jesus makes the point of the necessity of faith when dealing with the Eucharist.

† † †

Jesus, we believe. Help our unbelief.

When Jesus told the Jews in the synagogue in Capernaum that to please God they must believe in him, their reaction was in one way natural and in another way unnatural. They were correct in realizing that a miracle is a sure sign that God is working, because a miracle requires power beyond that of any human being or of any creature. Since only God can perform a miracle, a true miracle is divine proof that God is at work beyond the natural course of events. Therefore, the Jews were correct in believing that their religion had been established by God, because God had worked so many miracles for them in the past. They reminded our Lord of one of them. Through the intercession of Moses God miraculously created a daily portion of a bread-like substance they called manna. God did this for the forty years the Jews were wandering in the Sinai desert after their departure from Egypt. So the Jews ask our Lord a very natural question: "What sign (miracle) will you give to show us that we should believe in you? What work will you do? Our fathers had manna to eat in the desert, as Scripture says: "He gave them bread from heaven to eat."

Yet their question was unnatural, when one considers the day before, when before their very eyes, Jesus had miraculously cured all those needing to be cured. Then he miraculously multiplied the five loaves of which they ate. Many, if not all, in the synagogue had witnessed those miracles. Moreover the Apostles undoubtedly had told some of them about Jesus' having walked on the water early that morning. In addition, after Jesus had landed with the Apostles that morning at the town of Genesareth, about two miles from Capernaum, the people there laid their sick in the streets where Jesus would pass, so the sick could touch the hem of his garment. Those who touched his garment were miraculously cured. Some Jews in the synagogue must have seen or heard about that. So why ask for another miracle, especially since they knew that Jesus had worked many other miracles throughout the Holy Land for the past two years?

The Jews, "experts" in the matter of miracles, wanted to see Jesus work a miracle greater than that of the manna, if Jesus claimed to be greater than Moses.

† † †

You are the Christ, the Son of the living God. (Mt. 16:16)

Jesus did not grant the Jews' request of a miracle greater than that of the manna. Instead he corrected their misunderstanding about that miracle, and went on to promise the true bread of God. "It was not Moses who gave you bread from heaven." In reality it was God who had created the manna, and he had created it on the ground. It had not come down from heaven. Jesus continues: "It is my Father who gives you bread from heaven, the true bread; for the bread of God is that which comes down from heaven and gives life to the world." Obviously the Jews could not have understood fully concerning the Eucharist, but they understood enough to have some interest in our Lord's words. They say to him, "Give us that bread always."

Now that the crowd is interested, Jesus goes on to teach them more explicitly. Jesus begins by using the great expression, I AM, which God had revealed to Moses when Moses asked him what his name was. Promising the Eucharist, Jesus says, "I am the bread of life." A little later he will say,

31

"I am the living bread that has come down from heaven." He is the bread that both lives and gives life, the bread come down from heaven.

St. John writes: Meanwhile the Jews were complaining to each other about him, because he had said, "I am the bread that came down from heaven." "Surely this is Jesus, son of Joseph," they said, "We know his father and mother. How can he now say, 'I have come down from heaven?' Nazareth, where Jesus spent most of his life, was only some 18 miles from Capernaum, so the people knew the mother and foster-father of Jesus. We see that the secret of St. Joseph's relationship to Jesus had been well kept. The crowd knew nothing of Jesus' divine origin from God the Father. Up to this time all of our Lord's miracles to prove his divinity had been in vain, at least for most of the people. The Jews in the synagogue at Capernaum suffered from an unreasonable lack of faith, which prevented them from accepting the words of Jesus concerning the Eucharist. Jesus tells them to stop complaining, that they have been rejecting the grace that God the Father has been offering them to believe. "No one can come to me unless he is drawn by the Father who sent me." "I tell you most solemnly, everybody who believes has eternal life."

† † †

O Lord, increase our faith. (Lk 17:5)

Continuing his discourse in the synagogue in Capernaum, Jesus now uses the starkest realism in speaking of the Eucharist. He begins by referring to the manna that some in the crowd had just reminded him of in exalting Moses. Jesus emphasizes what he had said by repeating it: "I am the bread of life. Your fathers ate the manna in the desert and they are dead; but this is the bread that comes down from heaven, so that a man may eat it and not die." Jesus here uses one of his favorite comparisons, that between the natural and the supernatural worlds. The Jews of old had eaten the manna, but eventually they all died the natural death of the body. But Jesus promises that the Eucharistic bread come down from heaven will give those who eat it the means to preserve their supernatural life and thus prevent their supernatural death by mortal sin. Sanctifying grace is that participation in God's life in the soul which makes one holy and pleasing to God, indeed a child of God. Mortal sin, that grave offense against God that one knowingly and willingly commits, extinguishes God's life in the soul and makes one spiritually dead. Jesus promises to institute Holy Communion precisely to give us the means to avoid mortal sin. When one commits mortal sin, he is guilty of spiritual suicide by neglecting to use the means that Holy Communion has given him to avoid spiritual death.

Again Jesus emphasizes his words by repeating them: "I am the living bread which has come down from heaven. Anyone who eats this bread will live forever." And then with all clarity: "And the bread that I shall give is my flesh for the life of the world." When Jesus speaks of living bread and bread come down from heaven, surely no one in his audience understood him to mean common, ordinary bread. "Anyone who eats this bread will live forever." Jesus promises that the worthy reception of Holy Communion and the proper use of the graces it provides assures one of entrance into heaven. Jesus calls the Sacred Host "bread, living bread," simply because it will look like bread. None of the appearances of the bread used at Mass is changed, when the substance of the bread is changed into Jesus. Consequently the "bread" that he will give in Holy Communion is the flesh of Jesus, his living body, that he will offer on the cross for the supernatural life of all mankind. In saying he will "give his flesh," Jesus uses a technically correct, sacrificial term, which many in the crowd understood from their acquaintance with the sacrifices ordered by God in the Old Testament.

That Jesus spoke clearly about the Eucharist, and that his Jewish listeners understood him literally, can be seen in how they reacted. "Then the Jews started arguing with one another: 'How can this man give us his flesh to eat?'" Had they not understood our Lord literally, they would never have asked that question. If they believed that Jesus was going to give them a symbol or figure or memorial of his body, but not his real body, they surely would have had no problem. But they understood him literally, that he would give them his real body, and so they wondered how Jesus could do that. In addition, they probably conjured up ideas of cannibalism, something very repugnant to them and to most people. They asked the wrong question: "How can this man give us his flesh to eat?" The truth is that God seldom tells us HOW he does anything; and in this case it would have done no good to explain the HOW of the Eucharist, since no human being can understand it. We must content ourselves with the WHAT. WHAT does Jesus give us? His body. HOW can he do that? Not even the angels understand that.

When Jesus hears their problem, how does he, the divine teacher, the best of teachers, reply? On two other occasions Jesus corrected the Apostles when they took his words literally, while he was speaking figuratively. Having no food, the Apostles went to town and brought some to Jesus, when he was speaking with the Samaritan woman at the well. The Apostles urged him: " Rabbi, do have something to eat." Jesus said: I have food to eat that you do not know about." So the Apostles asked one another: "Has someone been bringing him food?" But Jesus said: "My food is to do the will of the one who sent me and to complete his work"(John 4:31). Similarly, when the Apostles had forgotten to take food with them in the boat on one occasion, Jesus in teaching them said: "Be on your guard against the yeast of the Pharisees and the yeast of Herod." The Apostles said to one another: "It is because we have no bread." Jesus said: "Why are you talking about having no bread?"(Mark 8:15) But does Jesus correct the crowd now and tell them they misunderstood in taking him literally, as any merely human teacher would do under the circumstances? On the contrary, Jesus confirms their literal understanding: "I tell you most solemnly, if you do not eat the flesh of the Son of man and drink his blood, you will not have life in you..."

When Jesus told the Jews in the synagogue in Capernaum that he would give them his flesh to eat, they understood him literally and expressed their dismay: "How can this man give us his flesh to eat? Jesus confirmed them in their literal understanding of his words with an even stronger expression: "I tell you most solemnly, if you do not eat the flesh of the Son of man and drink his blood, you will not have life in you. Anyone who does eat my flesh and drink my blood has eternal life; and I shall raise him up on the last day. For my flesh is real food and my blood is real drink."

"I tell you most solemnly, if you do not eat the flesh of the Son of man and drink his blood, you will not have life in you." Obviously Jesus is not speaking of the natural life of the body, but of the supernatural life of sanctifying grace, which is a sharing in God's own life. With these words of his Jesus, teaches the importance of receiving Holy Communion. He puts its importance on a par with baptism. He told Nicodemus: "I tell you most solemnly, unless a man is born through water and the Spirit, he cannot enter the kingdom of God"(John 3:5). Without the actual reception of the sacrament of baptism an adult can be saved with the proper disposition of soul and with at least an implicit desire to receive the sacrament. Likewise, without the actual reception of the sacrament of the Eucharist, an adult must have the same proper dispositions of soul and at least an implicit desire to receive Holy Communion to be saved. Baptized infants are saved without the reception of Communion through the maternal desire of Holy Mother Church that they receive the sacrament. In some Eastern Rite Churches, Holy Communion is administered to infants at their baptism by the priest, who places a few drops of the Precious Blood into their mouths. At any rate, both baptism and the Eucharist are equally necessary for salvation.

† † †

When Judas was about to hand over Jesus
to His enemies unto death,
Christ first handed himself over to his disciples
As the food of life.

St. Thomas Aquinas

In discussing the Eucharist with the people in the synagogue in Capernaum Jesus used a word that further brings out the literal meaning of his doctrine. In the other passages when he spoke of "eating" the bread from heaven or "eating" the flesh of the Son of Man, he used the common word for "eating" ("phagein" in the original Greek). But when he said, "Anyone who does eat my flesh," he used a different word ("trogein" meaning "munch" or "crunch"; as with raw fruits or vegetables). That choice of word would dispel any doubt or misunderstanding in the minds of his listeners: "Anyone who does munch on my flesh and drink my blood has eternal life, and I will raise him up on the last day."

Notice our Lord says "has," not "will have" eternal life. Eternal life in heaven is the continuation and blossoming forth of the life of sanctifying grace in one's soul at the moment of death. This means that the Eucharist gives us eternal life now in its inchoative or beginning stage. With reason St. Ignatius of Antioch in Syria calls Holy Communion "the medicine of immortality." When Jesus promises to raise up the recipient of the Eucharist on the last day, he makes the Eucharist the pledge or pawn of a glorious resurrection from the grave. Let us think of this when we receive Holy Communion.

Can even God say it more clearly? "My flesh is real food and my blood is real drink." How could Jesus have said it more clearly?

"He who eats my flesh and drinks my blood lives in me and I live in him." With these words Jesus expresses the most intimate union possible between two persons. It implies a mutual give-and-take, a most intimate mutual love. With every reception of Holy Communion may we always be reminded of the love of Jesus for us and the love we must have for him.

† † †

Christ, the Word made flesh, by a word changes true bread into his flesh; and the wine becomes the blood of Christ.
And if the senses fail to perceive this, faith alone suffices to convince

the well disposed.
Bowing lowly, let us adore so great a sacrament.
Let the Old Law give way to the New Rite.
Let faith supply help where the senses fail.

St. Thomas Aquinas

Jesus goes on to teach that the life that God the Father communicates to him, God the Son, is passed on to us through the Eucharist. "As I, who am sent by the living Father, myself draw life from the Father, so whoever eats me will draw life from me." We learn from these words where our sharing in God's life by sanctifying grace originates. God the Father shares his entire life and being with Jesus, God the Son, and thus Jesus is equal to the Father in all things. Jesus in turn shares part of his life with us through the seven sacraments that he instituted, especially Holy Communion. Jesus thus makes us holy by sharing in his life. Although Jesus had spoken in proper sacrificial terms when speaking of eating his flesh and drinking his blood, the words ("whoever eats me") indicate that the whole Christ is received, and received under only one form or species. It is therefore Christ himself, not just his body and blood, that is contained in the consecrated Host.

Jesus concludes his discourse by referring again to the manna of the Old Testament. "This is the bread come down from heaven; not like the bread our ancestors ate; they are dead, but anyone who eats this bread will live forever." Again he contrasts natural and supernatural life; and again in typical biblical style he refers to the Eucharist as bread, simply because it looks like bread.

In recording Christ's discourse on the Eucharist St. John the Evangelist says: "He taught this doctrine at Capernaum, in the synagogue." Jesus taught so clearly, and with such emphasis and repetition, that his listeners could not help but understand his claim that he himself would really be present in the Eucharist, that he would offer himself to be eaten, and that his flesh would be real food and his blood real drink. They understood so well that they persisted with their former problem, namely, "How can that be?" "Many of his followers said, 'This is intolerable* language. How can anyone accept it'?" To them our Lord's words were offensive, because they wrongly interpreted them in a cannibalistic way. In their imagination** they could see Jesus cutting off his arms or legs and offering them to be eaten. Naturally this caused them to suffer a terrible crisis of faith in Jesus. Our Lord knew this and, as a good teacher, he tries to correct the misunderstanding they have, not due to anything he said, but due to their faulty imagination.

With infinite patience our blessed Lord tries to correct the false impressions his listeners had due to their faulty imagination. Jesus says, "Does this (my doctrine) upset you? What if you should see the Son of Man ascend to where he was before?" With this reference to his future ascension into heaven with his real body, Jesus indicates how, in what condition, or in what state his body will be present in the Eucharist. His body in the Eucharist will be his real, live body, but in a heavenly state or condition. It will be his real body in the state that it was when he rose from the dead and made himself present to the Apostles on Easter night despite the locked doors. It will be his real body, but not in the same natural, human, physical condition that it was when he taught in the synagogue in Capernaum. His real body will be present in a spiritual way, something like the way our soul is present in our body.

Because Jesus is both man and God, his body is not only human, but also divine; and in the Eucharist it is present in a spiritual, heavenly condition. He tries to eradicate from the minds of some of his followers their false, cannibalistic ideas: "It is the spirit that gives life; the flesh has nothing to offer." They were latched on to the product of their faulty imagination, namely, that Jesus would be present in the Eucharist with his body in its natural, human condition, and in that condition they would eat his body (dead, of course, as the cannibals do, or even alive as some animals do). Jesus tries to get them to leave off their gross, naturally fleshy imaginations, which are only deceiving them. He reminds them that even in the natural world it is the spirit or soul that gives life. Without the spirit the flesh of the body is dead. Jesus is present, alive in the Eucharist with his real body in a glorified, divine, heavenly condition.

Jesus wants them to follow the promptings of the Spirit, God the Holy Spirit, who will lead them to a proper understanding of his Eucharistic body, that body which will give them the spiritual life they need. "The words I have spoken to you are spirit and they are life."

† † †

What a wondrous thing!
The poor, the slave and the lowly eat their Lord!

St. Thomas Aquinas

After trying in vain to correct the wrong ideas that some of his listeners had concerning the status or condition of his real body in the Eucharist, after trying to rid them of their cannibalistic notions of eating his flesh in its natural state, Jesus said with sorrow, "There are some of you who do not believe." Because they did not understand how, in what way, he could be present in the Eucharist, they rejected the idea that he would be present. Then St. John the Evangelist records some of the saddest words in the New Testament: "After this, many of his disciples left him and stopped going with him." Some of them had followed our Lord for a year, or even two years. Some had left their regular occupations to be with Jesus, to hear him teach and observe his miracles. They had believed in him and in everything he had said. But now, his teaching on his real presence in the Eucharist they found intolerable. They did not find his teaching false, only unbearable and offensive, because they were duped by their own false imaginations about cannibalism. And in their pride they clung to their false notions despite our Lord's efforts to correct them.

How it must have saddened the heart of Jesus to see those disciples abandon him. If they had misunderstood his teaching, obviously Jesus, the divine teacher, the best of teachers, would have called them back to explain: "Come back, come back! You misunderstand me. I am not really going to be present in the Eucharist. I am not really going to give you my body and blood to eat and drink." That would have been the natural reaction of any teacher. But Jesus knew they did understand the WHAT of his doctrine. It was only their false notions concerning the HOW of his doctrine that was inducing them to leave. And since in their pride they rejected our Lord's efforts to disabuse them of their false notions, he could do nothing but let them go. A similar sad scenario would take place 1500 years later, when those who were baptized and reared in the Catholic faith would reject it, along with the true doctrine concerning the Eucharist, in order to establish various Protestant religions.

† † †

In Thee, sight, touch and taste are deceived,
But hearing alone is safely believed.
I believe whatever the Son of God has said;
Nothing is truer than that word of truth.

St. Thomas Aquinas

It should be noted that the Apostles were also present in the synagogue in Capernaum, when our Lord gave his discourse on the Eucharist. Since most of them were from that region of Galilee, more than likely they saw some of their friends or even relatives among those disciples who were leaving Jesus. Again, reinforcing his doctrine, Jesus turns to the Apostles and asks: "What about you, do you also want to go away?" Jesus will not retract or water down his teaching on his real presence in the Eucharist. Simon Peter answers for the Apostles: "Lord, to whom shall we go? You have the message of eternal life; and we believe; we know that you are the Holy One of God." Peter did not understand the HOW of our Lord's real presence in the Eucharist any more than those disciples did who were leaving our Lord. He simply accepted the WHAT of Christ's teaching without letting his pride lead him astray. And it is his faith, the faith of the first pope, that we Catholics are privileged to profess today.

✝ ✝ ✝

Sacris Solemniis, by St. Thomas Aquinas

Let joy be joined to this solemn celebration,
and from the depths of our hearts let praises resound...
Let everything be The Last Supper is recalled,
when Christ is believed to have given to his brothers
lamb and bread according to the legal prescriptions
that were given to the ancient patriarchs.
When the Feast of the Paschal Lamb was finished,
we believe that, with his own hands,
the Lord gave his body to the disciples.
What was given to all was given to each of them.
To the weak He gave the food of his body;
and to those who were sad He gave the cup of his blood.
He said, "Take this cup that I give you,
and all of you, drink from it."
Thus He instituted the sacrifice, whose celebration He willed to be
committed to priests alone.
It is proper, therefore, that they partake of the sacrifice
and share it with the rest.
The Bread of angels becomes the Bread of man;
the heavenly bread puts an end to the symbols.
How wonderful: the poor, the slave,
and the lowly eat their Lord!

* *Greek "skleros" is translated: hard, intolerable, offensive.*
** *The human faculty that often deceives us in matters of religion.*

Chapter III

CHRIST INSTITUTES THE EUCHARIST

Of the annual Feasts instituted by God for the Jews in the Old Testament the most important was Passover (Pasch), which commemorated the deliverance of the Jews from slavery in Egypt. Christ chose that Feast to institute the new Passover, which would deliver all mankind from the slavery of sin. This he did at the Last Supper, the night before he died.

Of the four Biblical accounts of the institution of the Eucharist we quote here from St. Paul's account, which gives us the most details in First Corinthians, Chapter 11:

"This is what I received from the Lord (probably through the teaching of the other Apostles), and in turn passed on to you: that on the same night that he was betrayed, the Lord Jesus took some bread, thanked God for it and broke it, and he said: 'This is my body, which is for you; do this as a memorial of me.' In the same way he took the cup after supper, and said, 'This cup is the new covenant in my blood. Whenever you drink it, do this as a memorial of me.' Until the Lord comes, therefore, every time you eat this bread and drink this cup, you are proclaiming his death; and so anyone who eats the bread or drinks the cup of the Lord unworthily will be guilty of the body and the blood of the Lord. Everyone is to recollect himself before eating this bread and drinking this cup; because a person who eats and drinks without recognizing the body is eating and drinking his own condemnation. In fact that is why many of you are weak and ill and some of you have died. If only we recollected ourselves, we should not be punished like that. But when the Lord does punish us like that, it is to correct us and stop us from being condemned with the world."

St. Paul adds the note of punishment, because some Catholics at Corinth had been guilty of abuses concerning the celebration of Mass there.

† † †

*Sing, my tongue, of the mystery of the glorious Body
and the precious Blood, which the King of nations, the Fruit of a royal
womb, poured out for the ransom of the world.*

St. Thomas Aquinas

With some conjecture we can reconstruct the Passover meal at which Christ instituted the Mass. The Bible tells us the Passover was instituted in the Old Testament as a family meal. The "family" at the Last Supper consisted of Christ and his twelve Apostles.

For the Passover supper the family would stand around the table as if ready for a journey, just as the Jewish slaves did the night of the first Passover before leaving Egypt. The father would begin the ceremony by passing a communal cup of wine to all present. They would then eat a few bitter herbs and some unleavened bread to remind them of the hardships of their forefathers' slavery in Egypt. The communal cup of wine was passed a second time. There followed the singing of Psalms with Alleluias. After that all were seated. The father of the family broke and blessed unleavened bread, then passed it to all present as a sign to start the meal proper. MOST LIKELY IT WAS AT THIS POINT THAT CHRIST CONSECRATED THE BREAD. There followed the meal proper with the Paschal lamb. After the meal the father took the communal cup refilled with wine, raised it slightly, pronounced a blessing over it, and passed it to all present. MOST LIKELY IT WAS AT THIS POINT THAT CHRIST CONSECRATED THE WINE. There followed the singing of more Psalms. It was probably at this point that Christ terminated the meal, as St. Matthew writes: "After Psalms had been sung they left for the Mount of Olives"(Mt 26:30).

At the Passover meal of the Jews there was a fourth and last communal cup of wine. It appears that Christ omitted this, for he was already in a sacrificial state and would do nothing except what served to complete the sacrifice. He clearly stated that he was offering himself in sacrifice, as we see in St. Luke's account. Using sacrificial terms, Christ said: "This is my body which will be given (in sacrifice) for you...This cup is the new covenant in my blood which will be poured out (in sacrifice) for you." Having offered himself in sacrifice to God the Father, he knew that his body was no longer subject to his own will, for he had placed it under the sole jurisdiction of the Father. After Christ had put himself in a sacrificial state; and after the Apostles had consumed his body and blood in the state of a sacrifical victim by anticipation, Christ had but to complete his sacrifice by enduring the immolation or victimization, which was completed by his death. Thus his sacrifice came to an end.

Christ's one, redemptive sacrifice began, as we saw, at the Last Supper with his offering himself to the death. The sacrificial immolation or victimization bringing about his death began immediately after the Last Supper with the bloody sweat. It was continued by his being captured, bound, buffeted, insulted, spat upon, illegally tried, mocked, scourged, crowned with thorns, condemned, betrayed, burdened with the cross, and finally crucified His sacrifice was completed by his death on the cross on Calvary.

For a sacrifice there must be an offering of a sacrificial gift to God. We noted that Christ offered himself as the sacrificial gift. And if the sacrificial gift was alive (e.g. an animal), it had to be immolated or killed, because by having been offered to God, it became God's special property and was thus withdrawn from human use by being killed. (In some Old Testament sacrifices of animals God ordered that the immolated, dead animal be eaten by those who had offered it. In this way they became holy by eating God's special, holy property.) Since Christ had made himself the sacrificial gift (the Paschal Lamb) at the Last Supper, Christ completed his sacrifice by enduring the sufferings and death of his passion, which ended the following day on Calvary.

That was Christ's one, complete sacrifice for the salvation of the world; and that was the sacrifice Christ commanded to be made present again and again until the end of time. In initiating his sacrifice at the Last Supper Christ commanded his Apostles: "Do this as a memorial of me"..."Until the Lord comes (at the end of the world), therefore, every time you eat this bread and drink this cup, you are proclaiming his death." THUS DOES

CHRIST GIVE HIS CHURCH THE POWER AND THE COMMAND TO MAKE HIS SACRIFICE PRESENT UNTIL THE END OF TIME.

Obviously this one, same sacrifice of Christ was, and is, to be made present in a manner entirely different from the way it was first effected. When men and angels beheld that sacrifice taking place for the first time, they saw a bloody sacrifice, a sacrifice in which the Victim poured out his blood and died a painful, physical, sacrificial death. But now men and angels behold that same sacrifice being made present in a glorious, unbloody manner. But how? We shall see.

We have seen that, at the Last Supper while Christ was offering his one sacrifice (begun at the Last Supper and completed by his death on Calvary the following day), he empowered the Church to offer that sacrifice and to offer it until the end of time. The Church does that at Mass. The Mass, therefore, makes Christ's one sacrifice present on our altars. How?

Since God did not explain how the sacrifice of Christ and the sacrifice of the Mass are the one, same sacrifice, the Church cannot offer any official explanation. She must leave the explanations to the theologians, those good people who dedicate their lives to assimilating God's word, attempting to understand it, and presenting it to us in a way that helps us to understand it better and receive more benefit from it. The theologians over the centuries have offered several different explanations of how the sacrifice of Christ and that of the Mass are one, same sacrifice. We offer here, in a very abbreviated form, some ideas from an explanation by Father Maurice de la Taille, S.J. in his monumental work entitled "Mysterium Fidei" (The Mystery of Faith).

At the Last Supper Christ began his sacrifice. Changing bread and wine into himself, he offered himself to the death in sacrifice to his Father: This is my body which is offered for you in sacrifice; this is my blood that is poured out for you in sacrifice; do this in remembrance of me. By an act of his will Christ put himself into the status of a sacrificial victim, the Victim-to-be of his sacrifice. He never withdrew that act of his will, so he remained in the status of the Victim-to-be until the following day, when his victimization was completed by his death on the cross.

† † †

At his birth Christ gave himself as our companion; at the Last Supper he gave himself as our food; dying he gave himself as our ransom; reigning in heaven he gives himself as our reward.

St. Thomas Aquinas

At the moment Christ died he actively completed his sacrifice and became the Victim-in-fact. The Bible shows that Christ never withdrew from the status of a sacrificial Victim into which he put himself at the Last Supper. He rose from the dead as the living Victim of his sacrifice, which he indicated by still bearing the marks of his victimization in his body, the wounds in his hands, feet and side. He ascended into Heaven still in the status of the Victim, still bearing his wounds. And he remains in heaven in the status of the Victim,where he intercedes for us for all eternity by showing his Father his wounds. The Bible puts it this way: "He not only died for us—he rose from the dead, and there at God's right hand he stands and pleads for us" (Rom 8:34); "He is living forever to intercede for all who come to God through him" (Hebr 7:25); "Then I (St. John the Evangelist) saw (in heaven) standing, a Lamb that seemed to have been sacrificed" (Rev 5:6).

To sum up, Christ the Priest at the Last Supper offered his one sacrifice for all mankind by putting himself into the permanent status of a sacrificial Victim. He remains in heaven continually offering himself as the triumphant, glorified Victim of Calvary. If we could make him present as he is in heaven, we could make present again that one sacrifice of his. And this is precisely what is done at Mass. The priest changes the bread and wine into Christ as he is present in heaven offering his one sacrifice. Christ need not offer himself actively again, because by offering himself actively at the Last Supper he put himself into the permanent status of a sacrificial Victim. Nor does he have to undergo his immolation or victimization again, because he remains in the permanent status of a Victim-

47

in-fact, albeit a glorious Victim. In this way the Church makes Christ's one sacrifice present on our altars and carries out his command, "Do this in memory of me." At every Mass we offer actively the one sacrifice of Christ, who is present as the Priest of Calvary offering himself passively as the Victim of his sacrifice. On Calvary, Christ the Priest offered himself actively as the bloody Victim; at Mass, Christ the Priest offers himself passively as the glorious, unbloody Victim—and he empowers us and commands us to join him. This the Catholic Church has done from its inception at the first Christian Pentecost nineteen centuries ago up until this very day, as we shall see from the historical testimonies that follow.

Chapter IV

THE EUCHARIST IN APOSTOLIC TIMES

DIDACHE (90-100 a.d.)

After treating the institution of the Eucharist at the Last Supper we pass over several allusions to the Eucharist in the New Testament and begin to trace its history from the days of the last Apostle, St. John the Evangelist, who died about the year 100 a.d.

One of the oldest Christian documents is entitled "Didache," short for "The Lord's Instruction to the Gentiles through the Twelve Apostles." It was written between the years 90 and 100 a.d. in the Middle East, probably in Syria. It is the oldest source of Church law that has yet been discovered. Our interest, of course, is what it says about the Eucharist. We see that, although the author or authors lived in a culture very different from ours, the faith they professed is the same as ours.

In quoting from the Didache here we use Johannes Quasten's two volume work entitled "Patrology." In writing about the Mass the Didache says: "Regarding the Eucharist. Give thanks as follows: 'First, concerning the cup: "We give thee thanks, our Father, for the holy vine of David thy servant, which thou hast made known to us through thy Servant Jesus. To thee be glory forever." Next, concerning the broken bread: "We give thee thanks, our Father, for the life and knowledge thou hast made known to us through Jesus thy Servant. To thee be glory forever. As this broken bread was scattered over the hills (as grains of wheat) and then, when gathered, became one mass (of dough), so may thy Church be gathered from the ends of the earth into thy kingdom. For thine is the glory and the power through Jesus Christ forever.' " We can see some similarities between these prayers and our Offertory prayers today.

The Didache also has a Communion prayer to be said after receiving Communion: "After you have taken your fill of food, give thanks as follows: 'We give thee thanks, O holy Father, for thy holy name which thou hast enshrined in our hearts, and for the knowledge and faith and immortality which thou hast made known to us through Jesus thy Servant. To thee be the glory forever. Thou, Lord Almighty, hast created all things for the sake of thy name, and hast given food and drink for men to enjoy, that they may give thanks to thee; but to us thou has given spiritual food and drink and eternal life through (Jesus) thy Servant. Above all we give thee thanks because thou art mighty. Glory to thee.' "

The Didache also contains instructions as to the proper dispositions of soul required both to join the priest in offering the Mass and to receive Holy Communion. "On the Lord's own day (Sunday, according to St. John in Rev 1:10) assemble in common to break bread ("To break bread" was the earliest name of the Mass) and offer thanks. But first confess your sins (probably as we do together at the beginning of Mass), so that your sacrifice may be pure. However, no one quarreling with his brother may join your meeting until he is reconciled. Your sacrifice must not be defiled. For here we have the saying of the Lord: 'In every place and time offer me a pure sacrifice; for I am a mighty King, says the Lord; and my name spreads terror among the nations.' Regarding Holy Communion: 'Let no one eat and drink of your Eucharist but those baptized in the name of the Lord; for concerning this also did the Lord say: "Do not give to dogs what is sacred.' "

The early Christians thought a lot about the end of the world, and prayed that it would come soon with the return of Christ for the final, general judgment. We see this attitude in the Didache in the prayers at Mass: "May grace come, and this world pass away!" And the reply in Aramaic, the Jewish dialogue that Jesus spoke: "Maran atha." This Aramaic expression is found in 1Cor 16:22. It means, "The Lord is coming." Sometimes we read: "Marana tha," meaning "Lord, come." The expression found its way into some early liturgies. Today it is sometimes found on our Advent banners.

† † †

O saving Victim, you open the gate of heaven. The wicked enemies press hard upon us. Give us strength; bring us help. To the one and triune Lord be everlasting glory. May he give us life without end in our homeland.

St. Thomas Aquinas

Chapter V

THE EUCHARIST IN THE SECOND CENTURY

ST. IGNATIUS OF ANTIOCH (died c. 110)

The first historical period after the Apostolic times is called the Patristic Period, the period of the Church Fathers. These are the men who lived between 100 a.d. and 800 a.d. and were outstanding for their holiness and orthodoxy (correctness of their teaching). Due to the ravages of time and wars and the destruction by the Vandals only a number of their writings remain. But enough do exist for us to trace the history of the Eucharist throughout the early years of the Church.

St. Ignatius, the second successor of St. Peter the Apostle as Bishop of Antioch in Syria, is a strong, colorful figure. During the persecutions of the Church by the imperial Roman government Ignatius was condemned to death by being thrown to the wild beasts in the amphitheater in Rome. On his way to Rome he was able to write seven letters to the principal Christian communities (Churches) along his route. Fortunately those seven letters are still extant, and they contain interesting material so early in the history of the Church.

St. Ignatius is the first to apply the word "catholic" to the Church established by Christ. He uses the term in its original meaning of "universal," since the Church was already spreading throughout the then known world. He speaks of the hierarchy of bishops, priests and deacons as already well established. The office of bishop is very important: "Where the bishop is, there let the people be, just as where Jesus is, there is the catholic (universal) Church."

St. Ignatius points out the preeminence of the Church of Rome with its privileges over the other Churches, and, being eager to die a martyr's death, he begs the Catholics in Rome not to interfere with his martyrdom: "Let me be food for the wild beasts, through whom I shall reach my God. I am the wheat of the Lord; and I must be ground by the teeth of the beasts to change me into very pure bread of Christ." But our interest here in St. Ignatius concerns what he writes about the Eucharist in the seven letters mentioned above.

† † †

Blessed be the Lord our God, blessed from age to age.

Although St. Ignatius does not always write with the precision we would like, he does state clearly several things about the Eucharist. He calls the Eucharist "the medicine of immortality," "the antidote against death," and "everlasting life in Jesus Christ." He writes: "Take care, then, to partake of one Eucharist; for one is the flesh of our Lord Jesus Christ, and one the cup to unite us with his blood, and one altar, just as there is one bishop assisted by the presbyterate (priests) and the deacons."

One of the earliest heresies in the history of the Church was called Docetism, meaning "appearances." It held that all material things are evil and consequently Christ's body was not a real human body but only an apparent body. In combating that heresy St. Ignatius gives us not only a very clear statement regarding the Eucharist, but also becomes the first theologian of the Blessed Mother. He defends her virginal conception of Jesus and her having given Jesus, both God and man, a real human body. He says that the Docetists refrain from going to Mass, because the real human body of Christ is present in the Eucharist: "From Eucharist and prayer (Mass) they hold aloof, because they do not profess that the Eucharist is the flesh of our Savior Jesus Christ, which suffered for our sins, and which the Father in his living kindness raised from the dead." St. Ignatius believes that the body of Christ in the Eucharist is his body that suffered and rose from the the dead—therefore his real body.

† † †

Devoutly I adore thee, hidden Deity,
Who truly lies concealed under these appearances.
To Thee my heart submits itself entirely,
For when contemplating Thee all else is wanting.

St. Thomas Aquinas

ST. JUSTIN, MARTYR (died c. 165)

St. Justin has been called "the patron of upright, sincere, and valiant souls." He was a layman. He was born in Palestine of pagan parents. As a young man he had a burning desire to know truth. After exploring different pagan philosophies he felt unsatisfied. One day while walking along the shore of the Mediterranean Sea he met an old man who told him to read the Prophets in the Bible. His search for truth in the Bible satisfied his hunger and eventually led him to accept Christianity. He tried to apply philosophy to the truths of Christianity in order to build a bridge between paganism and Christianity to bring the pagans into the Church. To this end he opened a school in Rome itself. It troubled him greatly to see the Christians being falsely accused, illegally tried, and put to death. He boldly addressed a written defense of Christianity, the Church and the Catholic faith to the pagan Emperor and another to the pagan Senators in the vain hope that they would stop the persecution of the Christians. For all his efforts he himself died a martyr's death about the year 165.

One of the false accusations that the pagans would make against the Catholics was that at their meetings the Christians would kill a baby and eat its flesh and drink its blood. (Someone must have heard something about the Real Presence and Holy Communion.) "The Discipline of the Secret," as it was called, was the custom of not letting the pagans know about the Real Presence of Christ in the Eucharist to avoid profanation of the Host. Either that discipline was not yet practiced in Rome, or St. Justin thought it necessary to break that secret in order to defend the Christians. In his written defense of Christianity to the Emperor he gives us what is the earliest known description of the Mass, as it was celebrated about the year 150 in Rome.

† † †

On the cross only His Deity lay hidden,
But here lies hidden also His humanity.

57

> *Nevertheless, believing and professing both,*
> *I request what the penitent thief requested.*

St. Thomas Aquinas

St. Justin's partial description of the Mass in his day in Rome follows:

"On the day we call the day of the sun (Sunday), all who dwell in the city or country gather in the same place. The memoirs of the apostles and the writings of the prophets are read, as much as time permits. When the reader has finished, he (priest or bishop) who presides over those gathered admonishes and challenges them to imitate these beautiful things. Then we all rise together and offer prayers for ourselves ...and for all others, wherever they may be, so that we may be found righteous by our life and actions, and faithful to the commandments, so as to obtain eternal salvation. When the prayers are concluded we exchange the kiss. Then someone brings bread and a cup of water and wine mixed together to him who presides over the brethren.

He takes them and offers praise and glory to the Father of the universe, through the name of the Son and of the Holy Spirit and for a considerable time he gives thanks that we have been judged worthy of these gifts. When he has concluded the prayers and the thanksgivings, all present give voice to an acclamation by saying 'Amen.' When he who presides has given thanks and the people have responded, those whom we call deacons give to those present the "eucharisted" bread, wine and water and take them to those who are absent" (Catechism of the Catholic Church #1345).

"And this food is with us called 'Eucharist'; and it is not lawful for anyone to partake of it but him who believes our teaching to be true, and has been washed (baptism) with the washing which is for the forgiveness of sins and unto a new birth, and lives as Christ commanded. For it is not as common bread or common drink that we receive these, but just as by God's word Jesus Christ our Savior became flesh and blood for our salvation, so also we have been taught that the food made Eucharist by the word of prayer that comes from Him is both flesh and blood of that Jesus who was made flesh. For the Apostles in the memoirs they composed, which are called

Gospels, have thus recorded that they were given command ...that Jesus took bread ...and said, 'This is my body'; and took the cup and said, 'This is my blood' "(John J. Laux,"Church History").

ST. IRENAEUS, BISHOP OF LYONS, FRANCE
(died c.202)

Irenaeus is like a golden chain linking the last disciples of the Apostles with the rest of the Church Fathers. He was born in what is now Turkey, where as a young man he was a pupil of St. Polycarp, Bishop of Smyrna, who in turn had been a pupil of St. John, the last of the twelve Apostles. St. Irenaeus moved to Lyons, in what is today France, and was subsequently elected bishop of that city.

St. Irenaeus is known mainly as a great apologist, a defender of the faith. In his many writings he systematized Catholic doctrine and thus gained the title of "Father of Catholic Theology." He also authored the earliest known catechism containing the principle doctrines of the Christian faith in a form in which the less educated could understand them. He presented a "rule of faith," by which one can know what is the true doctrine revealed by God. He explained that the rule of faith is the living magisterium (teaching office of the pope and bishops, the successors of the Apostles). Of prime importance, he said, is the magisterium of the Church of Rome, where the Apostolic tradition is preserved and with whom all other Churches must be in agreement. St. Irenaeus expanded on St. Justin's Mariology by explaining in more detail Mary's share in the work of our redemption.

The greatest achievement of St. Irenaeus was that he dealt a death blow to the heresy known as Gnosticism. That heresy took many forms (as it does today), but in general it claims to have a knowledge of God and things divine, a knowledge superior to that which the Church has received from God himself. It claimed that matter (material things) was the product of an evil god and was therefore evil. Naturally this led to false ideas about the material things we use, about our bodies, about the body of Christ, and therefore about the Eucharist. It was in this regard that St. Irenaeus wrote about the Eucharist to point out errors in Gnosticism.

✝ ✝ ✝

I see no wounds, as Thomas did; nevertheless I confess Thee to be my God. Always make me believe in Thee more, hope in Thee more, and love Thee more.

St. Thomas Aquinas

Concerning the Eucharist, St. Irenaeus writes: "When, therefore, the mingled cup (with water and wine) and the manufactured bread receive the word of God (the Consecration using Christ's own words) and the Eucharist becomes the body and blood of Christ, from which things the substance of our flesh is increased and supported, how can they (the heretics) affirm that the flesh (our body) is incapable of receiving the gift of God, which is life eternal? (The Gnostics denied the resurrection of the body.) As a grain of wheat falling into the earth becomes decomposed and rises with manifold increase by the Spirit of God, and becomes the Eucharist, which is the body and blood of Christ, so also our bodies, being nourished by it, and deposited in the earth, and suffering decomposition there, shall rise at their appointed time." (Quasten op. cit.) Just as Jesus joined the resurrection of the body to Holy Communion ("He who eats my flesh...I shall raise him up on the last day."), so does St. Irenaeus in different words.

✝ ✝ ✝

Prayer After Communion
Soul of Christ, make me holy.
Blood of Christ, inebriate me.
Water from the side of Christ, wash me.

Passion of Christ, strengthen me.
O good Jesus, hear me.
In your wounds, hide me.
Never let me be separated from you.
From the wicked enemy defend me.
In the hour of my death call me,
And bid me come to you,
So that with your saints I may praise you forever.
Amen.

The Lord has saved me because he loves me; he wanted me for his own.

THE EPITAPH OF ABERCIUS, c.200

The gravestone containing the epitaph of Abercius is of interest to us, because it is the oldest known inscription in stone concerning the Eucharist. Abercius was the Bishop of Hieropolis in what is today Turkey. He had his tombstone inscribed prior to his death. He felt inspired to visit the Church in Rome, which he praises highly, and to travel throughout a large part of the Roman Empire to see how the Church was faring. Everywhere he found the Eucharist, which he describes in a mystical or symbolic way in accord with the ancient Discipline of the Secret, so that the Christians would understand and the pagans would not. He refers to Christ in the Eucharist as the fish, a very ancient symbol of Christ. (In Greek the first letter of the words, "Jesus Christ, Son of God, Savior" spells "Fish.")

The epitaph of Abercius reads as follows: "The citizen of an eminent city (He is a citizen of the Roman Empire) I made this (epitaph on tombstone) in my lifetime, that I might have here a resting-place for my body. Abercius by name, I am a disciple of the chaste shepherd (Christ), who feeds his flocks of sheep (Christian communities or Churches) on mountains and plains (throughout the Roman Empire). He has great eyes that look on all sides (He is God). He taught me faithful writings (Bible). He sent me to Rome to behold a kingdom and to see a queen with golden robe and golden shoes (praise for the Church of Rome). There I saw a people bearing a splendid seal (indelible character of Baptism). And I saw the plain of Syria and all the cities, even Nisibis (in today's Iraq), having crossed the Euphrates (river in Iraq). And everywhere I had associates (probably the Letters of St. Paul or the cities Paul had visited), having Paul as my companion. Everywhere faith led the way (He found the Church everywhere he went) and set before me for food the fish (Christ in the Eucharist) from the spring, the fish mighty and pure, whom a spotless virgin (the Church) caught; and gave this to friends (Christians) to eat, always having sweet wine and giving the mixed cup (wine with water) with bread (Communion under both species). These words I, Abercius, standing by, ordered to be transcribed. In truth I was seventy-two years old. Let him who understands this and believes pray for Abercius." [The epitaph is in the Lateran Museum in Rome.]

THE EPITAPH OF PECTORIUS, c. 200

Another tombstone, mentioning the Eucharist and dating from sometime after that of Abercius, was found in an ancient Christian cemetery near Autun in southern France. Pectorius, the author, not only prays for his deceased mother, but also asks his parents and deceased brothers to pray for him. This is a very early witness to the doctrine that holds that, not only can we assist the souls in Purgatory with our prayers, but also that they can assist us on earth. This epitaph was also written in very symbolic language, in accord with the Discipline of the Secret, to protect the Eucharist from profanation. This epitaph is preserved in the Museum of Autun.

The epitaph is addressed to the Christian who reads it. "You, the divine child of the heavenly fish (You, follower of Christ), keep pure your soul among the mortals. Because you receive the immortal fountain of divine water (Baptism), refresh your soul, friend, with the ever flowing water of wealth-giving wisdom (divine Revelation, Church teaching). Take from the Redeemer of the saints as the food sweet as honey (Eucharist): eat with joy and desire, holding the fish (Christ) in your hands (Communion in the hand). I pray, Lord and Savior, give as food the fish. I pray to thee, Light of the dead, may she, my mother, rest peacefully. Aschandius, father, my heart's beloved, with my sweet mother and my brothers, in the peace of the fish remember your Pectorius."

† † †

"O sacred banquet, in which Christ is received, the memory of his Passion is recalled, the soul is filled with grace, and a pledge of future glory is given to us."

"O how pleasant is thy spirit, O Lord. In order to show your sweetness to your children, having provided Bread most sweet from heaven, you fill the hungry with good things and you send away empty the finicky rich."

TERTULLIAN, c.160 - c.220

Tertullian was born about the year 160 in the prominent city of Carthage (in today's Tunisia) on the northern coast of Africa. His father, a pagan, was a centurion in the Roman army stationed in that city. Tertullian was given an excellent training in Greek and Latin literature and in Roman law. He went to Rome, where he practiced law for a number of years, and about the year 195 he was baptized into the Church.

Almost immediately he took up the defense of the Christians, who were being persecuted and martyred especially due to slanderous accusations by the pagans and the Jews. His training in Latin and law, along with his fiery and passionate character, made Tertullian ("the severe African," as they dubbed him) a formidable and outstanding apologist, defender of the faith. He showed how the Roman government's persecution of the Church only made the Christians grow in number. "Semen est sanguis christianorum," he wrote (The blood of Christians is the seed—of Christians.) Tertullian wrote profusely, so much so that he has been called "the father of ecclesiastical Latin"; and his precise concepts, due to his training in law, has earned him the title of "the father of Western (Latin) theology."

Unfortunately Tertullian's fiery character led him to a love of extremes; and, in turn, this led him out of the Church. His regrettable exit came about in this way. The many charismatic gifts that we read about in the New Testament, and which were necessary to get the Church established, had almost all disappeared by 100 a.d. A man by the name of Montanus pretended to bring them back. He claimed to have visions and that he was an organ of the Holy Spirit. His followers embraced a very severe moral code. Tertullian with his bent for extremes naturally felt comfortable with that teaching. He left the Church formally and joined the Montanists, whom he defended as being the real Church of Christ, not the Church of bishops but of the Holy Spirit, the Church where authority is exercised not by those having received the sacrament of Holy Orders, but by those receiving special gifts of the Holy Spirit! (Does that not sound familiar in our day, just as it did in different periods throughout the history of the Church?)

It appears that poor Tertullian never returned to the Church, just as he never denied the Real Presence of Christ in the Eucharist. His Eucharistic teachings during the Catholic period of his life are what interest us now, because they give evidence of what the Catholic Church believed about the Eucharist in Rome and Carthage, Africa, around the year 200 a.d.

Tertullian was the first to apply the ancient Latin word, "sacramentum," to the Eucharist and likewise the word, "consecrare," to the action of the priest at Mass when changing the bread and wine into the body and blood of Christ. Later the Church would "canonize" these terms by giving them specific meanings in her official teaching and in theology.

Tertullian writes about the serious difficulties for a Christian wife married to a pagan husband during the government's persecutions of the Church. "The more you try to hide your religious practices (from your husband), the more suspicious you make them look, and the more you arouse the pagan curiosity to see them. Will you remain unseen when you sign the bed and yourself with the sign of the cross?...When you get up during the night to pray, will it not seem that you are performing some magic? Will your husband not know what you eat in secret before you take any other food?" (Because of the danger of being suddenly arrested and put to death during the persecutions, in some places the Christians were permitted to take home from Mass consecrated Hosts to give themselves Communion daily. Incidentally the Eucharistic fast is implied here in Tertullian's statement.) "And if your husband knows that you are eating Bread, will he not believe that it is the bread that people talk bad about? (Some pagans said Christians eat babies and drink their blood.)...

"Many women, having not forseen these difficulties, have come to recognize them either with excruciating pain or with the loss of the faith."

† † †

Let us approach the Lord in the Blessed Sacrament with thanksgiving.

Against the Gnostics, who held that all matter is evil, Tertullian wrote: "Christ has not rejected the Creator's water with which he washes (baptizes) his own, nor the oil with which he anoints them (in Confirmation), nor the bread with which he makes present his very own body. Of necessity he must beg the Creator for these things even for the sacraments themselves."

"For the sacrament of the bread and the chalice we have already proved from the Gospel the truth of the body and blood of the Lord against the imagination propose by Marcion (a heretic)."

Again against the Gnostics: "When the soul is intimately united to God, it is the body that makes it possible for the soul to be so united. For example, the body is washed (in Baptism) that the soul may be clean; it is anointed, so that the soul may be consecrated; it is signed with the cross, so that the soul too may be fortified; it is overshadowed by the imposition of hands, so that the soul may be illuminated by the Spirit; the body is fed with the body and blood of Christ, so that the soul may be filled with God. Since the one action (of the sacraments) unites both body and soul, they both must share in the reward." (The Gnostics denied the resurrection of the body.)

"The sacrament of the Eucharist was entrusted by the Lord at the Last Supper to all; and we receive it in the meetings (Mass) that we hold before dawn. And we receive it from the hand of no one except that of those who preside...We suffer anxiety, if anything falls to the floor from our chalice or our bread."

Tertullian condemns the grave sin of those Christians who manufacture idols and yet receive Communion. "To receive the body of the Lord they stretch out those hands that make the bodies of demons...What a crime! The Jews put their hands on Christ only once; these people violate his body every day. Oh hands worthy to be cut off!...What hands must be amputated with more reason than those in which the body of the Lord suffers violation!"

***(All quotes by Tertullian are from the 2 volume work,"TEXTOS EUCARISTICOS PRIMITIVOS," by Jesus Solano, S.J. Abbreviated TEP)

(All quotes from St. Ignatius were taken from Quasten, op. cit.)

Chapter VI

THE EUCHARIST IN THE THIRD CENTURY

CLEMENT OF ALEXANDRIA, died c. 214

Around the year 200 a.d. the city of Alexandria on the northern shore of Egypt was the center for scientific speculation and the home of the Christian intellectual movement. It has been said that, at that time, Rome was the heart of the Church and Alexandria was its brain. Clement was at the head of the catechetical school of Alexandria. He was untiring in his study of Sacred Scripture. His noble attempt to incorporate philosophy with Christian doctrine has been called "the boldest literary undertaking in the history of the Church." Unfortunately some of his writings are not only difficult to understand but also contain some definite doctrinal errors. During the persecution of 202 a.d. he had to close his school in Alexandria and moved to Cappodocia (Turkey), where he died. His school was later opened by his most famous pupil, Origen. Clement joined the other African writers in calling the Church "Mother," "Mother Church," as we still do today.

Clement apparently did not have much occasion to write about the Eucharist. He considered the sacrifice of Melchisedech (a sacrifice of bread and wine) a figure or type of our Eucharist.. "He (Melchisedech) gave bread and wine as a sanctified nourishment in a figure of the Eucharist." Clement speaks of the heretics who, "contrary to the rule of the Church, use bread and water in their offering; indeed there are those who 'eucharisticize' (consecrate) water alone." (Such consecrations are invalid.) In writing about Jesus the Savior Clement says: "I (the Savior) am your Nourisher, who has given myself as bread. He who eats of it no longer has experience of death. And I have given myself as the drink of immortality."

† † †

His flesh is food and his blood is drink,
but Christ remains whole under each species.

He is received whole, not cut up, broken, or divided.
Both good and evil men receive him,
but with the unequal destiny of life or damnation.
It is death for the wicked, life for the good.
See how unequal is the outcome of the same reception.

St. Thomas Aquinas

ST. HIPPOLYTUS, died 235

St. Hippolytus was a priest in Rome. Like Tertullian he was a vigorous defender of the faith against heresy; and like Tertullian he went too far. His personal animosity against one of the popes led him to accuse the pope falsely of error. However his greatest complaint was that the popes were not fighting heresy with enough zeal to please Hippolytus. In his pride he allowed some priests in Rome to elect him antipope, the first antipope in the Church's history. For twenty-five years he wrote and spoke against the real popes. In a subsequent government persecution both he and the the real pope were condemned to work in the mines on the island of Sardinia off the coast of Italy. It was there that St. Hippolytus swallowed his pride and was reconciled with the real pope. Both he and the pope died as martyrs.

The most outstanding work of St. Hippolytus is called the "Apostolic Tradition." The author claims to incorporate traditions going back to the Apostles. The work contains an ordinal, a book containing directions to be followed in the consecration of a bishop. Most precious for our interest is that it contains the TEXT of a Eucharistic Prayer, the oldest such text ever discovered. St. Hippolytus offers it not as THE text for Mass in Rome, but as a model text, which need not be followed word for word. (At that time there were no fixed Mass texts or Mass formulas.) [TEP]

✝ ✝ ✝

*At the Last Supper of the new King the new Passover puts to flight
the old one. What Christ did at that Supper he commanded to be
done in his memory.
Instructed by the sacred teachings, we consecrate bread and wine into
the Victim of our salvation.
A dogma is given to Christians that the bread is transformed into flesh
and the wine into blood.
Beyond the order of nature a lively faith affirms what you neither
grasp nor see. Excellent things lie hidden under the different
appearances
which are signs and not the reality beneath.*

St. Thomas Aquinas

The model text of an Eucharistic Prayer by St. Hippolytus follows. "The Lord be with you. And with thy spirit. Lift up your hearts. We have lifted them unto the Lord. Let us give thanks to God. It is right and just. [And thus now proceed.] We render thanks to Thee, O God, through Thy beloved Son, Jesus Christ, Whom Thou hast sent to us in these latest times as Savior and Redeemer and an Angel of Thy will. He is Thy inseparable Word, through Whom Thou hast made all things, and Who was well pleasing to Thee. He, fulfilling Thy will and acquiring for Thee a holy people, extended His hands when he suffered, that He might free from suffering those who have believed in Thee.

When He was given over to his voluntary passion that He might dissolve death, and break the bonds of the devil, and trample hell under foot, and enlighten the just, and fix the goal, and manifest the resurrection, He...taking bread and giving thanks to Thee, said: 'Take, eat, this is My Body, which shall be crushed for you.' Likewise the chalice also, saying: 'This is My Blood, which is poured out for you. When you do this, you make a commemoration of Me.'

"Mindful, therefore, of His death and resurrection, we offer to Thee the Bread and Chalice, giving thanks that thou hast held us worthy to stand before thee and to minister to Thee. And we beg that Thou send the Holy Spirit over the oblation of the holy Church. Bringing them together, grant to all who partake of the holy Things a fullness of the Holy Spirit and the confirmation of the faith in truth, so that we may praise and glorify Thee, the Father, and the Son, together with the Holy Spirit in Thy holy Church now and forever. Amen."[TEP]

You might notice that today our Eucharistic Prayer 2, which is often said on weekdays without a special feast, is based on St. Hippolytus' text.

✝ ✝ ✝

O memorial of the Lord's death,
Living Bread, giving life to man,
Grant to my soul to live from Thee
And always relish Thee as sweet.

St. Thomas Aquinas

ORIGEN, died c. 215

Origen was the most prolific writer of the early Church. Thousands of works have been attributed to him. His tenacity in writing earned him the name, "man of steel."

Origen was born in Alexandria on the northern coast of Egypt. His saintly father, Leonidas, gave him a sound foundation in religion. When his father was being tortured in prison because of the faith, Origen, still a teenager, wrote his father not to avoid martyrdom for the sake of his wife and children. Origen himself wanted to turn himself over to a pagan judge to be sent to prison and martyred for the faith. His mother was forced to hide his clothes to prevent him from carrying out his desire for martyrdom.

Origen studied for a while in the famous theological school of Alexandria under Clement of Alexandria and later opened his own school in Caeserea in Palestine. This school came to be more famous than even that of Alexandria. It was at Caeserea that Origen was arrested during one of the government's persecutions and was tortured almost to death. He died a few years later around the year 215.

Origen's commentary on the Our Father is the oldest that has yet been found. But his most famous work is entitled "Hexapla" (sixfold). It was a tremendous undertaking. To facilitate study of the Old Testament he compared the original Hebrew text to four current Greek translations. In six parallel columns he wrote, word for word, the entire Old Testament in its original Hebrew letters, next to that the Hebrew letters in Greek characters, and then next to that the four Greek translations, side by side, for easy comparison and study.

† † †

When the Host is finally broken (at Mass), do not doubt; but remember there is as much concealed in the fragment as in the whole Host.
Christ is not broken. There is a fracture of the sign, which diminishes neither the condition nor the stature of the One signified.

St. Thomas Aquinas

We quote here a few things Origen wrote about the Eucharist. First, concerning the great care one must use when receiving Communion in the hand: "You are aware that, when you assist at the divine mysteries (Mass) and receive the body of the Lord, you guard it with every precaution and veneration in order that not even a particle of it fall to the floor, lest part of the consecrated gift be lost. You consider yourselves guilty, and rightly so, if anything of the Host is lost through negligence."

In teaching that one must have the proper dispositions of soul to receive Communion, Origen recalls that before the first multiplication of the loaves Jesus cured those who were sick (Matthew 14:14). He joins that idea to St. Paul's warning in 1 Cor 11:28 about examining one's self before receiving Communion. "In the first place observe that, when Jesus was about to give the loaves of benediction to the disciples to give to the multitude, 'he cured the sick,' so that having been restored to health, they partook of the loaves of benediction. Those who are sick are not capable of receiving the loaves of benediction. And further, if anyone should hear the words, 'Let each one examine himself and so eat the bread,' and he pays no attention to those words, but inconsiderately partakes of the bread of the Lord and his chalice, he becomes weak or sick or dies." [All quotes from Origen are from TEP]

† † †

Jesus Lord, kind Pelican,
Cleanse my filth with Thy blood,
One drop of which can save
The whole world from all its sin.

Jesus, whom now I behold veiled,
I pray that what I so thirst for will come to pass,
So that beholding Thee with face unveiled,
I may be blessed by the sight of Thy glory. Amen.

St. Thomas Aquinas

ST. CYPRIAN, died 258 a.d.

St. Cyprian was born of a wealthy pagan family in Carthage, which at that time was an important city on the northern coast of Africa in modern Tunisia. He received a very good education, especially in law, and enjoyed life and this world to the full. He owned a lot of property and moved in the best intellectual and social circles of Carthage. However, a persistent, vague dissatisfaction seemed to haunt him, until he studied the Christian faith and was received into the Church at the age of about 35.

Almost immediately after his baptism Cyprian made a vow of continence and sold much of his possessions to give the proceeds to the poor. Two years later he was ordained a priest. Not long afterwards, when the See of Carthage was open, the priests and people used their current privilege and elected St. Cyprian Bishop of that important diocese.

By the time of St. Cyprian the Church had spread well along the northern coast of Africa bordering the Mediterranean Sea. There were 90 bishops in Africa, and 87 of them came for the Council of Carthage at the request of St. Cyprian to study the validity of baptism administered by heretics. The Council voted to reject heretical baptism as invalid; but the Pope insisted that the traditional stance be followed by admitting its validity, as is still done today when certain conditions are met.

For 40 years the Roman government had not persecuted the Church, so the Church thrived and Christians gained respect and prestige in the social circles. Then a new and most vicious persecution broke out throughout the Roman empire. St. Cyprian died a martyr in that persecution. The Church in Rome recognized his sanctity as a martyr by mentioning him in its holiest prayer, the Canon or Eucharistic Prayer, of the Mass. His name is still found there in Eucharistic Prayer 1, along with two other African martyrs, Sts. Perpetua and Felicitas.

† † †

Praise and glory, honor and thanksgiving to our Eucharistic King now and forever.
Amen.

The extant writings of St. Cyprian contain more references to the Eucharist than those of any earlier writer. He mentions several points of

Eucharistic doctrine and customs, which we shall mention in our quotations from his works. He lived in times of religious controversy.

St. Cyprian criticizes a bishop who had permitted a priest to act as a tutor. "Let no one call to worldly troubles priests and ministers of God, who have been dedicated to his altar and to the Church."

He mentions annual Masses in honor of the martyrs. "We offer sacrifice for them (martyrs). As you recall, we always celebrate the days of the sufferings of the martyrs with an annual memorial."

It was the practice in both Rome and Carthage to deny the sacraments of Confession and Holy Communion to those who had apostasized (denied their faith) during a persecution. Only in danger of death could apostates receive the sacraments. St. Cyprian, in a letter to the Pope, believes that practice should be mitigated in the face of an upcoming persecution. He believes that those who denied their faith, but now want to do what is right, would not have the strength to avoid denying the faith again, if they could not receive Holy Communion. "Let us not leave unarmed and naked those we encourage and exhort to do battle, but let us defend them with the protection of the blood and body of Christ. And since the Eucharist exists for this, namely, to be able to be protection for those who receive it, those that we wish to be secure against the enemy, let us arm them with the fullness of the Lord. For, how can we teach them and encourage them to shed their blood in confessing the name of Christ, if we deny the blood of Christ to those about to do battle? Or, how can we make them capable of drinking the chalice of martyrdom, if we do not first admit them to drink the chalice of the Lord in church by way of Communion?" And in the same letter St. Cyprian goes on to mention the daily celebration of Mass. "It is a great honor and glory of our episcopacy, that we have given peace (absolution of sins) to the martyrs (martyrs-to-be), so that as we priests daily celebrate the sacrifices of God (Masses), we prepare the victims (martyrs) for God."

In a letter to the faithful of a neighboring town, St. Cyprian mentions the daily reception of Communion by the laity, something that he recommends in view of the imminent persecution. "Let us not think that the things (persecution) that are coming will be like those that have passed. Now a worse and fiercer struggle threatens, for which the soldiers of Christ must prepare themselves with strong faith and robust virtue. Let them consider that it is for that reason they daily drink the chalice of the blood of Christ, so that they themselves will be able to shed their blood for Christ."

Ancient, non-biblical sources mention that the Jews mixed water with the wine they used for the Paschal supper. In all probability, Christ also did that at the Last Supper when he instituted the Eucharist. From earliest times the Church used a mixed chalice for Mass. St. Cyprian not only mentions that Christ mixed water with wine at the Last Supper but adds a significance to this custom. "In the consecration of the chalice of the Lord one cannot offer only water nor only wine. Because if one offers only wine, the blood of Christ begins to be present without us; and if there be only water, the people begin to be present without Christ."

St. Cyprian fought the abuse of those priests who tried to say Mass with water only. He declares such Masses invalid. He also states that the proper sanctification is not present if the priest and people do not unite the offering of themselves to the Mass. "It is clear that there is not offered the blood of Christ, if the chalice lacks wine. Nor is the sacrifice of the Lord celebrated with proper sanctification, if the immolation and sacrifice of ourselves is not united to his suffering." [TEP]

† † †

Prayer of St. Thomas Aquinas
When Receiving Communion at the Hour of His Death

I receive you, the price of the redemption of my soul.
I receive you, theViaticum (food)
of my pilgrimage (to heaven).
For love of you I have studied, kept vigil, labored,
preached, and taught.
Never did I say anything against you.

> ***But if in ignorance I said something against you,***
> ***I do not persist in my ignorance.***
> ***But if I have said something wrong,***
> ***I submit everything to correction by the Roman Church. Amen.***

The death of Christ on the cross concluded the essential elements of his sacrifice for our redemption. Nevertheless, his resurrection from the dead was a necessary complement of his sacrifice, as were also his ascension into heaven and his sending the Holy Spirit to initiate the Church on Pentecost. In defending the celebration of Mass in the morning, which St. Cyprian believed to be the universal practice in his day, he shows the close relationship of Christ's resurrection to his sacrifice by simply calling the Mass the resurrection of the Lord: "We celebrate the resurrection of the Lord in the morning."

Although just in passing, it is with simple clarity that St. Cyprian teaches that the Mass makes the passion of Christ present again. But he does not elaborate on the manner in which Christ's passion is present again; i.e., in an unbloody manner. Graphically, he calls the Mass the passion of the Lord. "And because we make mention of his passion in all the sacrifices of the Mass—the passion is the sacrifice of the Lord that we offer—we must not do anything else but what he did. Now the Scripture says that as often as we offer the chalice in memory of the Lord and his passion, we do that which, it is clear, the Lord did."

As we saw, St. Cyprian used to move in the circles of high society and was thus acquainted with the wealth of some of the pagans of his day. He recalls this in his letter to his friend Donatus, who had recently been received into the Church as an adult. "No one can make poor him whom God has made rich. Once the heavenly food (Holy Communion) has enriched the breast, one can suffer no want. Now the ceiling panels incrusted with gold and the mansions decorated with precious marble will seem cheap to you, now that you know it is rather you who should be decorated, you who should be adorned, because your body is the principle house in which the Lord resides as in a temple, and which the Holy Spirit has begun to inhabit."

✝ ✝ ✝

Jesus Christ, our Lord and our God, really present in the Blessed Sacrament, we look forward to praising you in the fellowship of all your saints in our heavenly homeland.

St. Cyprian praises the "confessors," as they were called, those who suffered torture during the persecutions but lived and refused to deny their faith by taking part in pagan sacrifices to idols. "Noble hands, which were not made except for divine works, resisted the sacrilegious sacrifices. Mouths that had been sanctified with the heavenly food of the body and blood of the Lord rejected profane contagion and the leftovers of the sacrifices to idols."

As we saw, Christians who, out of fear or weakness, had denied their faith during a persecution, ordinarily were not forgiven and received back into the Church unless they were in danger of death. This was the regular practice in Rome and in Carthage. However, sometimes the "confessors" who had endured the persecution bravely would write letters to the bishop, in which they pleaded for clemency for the "fallen" who had denied their faith. After the "fallen" had shown what the bishop considered sufficient penance, he would sometimes hear the Confession of the "fallen" and forgive them while extending his hand over them. At times the bishop would delegate priests to do this. St. Cyprian complains about lax priests who would admit the "fallen" to Communion without their having made proper Confession or done penance for their sins. "Some priests reject with contempt the proper procedure. Before having expiated their faults, before having confessed their crime, before having purified their conscience with the sacrifice of the Mass and the hand of the bishop, before having placated their offenses against the Lord, who is indignant and threatening, the "fallen" do violence to the body and blood of the Lord and sin against the Lord now with their hands (Communion in the hand) and their mouth more than when they denied him."

79

On the conduct of sacrilegious persons, those who knowingly receive Holy Communion without the proper dispositions of soul St. Cyprian says: "The person gets angry with the priests, when he cannot promptly receive the body of the Lord with contaminated hands or drink the blood of the Lord with polluted mouth." [TEP]

† † †

Lord, may our love for you grow into a love which reaches our neighbor.

Throughout the history of the Church there have been numerous miracles attributed to the Eucharist. St. Cyprian says he was present at one such miracle. Christian parents once left their baptized child with a pagan wet nurse, who took the infant with her to a pagan sacrifice. Some sacrificial bread dipped in wine was given to the baby. Later the mother of the child took her to Mass, where the baby behaved exceptionally badly. It was the custom there, as it still is in some places, to give Holy Communion to infants by letting them sip few drops of the precious blood from the chalice. When the deacon approached this infant with the chalice containing the precious blood, St.Cyprian describes what happened. "The child instinctively turned her head away from the divine Majesty, closed her mouth, pressed her lips together and refused the chalice. Nevertheless the deacon insisted, and despite the fact that the infant refused it, he poured some precious blood into her mouth. Then the infant began to become nauseated and vomited. The Eucharist could not remain in the body and mouth that had been polluted (by the pagan sacrifice), and the drink that was sanctified in the blood of the Lord came out of her violated body. So great is the power and majesty of the Lord that the secrets of (diabolical) darkness were discovered under the light; and the occult crimes did not deceive the bishop of God." [TEP]

† † †

Prayer of St. Thomas Aq. to the Blessed Mother
After Communion

O Mary, Virgin and most holy Mother,
behold I have received your most beloved Son,
whom you conceived in your immaculate womb,
to whom you gave birth, nursed,
and whom you fondled with the sweetest caresses.
Behold him, whose sight filled you
with joy and all delight,
I humbly and lovingly present and offer to you
to be embraced and loved by you,
and to be offered in supreme worship
of the most holy Trinity for your honor and glory
and for my needs and those of the entire world.
Therefore, I ask you, most holy Mother,
beg for me forgiveness of all my sins,
abundant grace to serve Jesus Christ
more faithfully from now on,
and at last the final grace
that I may praise him with you forever.
Amen.

St. Cyprian mentions that a woman secretly tried to steal a Host during Mass, but when she swallowed it, it acted like a deadly poison. She began to choke and faint and fell to the ground panting and trembling. He remarks: "She did not remain long without punishment, nor did the sin of her secret conscience remain hidden. She who had deceived a man (bishop) experienced the vengeance of God." Another woman with bad dispositions of soul was going to give herself Communion from the chest containing the Eucharist in her home (as was the custom in some places during the persecutions). When she went to open the chest, fire shot out of the chest which prevented her from opening it.

A man with improper dispositions of soul received the Host in his hand. When he was about to put the Host in his mouth, he saw that he had only ashes in his hand. St. Cyprian remarks: "From the testimony about that man it is clear that the Lord withdraws when he is denied, and that when one is not disposed, what he receives profits him nothing for salvation. When the Holy One withdraws, saving grace turns into ashes."

In his commentary on the Our Father, St. Cyprian interprets our Lord's words, "Give us this day our daily bread," as referring to Holy Communion. "We ask that every day there be given to us our bread, that is, Christ, so that we who remain and live in Christ do not withdraw from his sanctification and his body."

In chastising a wealthy Christian woman, we learn from St. Cyprian that it was the custom in Carthage for the faithful to bring bread and wine to be consecrated at Mass. "You are very wealthy, and do you believe that you celebrate the sacrifice of the Lord (Mass), you who pay no attention to the sacred treasure, you who come to the sacrifice of the Lord with no gift for the sacrifice, you who in the sacrifice take part of that which some poor person has offered?"

St. Cyprian on the necessity of good works: "It is of little value to be baptized and receive the Eucharist, if one does not profit by it in actions and works."

Finally St. Cyprian says: "It is with reverential fear and with honor that the Eucharist is to be received." [TEP]

THE FIRST KNOWN MARTYRS OF THE EUCHARIST, 257 - 259 a.d.

It was in the Roman imperial persecutions of the late 250's that Pope St. Sixtus and his deacon St. Lawrence, and St. Cyprian in Carthage and St. Fructuosus in Spain were martyred for the faith. It was also the time of the first known martyrs of the Eucharist.

In some places it was the custom to bury the dead in underground passageways called catacombs. The imperial government respected these cemeteries and forbade any violence or arrests in the catacombs. During times of persecution, when they could not assemble openly, Christians would take advantage of the law and hold their assemblies and celebrate Mass in the catacombs. In their "History of the Catholic Church" Rev. Fernand Mourret, S.S. and Rev. Newton Thompson, S.T.D. (Vol. 1, p.415) speak of the first known martyrs of the Eucharist, as follows:

"In a crypt on the Via Salaria (in Rome) some Christians holding a liturgical meeting were discovered by soldiers, who quickly blocked the entrance to the cavern with stones and earth. After the peace of the Church (after the persecutions ceased in 313 a.d.) the skeletons of these Christians were found, as also the silver vessels that had been used in the Eucharistic sacrifice. Pope Damasus, when restoring the catacomb, did not disturb these venerable relics, but simply made a little window in the wall, so that pilgrims might venerate the remains of these martyrs of the Holy Eucharist."

It was probably during the same persecution that a more well known martyr, St. Tarsicius of Rome, gave his life for the Eucharist. On the same page noted above the same authors state the following: "The acolyte St. Tarsicius was attached to the service of one of the Roman catacombs. While bearing the sacred species (the Host), which had been consecrated in the crypt (catacomb), to some Christian home, he was seized by soldiers, who ordered him to hand over what he carried. (He refused) and the soldiers clubbed him to death, while he pressed to his heart the sacred pyx holding the body of the Lord." Legend has it that St. Tarsicius was only a boy when he died. Pope Damasus (366-384) had the following inscription carved on his tomb: "When... violent hands were laid on holy Tarsicius carrying the body of Christ, he preferred to die rather than surrender to mad dogs the heavenly Body."

ST. DIONYSIUS THE GREAT, died c. 264

St. Dionysius, a native of Alexandria on the northern coast of Egypt, was born of a pagan family and baptized as an adult after much searching and study, especially at the Didascalia, the theological school in Alexandria. He later taught at that school and was made Bishop of Alexandria. Few of his writings are extant. The one we mention here teaches us about some Eucharistic practices in the Church of Alexandria toward the end of the third century.

In a letter to Fabian, Bishop of Antioch in Syria, St. Dionysius writes about Serapion, an old man, who had been a faithful Christian for a long time. However, during a persecution, "he fell into temptation," that is, he sacrificed to a pagan idol. He frequently asked priests to hear his confession, but they paid no attention to him. They followed the rule that apostasy from the faith would not be forgiven except in danger of death.

One day Serapion fell ill, and for three days he was unconscious and unable to speak. When he recovered a little, he sent his young nephew to fetch the priest. However, it was at night, and the priest himself was so ill that he could not leave to attend to the old man. But the priest recalled that Bishop Dionysius had given the order that no one in danger of death was to be denied the consolation of Confession, especially those who had requested it before.

The priest, undoubtedly believing that the old man had made or could make an Act of Perfect Contrition, gave the boy a small piece of a consecrated Host. He told him to take it to his uncle, moisten it, and immediately put it in the old man's mouth. When the boy returned, Serapion said, "Have you returned, my son? Since the priest has not been able to come, do quickly what he ordered you to do, and then leave me." The boy moistened the

Host and immediately put it in the mouth of the old man. The man had hardly swallowed the Host when he died.

In a letter to the Pope on rebaptizing Dionysius writes: "I would not dare to rebaptize one, who for some time, has listened to the Action of Thanksgiving (Mass), who has answered (the Great) 'Amen'...who has approached the Eucharistic table, who has extended his hands to receive the holy food, and who has taken and partaken of the body and blood of our Lord Jesus Christ." [TEP]

(All quotes from TEP-Textos Eucaristicos Primitivos)

Chapter VII

THE EUCHARIST IN THE FOURTH CENTURY

EUSEBIUS OF CAESAREA, died 340 a.d.

Eusebius, a native of Palestine, was Bishop of Caesarea in Palestine from about 313 to 340. He is known as the Father of Church History chiefly because of his monumental work of 10 books entitled "Ecclesiastical History." He begins with Christ and reviews the history of the Church down to the year 323. Without this great work of his we would know little of the history of the Church in its first 300 years. However, what interests us here is what he wrote about the Eucharist.

Eusebius speaks of Mass being said daily. He understands the Mass to be the sacrifice of Christ, which he left us as a memorial of him: "Having presented to the Father a marvelous sacrifice and a choice Victim, Christ offered that Victim for the salvation of us all. He also bequeathed to us as a memorial the fact that we can offer that Victim to God constantly as a sacrifice."

Regarding Holy Communion, Eusebius writes: "We who live on the earth are made partakers of the bread that came down from heaven and of the Word (Christ) who emptied himself... He will be able to delight in the Lord, he who is purified in the affections of his soul, so that he can eat the living bread and the life-giving flesh and drink his saving blood. Having been nourished and strengthened with these, he rejoices in divine rapture."

Not like the Pasch in the Old Testament Eusebius says they celebrate our Pasch every Sunday and even daily. "We celebrate our Pasch every Sunday; we are always filled with the body of the Savior; we always partake of the blood of the Lamb... and the Gospel wants us to do this not only once a year but always and daily. Therefore, every week on the day of the Savior and Lord we celebrate the feast of our Pasch, making present the mysteries of the true Lamb, by whom we have been redeemed. We celebrate these same mysteries throughout the whole year. We commemorate the passion of the Savior every Friday with the fast that the Apostles first observed, when the Bridegroom (Christ) had been taken from them. And every Sunday we are renewed by the body that was sanctified in the same saving Pasch, and our souls are sealed with his precious blood."

The Jews in Egypt, at God's command, smeared blood of the paschal lamb on the lintels of their homes to avoid the angel killing the firstborn of the Egyptians. Likewise, Eusebius writes, "We mark the lintels of our souls with the blood of the Lamb that has been sacrificed for us in order to make our mortal enemy (Satan) flee from us."

Eusebius lived to see the end of the Roman government's persecutions of the Church. In the year 313 by imperial decree the Christians were permitted to practice their religion freely throughout the Roman Empire; and their property, confiscated during the persecutions, was returned to them. Consequently Eusebius could speak of altars being built and churches being consecrated everywhere. "And who, but only our Savior has bequeathed to his adorers the mandate to offer unbloody and spiritualized sacrifices through the prayers and ineffable invocation of God (at Mass)? Therefore wherever men live, altars have been constructed, and there are consecrated churches. On the part of all people there are offered to the one God and King of the universe rites of spiritualized sacrifices. (Eusebius uses the term "spiritualized sacrifices" to distinguish the Mass from the pagan sacrifices that lacked any true spiritual element, because the gods to whom they were offered did not exist.) And who, with a hidden and invisible force, has brought about the absolute extinction of those bloody sacrifices with their foul blood and smoke (former Jewish sacrifices), and of those cruel and wild sacrifices (of the pagans) with their human victims? ...Not before, but after the divine teaching of our Savior did the sacrifices of human victims cease completely everywhere." (TEP - Textos Eucaristicos Primitivos)

✝ ✝ ✝

Help us, O Lord, to live
The faith which we proclaim,
That all our thoughts and words and deeds
May glorify your name.

W.W.Reid

FIRST ECUMENICAL COUNCIL OF NICEA, 325a.d.

The early years of the fourth century were very turbulent times for the Church and for the entire Roman Empire. Savage persecutions were unleashed by the Emperors in a last ditch effort to stamp out Christianity and maintain paganism as the State religion. But the government persecutions, which had gone on periodically for nearly 300 years, finally came to a definite end in the year 313 by the order of Emperor Constantine. Although not baptized until on his death bed, he favored Christianity and helped the Church prosper throughout the Empire.

But there was to be no peace within the Church herself. She was now facing what would probably be the greatest threat to her existence that she would ever face, the heresy called Arianism. Arius, a priest from Alexandria in Egypt, found many followers among priests and bishops with his novel teaching that Jesus Christ is not really God, but only like God and the greatest creature that God created.

The danger created by that heresy was so great that, at the insistence of Emperor Constantine himself, the first ecumenical council was held in Nicea (in modern Turkey). As successors of the Apostles, all bishops were invited and expected to attend, if possible. There were 318 bishops who attended from all over the Roman Empire. The Pope could not attend personally, so he sent his legate, Hosius, Bishop of Cordova in Spain, and two priests. The three were to preside over the Council in the Pope's name. Many of the bishops like Hosius himself, bore the physical marks of the persecutions they had endured for their belief in the divinity of Christ, and consequently were not well disposed to be deceived by the smooth-talking Arius and his noisy followers.

PRAYER AFTER COMMUNION

Most sweet Jesus, may your most holy body and blood be the sweetness and delight of my soul, my salvation and strength in every temptation, my joy and peace in every trial, my light and strength in every word and deed, and my final protection in death.

St. Thomas Aquinas

Arianism posed a mortal threat to the Church, because she was very young and none of her doctrine had yet been formally defined. Nearly 300 years of physical persecution hampered the Church's growth but could not kill her. However, heresy could, and still can, destroy her, if God would not intervene to assist her. But God raised up the young deacon, St. Athanasius of Alexandria in Egypt, who had accompanied his Bishop to the Council. He turned out to be the shining star of the Council despite the fact that he was only 30 years old. The Arians simply could not resist his wisdom and his ability to debate. He championed the doctrine of the divinity of Christ and won for himself the title, "Great." We shall meet him soon as the Bishop of Alexandria.

With all of the doctrinal authority that Christ left to his Church the First Ecumenical Council of Nicea formulated a new Creed, which expanded the Apostles' Creed that had been used in the Church since earliest times. The Nicene Creed specifically clarifies the divinity of Christ, that he is truly God and of the same substance or nature of God the Father. Later this Creed would be added to in order to refute other heresies.

This is the Nicene Creed: "We believe in one God, the Father almighty, Maker of all things visible and invisible; and in one Lord Jesus Christ, the Son of God, the only-begotten of the Father, that is, of the substance of the Father, God of God, light of light, through whom (Christ) all things were made both in heaven and on earth; who for us men and for our salvation descended, became incarnate, and was made man, suffered and rose again the third day, ascended into heaven and will come to judge the living and the dead. And (we believe) in the Holy Spirit." To clarify the divinity of Christ still further the Council added the following: "The Catholic and Apostolic Church anathematizes (condemns) those who say: 'There was a time when he (Christ) did not exist, and he did not exist before he was begotten, and he was made out of nothing.' Or those who say, 'He is of another essence or substance (than that of the Father), or that the son of God is created or is susceptible of change or alteration.' "

The First Council of Nicea did not take up doctrine of the Eucharist, simply because no objections to that doctrine had been registered. However, the Council did correct two abuses regarding the distribution of Holy Communion. Those who had been excommunicated were barred from Confession and Communion except when they were in danger of death. The Council forbade the practice, prevalent in some places, of deacons giving Communion to priests and receiving Communion before the bishops present at Mass.

✝ ✝ ✝

PRAYER BEFORE COMMUNION

Almighty and eternal God, behold,
I approach the sacrament of your only begotten Son,
our Lord Jesus Christ.
I come as one sick to the doctor of life,
unclean to the fountain of mercy,
blind to the light of eternal radiance,
poor and needy to the Lord of heaven and earth.
Therefore I beg the abundance of your immense generosity
to heal my sickness, wash away my defilement,
enlighten my blindness, enrich my poverty,
and clothe my nakedness.
May I receive the Bread of angels,
the King of kings, the Lord of lords,

with such reverence and humility,
with such contrition and devotion,
with such purity and faith,
with such resolve and intention
as befits the salvation of my soul.
Grant me, I implore you, to receive
not only the sacrament of the Lord's body and blood,
but also the reality and power of the sacrament.
O most gentle God, allow me
to receive the body of your only begotten Son,
our Lord Jesus Christ,
which he took from the Virgin Mary,
so that I may be worthy to be incorporated into
his mystical body and be numbered among his members.
O most loving Father, grant me finally to contemplate forever face to
face your beloved Son,
whom I now propose to receive veiled
on my earthly pilgrimage.
Amen.

St. Thomas Aquinas

JUVENCO, died c. 330

The early years of the fourth century were outstanding for several reasons. The imperial government's persecutions of the Church finally stopped after nearly 300 years. The Church gained her freedom to exist and expand. The first ecumenical council, that of Nicea, spelled out the divinity of Jesus Christ. And the early fourth century saw the beginning of Christian Latin poetry, which would grow and blossom within the Church for a thousand years. Until the fourth century Christian poetry was written in Greek, Syriac, Coptic, or other eastern languages. The first, or one of the first Christian poets to write in Latin was a priest by the name of Juvenco (Juvencus), who was born and lived in Spain.

In one of his poems he attempts to harmonize the events contained in the four Gospels. He tries to put the message of all four Gospels to poetry, a gigantic task indeed. Juvenco says: "I have wished to adorn the majesty of the divine law with the ornamentations of earthly poetry. It is Christ who has given me this leisure by granting peace to our age (a reference to the end of the persecutions)" [Murret-Thompson], Vol 2, p.93].

The following quotation, in which he describes the scene at the Last Supper, shows that he availed himself of the license and freedom that a poet enjoys. "Having said this, the Lord began to break the bread with his hands. Having divided it, he gave it to his disciples. Then he offered holy prayers, and taught the disciples that they were thus to eat his own body. Afterwards, the Lord takes the chalice full of wine. He sanctifies it with words of thanksgiving and gives it to them to drink. He taught them that he had distributed to them his blood and said, 'This blood redeemed the sins of the people. Drink this, my blood. Believe the true words...' "[TEP]

† † †

POEM TO THE HOLY SPIRIT

Breathe on me, Breath of God,
Fill me with life anew,
That I may love the things you love,
And do what you would do.

Breathe on me, Breath of God,
Until my heart is pure
Until with you I have one will
To live and to endure.

Edwin Hatch

ST. ATHANASIUS, died 373

We met the young deacon, St. Athanasius, as the shining star of orthodoxy and the staunch defender of Christ's divinity during the First Ecumenical Council of Nicea in the year 325. The Council had condemned Arianism, but did not kill it. The heresy continued to spread especially in the East through the efforts of the Emperor. It gained so much ground among Christians that later St. Jerome would say, "The world groaned and was astonished to find itself Arian."

Meanwhile, St. Athanasius was made Bishop of Alexandria in Egypt. He continued his fight against the Arian heresy. This caused the Emperor to banish him into exile. He would be returned more than once to his bishopric only to be exiled again through the evil machinations of the Arians. However, he and others like him, such as Bishop Hosius of Cordova in Spain and St. Hilary in France, kept up the fight for the true faith of Nicea. By the time St. Athanasius, "the pillar of orthodoxy," died in 373 Alexandria had become the center of Catholic life in the East. The saintly Bishop saw Arianism declining as rapidly as it had arisen. Christ had not abandoned his Church.

In the literary works of St. Athanasius that are still extant we find several references to the Eucharist. In pastoral letters to the faithful of his Diocese of Alexandria he invites the people to prepare properly for the coming Paschal feasts. He compares the Paschal lamb offered by the Jews in the Old Testament to the true Lamb we offer at Mass: "Now we do not offer a material lamb but that true Lamb, which was immolated, our Lord Jesus Christ...Then the Jews celebrated the feast of the Pasch with the meal of the flesh of an irrational lamb, and they warded off the (angel) exterminator with branches dipped in the blood of the Paschal lamb. But now we eat the Word of the Father (God the Son), and we sign the lips of our hearts with the blood of the New Testament." [TEP]

† † †

Jesus in the Blessed Sacrament, through your presence guide the college of bishops in union with the Pope, and give them the gifts of unity, love, and peace.

In another letter to the members of his diocese St. Athanasius reminds them to celebrate the Paschal feast with the proper dispositions of body and soul: "Let us pray that we not eat the Pasch unworthily, so as not to be entangled in the dangers (mentioned below by St. Paul). The Pasch will truly be heavenly food for those who celebrate the Feast with purity; but for those who are impure and indifferent it will be danger and shame. Because it is written: 'He who eats and drinks unworthily will be guilty of the death of the Lord' (1 Co. 11:27). Therefore in order not to approach the celebration of the festival rite without preparation, and in order to be worthy to approach the divine Lamb and taste the heavenly foods, let us purify our hands, cleanse our body, and have our conscience free from all deception."

In explaining the false, cannibalistic understanding that many Jews had in the synagogue in Capharnaum, when our Lord first announced his real presence in the Eucharist, St. Athanasius writes the following: "What body would be necessary to be able to be nourishment for the whole world? For this reason Christ reminded them of the ascension of the Son of Man to heaven, namely, that they learn that the flesh about which he had been speaking would be given as heavenly nourishment and spiritual food. He said: 'The words which I have spoken to you are spirit and life'(Jn 6:63), as if he were to say that what is seen and what is given for the salvation of the world is the flesh which I carry; and this same flesh with its blood I shall give you spiritually as nourishment, so that in this way it is distributed spiritually to each one, and is for all of you a defense for the resurrection to eternal life." [TEP]

† † †

From all that dwell below the skies
Let the Creator's praise arise:

95

Let the Redeemer's name be sung
Through every land, by every tongue.
Eternal are thy mercies, Lord;
Eternal truth attends thy word:
Thy praise shall sound from shore to shore,
Till suns shall rise and set no more.

Isaac Watts

St. Athanasius has some advice for those who in his day practiced virginity in order to be free to serve God and neighbor better. "Employ your time in fasting, praying and giving alms. Happy is he who hears this advice and follows it. Let not the word of God leave your lips day or night. Let your continuous occupation be the meditation on the Sacred Scriptures. Have a psalter (book containing the 150 Psalms of the Bible) and learn the Psalms by heart. As the sun rises, contemplate the sacred book in your hands. Afterwards, at nine o'clock, celebrate Mass, because at that hour the wood of the Cross was formed."

In a sermon to the recently baptized adults St. Athanasius teaches them about the Consecration at Mass, which makes Christ truly present. "You will see the deacons who bring the bread and chalice with wine and place them on the altar. And as long as prayers and invocations are not finished, it is only bread and chalice. But once the great and admirable prayers are finished, then the bread becomes the body and the chalice the blood of our Lord Jesus Christ. Again, let us come to an understanding of the mysteries. This bread and this chalice, as long as the prayers and invocations have not been made, are only bread and chalice; but as soon as the great prayers and holy invocations are said, the Word (God the Son) descends to the bread and chalice, and they become his body." (Let us mention here that it is still a popular, but incorrect, way of explaining the Consecration at Mass to say that Christ descends into the bread and wine. As the Council of Trent says, the substance of the bread and wine is changed into the body and blood of Christ. Therefore Christ does not "descend" into the bread and wine. Christ becomes present by the priest's changing the bread and wine into him with Christ's own power, which was given to the priest in the sacrament of Holy Orders, which made him a priest.)

† † †

Help us, O Lord, to teach
The beauty of your ways,
That yearning souls may find the Christ,
And sing aloud his praise.

W.W.Reid

AFRAATES. died c. 350

From his writings that are extant we learn that Afraates was a monk and later a bishop in Mesopotamia in modern Iraq. He is surnamed "the Wise Man of Persia," and he gives us the earliest known witness to the faith in his country. His writings contain 22 "Demonstrations" or dissertations on religion. He said he wrote the first ten after a friend had consulted him on religious matters. What interests us, of course, is what he wrote about the Eucharist in the fourth century in that part of the world.

He writes of how a Christian should act after having received Holy Communion. "If one deprives himself of bread and water, let him not mix curses and insults in his fasting. Your house (body) is the temple of God, and there is but one door to that house. It is not fitting for you, O man, that filth and dirt come out of that door through which the King (God) enters. If one avoids whatever sins to receive the body and blood of Christ, he must guard well the mouth through which the Son of the King enters. With that mouth you cannot say filthy words. Listen, man, to what our Vivifier (Christ) says: 'What enters the mouth does not defile a man, but what comes out of the mouth, that defiles him' " (Math 15:ll).

Afraates comments on the incident in the Old Testament, when God ordered Gideon to march into battle with only the 300 soldiers who had lapped water, as dogs do, and to send home the vast number that had knelt down to drink. "Of all the animals that were created along with man only the dog joins his master watching day and night. And even if the master strikes the dog frequently, it never abandons him. When the dog accompanies his master on the hunt, if the master comes upon a powerful lion, the dog goes to his death in place of his master. That is the way the valiant men conducted themselves, who were chosen by the waters. Like dogs, they follow their master; they offer to die in his stead; they fight bravely in battle; they keep guard day and night; they bark like dogs, while they meditate day and night on the law (of God); they love the Lord and lick his wounds, when they receive his body and lift it to their eyes (a liturgical custom we shall meet later); and they lick Him with their tongue, as the dog licks its master.

"But those who do not meditate on the Law are like mute dogs who cannot bark; and those who are not disposed to fasting are like greedy dogs who are never satisfied."

As we know, Christ was buried on a Friday evening and rose from the dead the following Sunday morning. According to our way of reckoning time Christ would have been in the grave for about a day and a half. But the Jews reckoned any part of a day as a whole day. Therefore the Bible speaks of Christ's being in the grave three days, just as we say, "He was buried and on the third day rose again from the dead." Apparently Afraates was not aware of the Jewish way of reckoning time, but was rather inventive in having Christ dead for three nights. In writing about the Last Supper he says, "Christ who gives his flesh to eat and his blood to drink will be counted among the dead." [TEP]

PRAYER AFTER COMMUNION, by St. Thomas Aquinas

I thank you, Lord, holy Father, almighty and eternal God, for having deigned to feed me, a sinner and your unworthy servant, with the precious body and blood of your Son, our Lord Jesus Christ, not for any merits of mine but solely out of the kindness of your mercy.
I pray that this Holy Communion will not be for me condemnation and punishment but forgiveness and salvation. Let it be for me a defense of faith and a shield of good will. Let it put an end to my evil ways and root out concupiscence and lust.
Let this Communion be for me an increase in charity and patience, humility and obedience, and all the virtues. Let it be for me a strong defense against the wiles of all enemies, both visible and invisible,
May it be the perfect calming of my impulses, both carnal and spiritual. May it make me adhere to you, the one true God, and give me a happy death.
I pray you, Father, that you will deign to lead me, a sinner, to that amazing banquet, where you with your Son and the Holy Spirit are for your saints true light, total fulfillment, everlasting joy, exquisite pleasure, and perfect happiness. Through Christ our Lord. Amen.

ST. EPHRAEM, died 373

Like Bishop Afraates, St. Ephraem was from Mesopotamia in modern Iraq. He remained a deacon all his life. When the Persians of what is today Iran waged war on Mesopotamia, St. Ephraem fled north to Edessa in modern Turkey. Since all of that territory was part of Syria at that time, St. Ephraem, like Bishop Afraates, wrote in Syriac. St. Ephraem was mainly a poet. He wrote to spread Christian teaching and to give greater solemnity to the ceremonies of the Church with his poems. His writings on the Eucharist stress the real presence of Christ in the Blessed Sacrament.

"The crowd in the desert were like sheep wandering without a shepherd. In his compassion he (Christ) gave them food, the nourishment of bread which he multiplied. How fortunate are you, lambs branded by Christ, who have been made worthy of the body and the blood. The shepherd himself has become food for you."

Referring to the church building, St. Ephraem says: "Oh blessed place! No other place has seen or will see what you have seen, that is, the Lord who has become the true altar, priest, bread and chalice of salvation. By himself he suffices for everyone; and no one can be enough for him. He himself, is the altar and the lamb, the victim and the sacrificer, the priest and the food."

St. Ephraem refers to the slaughter of the innocents in Bethlehem in a failed attempt to kill the Christ Child. "The soldiers harvested tender flowers in Bethlehem, so that with them the new seed (Christ Child) would perish, the seed in which was hidden the bread of life. But the seed of life had fled in order to become a sheaf at the time of the harvest. The grape which, when it was new and young had fled, handed itself over to be trodden upon (in his passion), in order to give life to souls with its wine. Glory to You, treasure of life." [TEP]

† † †

Lord, open my mind to bless you and my heart to love you, so that I may spend this Holy Hour in your Eucharistic presence with attention and devotion.

In a sermon St.Ephraem says: "Brothers, in the waters of baptism you put on white garments. Do not stain your garments with sinful works. Behold, you sit at a banquet, which is the holy Church; in it you eat the living body and drink the propitiatory blood. He who sits at this banquet and delights in these pleasures, and at the same time does evil and sins—woe to him on the day of the resurrection, on that day when the King will come in glory to establish his throne of judgment. He will sit on his throne to take vengeance and to judge the peoples ... And on that day a thousand woes to him, who on Sunday neglects Christ immolated (at Mass) and sits in the plaza!"

"Sprinkle with the hope of life, O Lord, the faces of all the deceased, and place them at your right hand when you come (for the Last Judgment). O Son of God, let the dead who ate your body and blood be raised by you and be with you on the day of your manifestation. ... The Mass offerings do not benefit all the dead. The bodies that had been clothed with Him will be clothed with glory on the day of the resurrection, and the mouths that ate Him will sing his praises in the heavenly kingdom."

Just as the Jews were ordered by God to eat the Paschal meal while standing, so St. Ephraem says no one is to eat Christ, our Paschal meal, while one is seated. "Let no one eat Him while one is seated. If it is with fear that the Seraphs (angels in Isaiah 6) are in his presence, who will dare to eat Him while one is seated? No one is permitted to receive the living body while one is seated."

"Praised be Him who gave us hands, in which we receive his body. ...The mouth that he gave us is for his flesh and his chalice; the eyes that He created are for his Scriptures (Bible); and it is for the church that he gave us feet (i.e. to go to church)."

"It is you, O Lord, that we eat, and it is you that we drink, not in a way that we annihilate you, but so that we live for you." [TEP]

† † †

Lord God, to you all the angels in heaven
and around this altar sing in endless praise:
Holy, Holy, Holy Lord, God of power and might.

ST. ZENO, died c. 373

St. Zeno was of African origin, but as bishop he ruled the Diocese of Verona in northern Italy for the last ten years of his life. His extant writings are of value from a literary and doctrinal point of view, especially as regards the Trinity and the Blessed Mother. We shall quote from his writings that pertain to the Eucharist.

St. Zeno writes to warn Christian women not to marry pagans. He writes where pagan sacrifices were still being offered in public, and where Christians would still keep the Blessed Sacrament in a secret place in their homes, so that they could give themselves Holy Communion even daily. "What? His (the pagan husband's) sacrifice in public, and yours (receiving Communion) in secret? His sacrificial food can be handled by anyone, and yours cannot even be seen without committing sacrilege, even by those Christians (catechumens) who have not yet been baptized. And if (what your husband wants) is not done, or if what is done does not please him, then the whole house will grow with quarreling and God will be blasphemed. Your sacrificial food (consecrated Hosts) may even be snatched away. He will strike your breast and disfigure your face. Sometimes he will do you a 'favor' by ordering you not to come to church. But if you please your husband, it will be much worse; for you cannot please a sacrilegious person without committing sacrilege."

St. Zeno compares the empty sacrifices of the pagans and the Jewish sacrifices that had been repudiated by God with the Christian sacrifice, which he insists must be offered with proper dispositions of soul. "If it is proper that a bodily sacrifice be offered to bodily gods (of the pagans), surely a sacrifice offered to the spiritual God must likewise be spiritual. It must not take its origin from the pocket (money), but from the heart; nor must it come from a foul-smelling herd, but be prepared with very good conduct; nor must it be offered with bloody hands but with pure intentions. The sacrificial victim (Christ at Mass) is not killed, so that he perishes; but, like Isaac, it is offered in a way that it lives...This is what is pleasing to God, that the sincere spirit itself be offered. The rest is useless, if the soul of the adorer is not pure...Let each one watch how he takes and offers the sacrifice; for it is a sacrilege to offer it unworthily; it is deadly to eat it unworthily." [TEP]

JULIUS FIRMICUS MATERNUS, died after 348

Although Christianity was growing steadily after the persecutions ended in 313, and although paganism was steadily declining, yet in the second half of the fourth century there were still several pockets of paganism that presented stubborn resistance to the Church. This prompted Julius Firmicus Maternus of Italy to write spirited letters to the Christian Emperors exhorting them to greater efforts to stamp out paganism completely. Maternus was an educated layman and a convert from paganism. We quote from one of his letters written most likely in the year 348.

"There is another food that gives health and life, another food that really commends man to God and returns him to God, another food that strengthens the weak, calls back those who stray, lifts the fallen, and gives to the dying signs of eternal immortality. Seek the bread and the chalice of Christ, so that, having overcome earthly weakness, the substance of man maybe fed with immortal food."

"This divine bread is given to the baptized by God. So says the Holy Spirit through Isaiah: 'Thus says the Lord: "You shall see my servants eat, while you go hungry. You shall see my servants drink, while you are thirsty. The Lord will destroy you." Not only does the most high God deny this bread to the wicked and sacrilegious persons, but he also threatens them with punishment and decrees their end to be a terrible death. Their hungry gullets will swallow the consequence of divine aversion. Likewise the sacred verses of Psalm 33 teach the same thing, where the Holy Spirit through David says: "Taste and see that the Lord is sweet." Sweet is the heavenly food, sweet is the nourishment of God. It does not have in itself the sad torment of a miserable hunger, and it relieves one of the infection of former poison (sin).' "

✝ ✝ ✝

May this gracious God through all our life be near us,
With ever joyful hearts, and blessed peace to cheer us;
Preserve us in his grace and guide us in distress,

And free us from all sin till heaven we possess.

Martin Rinkart; translated by Catherine Winkworth

We continue to quote from a letter on the Eucharist that Maternus wrote about the middle of the fourth century. "In order to manifest more clearly the type of that bread by which the scourge of a miserable death is avoided, the Lord himself taught with his holy and venerable mouth, so that the hope of mankind would not falter by the bad interpretations of some writings: 'I am the bread of life. He who comes to me will never hunger; and he who believes in me will never thirst. If you do not eat the flesh of the Son of Man and drink his blood, you will not have life in you.' Therefore, you miserable mortals, have nothing to do with the food of the drum. (The drum was used in some pagan sacrifices.) Seek the grace of the saving food and drink the chalice. Christ will lead you to the light of his banquet, and he will restore those members who are sick and morbid due to the deadly poison (sin). Renew the lost man with the heavenly food, so he who was dead among us will come to life through the divine gift. You have learned what you should do. Choose what you wish. There (in pagan sacrifices) death is born; here (at Mass) is given immortal life."[TEP]

Firmly I believe and truly
God is three and God is one;
And I next acknowledge duly
Manhood taken by the Son.
And I trust and hope most fully
In that manhood crucified;
And I love supremely, solely,
Christ, who for my sins has died.
And I hold in veneration
For the love of him alone,

Holy Church as his creation,
And her teachings as his own.
Praise and thanks be ever given
With and through the angel host,
To the God of earth and heaven,
Father, Son and Holy Ghost.

John Henry Newman

ST. HILARY OF POITIERS, c.310-367

St. Hilary of Poitiers in modern France was born of pagan parents and received an excellent education. He was an orator, a philosopher and a poet. He received the gift of faith upon reading the Bible, especially the prologue of St. John's Gospel, in which it is explained that the Word (God the Son) was made flesh (became a man) in order to make us sons of God. Hilary was baptized when he was about 35 years old. He himself states that, when the clergy and people of the city of Poitiers asked him to be their bishop, he was already married and had a daughter named Abra. Since the law of continence was imposed strictly on the clergy, St. Hilary's wife agreed to leave him and never to look upon him again except at the altar, and henceforth to love him only as a daughter or a sister.

Hilary's good education made him an excellent apologist against the Arian heresy, which had flared up at that time in Gaul (France). He was so successful in his fight against Arianism that he was called "the Athanasius of the West." And just as the success of St. Athanasius of Alexandria in Egypt against the Arians caused him to be banished by the Emperor, so too was St. Hilary banished. During his exile in modern Turkey he wrote a theological treatise on the Trinity that earned him the title of Doctor and Father of the Church.

We quote here from one of St. Hilary's writings on the Eucharist. On Psalm 128, 3: "Your sons shall be round your table like shoots round an olive tree." It does not say they will be round your banquet, but round your table. Now the table is that of the Lord, from which we take the nourishment of the living bread. Just as he (Christ) himself lives, that living bread has the ability to make those live who receive it."

✝ ✝ ✝

Faith of our fathers! Faith and prayer
Shall win all nations unto thee;
And through the truth that comes from God,
Mankind shall then indeed be free.
Faith of our fathers, holy faith!
We will be true to thee till death.

Frederick W. Faber

St. Hilary writes on how Christ's presence is among us and in us through the Eucharist: "Now if the Word (God the Son) really was made flesh, and if by taking the Lord's food we truly receive the Word made flesh, then how can He not be expected to remain in us naturally? For when he was born man, he took to himself in an inseparable way the nature of our flesh; and he joined the nature of his flesh with his eternal nature in the sacrament in which he was to give us his flesh...The flesh in which the eternal Word, the Son of God, was born remains among us through the sacrament...'Give us this day our daily bread." (We recite this because) what does God want more than that Christ live in us daily, Christ who is the bread of life and the bread from heaven? And since this is a daily prayer, we ask that this bread be given to us daily."

✝ ✝ ✝

O Christ , you are the light and day
Which drives away the night,
The ever shining Sun of God
And pledge of future light.

O God of truth, prepare our minds
To hear and heed your holy word...
Teach us to love eternal truth
And seek its freedom everywhere.

Stanbrook Abbey

Father of unfading glory,
Rich in grace and strong to save,
Hear our prayers and come to save us,
Keep us far from sinful ways.

Mount St. Bernard Abbey

O most Holy Trinity,
Undivided Unity;
Holy God, Mighty God,
God Immortal, be adored.

Anon.; Tr. J. Rothensteiner

ST. CYRIL OF JERUSALEM (313-386)

At the close of the first ecumenical council, that of Nicea in 325, Emperor Constantine believed it to be his duty to restore or preserve some of the holy places in Palestine, where our Lord lived and died. In 327 his wife, St. Helena, visited Palestine. It was believed that she had discovered the True Cross, the one on which Christ had died. St. Cyril of Jerusalem says that in his day relics of the True Cross were to be found throughout the Roman Empire.

Throughout the fourth century the Church was torn by bitter theological disputes; but in the writings of St. Cyril, Bishop of Jerusalem, we find a haven of calm. The reason is simple. During Lent of the year 348 a scribe took down the 19 instructions that St. Cyril gave to the adult catechumens, who were preparing for baptism at the Easter Vigil. The scribe did the same for the 5 instructions that the Saint gave to the newly baptized on the sacraments of Baptism, Confirmation and the Eucharist, together with instructions on the meaning and symbolism of the Mass ceremonies. Just as the Didache tells us what the Mass ceremonies were like in the Middle East about the year 90 a.d., and just as St. Justin describes the Mass ceremonies in Rome around the year 150, the writings of St. Cyril tell us what the Mass ceremonies were like in Jerusalem in the year 348.

Referring to St. Paul's instruction on the Eucharist in 1 Cor 11, St. Cyril says to the newly baptized converts: "And this teaching of Blessed Paul is fitting to convince you completely of what refers to the divine mysteries. Having been judged worthy to receive them, you have become concorporate and consanguine with Christ. (The meaning of the underlined words is clear and graphic, namely, having received Holy Communion, you share with Christ his body and his blood. The Spanish words in TEP are "concorporeos" and "consanguineos.")

St. Cyril explains: "On another occasion with one of his miracles he (Christ) changed water into wine in Cana of Galilee, and are we not to believe when he changes wine into his blood?" It appears that when the Saint used the word "change" (Greek: metaballein; Latin: convertere; Spanish: convertir) he understood the doctrine of transubstantiation, which the Council of Trent would solemnly define 1200 years later.

In explaining the real presence of Christ in the Eucharist St. Cyril states: "With no doubt whatsoever we partake of the body and blood of Christ; for in the form of bread his body is given to you, and in the form of wine his blood is given to you, so that having partaken of the body and blood of Christ, you become concorporate and consanguine with him. In this way we become bearers (carriers) of Christ, as his body and blood are distributed through the members of our body. And so, according to Blessed Peter (2 Peter 1:4) we are made 'sharers (partakers) in the divine nature.' "

"Do not take them for mere bread and mere wine, because they are the body and blood of Christ according to the solemn affirmation of the Lord. Now although the senses suggest to you that it is mere bread and wine, yet faith must convince you. In this matter do not judge according to taste, but according to the faith. Believe firmly without doubt that you have been made worthy of the body and blood of Christ."

St. Cyril instructs the newly baptized on the manner of receiving Communion. "(After the Our Father) the bishop (celebrant) says: 'The holy things for the holy people'...Now when you approach do not approach with the palms of your hands stretched out nor with your fingers separated, but make your left hand a throne for your right, as if the right was to receive a king; and with the hollow of your hand receive the body of Christ, while you answer the Amen. Carefully then, having sanctified your eyes by touching them, receive the holy body, being careful not to lose any of it. Because if you lose any of it, you clearly do damage to yourself, just as you would to something of your own body. Because, tell me: if someone gave you gold filings (fragments), would you not guard them with all diligence, while you were careful not to lose any of them...

Shall you not take care with much mere diligence that there not fall even one crumb of that which is more precious than gold...?'"

† † †

Blessed are you, Lord, for you graciously called us into your holy Church. Keep us within the Church until death.

After explaining to the newly baptized the proper manner of receiving the Sacred Host in Holy Communion, the Bishop of Jerusalem continues by explaining how to receive the Precious Blood. "Then, after the communion of the body of Christ approach also the chalice of the blood. Do not extend your hands, but bow, and in an attitude of adoration and veneration bless yourself while saying the Amen and partaking of the blood of Christ. And while your lips are still moist, touch them with your hands and sanctify your eyes, your forehead, and all the other senses. Afterwards, while you spend time in prayer, give thanks to God who has made you worthy of such great mysteries." [TEP]

St. Cyril carefully explains the proper manner of receiving Communion in the hand and from the chalice. It is clear what the custom of receiving Communion was in his day in the Diocese of Jerusalem. Religious customs change and eventually become law. We, of course, may not touch the Host to our eyes or to any other part of our body except the tongue. Nor are we permitted to touch our lips with our hands, when they are moist with the Precious Blood. With our tongues, we remove any Precious Blood from our lips. But we can learn from St. Cyril that we are to receive Holy Communion reverently and carefully. Do we? Do we receive Communion properly?

† † †

Lord Jesus, once you spoke to men
Upon the mountain, in the plain;
O help us listen now, as then,
And wonder at your words again.
We all have secret fears to face,
Our minds and motives to amend;
We seek your truth, we need your grace,
Our living Lord and present Friend.
The Gospel speaks, and we receive
Your light, your love, your own command.
O help us live what we believe
In daily work of heart and hand.

H.C.A.Gaunt

ST. OPTATUS, BISHOP OF MILEVE, died c.385

St. Optatus, Bishop of Mileve in Northern Africa, is best known for his struggle against the Donatist schism. Several African bishops under the leadership of Donatus, Bishop of Carthage, erroneously came to the belief that one lost his membership in the Catholic Church through the commission of any mortal sin, and that the value of a sacrament depends on the sanctity of the priest administering the sacrament. They believed, for example, that a person baptized by a priest in mortal sin remained unbaptized. By the end of the fourth century nearly half the bishops of Africa were Donatists. The main errors of the Donatists were renewed some 1200 years later by some of the Protestant Churches.

The Donatists, encouraged by Julian, the apostate Emperor, turned very violent against the Catholics. In many places they desecrated Catholic churches, while they took special delight in wrecking altars on which their own bishops and priests had formerly said Mass. St. Optatus took up the pen to battle the Donatists. Some of his theological works were received soon afterwards by the great St. Augustine of Hippo in Africa, who developed and refined them.

We quote from some of St. Optatus' writings against the Donatists, in which he refers to the sacrileges committed by them against the Eucharist. "They (the Donatists) ordered the Eucharist to be thrown to the dogs, but not without a sign of divine judgment. For the dogs, turning wild with madness and using their teeth as judges, tore to pieces their own masters, as if they were thieves and unknown enemies—those who were guilty of the holy body."

"Now what is more sacrilegious than to break, scratch, and remove the altars of God on which you yourselves offered Mass, the altars on which were laid the gifts of the faithful, the altars which held the members of Christ, the altars on which the Holy Spirit descended at your invocation, the altars from which many have received the pledge of eternal salvation and the defense of the faith and the hope of the resurrection."

✝ ✝ ✝

Lord, let not temptation ever quench the fire your love enkindled in us.

St. Optatus continues to deplore the sacrilegious vandalism of the schismatic Donatists, who were formerly practicing Catholics. "What is the altar but the resting place of the body and blood of Christ? ... Why do you harm yourselves by breaking those altars on which, for a long time and apparently devoutly, you offered Mass before we did? While the wicked persecute our hands (offering Mass) there where the body of Christ dwells, you do harm to your own hands. In this way you have imitated the Jews. They laid hands on Christ, when he was on the cross; but you have struck him here on the altar. If you wanted to persecute Catholics here at the altar, you should have respected at least your own former sacrifices (Masses)."

✝ ✝ ✝

HYMN TO THE WORD OF GOD

Lord, your word abiding,
And our footsteps guiding,
Gives us joy forever,
Shall desert us never.
Who can tell the pleasure,
Who recount the treasure,
By your word imparted
To the simplehearted?
Word of mercy giving
Succor to the living;
Word of life supplying
Comfort to the dying.

O that we, discerning
Its most holy learning,
Lord, may we love and fear you,
Evermore be near you.
Henry William Baker, Anthony G. Petti
Lord God, look kindly on all who put their trust in our prayers and fill
them with every bodily and spiritual grace.

ST. AMBROSE, c.340-397

As the turbulent fourth century was drawing to a close, there died one of the great figures in the history of the Church, namely, St. Ambrose, Bishop of Milan in northern Italy. With good reason the Church has declared him a Father and Doctor of the Church.

St. Ambrose was born about 340 in Treves in modern Germany. His father was the Prefect (chief ruler) of the Province of Gaul, which comprised all of today's western Europe and northwestern Africa. Since his father died when Ambrose was but a boy, his mother moved to Rome, in order to give her three children the opportunity for a good education. With his keen mind and retentive memory Ambrose excelled in the study of Greek literature and Roman law. For a while Ambrose practiced law in Rome and came to be known as an orator. Later, he would use his oratorical ability to become an outstanding preacher with a facility to reach and move his listeners. In matters of doctrine he spoke with the firmness of a Roman magistrate, but he tempered his words with a suavity that inclined his listeners to accept his teaching. The most famous of all his converts was the great St. Augustine of Hippo in Africa. The Emperor in Rome recognized the ability of Ambrose, the lawyer and orator, and appointed him Governor of Liguria and Aemilia in northern Italy. The city of Milan came under Ambrose's jurisdiction. After the Bishop of Milan had died, the clergy and laity met in the cathedral to elect a new Bishop, as was their custom. A great disturbance broke out in the cathedral during the election.

The former Bishop had been an Arian. Some of the clergy and laity present were Arians, while most were Catholics. When Governor Ambrose was called to quiet the disturbance, a boy in the cathedral shouted, "Ambrose, bishop!" The crowd kept repeating, "Ambrose, bishop!"

† † †

HYMN TO THE APOSTLES

The eternal gifts of Christ the King,
The Apostles' glory, let us sing,
And all with hearts of gladness, rise
Due hymns of thankful love and praise.

St. Ambrose, Tr.: J.M. Neale

When the crowd in the cathedral of Milan kept shouting for Ambrose to be their Bishop, he protested vehemently, and for a few days even went into hiding. His Christian parents had followed the bad custom of allowing the children to choose Baptism for themselves. At this time Ambrose had not been baptized; but he reluctantly yielded to the wish of the laity and the clergy. Even the Emperor was delighted that one of his Governors had been chosen Bishop of an important Diocese like Milan. After receiving the proper instructions Ambrose was baptized and ordained bishop. Immediately he divested himself of his great wealth, which he gave to the poor. Then, realizing his deficiency in religious doctrine, he immersed himself in the study of the Greek Fathers of the Church and Sacred Scripture.

As Bishop, St. Ambrose put himself at the service of all who wanted to speak with him. His fame as a preacher grew far and wide. To counteract the heresy of Arianism he used a tool that the Arians used so successfully, namely, doctrinal hymns. St. Ambrose composed a number of hymns, of which a few still survive. The Ambrosian Rite (liturgy), in which Mass is still offered in the cathedral of Milan, takes its name from St. Ambrose, although he himself most likely did not introduce it. As Bishop, he spread devotion to the Saints, especially to the Blessed Mother. St. Ambrose was not a theologian in the proper sense of the term, but theologians were able to glean much material from his many writings, many of which are still extant. He is remembered for his famous saying, "Where Peter (the Pope) is, there is the Church."

† † †

ST. AMBROSE'S HYMN TO THE APOSTLES

Their faith in Christ the Lord prevailed;
Their hope, a light that never failed;
Their love ablaze o'er pathways trod
To lead them to the eternal God.

Translator: J.M.Neale

Given his background, it was only natural that St. Ambrose counted several Emperors among his personal friends. Some sought advice from him; others sent him on diplomatic missions. He was indeed a statesman, but a Christian statesman. Now that a great part of the Roman empire had become Christian, he used his political influence to abolish laws that had sprung from paganism and that hindered the growth of the Church. Despite his friendship with Emperors, St. Ambrose was adamant in upholding the rights of the Church. He formulated principles to establish a correct relationship between the Church and the State. When Emperor Theodosius, a Catholic, ordered and carried out the massacre of several thousand civilians in Thessolonica (Greece) in revenge for a mob's having murdered its unpopular Governor, St. Ambrose placed the Emperor under excommunication. (This was probably the first time that a high-ranking ruler was excommunicated.) St. Ambrose not only refused Holy Communion to the ruler of the whole known world at that time, but apparently he even barred him from entering church, until he had done public penance. It was to the Emperor's credit that his faith was strong enough that he performed the public penance that the Bishop had imposed, and was reconciled with God and the Church. In this and other ways St. Ambrose paved the way for the tremendous influence the bishops would have in the newly formed world, which would be almost entirely Christian and Catholic.

On Good Friday of the year 397 St. Ambrose left off writing his commentary on the Psalms, went to the cathedral of Milan, and for five hours lay prostrate on the floor with his arms outstretched in the form of a cross—and then died.

† † †

FROM ST. AMBROSE'S HYMN TO THE APOSTLES

In them the Father's glory shone,
In them the will of God the Son,
In them exults the Holy Ghost
Through them rejoice the heav'nly host.

Translator: J.M. Neale

We begin quoting now from some of the writings of St. Augustine concerning the Eucharist. Christ offers the Mass through the priest. "If indeed it appears that Christ does not offer the sacrifice, nevertheless, he himself is offered on earth, because the body of Christ is offered. Moreover, it is clear that he himself offers in us, he whose word sanctifies (consecrates) the sacrifice that is offered."

On daily Communion: "Christ is for me, food; Christ is for me, drink. The flesh of God is food for me; and the blood of God is drink for me. Now for my fill I do not wait for the annual harvests, since Christ is served to me every day."

On the sacraments, especially the Eucharist: "Who is the author of the sacraments but the Lord Jesus? From heaven came these sacraments... Maybe you will tell me, 'My bread is ordinary bread.' But this bread is bread before the sacramental words; but once it receives the consecration, from bread it is made the flesh of Christ. Now let us demonstrate this. How can that which is bread come to be the body of Christ? And the consecration, with what words is it realized, and who said those words? With the words that the Lord Jesus said. Because everything which is said before (at Mass) are the words of the priest, praises offered to God, prayers for the people and the rulers and all others; but once the moment arrives in which the venerable sacrament is confected (made present), the priest no longer speaks with his own words, but uses the words of Christ. Therefore, it is the word of Christ that confects this sacrament. Now what is the word of Christ? That word with which everything has been made. The Lord gave the order and heaven was made; the Lord gave the order and the earth was made; the Lord gave the order and the seas were made; the Lord gave the order and every creature was produced. Just look what power the word of Christ has. And if there is so much power in the word of the Lord Jesus that there began to be what before did not exist, how much more powerful is his word to change things that already exist into something else?" [TEP]

† † †

Father, may our lips praise you; our lives proclaim your goodness; our work give you honor; and our voices celebrate you for ever.

On why the appearances of bread and especially of wine are not changed by the consecration: "Now do you not understand from all this (miracles he just mentioned from the Old Testament) the power that the heavenly word has? If it had power over an earthly spring (the spring of bitter water that was changed into sweet water by the piece of wood that Moses threw into it), and if the heavenly word was able to accomplish other things, shall not that word also work in the heavenly sacraments? Now you have learned that from bread there is made the body of Christ, and that wine and water are poured into the chalice; but by the consecration through the heavenly word it becomes blood. But you might say, 'I don't see the appearance of blood.' No, but it has the likeness (of blood, in so far as the wine is red and liquid). Just as you received the likeness of death (in baptism), so too you drink a likeness of the precious blood, so that the blood is not repugnant to you, while it, the price of your redemption, works its effects in you. You have learned, therefore, that what you receive is the body of Christ."

What St. Ambrose says about the appearances of wine, removing any feelings of repugnance in drinking Christ's blood, applies equally to the appearances of bread. We know that when Christ first announced the Eucharist, many of his disciples abandoned him for the horror they experienced at the thought of eating his flesh and drinking his blood in the natural condition of those elements. They thought wrongly, and they persisted in relying on their own thoughts and feelings rather than on the words of Christ. In a word, they believed in themselves, not in Christ. We witness the same thing today with many Catholics, who rely on their own misunderstandings and feelings rather than on the teachings of the Church. They believe in themselves, not in the Church, even though every Sunday they may say, "I believe in the Holy, Catholic Church."

✝ ✝ ✝

FROM ST. AMBROSE'S HYMN TO THE APOSTLES

To thee, Redeemer, now we cry,
That thou wouldst join to them on high
Thy servants, who this grace implore,
For ever and for ever more.

Translator: J.M.Neale

On saying the "Amen" when receiving Communion: "It is not, therefore, in vain that you say 'Amen,' confessing in spirit that you receive the body of Christ. When you approach, the priest says to you, 'Body of Christ,' and you say 'Amen,' that is, 'It is true.' What your tongue confesses retain in your consent."

In explaining the Our Father St. Ambrose refers the words, "daily bread" to the Eucharist: "If it is daily bread, why do you receive it only annually? ... Receive daily that which is of daily benefit to you. Live in such a way that you are worthy to receive it every day. He who is not worthy to receive it daily is not worthy to receive it annually."

On the difference between what the Eucharist is and what it appears to be: "Perhaps you will say, 'What I see is something else. How can you assure me that I receive the body of Christ?' And this is something that we have not yet discussed. What examples shall we use? Let us show that this (what happens in the Eucharist) is not something that nature has made but what the blessing (consecration) has consecrated. And let us show that the force of the blessing (consecration) is greater than the force of nature, because by the blessing even nature itself is changed. (Here St. Ambrose recalls several miracles from the Old Testament in which the nature of things were changed miraculously by Moses and the Prophets; e.g. Moses' staff changed into a snake, then back to his staff; the crossing of the Red Sea and the Jordan on dry land; etc.) Now if the blessing of a man was so powerful as to change the nature of things, what shall we say of the divine consecration itself, where the very words of our Savior are operative? Now this sacrament that you receive is confected by the words of Christ. Now if the word of Elias was so powerful that it rained down fire from heaven, will not the word of Christ be able to change the nature of the elements? Concerning the works of the universe you have read, 'He spoke and they were made; he commanded and they were created.' Now the word of Christ, which was able to make from nothing that which did not exist, is it not able to change the things that are into something that they were not?

✝ ✝ ✝

I lift up my heart to you, O Lord, and you will hear my prayer.

St. Augustine continues to explain the difference between what the Eucharist is and what it appears to be: "But why use arguments? Let us use the example of Christ himself and establish the truth of the mystery of the Incarnation. Did nature's way precede the birth of the Lord Jesus from Mary? If we seek the natural order, the woman conceives in union with a man. Therefore it is very clear that the Virgin gave birth outside the natural order. And this body that we confect (at Mass) is from the Virgin. When then do you seek here the order of nature in the body of Christ, when the Lord Jesus himself was born of the Virgin outside the natural order? It was the true flesh of Christ that was crucified and buried; and therefore it (the Eucharist) is truly the sacrament of that flesh."

St. Ambrose refers to the practice in the Old Testament where those who gathered a greater amount of manna never had too much to eat, while those who gathered a smaller amount never had too little to eat. "This is understood with greater fullness with reference to the blood of Christ, whose grace is not diminished nor added to. Whether you drink a little or a lot, the same measure of redemption (grace) is perfect for all." (The same can be said of receiving a whole Host or only a particle, for Christ is whole and entire in the whole Host and in every particle, even before the Host is broken.)

In a letter to his sister St. Ambrose writes about the finding of the bodies of two martyrs, and his placing the bodies under the altar where he celebrated Mass. "The triumphant victims (the martyrs) are put beneath the place where Christ the Victim resides. But He who suffered for all is placed above the altar, while those who have been redeemed by his passion are put beneath the altar. I have reserved this place for myself, for it is fitting that a priest rest where he used to offer Mass. But I cede to the sacred victims (the martyrs) the right side (of the altar): that place must be for them." (All quotations, as usual, are from TEP)

120

† † †

Lord, from the rising of the sun to its setting you are worthy of all praise. Let my prayer come before you like fragrant incense.

ST. SIRICIUS, Pope from 384 to 398

Himerius, Bishop of Tarragona in Spain, wrote to the Pope concerning what was to be done about certain buses. In the year 385 Pope St. Siricius answered Bishop Himerius in a letter which has become noteworthy, because it is the oldest papal document that has yet been discovered. Among other things in his letter the Pope reinforced the moral directives given by the First Ecumenical Council of Nicea in 325.

The Pope writes: "It is to be added also that some Christians, going over to apostasy (complete denial of one's faith), which is a crime even to mention, have profaned themselves with the adoration of idols and the contamination of (pagan) sacrifices. Now we command that these persons, who once had been redeemed through rebirth (baptism), be cut off from the body and blood of Christ. And if, coming to their senses, they ever shed tears of repentance, they are to do penance as long as they live, and at the end of their life they are to be granted the grace of reconciliation; because, as the Lord teaches, we do not desire the death of the sinner but only that he be converted and live."

† † †

EVENING HYMN TO THE TRINITY

O blessed light, Trinity and Unity, Source of all, now that the bright sun disappears, pour thy light into our hearts.
We praise thee with our hymns morning and evening, humbly we

121

glorify thee through all ages.
To God the Father be glory and to his only Son, with the Holy Ghost,
the Comforter, for all ages.

Attributed to St. Ambrose; translator: Adrian Fortescue

† † †

HYMN FOR SUNDAY

On this day, the first of days, God the Father's name
we praise;
Who, creation's Lord and spring, did the world from darkness bring.
On this day the eternal Son over death his triumph won;
On this day the Spirit came with his gifts of living flame.

Le Mans Breviary; translator: Henry W. Baker

ST. BASIL THE GREAT, 330-379

In the history of the Church there are three Saints who are known as The Cappadocian Fathers. They are St. Basil the Great, his friend St. Gregory of Nanziansus, and his brother, St. Gregory of Nyssa. All three were from the Roman Empire's Province of Cappadocia, which today is part of eastern Turkey. Although St. Basil is the only one given the title of "Great" in the Eastern Church, all three are recognized as Doctors of the Church and defenders of the faith against Arianism.

St. Basil received a classical education in Greece at Constantinople and Athens. For a time he followed the monastic life and wrote a Rule of Life for monks. It is the only monastic Rule recognized by the Greek Church today. After being made Bishop of Caeserea in Cappodocia, he devoted his efforts to fighting Arianism and promoting works of charity. He is sometimes pictured holding up a church with one hand and feeding the poor with the other. In order to defend the rights of the Church in his diocese St. Basil consecrated as bishops his brother Gregory and his friend Gregory Nazianzen, whom he sent to Nyssa and Sasima respectively on the limits of his diocese.

St. Basil on faith: "Now it is necessary not to be doubting the things the Lord says, but on the contrary to convince one's self that every word of God is true and possible, even though it be contrary to nature, because here is precisely the battleground of the faith."

"Partaking of the body and blood of Christ is likewise necessary for eternal life. (As Christ said:) 'Amen, amen, I say to you: If you do not eat the flesh of the Son of Man and drink his blood, you do not have life in you. He who eats my flesh and drinks my blood has eternal life.' "

"He who approaches Communion without considering that there is given to him a partaking of the body and blood of Christ receives no benefit from it; and he who receives unworthily is condemned." [TEP]

† † †

FROM A HYMN TO THE EUCHARIST USED IN GERMANY

O most sweet bread, life-giving food of faithful souls.
O meek Lamb, lawful offering of the Paschal sacrifice.
Immortal flesh veiled by God under the form of bread.

Translator: Adrian Fortescue

St. Basil on the Bible and Sacred Tradition, the two sources from which the Church draws her teaching: "Of the dogmas and teachings preserved in the Church, some we have through the written teaching, while others we have received transmitted to us in mystery through the tradition of the Apostles; and both are equally useful for piety. And no one who has experience in ecclesiastical matters will contradict either of them. If we try to reject the customs that have not been transmitted to us in writing, as if they did not have great force, without realizing it we shall do damage to the Gospel even in important matters; even more, we shall reduce the preaching to nothing. Just to recall what is important and quite common, take for example the fact that those who place their trust in the name of our Lord Jesus Christ sign themselves with the sign of the cross. Who has taught that in writing (in the Bible)? What Scripture taught us to face east when praying? Which of the saints (human authors of the Bible) left us in writing the words of the Invocation (calling down of the Holy Spirit at Mass, the epiclesis) in the Manifestation (consecration) of the Eucharistic bread and the chalice of benediction? We do not content ourselves (at Mass) with the words that the Apostle (Paul) recalled or the Gospel, but before and after (the consecration) we say other words to give great force to the mystery, words that we have received through unwritten Tradition."

On reserving consecrated Hosts at home: "To receive Communion every day and partake of the holy body and blood of Christ is good and very useful ... All the monks (those who were not priests) who live in the deserts, where there is no priest, reserving Communion at home, receive it by themselves. In Alexandria and in Egypt everyone, even lay people, regularly have the Eucharist in their homes and receive Communion by themselves when they wish ... It has the same effect if one receives from the priest a part (of the Host) or many parts at the same time." [TEP]

† † †

The Lord shall wipe away every tear from the eyes of his saints, And there shall no longer be mourning, nor crying, nor pain; for all that used to be has passed away.

St. Basil on the practice of public penance in Cappadocia (modern Turkey) for fornicators (single persons who had committed sins of the flesh with one another): "It is necessary to recognize as guilty of fornication one who retains a woman by force, be it hidden force or more violent. It has been determined that four years is the penalty for fornicators. It is proper that for the first year they be excluded from the prayers (Mass), and that they weep at the doors of the church. In the second year let them be admitted to hear (the foreMass with the Bible lessons and sermon). During the third year let them do the penance (imposed by the bishop or priest, in addition to assisting at the foreMass). During the fourth year let them join the people (at Mass), while they abstain from Communion. And afterwards let them be permitted to receive Communion of the Greatest Food."

On the proper dispositions required for Communion: "Let us approach the sacred things in such a way as to escape the judgment of those who killed the Lord, for 'whoever eats this bread or drinks the chalice unworthily, will be guilty of the body and blood of the Lord.' And let us possess eternal life as the true Lord and our God Jesus Christ promised, if when eating and drinking we remember him who died for us. And let us observe the word of the Apostle (Paul) who says: 'The love of Christ moves us to consider that if one died for all, then all died; and he died for all, so that those who live, no longer live for themselves but for him who died and rose for them' — and this is what we contracted to do at baptism."

A type of Byzantine Liturgy is attributed to St. Basil. In it the priests distributing Holy Communion are directed to say to each communicant, "This is the body of Christ that he offered for our sins." [TEP]

† † †

FROM A EUCHARISTIC HYMN USED IN GERMANY

Strengthen us in every way by the food of grace sevenfold from the Holy Spirit. When thou art received, not consumed, thou dost give eternal life to him who receives thee. For by so great a gift thou dost cleanse mercifully the stain of sin. To unite us to thee, to strengthen us in good, grant us to receive thee worthily.

Tr.: Adrian Fortescue

ST. GREGORY OF NYSSA, c.335 - c.395

St. Gregory of Nyssa was the youngest brother of St. Basil the Great. As a young man he taught rhetoric until his older brother and their mutual friend, St. Gregory of Nazianzus, made him understand the vanity of this world. He went into retreat for ten years, after which St. Basil ordained him priest and bishop and sent him to the small town of Nyssa on the border of St. Basil's Diocese to protect the rights of the Church, which were being threatened by heretics.

As the Bishop of Nyssa, St. Gregory demonstrated that he had very little administrative ability, but that he was outstanding as a theologian and philosopher. At the end of the second ecumenical council, that of Constantinople 1 in 381, St. Gregory was acclaimed as a "column of orthodoxy" for his brilliant defense of the faith against the heretics, especially the Arians. (While Arianism was dying in the West, it was growing in the East.) St. Gregory was considered the intellectual successor of his brother, St. Basil. In his philosophy his chief aim was to show that faith and reason are not opposed to one another, but that there is perfect harmony between the two. He taught catechists that the explanation of Christian truths should be based on reason, on principles that were held by Jews and pagans, whom it was necessary to convince.

With reference to the Eucharist St. Gregory says that Saturday, the day on which God rested after creation, is "Sunday's brother," and consequently Mass was said publicly on Saturdays for the devotion of the people. He writes that all take part in singing the Sanctus at Mass, for we on earth should join the angels in heaven singing the Sanctus, as is recorded in the Prophet Isaiah. Although we saw that some Church Fathers in both the East and West held that the petition for bread in the Our Father has a Eucharistic meaning, St. Gregory, along with others who used the Greek liturgy, makes an explicit denial of the Eucharistic sense.

FROM A EUCHARISTIC HYMN USED IN GERMANY

Driving away temptation, make us live in holiness with thee. So, comforted by the cup of thy blood, by the holy banquet of thy flesh, for ever and ever may we rejoice, called to the high feast of thy eternal pasch.

Translator: Adrian Fortescue

St. Gregory on the Real Presence: "Jesus says, 'My flesh is real food and my blood is real drink.' Now he who loves this flesh is no friend of his own flesh; and he who loves this blood will not be guilty of natural blood. Because the flesh of the Word (Christ) and the blood that is in this flesh do not have an ordinary grace; but they are pleasing to those who taste them, appetizing to those who desire them, and attractive to those who love them."

On the proper dispositions for Communion: "On the occasion of the holy passion (of our Lord) that noble senator (Joseph of Arimathaea) put the body of the Lord in a white and clean shroud and placed it in a new and uncontaminated sepulcher. Consequently let the precept of the Apostle (Paul concerning the proper dispositions for receiving Communion) as well as the teaching of the evangelist (John in his Gospel) be a law for all of us for receiving the sacred body with a clear conscience. And if there be any little stain of sin, let us wash it away with the water of tears."

On how ordinary things are used for our sanctification: "Do not despise holy baptism, or think little of it, as if it were some ordinary thing for the use that is made of water; for what it does is great, and the effects it produces are admirable. Likewise this holy altar at which we assist is ordinary stone according to its nature, and is no different from the other stones with which our walls are built and our paving adorned. But because it was consecrated to the worship of God and received the blessing, it is a holy table, and immaculate altar, which cannot be touched by everyone, but only by the priests, and by them only for praying. In like manner, the bread at first is ordinary, but once the mystery consecrates it, it is called and becomes the body of Christ. Likewise, the holy oil and the wine, although things of small value before the blessing, after the sanctification brought about by the Holy Spirit each of these things produces marvelous results." [TEP]

† † †

O glorious cross, you are worthy of our praise.
Your precious wood is the wonderful sign by which
the devil was conquered and the world redeemed
through the blood of Christ.

Although any scientific explanation of the Eucharist would necessarily be imperfect, nevertheless St. Gregory offers what may well be the first attempt at such an explanation. He says that the bread that Christ ate during his earthly life was gradually changed into his body, just as it is with us. In a similar way the bread that is consecrated at Mass by Christ's own words is instantly changed into the body of Christ. Although the two changes of the bread are different, the one gradual and the other instantaneously, nevertheless the result of the changes is the the same body of Christ. And St. Gregory adds that we ourselves are divinized by our union with that body in receiving Holy Communion.

† † †

COMMUNION HYMN OF THE GALLICAN RITE
(From 7th century; oldest known Latin Eucharistic hymn. Tr: A.Fortescue)

Come all ye holy, take the body of your Lord,
Drink of his chalice, take the blood for you outpoured.

Saved by his body, by his sacred blood, we raise
Grateful our voices unto God in hymns of praise.

Giver of life, he, Christ our Savior, Son of God,
Bought our redemption by his cross and precious blood.

Dying for all men, he, the Lord prepared this feast,
Offered as victim, offering himself as priest.

God to our fathers ordered sacrifice of old;
So he in symbols Christ the victim true foretold.

Giver of light, the one Redeemer of our race,
He to his holy servants gives abundant grace.

ST. GREGORY NAZIANZUS, c.330 - c.390

The third member of the trio known as the Great Cappadocians was St. Gregory of Nazianzus. Although he was a gifted orator, he preferred the solitary life of the hermit. His close friend, St. Basil the Great, prevailed upon him to be consecrated a bishop.

At that time the great City of Constantinople in Greece (formerly called Byzantium and today called Istanbul and belonging to Turkey) was the residence at times of the sole Emperor of the worldwide Roman Empire and at times of the Eastern Emperor while the Western Emperor resided in Rome. It was a stronghold of Arianism. The Catholics of Constantinople invited St. Gregory to be their bishop. He accepted reluctantly; but within a short time Catholicism gained preeminence over Arianism.

A Council of Eastern bishops was held at Constantinople in 381 to combat heresy. (Later this Council was recognized by the universal Church as the second ecumenical council, that of Constantinople 1.) For a while St. Gregory headed the Council, and his brilliant interventions earned him the name of "theologian." However, in face of opposition, which his gentle soul could not tolerate, Gregory resigned not only as head of the Council but also as Bishop of Constantinople. He retired for a while to his beloved solitude in his home town and later served as Bishop of the small town of Nazianzus. He devoted his spare time to writing poetry.

† † †

FROM A COMMUNION HYMN OF THE GALLICAN RITE

Come, who with pure hearts in the Savior's word believe;
Come, and partaking saving grace from him receive.

God our defender, guardian sure in this our strife,
Gives to his faithful after death eternal life.

He to the hungry gives as food this heavenly bread;
Fountain of life, he gives to drink the blood he shed.
Christ, source of all things, who here feeds us sinful men,
When his great day dawns, judge of all, will come again.

In his extant works St. Gregory mentions the Eucharist only in passing. In one of his sermons he spoke against the Emperor known as Julian the Apostate. (He had been baptized a Catholic but became a pagan and tried to make paganism the official religion of the Empire again.) About him Gregory says: "He had hardly obtained the Empire as his inheritance, when he began to make public profession of his impiety by being ashamed of having been a Christian and by seeking vengeance for it against the Christians with whom he shared the same name. To be sure, the first of his arrogant deeds, according to those who boast of being privy to his secrets (Oh what tales I see myself obliged to be involved in!) — the first thing he tried to do was erase his baptism with impure blood. He did this by opposing the initiation of the abominable (pagan initiation) to our initiation (baptism). As the proverb goes, he was a pig wallowing in the mud. And he removed (tried to remove) the holiness of his hands by purging them of the unbloody sacrifice (Mass), through which we take part with Christ in his passion and in his divinity." (The holiness of the hands is a reference to receiving Communion in the hand.)

In one of his poems St. Gregory gives a short autobiography. "First, I am a gift of God to the prayers of my illustrious mother. Second, God received from my mother a beloved gift. (His mother, Nonna, prayed to have a boy and offered him to God before his birth.) Third, when I was about to die, the immaculate table (Eucharist) saved me. Fourth, the Word (Christ) granted me a two-edged sword (oratorical ability). Fifth, virginity enfolded me in its sweet dreams (probably a reference to a vow of virginity). Sixth, I exercised the sacred ministries in company with Basil (the Great). Seventh, the giver of all life freed me from the deep abysses (perhaps sicknesses). Eighth, again I purged my hands (myself) of diseases. Ninth, O King, I took the Trinity to new Rome. (Constantinople was called "new Rome," and there St. Gregory vigorously defended the doctrine of the Trinity against the Arians.) Tenth, I was stoned (persecuted) even by my friends (not only by the Arians but also by the Catholics)." [TEP]

† † †

Bind all Christians more closely to yourself, O Christ our Lord, and lead them to proclaim your kingdom by the witness of their lives.

DIDYMUS THE BLIND, c.313 - c.398

Didymus the Blind was born in Alexandria on the northern coast of Egypt and lived there all his life. At the age of four he lost his sight. Although he was not gifted with superior intelligence, he did have an exceptionally good memory. He would spend hours, sometimes whole nights, meditating on what he had heard in class. He dedicated himself to study, especially in the fields of philosophy and theology. His piety, together with his sweet and gracious kindness, was admired even by the Arians. He died at the age of 85 about the year 398.

When the Pope asked St. Jerome to write an exposition on the Holy Spirit, the Saint could do nothing better than to translate the exposition by Didymus. The most important theological work of Didymus was on the Blessed Trinity.

Didymus refers to the Mass as "the unbloody sacrifice, which is offered piously and in a holy manner." He comments on the words of the Prophet Isaiah, who writes in Chapter 55:1: "Oh, come to the water all you who are thirsty; though you have no money, come. Buy corn without money and eat, and wine and milk at no cost." Writes Didymus: "The Prophet called water the Holy Spirit and the streams (of grace) flowing from the baptismal font. By wine and milk he signified for the Prophet's times things pertaining to the Jews, and for our times the immortal communion of the body and blood of the Lord, which we buy surely along with our renewal (in baptism), paying for it not with money but with faith, with faith that we receive also as a free gift."

Didymus alludes to the then current practice in Egypt of keeping the Blessed Sacrament in one's home and taking Communion daily. "O why do we celebrate with faith and full of fear that most desirable and most providential Pasch every year, and even every day, and, yes, also every hour, receiving the body and blood of Christ? Those worthy of this supreme and eternal mystery know of what I speak, for there is due honor and thanksgiving to Him, who of his own will and without regret has given something of his very own goodness."   [TEP]

† † †

God our Father, look upon
the many wounds of your Church.
Restore it to health by your risen Son,
so that it may sing a new song in your praise.

ST. JOHN CHRYSOSTOM, C.344 - 407

St. John Chrysostom was the first in the history of the Church to be given the title, "Doctor of the Eucharist." As we shall see, his extant writings on the Eucharist are numerous and explicit. Among the early Church Fathers no one taught the doctrine of the Real Presence of Christ in the Eucharist more forcefully than did St. John Chrysostom. Naturally we shall quote at length from his many writings and sermons on the Eucharist.

St. John came to be called Chrysostom, meaning "golden mouth" because of his exceptional ability as an orator and preacher. Historians often refer to him simply as "Chrysostom." He was born in Syria. His father died shortly after John's birth, and his mother, Anthusa, was determined to remain a widow, although she was only 20 years old. She dedicated her life to the proper rearing of her only son, John. He received a classical education from the best masters of the time, while his mother saw to it that he was schooled in piety and asceticism. It was probably after his mother's death that John followed the life of a hermit for some ten years, during which he did a great deal of writing, much of which is still extant. When he was about 40 years old the Bishop of Antioch called John to the priesthood.

During the twelve years that St. John served as a priest in Antioch, his chief duty was to preach. He exercised that ministry so well, that it was there he was given the name "Chysostom." His sermons consisted primarily of commentaries on the various books of the Bible.

† † †

Called from worship into service,
Forth in your great name we go
To the child, the youth, the aged
Love in living deeds to show.

Hope and health, goodwill and comfort,
Counsel, aid, and peace we give,

That your children, Lord, in freedom
May your mercy know and live.

Albert Bayly

In the year 398 Chrysostom was chosen to be Bishop of Constantinople, the city in Greece that was then occupied by the Eastern Emperor of the Roman Empire. As Patriarch of Constantinople, St. John spread the faith not only in the Capitol of Constantinople but also in the surrounding districts. He also sent missionaries to the pagan Goths, who were living on the borders of the Empire at that time. These were part of the Germanic tribes, who, in the following century would defeat the Roman Empire, overrun Europe and form the core of today's European population.

As Bishop of Constantinople Chrysostom had the unpleasant task of reforming some of the lax practices in the Capitol among both clergy and laity. Naturally this caused opposition, even by the Empress herself. After serving as Patriarch for only six years, Chysostom was forced into exile by the Emperor. Even during his exile his enemies continued to persecute him. He died from the hardships of his exile on Sept. 14, 407. His last words were, "Glory be to God in all things."

In addition to his all-pervasive doctrine on the Real Presence his other Eucharistic doctrine can be summed up as follows:

Thanksgiving (Eucharist) is a basic Christian idea.

He complains of wealthy Christians who own entire villages, but who do not build churches. He demands that they erect churches and provide for a priest and deacon, so that divine services and Sunday Mass can be conducted.

He warned about excessive zeal in decorating the altar with precious cloths and leaving other things undone, such as feeding and clothing the poor.

He speaks of three Bible readings at Mass: prophetic (Old Testament), apostolic (New Testament) and the Gospel. He says that the readings should be given their setting, that the lector should not only state from what book the reading is taken, but also give the motive behind what is being related.

† † †

Lord God, look kindly on all who put their trust in our prayers and fill them with every bodily and spiritual grace.

We continue a summary of St.John's Eucharistic doctrine:

The doxological (prayer of praise) ending of a sermon was a fixed rule with Chrysostom and generally in ancient Christianity.

He often extols the value of community singing at Mass, such as at the Sanctus. He says, "Above (in heaven) the Seraphim shout the thrice holy hymn (in Isaiah), and below (on earth) all mankind sends it aloft." "After Christ removed the wall between heaven and earth ... he brought us this song of praise from heaven."

Chrysostom sees in the Memento for the Dead a practice going back to Apostolic times. He also sees its value: "When ... that awe-inspiring sacrifice (Mass) lies displayed on the altar, how shall we not prevail with God by our entreaties for them (the deceased)?"

We begin now many quotations from the writings and sermons of Chrysostom on the Eucharist. Many can be applied to our own times.

"Today many of the faithful have arrived at such a state of insensitivity and apathy that, while they are full of evil and take no precaution for their own life (referring to St.Paul's condemnation of those receiving Communion unworthily), they dare to approach negligently and distractedly this table (altar) on feast days without considering that the time to receive Communion does not depend on the feast day ... but on a pure conscience and a life withdrawn from all (mortal) sin." For just as it is proper for one who is not conscious of any evil to approach daily, so no one who is entangled in sin and does not repent cannot approach with confidence on feast days. Neither does the reception of Communion once a year free us from sin, if we approach unworthily. On the contrary, it increases our condemnation to receive only once a year unworthily ...Therefore I exhort all of you not to participate in the divine mysteries negligently, as if obliged by the feast; ...but purify yourselves many days before by penance, prayer, almsgiving, and spiritual exercises; and do not return to what you have cast off, as do the dogs." [All quotations from St. John are from TEP]

† † †

I lift up my heart to you, O Lord,
and you will hear my prayer.

St. John continues his homily on the proper preparation for receiving Holy Communion: "Is it not absurd to take so much care about what pertains to the body, as the feast approaches? For many days beforehand you carefully prepare a very beautiful dress after taking it from the chest; and you buy footwear; and you prepare a more abundant and splendid table. Finally you give thought to various supplies of all sorts of things; and you adorn yourself and beautify yourself in every possible way. Yet you take no care of your soul, which is abandoned, dirty, squalid, consumed by hunger and remains impure. And you take to the feast a body all decked out and a soul naked and abandoned? And only another servant like you sees the body, and you suffer no harm no matter how you are dressed. But the Lord sees the soul and punishes negligence rigorously. Do you not know that this table (altar) is full of spiritual fire? And just as fountains make water shoot out with force, so also this table has an unspeakable flame. Therefore do not approach carrying sticks or wood or hay, so that you do not increase the fire and burn your soul, if you approach to receive Communion."

On the cross: "The royal crown does not bring as much beauty to the head as does the cross, more precious than the entire world. And now the image of what everyone abhorred is so greatly desired that it can be found everywhere, on princes and subjects, women and men, virgins and married women, slaves and freemen. For everyone imprints that sign on the most noble part of his body, and as if engraved on a column they carry it on their forehead every day. It shines forth on the sacred table (altar), at priestly ordinations, and again together with the body of Christ at the mystical supper." [TEP]

† † †

FROM A 14th. CENTURY GRADUAL AT LIMOGES

Hail true Body, born of Mary the vigin;
suffering, sacrificed truly on the cross for men;
from whose pierced side water flowed and blood.
Be merciful to us at the judgment of death,
O sweet Jesus, O merciful Jesus,
O Jesus, Son of Mary.

Translator: Adrian Fortescue

As a priest in Antioch of Syria St.John preached on one occasion to calm the people who were living in dread of punishment by the Roman soldiers for having destroyed statues of the Emperor when he raised their taxes. "Now Elijah left his mantle to his disciple, but the Son of God, when ascending into heaven, left his own flesh. Elijah had to remove his mantle, but Christ gave us his flesh and took it with him when he ascended.

"Do not be fainthearted, do not cry, do not fear the difficult times. For he who did not refuse to shed his own blood for everyone and even made us partakers of his body and blood, what will he refuse to do for our salvation? Take heart, therefore, with this hope. Let us call on him continually and give ourselves to prayer and supplication. With all diligence let us give thought to the other virtues, so that we may escape the danger that threatens us. Let us be worthy of the good things to come, which, I hope, all of us will obtain through the grace and kindness of our Lord Jesus Christ, through whom and with whom be the glory to the Father together with the Holy Spirit for ever. Amen."

137

After consoling the citizens of Antioch Chrysostom tried to eradicate vices that were prevalent there, especially that of taking vain or useless oaths. "Through the Prophet (Isaiah) God told the Jews, 'If you fast only to criticize and hold grudges, why fast?' But through me God says to you, 'If you fast only to take oaths and commit perjuries, why fast?' For how can we see the holy Pasch (that is, assist at Mass)? How can we receive the sacred Host? How can we take part in the holy sacraments with the same tongue with which we trample the law of God, with the same tongue with which we stain our soul? Now if no one would dare touch the imperial purple cloak with dirty hands, how shall we receive the body of the Lord with a dirty tongue? For the oath is of the devil, and the Host is of the Lord. Now 'What has light to do with darkness, or what relation does Christ have with Belial(Satan)' (2Cor,6)." [TEP]

† † †

Lord God, may those who are in danger for love of you,
find security in you now; and in the day of judgment
may they rejoice in seeing you face to face.

On the necessity of forgiving injuries: "Just as a fornicator or a blasphemer cannot partake of the sacred table (altar), so too anyone who retains enmities and rancor cannot receive Holy Communion. One who commits fornication or adultery stops sinning, once his appetite is satisfied. And if he comes to his senses and wants to rise from his fall and give definite signs of repentance, he has some consolation; but one who retains rancor commits the sin every day and never stops. In the first case, once the bad deed is done, the sin stops; but in the latter case the sin is committed every day. Tell me, what pardon shall we gain, if we willingly pit ourselves in the claws of so wild a beast? And how can you wish that the Lord be kind and merciful to you, while you are so hard and implacable with your fellow servant? ... You dare not touch the sacred Host with dirty hands, even if grave necessity urged you. Likewise do not approach (for

Communion) with dirty soul, because that would be much graver and carries a more terrible punishment. There is nothing that fills the soul with uncleanness more than constant anger in it. For where there is fury and anger the Spirit of meekness does not rest its wings. And what hope does a man have who is deprived of the Holy Spirit?

On missing Mass through one's own fault: "Where do these calamities come from? Because some of you frequently do not assist at the prayers, and others skip the divine reunions (Mass). Don't you notice how alert they are who want to receive some dignity from an earthly king, how they get others to help them attain what they desire? To those who forget about the divine reunions, and to those who at the hour of the awesome and mystical supper are occupied in useless chatter and gossip, to them I say, 'Man, what are you doing?' " [TEP]

✝ ✝ ✝

COMMUNION ANTIPHON OF THE GALLICAN RITE

Come, people, to offer the holy, immortal mystery and sacrifice. Let us approach with fear and faith to receive the gift of pardon with clean hands. For the Lamb of God is offered as a sacrifice to his Father. Him alone we adore, him we glorify, crying with the angels: Alleluia.

Translator: Adrian Fortescue

St. John continues his sermon on missing Mass through one's own fault: "When the priest said, 'Lift up your thoughts and your hearts,' did you not make him a promise when you said, 'We have them lifted up to the Lord?' Are you not embarrassed and ashamed to be found a liar at that hour (of Mass)? What a strange thing! The mystical supper is prepared, and the Lamb of God is immolated for you; the priest is greatly concerned about you; spiritual fire shoots out from the sacred table (altar); the Cherubim are present; the Seraphim fly round about; the angels with six wings cover their faces; all the spiritual Virtues together with the priest intercede for you; the spiritual fire (God) descends from heaven; the blood is poured out from the immaculate side into the chalice for your purification — and you, have you no fear and no shame to be found a liar at that tremendous hour?"

"A week has one hundred and sixty-eight hours, and God set aside only one for himself; and you use that hour to do works that are profane and silly and to gossip idly. With what confidence can you later approach the mysteries (Communion)? If you have filth on your hand, would you dare touch the hem of a garment of an earthly king? By no means."

In a homily on Christmas day Chrysostom speaks about the proper conduct in church and at Mass, and the proper dispositions of soul for receiving Communion: "When you approach the awesome and divine table (altar) and those sacred mysteries, do it with fear and trembling, with a clear conscience, with prayer and fasting. Do not approach in disorder, kicking and pushing others, because that would show great arrogance and no small disrespect; and those who do such things merit a severe punishment. Man, think to yourself what a great Victim (Christ) you are going to touch, what table you are approaching. Consider that you, being earth and ashes, take the blood and body of Christ." [TEP]

† † †

O God, who in this wonderful Sacrament hast left us a remembrance of thy passion, grant us, we beseech thee, so to reverence the sacred mysteries of thy body and blood that we may feel within us the fruit of thy redemption.
(Prayer at Benediction with the Blessed Sacrament)

Translator: Adrian Fortescue

Chrysostom continues his Christmas homily on the proper dispositions for receiving Communion: "If some king invites you to a banquet, you sit with fear; and with respect you eat the food that is offered. But when God invites you to his table and there offers you his Son, where the angelic powers are present with fear and trembling, where the Cherubim cover their faces and the Seraphs cry out with fear: 'Holy, holy, holy Lord' —and you dare to approach this spiritual banquet shouting and shoving? Don't you realize that at that moment it is proper that your mind be perfectly tranquil? Great calm and quiet are necessary, and not confusion, anger, and noise; because such things make impure the soul of one approaching for Communion.

"Therefore let us come to church with fear and thanksgiving. Let us kneel while confessing our sins, and with tears let us lament our wrongdoing. Before the Lord let us pour out long and silent petitions. And cleansing ourselves in this way let us go quietly and with proper modesty to meet the King of heaven. And upon receiving this holy and immaculate Host, let us kiss it ardently; and embracing it with our gaze, let us warm our mind and soul, so that we do not come together for judgment and condemnation, but for calmness of soul, for love, for virtue, for reconciliation with God, for lasting peace, for an occasion of a thousand good things, and in order to become holy and edify our neighbor." [TEP]

† † †

HYMN TO THE HOLY TRINITY (10th. century)

Thee we invoke and adore, thee we praise, blessed Trinity; do thou grant to us forgiveness of all sins,
That we may, with devout mind, give worthy praise to thee day and night, at all hours and moments, saying always:
All glory without end be to the Trinity, the high God, for all ages.
And together with one voice let us say: Amen.
Translator: Adrian Fortescue

Father, gather into one body all who bear the name of Christian, so that the world may believe in Christ whom you have sent.

141

In concluding his homily on the Feast of the Baptism of our Lord, Chrysostom spoke on receiving Communion on the big Feast days and on leaving Mass before it is finished. "I know that most of you are going to approach the sacred table, because it is the custom to do so on the Feast. It would be well to remember what I have said repeatedly many times, namely, to observe the Feast does not create the proper time to receive Communion, but purifying the conscience does; and after that approach the holy sacrifice. For one who is stained and dirty (spiritually) must not become a partaker of that sacred and awesome flesh even on the Feast day. But one who is clean (spiritually) and has washed away his faults with proper penitence, both on the Feast day and always is worthy to receive Communion of the divine mysteries and enjoy the gifts of God. But I don't know why some are so careless about this matter, and many, being full of a thousand sins and feeling compelled when they see the Feast day arriving, approach the sacred mysteries, mysteries which they should not even look at when they are so disposed. Surely if we know who they are we will refuse them; those whom we do not know, we leave to God, who knows the secrets of every conscience...

"Do you want that I tell you why there is this noise and disorder? Because we do not lock the doors during the entire sacred time, and we endure your leaving and returning to your homes before the last act of thanksgiving. That is a matter of serious disregard. Man, what are you thinking about? Christ himself is present, the angels are present, the awesome table is prepared, and while your brothers are being instructed in the mysteries, you leave them and go away? Now if you are invited to a banquet, even if you are already full, you do not dare to leave while your friends are still at table; but here when the mysteries of Christ are being celebrated, when the holy sacrifice is still in progress, do you leave things half finished and go away? Who will believe that this can be pardoned? Who will excuse them with some defense?"

Father, hear us during times of trouble and protect us by the power of your Son, so that we who share his struggle on earth may merit a share in his victory in heaven.

St. John continues to reprimand those who leave Mass before it is finished: "Do you want me to tell you what they do who leave Mass before it is finished and do not offer hymns of thanksgiving at the end of Mass? On that last night (night of the Last Supper) while all the others were at table, Judas left hurriedly. Those who leave Mass before the last thanksgiving imitate Judas ... Judas went out to the Jews; but the Apostles, after singing a hymn, went out with the Lord. Don't you see how the last prayer after the sacrifice of the Mass is in conformity with that example?

"Now, my dearest people, let us keep these things present in our minds; let us think about them and have fear of the punishment prepared for this offense. He (Christ) gives you his flesh, and you do not repay him even with words and give no thanks for what you have received? After you have eaten bodily food you offer a prayer; when you partake of spiritual food which is greater than any visible or invisible creature, being a man with a fickle nature are you not going to wait to give thanks with words and deeds? What is that except to hand oneself over to the ultimate punishment?"

Chrysostom offers a unique explanation of how the Consecration at Mass takes place through Christ's power and how the human priest acts in the person of Christ: "Now it is time to approach this tremendous altar. Let us approach with the calmness and awareness that are proper, ...Christ is present, and He who prepared the altar now adorns it. Because it is not the man (human priest) who makes the offerings come to be the body and blood of Christ, but Christ himself, who was crucified for us. The priest is present fulfilling the figure of Christ, pronouncing those words; but the power and the grace is from God. 'This is my body' he says. That word transforms the things that have been offered, just as that word, 'Increase and multiply and fill the earth,' although it was said only once, fills our nature with the power to procreate children. So also that other word, having been said only once, from that time till now and until the coming of Christ (at the end of the world) makes present the perfect sacrifice on every altar in the churches." [TEP]

Chrysostom on the Church's having been born from the side of Christ crucified: "How can one show that the Church was born from the side of Christ? Scripture also indicates this to us. After Christ died nailed to the cross on high, (we read) 'One of the soldiers drew near and transpierced his side, and there came out blood and water.' The entire Church was formed from that water and that blood. Christ himself attested to that for us when he said, 'He who is not born again of water and the spirit cannot enter the kingdom of heaven.' He calls the blood 'spirit.' And in reality we are born through the water of baptism, and we are nourished with the blood. Do you see how we are of his flesh and his bones, we who have been born and nourished by that blood and water? And just as the woman was created while Adam was sleeping, so too the Church was formed from the side of Christ already dead."

On helping the needy: "What pardon can they look forward to who, after this exhortation and advice, neglect the needy? Moreover — and listen, you who have been initiated into the sacred mysteries (i.e. baptized) — when it was necessary to feed you, Christ did not spare his own flesh; when it was necessary to give you a drink, he did not spare and was not stingy with his own blood. And you do not share your bread and drink? And what pardon can you look forward to, you who have received so many and so precious good things, while you show how stingy you are with the things of no value?"

On the superiority of the New Testament over the Old: "The Jews of old offered their thanksgiving celebration, when the army of the Egyptians was drowned in the sea. They said, 'Let us sing to the Lord, for he has been gloriously glorified.' But our thanksgiving celebration is much greater, for the Egyptians have not been drowned, but the demons; Pharaoh has not been conquered, but the devil; material weapons have not been captured, but wickedness has been done away with, and not in the Red Sea but in the water of regeneration (baptism); we have not gone out to the promised land, but we have been directed to heaven; we do not eat manna, but we are nourished with the body of the Lord; we do not drink the water from the rock, but the blood from the side (of Christ) ..."

St. John speaks of the spiritual aids Christ offers us in our battle against the devil: "He (Christ) has restrained your flesh (body); he gave you armament: the breastplate of justice, the cincture of truth, the helmet of salvation, the shield of faith, the sword of the Spirit; and he gave you the pledge (of the Holy Spirit); he nourishes you with his body; he gives you his blood to drink; he put in your hands the cross as a lance that never bends; and he bound the devil and hurled him to the ground. So then, if you are conquered, now you have no excuse; if you are defeated, you are not worthy of pardon; for you have innumerable means to conquer."

On proper use of the tongue: "Remember that the tongue is the member with which we speak with God, and with which we celebrate the praises. It is the member with which we receive the venerable sacrifice (Holy Communion). The faithful know what I am talking about. Therefore it is proper that this member be free of all accusation, cursing, obscene words and calumny."

From a commentary on Isaiah 6:6, where one of the Seraphim (angels) took a live coal from the altar with a pair of tongs and touched the Prophet's mouth with it: "That altar is a figure and image of this altar of the church, and that fire is an image of the spiritual fire of this same church. The Seraph did not dare touch the live coal with his hand, but with tongs. We, nevertheless, take it (the Host) in our hands. If we consider the grandeur of the things that are offered to us to touch, it is without doubt that it exceeds the greatness of anything else, so that even the Seraphim did not dare to touch it. And if we reflect on the goodness of the Lord in making such exceedingly great grandeur descend in our poor hands, we cannot but cover our face with the mantle of shame ... For that reason now, at this time, from this altar, in a loud voice I make you know, I implore you, I beseech you, and I demand it of you, that you never approach this sacred altar with a soiled conscience, with a contaminated soul. Such an approach, even though you touch the body of Christ a thousand times, can never be called and entrance to or union with the Lord, but condemnation and an increase of sufferings and punishments." [TEP]

St. John points out the Eucharist as a spiritual remedy: "How can we rid ourselves of this plague (anger)? By drinking that drink that has the power to kill the worms and serpents that we have within us. And what could be the drink that has that power? The precious blood of Christ, if it is drunk with confidence; for it is able to cure all sickness. Add to that the listening attentively to the Sacred Scriptures, and also add almsgiving. Without doubt with these measures the passions that corrupt our soul can be mortified."

On giving thanks to God: "Therefore the tremendous mysteries, full of every kind of benefit, which are celebrated in every Mass, are called Eucharist (thanksgiving) because they are the memorial of many benefits. They present to us the principle things of the divine economy, the new order of things through the Incarnation. And they move us from every side to give thanks. Now, if having been born of a virgin is a great miracle, so that the Evangelist, full of amazement, says, 'and all this was done,' having also been immolated — what consideration does that not deserve? If the Evangelist calls Christ's having been born 'all this,' what can he call having been crucified, his having shed his blood, and his giving himself to us as food in the spiritual banquet? Let us then give him thanks continuously, and let this be the principle thing in our works and words. ... Passing over all other benefits, which are more numerous than the grains of sand, what can equal the Incarnation that was done for us? What was most precious to God the Father, namely his only begotten Son, he gave to us, his enemies. And he not only gave him to us, but after giving him to us, he puts him on the altar as food." [TEP]

† † †

To you who stooped to sinful man
We render homage and all praise;
To Father, Son and Spirit blest
Whose gift to man is endless days.
In ancient times God spoke to man

Through Prophets and in varied ways,
But now he speaks through Christ his Son,
His radiance through eternal days.

Stanbrook Abbey

St. John on how the Eucharist should move us to practice Christian charity: "We have partaken of the spiritual altar; let us also partake of spiritual charity. Now if robbers who eat together mutually put aside their ways (of robbing), what excuse shall we have who partake of the body of the Lord, if we do not even imitate the mutual kindness of robbers? And if not only the meals, but the mere living together in a city was sufficient for many to form friendships, then what pardon shall we be worthy of, if we live divided — we who are in the same city, live in the same house (the Church), have the same road (Christ), the same King, the same doctor, the same judge, the same Creator, the same Father and all things in common?"

From one of Chrysostom's homilies on the Eucharist: "Let us obey God anywhere, and let us not contradict him, even though what he says appears contrary to our reason and contrary to our eyes; rather let his word be of more authority than our reason and our eyes."

"Let us do that also in what pertains to the Eucharistic mysteries. Let us not only look at what we have before us, but also remember his (Christ's) words; for his word is infallible and our senses are very fallible. His word was never wrong, while our senses were deceived innumerable times. Therefore, now that his word says, 'This is my body,' let us obey and believe, and let us see him with eyes of the spirit. Christ did not give us anything we can detect with the senses, but through such things he gave us nothing but what is spiritual. Thus in baptism, through what we can perceive with our senses he gives us the gift of water, but the birth and renewal that are accomplished are spiritual. If you had no body, he would have given you only those gifts that are not physical; but since the soul is united to the body, he gives you spiritual gifts through things perceptible by the senses. How many now say,

'I would like to see his form, his shape, his clothes, his shoes!' Well, behold here you see him, you touch him, you eat him. You wish to see his clothes; but he gives himself to you, not only so you can see him, but also that you touch him and eat him and receive him within yourself. Let no one approach with nausea; let no one approach with lukewarmness. Let all be on fire, fervent, animated." [TEP]

Chrysostom continues his homily on the Eucharist: "For if the Jews (at the Pascual supper in Egypt) stood, wearing shoes and holding staffs in their hands, ate rapidly, how much more fitting is it that you be attentive? Now they had to be on their way to Palestine, and for that reason they looked like those on a journey; but you must be on your way to heaven."

"Therefore great vigilance is necessary in every respect, for the punishment that threatens those who receive Communion unworthily is not moderate. Consider how you are indignant against the traitor and those who crucified Christ. Look then, don't you become guilty of the body and blood of Christ. They sacrificed his most holy body, but you receive it with a filthy soul after so many benefits! He was not content with becoming man and being buffeted and crucified, but he also unites himself with us and enters into us — and that not only through faith, but in reality he makes us his own body. What purity should impel one who partakes of such a sacrifice? With what rays of light should the hand that divides this flesh be illuminated, and the mouth that is filled with this spiritual fire, and the tongue that is red with such venerable blood?"

"Consider what great honor has been given to you, and what altar you partake of. He, upon whom the angels gaze with trembling, and because of the splendor he radiates they do not dare look him in the face; he is the same one with whom we nourish ourselves, with whom we are commingled and become one body and flesh of Christ. 'Who will tell of the multiple power of the Lord and make all his praises resound?'(Psalm 106:2) What shepherd feeds his sheep with the members of his own body? And why speak of shepherds? There are mothers who, after the pains of birth, often give their children to other women to nurse. But Christ did not consent to that. Instead he nourishes us with his own blood, and in every way unites us with himself. Pay close attention!

He was born of our very own substance. But you say that was not for everyone. Yes, surely it was for everyone. Because if he came to take our nature, it is evident that he came for all; and if for all, then for each one." [TEP]

We continue with St. John's homily on the Eucharist: "How is it, you ask, that not everyone takes advantage of this benefit? Surely not through the fault of him who chose to do this for everyone, but through the fault of those who do not want it. With each one of us he unites himself and commingles us with himself by means of the sacrament; and those to whom he gave birth (by baptism) he nourishes with himself. He does not give them to another, and in this way he convinces you that he took your flesh. Let us not be sluggish then, after we have been judged worthy of so great love and honor. Do you not see with what eagerness the little ones adhere to the breasts of their mothers, with what force they apply their lips to them? With much more eagerness than that of children at the breast let us draw the grace of the Holy Spirit; and let us have no other anxiety than not to partake of this food. The Eucharist is not a work of human power. He who brought it about at that supper (Last Supper) is the one who also brings it about now. We have the place of his ministers; but the one who sanctifies the offering and transforms it is Christ."

"Therefore let no Judas, no miser assist at this altar. If one is not a disciple, let him leave. Such are not admitted to the sacred table. 'With my disciples,' he said, 'I shall celebrate the Pasch.' This is the same table as that. It is not that Christ prepared that table and a man prepares this one. Christ prepares both."

† † †

O Lord, who in the desert fed the hungry
thousands in their need,
Where want and famine still abound,
let your relieving love be found;
And in your name may we supply your hungry
children when they cry.
O Spirit, your revealing light

149

has led our questing souls aright;
Source of our science, you have taught
the marvels human minds have wrought,
So that the barren deserts yield the bounty
by your love revealed.

Donald Hughes

You enabled the blind to see,
the deaf to hear — help our unbelief.

In a homily on St. John's Gospel Chrysostom uses the realistic style of speech of the people of Antioch in Syria, where he was born and reared, to present the doctrine of the Real Presence of Christ in the Eucharist. With the passage of time, with the guidance of the Holy Spirit given to the teaching office of the Church, and with the aid of holy and dedicated theologians, this doctrine, like others, would grow, develop and be better understood. However the substance or core of the doctrine is already presented by Chrysostom in a manner that is forceful, graphic, and realistic. Chrysostom quotes St. Paul (Eph. 5:30): "We become one body with Christ and members of his flesh and blood." Then he continues: "Let the baptized follow this thought. Well now, so that we come to be that (one body with Christ) not only through love but also in reality, let us commingle ourselves with that flesh of his. For this is what is brought about through that food that he gave us, when he wished to give us a proof of the burning love he has for us. For that reason he commingles himself with us, puts his own body in us as ferment, so that we come to form a unit with him, just as a body is united with its head. This is a proof of ardent lovers. Job makes something similar understood, when he speaks of his servants who had a very great love for him and wanted to be grated into his body. To show their ardent love for him they said, 'Who will give us of his flesh that we may be satisfied?' " (Job 31:31 in Vulgate) [TEP]

† † †

BYZANTINE EVENING SERVICE HYMN,
probably 2nd Century

Kindly light of glory, fount of light from light, blessed Jesus, coming from the Father in heaven,
The bright rays of the day, the light of the sun fade; and we at the evening hour confess thee with our hymn.
We praise the one God, almighty Father, Son and Holy Ghost the Comforter, in the glory of the Trinity.
Son of God, worthy to be glorified at all times by pure tongues, giver of life, all ages proclaim thee.

Translator: Adrian Fortescue

St. John continues his homily: "For that reason Christ did the same thing by inducing in us a greater friendship and showing his most ardent love for us. Those who love him he permitted not only to see him but also to touch him (Communion in the hand), and to eat him, and to sink their teeth in his flesh, and to become most intimate with him, and to satisfy all their ardent desires for love. Let us leave that altar like lions, breathing fire, frightful to Satan, with our thoughts fixed on our leader and on the love he has shown us. It is true that many times parents give their children to others to be fed; but Christ says, 'Not I; rather I feed you with my own flesh, I offer myself to you as food. I desire that all of you be noble; and I offer you great hope for the good things to come. For he who gives himself to you now will surely do so in the life to come. I want to be your brother. For you I took on flesh and blood. Again I give you that flesh and blood, through which I make myself your parent.' "

"This blood makes the image of our King flourish within us; it produces inconceivable beauty; it does not permit the beauty of the soul to fade by continually watering and nourishing it. The (natural) blood that food

151

forms within us is not formed immediately, but first becomes another substance. But it is not like that with this other blood (of Christ), which immediately irrigates the soul and floods it with great strength. This blood, worthily received, puts to flight and banishes the demons, and draws the angels to us and even the Lord of the angels. Wherever they see the blood of the Lord, the demons flee and the angels gather. This blood, when poured out, cleansed the entire world ... This blood is the health of our consciences; with it the soul is cleansed; with it the soul is beautified and inflamed. It makes the soul more resplendent than fire. This blood, when poured out, opened heaven ... This fountain (of Christ's blood) is a fountain of light, which sends out its rays of truth. Even the powers of heaven assist at its presence with their gaze fixed on the beauty of its rays; for they contemplate with greater clarity the efficacy of the Eucharistic oblation and its unseen rays of light." [TEP]

Chrysostom continues his homily on the Eucharist: "This blood (in the chalice at Mass) is the price of the world. With this blood Christ bought the Church; and with it he beautified the Church completely. Just as with a man who gives gold to buy slaves and uses gold if he wants to adorn them, so too Christ bought us with his blood, and with his blood he makes us beautiful. Those who partake of this blood assist at Mass together with the angels, with the archangels and with the sovereign powers, dressed with the same royal stole of Christ and fitted out with spiritual armaments. But I have not yet said anything great. They are dressed with the King himself." [TEP]

St. John begins his homily on 1Cor 10:16, which he quotes as: "The chalice of blessing which we bless, is it not the communion with the blood of Christ?" He continues thus: "St. Paul has spoken with great fidelity and with great awe; and what he says is, 'That which is in the chalice is that which flowed from his side; and from that we partake.' He calls it a chalice of blessing, because, holding it in our hands, we praise with admiration and astonishment at such an ineffable gift. We bless the blood, because he poured it out, so that we would not remain in error. Not only did he pour it out, but he also distributes it among all of us. 'So,' he says, 'if you want blood, do not bloody the altar of the idols with the blood of irrational victims, but bloody my altar with my own blood.' Tell me, what can be more awesome, and at the same time, more lovable than this?"

† † †

ADVENT HYMN, VERBUM SUPREMUM PRODIENS,
10th Century

High Word of God, coming forth from the eternal Father, who being born in the fullness of time dost succor the world;
Enlighten now our hearts and burn them with love of thee, that leaving earthly things they be filled with heavenly joy.
And when the tribunal of the great judge condemns the wicked to fire, when his voice calls the good to their reward in heaven,
Let us not be cast into the darkness to burn in flames, but may we share the joy of heaven, seeing the face of God.

Translator: Adrian Fortescue

Chrysostom continues his Eucharistic homily on 1 Cor. 10:16: "Christ transformed the priestly function into something infinitely more august and admirable than it was before (in the Jewish religion); and he commanded that he himself be offered in place of the sacrifice of animals. 'The bread that we break, is it not a communion with the body of Christ?' Why did Paul not say 'participation' instead of 'communion?' Because he wanted to show something more, and manifest a great union. For we communicate not only by partaking and receiving, but also by being united. As that body (his human body) is united to Christ, so we also are united to him by means of this bread. Because Paul adds: 'That which we break.' This can be seen realized in the Eucharist, but by no means on the cross. Rather it says, 'Not one of his bones shall be broken.' And what Christ did not suffer on the cross, he suffers for you in the offering of the Mass; and he allows himself to be divided into fragments, so that all may be filled." [Unfortunately here, the realism of Chrysostom in describing the Eucharist is exaggerated. Later the theologians would rightly explain that, when the Host is broken, only the species or sign or appearance is broken, not the body of Christ. And the Holy Spirit, speaking through the Council of Trent, declared that Christ is whole and entire, not only under each form or species of bread and wine, but also in each particle after the species is divided. However, what Chrysostom declares so forcefully and clearly is the Real Presence, that Christ is really and truly present and alive in the Eucharist.]

† † †

MEDIEVAL HYMN DISMISSING THE ALLELUIA BEFORE LENT

Alleluia, glad song, word of eternal joy. Alleluia is the praise of heavenly choirs, sung for ever by those who dwell in the house of God. Jerusalem, happy mother, thou singest Alleluia. Alleluia is the word of the joyful citizens. But the waters of Babylon make us exiles weep.
We are not worthy here always to sing Alleluia. Our sins compel us to interrupt our Alleluia. Now comes the time when we must mourn our past crimes. Wherefore, holy Trinity, praising thee we pray thee to let us see thine Easter on high, in which joyfully forever we may sing to thee Alleluia.

Translator: Adrian Fortescue

St. John continues his homily on 1 Cor. 10:16: "Now what is the bread? The body of Christ. What do they become who receive it? The body of Christ. Not many bodies, but only one body. Just as the bread is made of many grains united in such a way that they are not seen anywhere but are surely in it, and the different grains disappear completely by being mutually fused together, so too we are mutually united to one another and to Christ. Now you do not feed on one body and your neighbor on another, but we all feed on the same body. Therefore Paul adds, 'We partake of one and the same bread.' Now if we all partake of the same bread and all become the same thing (the body of Christ), why then, do we not show the same love and change into the same thing?"

"Please, let us not kill ourselves with our own effrontery. Rather let us approach him (Christ in the Eucharist) with fear and absolute purity. When you see him exposed before you, say to yourself, 'Because of this body I am no longer dust and ashes, no longer a captive but free. Because of this body I hope to attain heaven and the blessings in it, such as eternal life, the lot of the angels, and the cordial fellowship with Christ. Death did not carry off this body, pierced with nails and wounded with lashes. Even the sun, at seeing this body crucified, turned away its rays. Because of this body the (Temple) curtain was torn in two, the rocks broke open and the whole earth trembled. This is that body that was bloodied, wounded by the lance, and which made the fountains of salvation gush forth for the whole world, one of blood and the other of water.' "

"This body, which death could not hold, is the body that he gives to us to hold and eat. In that we have a proof of his intense love ... And so Christ lets us fill ourselves with his flesh, and thus brings us into greater friendship."

† † †

Mine is the sunlight! Mine is the morning,
Born of the one light Eden saw play!
Praise with elation; praise every morning,
God's re-creation of the new day!

Eleanor Farjeon

We continue St. John's homily on 1Cor 10:16: "The Magi adored this body, even when it was lying in a manger. Those men, strangers and without religion, left their home and country and set out on a long journey. Approaching with reverence and fear, they adored that body. Let us, citizens of heaven, at least imitate those strangers ... Let us rouse ourselves and tremble, and show greater piety than those strangers, so as not to heap fire on our heads by approaching for Communion thoughtlessly and with temerity. I say these things, not so that you do not approach, but so that you do not approach with temerity. Just as to approach without proper preparation is dangerous, so not to receive at all from these mystical suppers is hunger and death. For this altar is the nerves of the soul, the understanding of our mind, and the fountain of our confidence. This altar is hope, salvation, light and life. If we die after this sacrifice, we shall arrive with great confidence in those sacred regions, shielded on every side with golden armament."

"Just as in regal chambers the most magnificent thing of all is not the walls or the golden ceiling, but the body of the king seated on his throne, so also in heaven the greatest thing is the body of the King. And you may now see that body already here on earth. I show you not the angels, archangels, or the heaven of heavens, but the Lord of all that. Have you noticed how you can see on earth what is the most precious of all things? And how you not only see it, but hold it in your hands; and how you not only hold it but also eat it? ...Purify your soul, therefore, and prepare your spirit for the reception of these mysteries ...When receiving the only Son of God, tell me, do you not tremble with wonder and reject all love of things of this world? And do you not glory only in that honor, but still look to the things of this earth, and love money, and covet gold? What pardon will you be able to receive? What excuse will you offer? Do you not know how much the Lord hates all worldly pomp? Was it not for that reason that, when being born, he was placed in a manger and chose a humble mother?" [TEP]

† † †

Be calm but vigilant, because your enemy the devil is prowling round
like a roaring lion,
looking for someone to eat.
1Peter 5:8-9

From Chrysostom's homily on 1Cor 11:17, where St. Paul says that the Corinthians were doing themselves more harm than good by offering Mass, St. John speaks of committing mortal sin after receiving Communion, even on the day of reception. "Before you receive Communion, you fast in order to appear worthy of it; but after you have received it, when you should increase your resolve, you throw it all away. Nevertheless, to fast before or after Communion is the same. It is necessary to be serious at both times, but especially after having received the Groom. The fast before Communion is to make you worthy to receive it, and after Communion, so that you do not appear unworthy of having received it. Then, must I fast after having received Communion? I don't say that, nor do I require it. It would be good to do that, but I am not requiring you to do it. What I am exhorting you to do is not to hand yourself over to pleasure without restraint. Now it is never proper to give oneself over to pleasure without restraint, as St. Paul declared: 'One who thinks only of pleasure, although alive, is dead'(1Tim 5:6). To do so after Communion is much worse. If a pleasure means death for a woman, much more so is it for a man; and if it leads us to perdition at some other time, much more so after having received Communion. And you, are you not horrified when you do things worthy of death after having received the bread of life?" [St. John's statement regarding the gravity of sin for a man and a woman requires explanation.]

"Do you not know how many evils originate in pleasures? Excessive laughter, immoderate language, laxity that is full of perdition, useless jokes, and other things that it is not proper to mention. And you do all that on the same day that you partake of the table of Christ, on that day when you were made worthy to take his flesh on your tongue. Whoever you are, in order that this does not happen, wipe your right hand (in which you took the Host); clean your tongue and your lips, which formed the vestibule for the entrance of Christ." [TEP]

† † †

Lord, open wide the doors of your compassion to those who have died, or will die today. In your mercy receive them into your kingdom.

Chrysostom gave a homily on 1Cor. 11: 28-32, where St. Paul says: "Everyone is to examine himself before eating this bread and drinking this cup, because a person who eats and drinks without recognizing the body is eating and drinking his own condemnation. In fact that is why many of you are weak and ill and some of you have died. If only we examined ourselves, we should not be punished like that. But when the Lord does punish us like that, it is to correct us and stop us from being condemned with the world." We quote from Chrysostom's homily on these words.

"St. Paul discourses very energetically on these words, showing that the beginning of all good things is an approach to them with a pure conscience ... Not as we do now, approaching for Communion moved more by the circumstances than by a desire of the soul. For we are not preoccupied on how we will be able to approach well prepared, purified of our sins and full of compunction, but rather on how we do it at fiesta time, and when everyone is receiving Communion."

"But that is not how St. Paul ordered. He held it to be certain that there is only one fitting occasion to receive Communion, namely, with purity of conscience. Now if we do not partake of common food when we have fever and are very sick, so as not to lose our life, much less must we partake of this table with base desires, which are worse than fevers. When I say base desires I mean desires of the flesh, of riches, of anger, and in a word, all evil passions. He who approaches to touch this pure sacrifice should have stripped himself of all such things completely. Let him not consider himself obliged to receive Communion because of the fiesta, with a sluggish spirit and miserably disposed. By the same token one who is prepared and repentant should not think himself prohibited from receiving Communion simply because it is not a feast day. The feast day is a clear example of good works, piety of soul and exact fulfillment of your duties. If you are so disposed, you will be able to be in perpetual fiesta and receive Communion always." [TEP]

† † †

Father, let the nations recognize you as the one true God, and Jesus your Son, as the Messiah whom you sent.

Let us conclude our quotation from Chrysostom's homily on 1Cor. 11:28-32: "He who eats and drinks unworthily eats and drinks his own condemnation, says St. Paul. What does he say? The cause of so many blessings and the table that pours out life so profusely, those things themselves become condemnation? Not by their nature, he says, but by the will of the one who approaches. Just as the coming of Christ, which brought such great and ineffable blessings, brings greater condemnation to those who do not receive him (through their own fault), likewise the sacraments provide greater punishment for those who receive them unworthily ... If you recognize well Who it is that is set before you, and who it is to whom He is given, you would need no other reason (to examine yourself). It would be enough for you to approach with caution and avoid a great fall." [TEP]

Chrysostom's homily on St. Paul's Letter to the Ephesians explains how the body of Christ in the Eucharist is the same body that Christ has in heaven. "Now that we are speaking of the body of Christ, let us think that as many partake of the body and taste the blood we are partakers of that body which in no way is different from or distinguished from that body of Christ which is seated above in heaven, that body which is adored by the angels ... Poor me! How many are the roads to salvation! He made his (mystical) body (the Church), and he gives us his (real) body; and despite it all, nothing withdraws us from evil. What darkness, what deep abyss, what insensibility! St. Paul says, 'Look for the things that are in heaven, where Christ is, seated at the right hand of God' (Col.3:1-2). And yet there are those preoccupied with money, and others who are slaves of passion."

† † †

A MORNING PRAYER, by *James Quinn, S.J.*

Darkness has faded, night gives way to morning. Sleep has refreshed us, now we thank our Maker, singing his praises, lifting up to heaven hearts, minds, and voices.
Father of mercies, bless the hours before us. While there is daylight may we work to please you, building a city fit to be your dwelling, home for all nations.

We continue Chrysostom's homily on Ephesians; "I see many partaking of the body of the Lord rashly and routinely, more out of habit and custom than from consideration and desire. It is said that, when Lent arrives, whoever one is, he partakes of Communion, and likewise on the Feast of Epiphany. Nevertheless, these are not times to receive Communion, because Epiphany and Lent do not make one worthy of Communion; but the purity and sincerity of the soul make one worthy. With these dispositions receive Communion always; and without them, never ... You limit the times of your purification to certain days, when you approach the sacrifice which makes even the angels tremble."

"How will you be able to present yourselves before Christ's tribunal, if you have the audacity to touch his body with hands and lips that are soiled? Would you kiss the king with a mouth that smells bad? And yet you kiss the king of heaven with a foul smelling, stinking soul? (It was the custom there at that time to kiss the Host before swallowing it.) Truly this is a great offense. Tell me, would you approach the sacrifice (Communion) with dirty hands? I don't think so. You are so reverent and religious in that small matter, and yet you approach and dare to touch the body of Christ with a dirty soul? His body is retained in your hands only for a moment, but it dissolves completely in your soul. Do you not see how bright and clean are the vessels (for Mass)? But it is proper that our souls be brighter and cleaner than them. Why? ... Because they do not partake of what they contain; they do not understand, but we do. Undoubtedly you would not want to use a soiled, dirty cup; and you approach for Communion with a dirty soul!"

"In this matter I notice a great anomaly: on other days you do not approach for Communion, although many times your conscience is clean; but for the Pasch you do, even though you have committed some crime. What a custom! What presumption! In vain Mass is celebrated every day; in vain do we priests assist at the altar; no one approaches to receive Communion. I say this not so that you receive Communion rashly, but so that you prepare yourselves and make yourselves worthy to receive." [TEP]

† † †

Claim me once more as your own,
Lord, and have mercy on me.

Continuing his homily on Ephesians, Chrysostom says: "How is it that you say we receive Communion only once a year? Now it is a serious matter that you measure the worthiness to receive, not by the purity of soul but by the interval of time. And you consider it piety not to receive frequently. You ignore the fact that to receive unworthily, even though it be but once, imprints on the soul the sign of perdition; while on the other hand to receive worthily, even though it be frequently, brings salvation. It is not audacity to receive frequently but to do so unworthily, even though it be but once a year ... In no way is Mass celebrated for the Pasch superior to that celebrated now. It is the same, the same grace of the Spirit; it is always Pasch."

"Let nothing bitter come from the mouth that was made worthy to partake of so great a mystery. Let not the tongue that has been in contact with the divine body speak anything harsh; let us keep it pure and not utter curses with it."

(Christ speaks:) "For you I received spittle and blows to my face. For you I emptied myself of all my glory. I left my Father and came to you, you

161

who hated me, and were against me, and did not even want to hear my name. I followed you and ran after you to hold you. I united myself to you intimately; I said, 'Eat me, drink me.'   Again I came down to earth (at the Consecration of the Mass). I unite myself to you lovingly. I am food; I am divided into little pieces so that there be greater union and fusion between us. [See note of explanation on page 107] Now things that are united do not disappear but remain within their own proper limits. On the contrary I am identified, enmeshed with you. In the future I want nothing between us; I desire to be one with you." (Chrysostom speaks:) "Recognizing all of this and his providential care for us, let us do all we can to show that we are not unworthy of such great gifts, gifts which we all hope to acquire through the grace and mercy of our Lord Jesus Christ, with whom let there be to the Father and the Holy Spirit glory, power, and honor now and for ever and ever. Amen." [TEP]

† † †

My God, for you I long; for you my soul is thirsting.
My body pines for you like a dry,
weary land without water.

(Psalm 62:1)

St. John explains how the sacrifice of Calvary and the sacrifice of the Mass are not two sacrifices but one. The sacrifice of the Mass and that of Calvary are one and the same sacrifice. The Mass makes the sacrifice of Calvary present, the only difference being the manner in which Christ's one sacrifice of Calvary is offered: then in a cruel, bloody manner; at Mass in a glorious, unbloody manner. Chrysostom says: "Do we not present offerings every day? Surely, but in doing so we make a commemoration of Christ's death; and this oblation is one, not many. How can it be one and not many? Because this oblation was offered only once. ... We always offer the same Lamb, not one today and another tomorrow, but always the same one. And for that reason the sacrifice is always one; otherwise there would have to be many Christs, since it is offered in many places. But in no way are there many Christs, since in every place there is only one Christ, who is whole and entire here and whole and entire there with his one only body. Now just as Christ, who is offered in many places on earth, has only one body and not many bodies, so also is the sacrifice one. Our Pontiff (Christ) is the one who offered the victim that purifies us. And now we also offer that same Victim, which was offered then and which will never be consumed. This is done in memory of what took place then. As it says, 'Do this in memory of me.' We do not offer another sacrifice, as the Jewish priest used to do; but we always offer the same sacrifice." [TEP]

† † †

Lord Jesus, eternal priest, you exercised your priesthood on earth chiefly by offering yourself to the Father in the bloody sacrifice of Calvary. In heaven, showing the Father the wounds of Calvary, you continue to offer that one sacrifice of yours, but now in a glorious manner, while you make intercession for us constantly. In your infinite love for us you let us all share in your one priesthood: the laity through their baptism, the ministerial priests through their ordination also. Thus you have formed us all into a congregation of priests, who not only join you at Mass in offering in a glorious manner your one sacrifice of Calvary, but who also offer the Father daily the spiritual sacrifices of their holy lives.
(A prayer by the compiler based on the doctrine of the Eucharist.)

In a beautiful homily to the newly baptized adults Chrysostom speaks of Baptism, the Eucharist and the Church:

"God has given me another weapon for my defense. And what is it? He has prepared a table for me, he has given me a food that satisfies, so that, strengthened by a splendid banquet, I overcome the enemy (devil) victoriously. When the rabid demon sees you after you have approached the table of the Lord, the heavenly banquet, he flees as before a lion spewing fire from its mouth; he retreats rapidly like the wind and does not dare to approach. And if from a distance he sees your tongue moist with the blood of the Lord, believe me, he will put up no resistance. And if he sees your lips red with the blood of Christ, he will slip away and flee, overcome with fear."

"If the exterminating angel (in Egypt at the first Pasch), when he saw the blood of the Paschal lamb (a figure of Christ), dared not approach, how much more will the devil flee at seeing the blood of the reality (Christ) and remain at a distance at seeing the blood of Christ, not smeared on doorposts but in the mouths of the faithful, that is, on the doors of the living temple of God."

"If you want to understand better the strength of the blood of Christ, recall the first origin from which it flowed. This blood ran from the wound of the crucified Lord ... The soldier pierced the side of Christ and dug into the wall of the holy temple (Christ's body); and I found the treasure and took the riches. That is the way it also happened with the Paschal Lamb. The Jews immolated the Lamb, and I reaped the fruit of the sacrifice. From his side flowed blood and water ... The water is a symbol of baptism; the blood is a symbol of the most holy sacrament (Eucharist)." [TEP]

† † †

Silence before the Lord Yahweh! (Zephaniah 1:6)

I (God) will let him (ruler of the Jews) come freely into my presence, and he can come close to me; who else, indeed, would risk his life by coming close to me?
It is Yahweh who speaks.
(Jeremiah 30:21)

Chrysostom's homily to the newly baptized continues: "Do not pass over this deed superficially. It is full of meaning. Consider what other secret is hidden there. I said that water and blood are a symbol of baptism and the most holy sacrament. Now the Church is founded on the spiritual renewal by the bath of rebirth and on the most holy sacrament (Eucharist), both of which have their origin in the side of Christ. Therefore Christ built the Church from the side of Christ, just as he made Eve from the side of Adam. Therefore St. Paul says, 'We are of his flesh and of his bones.' "

"Now see how intimately Christ has been united to his spouse (Church); see with what food he satisfies us. He himself is our food and nourishment; and just as a woman nourishes her child with her own blood and milk, Christ also consantly nourishes with his own blood those to whom he has given birth (by baptism)."

† † †

LENTEN HYMN *from before the tenth century*

Hear, merciful Creator, the prayers which we make with tears in this holy Lenten fast.
Reader of hearts, thou knowest how weak is our strength; show mercy to us who turn to thee.
Much have we sinned, but spare us repentant. For the glory of thy name heal our sick souls.
Let our bodies be subdued by abstinence; so may our souls, fasting from all evil, leave the food of sin.
Grant, blessed Trinity, divine Unity, that the offerings of our fast be fruitful.

Translator: Adrian Fortescue

Spare, O Lord, spare thy people;
and be not angry with us for ever.

165

We conclude Chrysostom's homily to the newly baptized: "Now since we have been made worthy of so great graces, let us also lead a worthy life ... Do you want to understand better of what honor you have been made a partaker? The Jews were not allowed to see the transfigured face of Moses, who was simply a descendant of Adam, a man like them. But you have seen the face of Christ in his glory. As St. Paul says, 'We have all seen the glory of the Lord with uncovered faces.' And if we apply to our new Moses (the bishop) what was written of the former Moses, we will not be in error ... Then Moses lifted his hands to heaven, and there fell manna, the bread of angels; our Moses (the bishop) extends his hands to heaven and brings us bread from heaven. He (Moses) struck the rock and there shot out a fountain of water; our pastor (bishop) approaches the sacred table, touches the spiritual rock (Christ), and wrests from him a spiritual fountain. For that reason the sacred altar is raised in the middle of the faithful (in the middle of the church), like a flowing fountain, so that the thirsty little sheep find a place to drink round about—the well of salvation, manna in abundance, so that no one perishes from tortuous thirst."

"Now that we have a saving fountain that gives life; now that the table is loaded with an abundance of every good thing to shower on us most copious spiritual graces, let us approach with a heart full of faith and a clear conscience, so that we receive grace and mercy and help at an opportune time through the favor and compassion of our Lord Jesus Christ, through whom and with whom be honor to the Father with the Holy Spirit now and forever. Amen." [TEP]

With this we conclude our quotations from St. John Chrysostom, Doctor of the Eucharist.

✝ ✝ ✝

Lord, please keep us today from sin.

Would that today we heed the voice of the Lord, "Do not harden your hearts."
Open my heart, O Lord, to praise your holy name.

CYRILLONAS (CYRUS), PRIEST-POET OF SYRIA

Toward the end of the fourth century there lived in Syria a priest-poet by the name of Cyrillonas or Cyrus. Little is known about him outside of some of his hymns and homilies that are extant. We quote here from one of his homilies on the Paschal Feast. Although we find poetical ideas and expressions even in his prose, we see clearly his doctrine on the Eucharist, which is typically Syrian, that is, vivid and graphic, as is that of the Syrian, St. John Chrysostom.

"The true Lamb (Christ), full of joy, speaks to his table guests (at the Last Supper), who are about to eat him. The First-born announces the Pasch to his disciples in the festive chamber. Our Savior invited himself to his immolation and to the generous offering of his own blood. His bread of life was nutritious and well prepared; the bundle of stocks of wheat had arrived at their fullness. The matter of his body was penetrated with the leaven of his divinity. His mercy flowed generously, and his love forced him to make himself food for his own. He gathered the white wheat from Zion and entrusted it to his Church in holiness. He had prepared a new nuptial feast, and now he invited and called his companions to celebrate it. He prepared a feast to satisfy the hunger of his spouse (the Church)."

"The people (Jews), when leaving Egypt, took with them unleavened dough wrapped in their cloaks. The dough was cold, like a corpse, and without yeast. The synagogue (the Jews) took the unleavened dough in its cloak for the time of its Pasch; but the Church received in a new cloak the leaven of God. Mary is the cloak; and our Lord, the true leaven. The heat indicates his immortality, for divinity is immortal. The leaven was wrapped and kept in the cloak of the womb of Mary. Because of her virginity this cloak was closed as with a seal. The leaven (Christ) came out of that cloak without tearing its enclosure or breaking the seal. In the festive chamber (Mary's womb) he remained as the Paschal Lamb to make the dough of our body completely leavened. He kneaded our body with leaven, so that with it we would participate in immortality; and with the salt of his divinity we would remain immune to the poison of the serpent (sin)." [TEP]

We continue quoting from the Paschal homily of Cyrillonas: "Our Lord led his disciples and sat down in the banquet chamber (for the Last Supper). He sat down first and his disciples after him. There they were reclining with him at table and watching how he ate and was transformed. (Cyrus believed our Lord received Communion at the Last Supper. It is not certain that he did.) The Lamb (Christ) ate the Lamb (Christ), and the Pasch ate the Pasch. He put an end to the (Paschal) institution of his Father, and initiated his own. He closed the Law (Old Testament) and opened the new covenant of reconciliation."

"Then Christ began to announce what he had promised: 'With great desire I have desired to eat this Pasch with you before I suffer.' Come, receive me — I ask it of you. Eat me — I desire it. With your teeth of fire (i.e. of love) grind my bones to pieces, and with your tongue drink my warm blood in draughts." (As was explained before, in the Eucharist only the species or appearances are broken or affected, not the body of Christ.)

"This is the body on which the angels cannot fix their gaze because of its brightness. This is the bread of Divinity that I have given graciously to the inhabitants of the earth. This is the Most Holy, through whom the Seraphim on high are sanctified, while they extol it as holy. This is the fruit enabling one to become God, the fruit whose goodness Adam desired.

"Come, receive me, break me into pieces, taste me hidden under the species! I have made myself food and complete nourishment for the welfare of the world, to calm its hunger. Come, my disciples, receive me. I want to place myself in your hands. Look, in very truth I stand here; but at the same time chew me likewise in very truth. I do not burn (punish) one who eats me, but one who remains far from me; my fire causes no pain to one who chews me, but to one who does not love me." [TEP]

✝ ✝ ✝

Lord Jesus, dispel the darkness of error, so that we may live securely in you here and hereafter.
All praise and honor to Christ, who lives for ever to intercede for us

and to save us, who approach
the Father in his name.

We conclude our quotations from the Paschal homily of the priest-poet, Cyrus or Cyrillonas: "Come, my beloved, also drink my (Christ's) blood, which is the blood of the New Testament. Drink the chalice of fire, the blood which inflames all who drink it. This is the chalice which consoled the first Adam in his labors (by anticipation). This is the blood that replaces the blood of the animals sacrificed throughout the world."

"This is the blood that sanctifies body and soul with divinity ... This is the blood that establishes peace and concord between heaven and earth."

"So, take the chalice and drink from it, in order to put aside your sufferings; become inebriated with it; gain that mysterious power to make you intrepid before the persecutors. Drink from it and, full of zeal, drench the whole of creation with it. With its strength you will trample the serpents; and with its reception you will conquer death!"

"The ancient prophets desired me, and the just asked to contemplate me. They died with clamor and wailing, because they were not to see me despite their pleas. Blessed are you, my disciples, who have chewed me in your mouth."

"But in order that you do not forget this night, which for you must be more precious than the day; in order that you do not forget the hour in which you have tasted the Divinity, I also command this of you, my beloved and confidants of my secrets: this remembrance must not stop among you until the end of the world. Therefore, my brothers, you must make this remembrance at all times and remember me. You have chewed my body — do not forget me! You have drunk my blood — do not neglect me!" [TEP]

† † †

Come, let us adore the Lord on bended knee.
Inspire us to yearn for you always, as the deer does for running
streams, until you satisfy every longing in heaven.

When I found your words I devoured them; they became my joy and the happiness of my heart.

FRAGMENTS FROM BYZANTINE EUCHARISTIC POEMS BY UNKNOWN AUTHORS TOWARD THE END OF THE FOURTH CENTURY

We close our Eucharistic quotations from the fourth century by citing a few fragments of Byzantine poetry.

"Today we have gazed upon our Lord Jesus Christ on the altar ... Today we have heard the grand and sweetest voice that said: 'This body cuts the thorn bush of sins, and illumines the souls of men. The hemorrhaging woman, having touched this body, was freed from her illness. The daughter of the Canaanite woman, having seen this body, was cured. The sinful woman, having approached this body with full faith, cleansed the filth of her sins. Thomas, having grasped this body, exclaimed: 'My Lord and my God.' This great and most grand body is for us salvation."

"Again the Word (Christ) himself and our life said: 'This blood is poured out for you and given for the pardon of sins.' Beloved, we have drunk the holy and immortal blood. Beloved, we have drunk the blood that flowed from the side of the Lord, the blood with which we have been purchased, with which we have been redeemed, by which we are obligated and enlightened. Look, brothers, what body we have eaten; look, sons, what blood we have drunk. Look what covenants we make with God, so that we will not be ashamed on that terrible day of accounting. And who can praise sufficiently the mystery of your grace? We have been made worthy to partake of the gift. Let us keep it till the end, so that we may be made worthy to hear that blessed, sweetest, and holy voice of Him which says: 'Come blessed of my Father. Enter in possession of the kingdom which is prepared for you.' " [End of quotations from Vol 1 of TEP—TEXTOS EUCARISTICOS PRIMITIVOS by Jesus Solano, S.J.]

✝ ✝ ✝

Faith of our fathers! faith and prayer
Shall win all nations unto thee;
And through the truth that comes from God,
Mankind shall then indeed be free.
Faith of our fathers, holy faith!
We will be true to thee till death.

Frederick W. Faber

[All quotations from St. Gregory and from anyone else are from TEP unless otherwise specified.]

El fuerte es el' que sabe morir. (The strong person is the one who knows how to die.)
[From the liturgy of the Feast of the Holy Innocents]

Chapter VIII

THE EUCHARIST IN THE FIFTH CENTURY

TIMOTHY OF ALEXANDRIA IN EGYPT, c. 400 a.d.

Early in the fifth century there lived a man by the name of Timothy in Alexandria on the northern coast of Egypt. It is not certain whether he was the bishop of that great city or only a deacon. Some historians list him as a saint. What is certain is that at the beginning of the fifth century he wrote a history entitled, "History of the Monks." We quote here, a bit, from that work that pertains to the Eucharist. It should be noted he speaks of monks in a closed community known as a monastery. What he says cannot be applied to a public situation such as a parish church.

"The holy Abbot Apolonius had the custom that the brothers who were with him took no nourishment whatever, until they had received the Lord's Communion about three o'clock in the afternoon. Sometimes the monks remained fasting even until evening was approaching, while, listening to the word of God, they were taught how they were to fulfill the mandates of the Lord without intermission. After that, having eaten, some went to their desert habitats, where they spent the entire night memorizing the Sacred Scriptures. Others remained in the same place in which they had gathered and passed the night until dawn singing hymns and praises to God, as I myself saw when I was present. Some of them around three in the afternoon came down from their mountain, received the Lord's Communion, and then left content with only this spiritual feast; and this they did many times. They had so much joy and happiness and more exultation than a man on earth should have ..." [TEP, Volume 2]

† † †

FROM A HYMN TO THE CROSS, *of the sixth century*

The banners of the King go forth, the mystery of the cross shines, by which our Life bore death

and by death gave us life.
To wash us from the stain of sin he was pierced by the sharp point of
the lance and shed water and blood.
What David in his true hymn told to the nations is now fulfilled: God
reigns from the tree.

Text: Vexilla Regis Prodeunt by Venantius Fortunatus, Bishop of
Poitiers (France); died c. 600.
Translator: Adrian Fortescue

We continue quoting from Timothy's "History of the Monks': "Likewise
the Abbot taught that, if it were possible, the monks should receive
Communion every day; lest if they be withdrawn from it, they be separated
also from God. But it is seen that one who receives the Savior more
frequently receives him still more frequently. For the Savior himself said,
'He who eats my flesh and drinks my blood remains in me and I in him.'
Moreover the commemoration of the passion of the Lord (Mass), when
the monks offer it fervently, is for them very useful for an example of
patience. And notice is given that everyone should try always to be prepared
in such a way that he is not unworthy to receive Communion. And to this
the Abbot adds that also the forgiveness of sins is given to the believers
through the Mass." (Mass always forgives venial sin for those properly
disposed. It can likewise forgive mortal sin. However, one who committed
mortal sin may not receive Communion until he has made a good
sacramental Confession to a priest.)

"We saw another holy Abbot named Eulogius, who, when he presented
Communion, he had received such grace from the Lord, that he knew the
faults and merits of all who approached the altar of God. For that reason
he would detain some of the monks among those wishing to approach for
Communion and say, 'How have you dared to approach the divine
sacrament with your mind and intention set upon evil?' Then he would
add, 'You, this very night you were thinking about fornicating. You said in

your heart: 'It makes no difference in approaching Communion whether one is holy or a sinner.' And another monk was perplexed in his heart saying, 'What power does Communion have to sanctify me?' All these the Abbot would bar from communion saying to them, 'Refrain for a little while from receiving Communion and do penance, so that, having been purified properly and with tears, you may be worthy of Christ's Communion.' " [TEP, Vol. 2]

† † †

The Lord will strengthen us if we obey him.

Eternal God, help us remember that life is like a flower which blossoms in the morning, but withers in the evening.

Timothy writes about a St. Marcarius of Alexandria, who appears to have been venerated only locally, since he is otherwise unknown to us. "St. Marcarius of Alexandria added something else more terrible, which he saw when the monks were approaching for Communion. When they had extended the palms of their hands to receive the Host, the demons advanced and put coals in the hands of some; and the Body of Christ that was seen to have been given by the hand of the priest returned to the altar. And when those with merits of better deeds extended their hands, the demons went far away and fled with fear. St. Marcarius saw an angel of the Lord present at the altar, who put his hand over the hand of the priest in the distribution of Communion. From then on this grace of God remained with St. Marcarius. When the monks observed vigils, or at the time of Psalms and prayer, he saw when anyone was deceived by the devil and was thinking of other things. He was aware of the merits and the unworthiness of those who approached the altar." [TEP, Vol. 2]

✝ ✝ ✝

FROM A HYMN TO THE CROSS, *of the sixth century*

Fair and radiant tree, with royal purple adorned, chosen to touch so
sacred limbs with thy boughs.
Blessed cross, on whose arms the redemption of the world is borne;
thou, from whom his body hangs,
dost snatch from hell its prey.
O cross hail, our only hope! At this Passion-tide increase grace to the
good and take sin from the wicked.
Thee, holy Trinity, fount of salvation, let every spirit praise. To whom
thou givest the victory of the cross,
to them give also its prize.

Text:Vexilla Regis Prodeunt by Venantius Fortunatus, Bishop of
Poitiers (France); died c. 600 a.d. Translator: Adrian Fortescue

✝ ✝ ✝

Jesus, teach us to put our trust in the Father and to seek his kingdom
first of all rather than imitate the powerful and envy the rich.
Lord, let us seek and taste the things that are above, so that we may
direct our work and leisure to your glory.

ST. CHROMATIUS, BISHOP OF AQUILEA
IN ITALY, died c. 407

In his commentary on the Our Father St. Chromatius believes that the
fourth petition (Give us this day our daily bread) refers to both ordinary
food and the Eucharist.

He writes: "Give us this day our daily bread. We understand these words of our Lord in two ways. First, that we do not ask for food other than that of each day. He did not command us to ask for riches nor an abundance of temporal things, but our daily bread. That alone is necessary for the present life of Christians who live by faith, as the Apostle Paul says: 'We are content with food and clothing.' Solomon in the Book of Ecclesiastes demonstrates the same thing in all clarity: 'What is essential for man is bread, water, and clothing.' When Jesus says 'this day,' he teaches us to think only of the present day and not of the entire course of our life, so that our thoughts are not preoccupied with temporal matters. The Lord himself teaches clearly in another place, saying: 'Do not think about tomorrow. Tomorrow will have its own trouble' (Mt 6:34).

"And we must keep in mind that Christ treats of a spiritual command, that we ask for our daily bread, that is, that heavenly and spiritual bread that we receive every day for medicine for our soul and hope of eternal salvation. About that, the Lord says in the Gospel: 'The heavenly bread is my flesh, which I shall give for the life of this world' (Jn 6:51). And so he commands us to ask every day for this bread, that is, through the mercy of God we may merit to receive daily the bread of the body of the Lord. The holy Apostle Paul says: 'Let a man examine himself, and thus eat the bread and drink the chalice' (1 Co 11:28). And again: 'He who eats the bread of the Lord unworthily and drinks the chalice, will be guilty of the body and blood of the Lord' (Ibid.27). Therefore, not without reason are we to pray always to merit the daily reception of this heavenly bread, lest for some sin we be separated from the body of the Lord."[TEP]

† † †

Lord, to whom shall we go? You have the words of eternal life.
(Jn.6:68)
Let us serve the Lord in holiness all the days of our life.

ST. GAUDENTIUS, BISHOP OF BRESCIA (ITALY), died c. 410

There are extant some instructions that St. Gaudentius, Bishop of Brescia in Italy, gave in the early 400's on the Paschal Feast in both the Old and New Testaments. We quote from those instructions.

"One (Christ) died for many. And in all of the churches, in the mystery of the bread and wine, when he is immolated, he strengthens; when he is believed in, he gives life; when he is consecrated, he sanctifies those who consecrate. This is the flesh of the Lamb; this is his blood."

"The very Creator and Lord of nature, who produces bread from the earth, also (because he can and promised it) makes his own body from the bread. And he, who made wine from water, also makes his blood from the wine."

"In truth this is the hereditary gift of his new testament, that he bequeathed to us as a pledge of his presence, the night he was handed over to be crucified. This is the food for our journey, with which we are fed and nourished along life's way, until we come to him after leaving this world. For that reason the Lord himself said: 'If you do not eat my flesh and drink my blood, you will not have life in yourselves.' "

"Christ willed that his benefits remain with us. He wanted the souls, redeemed by his precious blood, to be forever sanctified by the re-presentation of his own Passion. And for that reason he commands his faithful disciples, whom he also made the first priests of his Church, to celebrate perpetually these mysteries of eternal life. It is necessary that all priests celebrate these mysteries in all the churches of the entire world, until Christ comes again from heaven. In this way not only the priests themselves but also all of the faithful, having before our eyes daily a representation of the Passion of Christ, we bear it in our hands, receive it in our mouth and heart, and have an indelible memory of our redemption. And against the poison of the devil we acquire a sweet medicine for our eternal protection, as the Holy Spirit exhorts us: 'Taste and see that the Lord is sweet.' "

✝ ✝ ✝

Father, may the fulfillment of your law be our aim in life, so that you yourself may be our inheritance, and we your chosen possession forever.

We conclude our quotations from the instructions by St. Gaudentius. "The true Lamb of God, whom John the Baptist pointed out, is Christ. He said: 'Behold the Lamb of God; behold him who takes away the sins of the world.' Not only we who are faithful to this sacrament, but also all believers in the faith, must eat his flesh and commend it to the very interior of our hearts in such a way that we not only have our loins girded with chastity, but also, as the Apostle Paul says, 'We are fitted with shoes for announcing the Gospel of peace.' The precepts of the divine laws are like earthly footwear that protects the feet against the harshness of the cold, or the bite of serpents, or the prick of thorns. Therefore, we who celebrate the Pasch of the Lord must use this footwear." [TEP]

✝ ✝ ✝

HYMN TO THE CROSS *(sixth century)*

Sing, my tongue, the victory of the glorious battle, sing the triumph of the cross; how the Redeemer of the world being sacrificed yet conquered.
The Creator, pitying Adam's race, when it fell by the taste of the forbidden fruit, then noted the tree; that by a tree the loss from a tree should be repaired.
So was the work of our salvation ordered, that art should destroy the art of the deceiver, that healing should come from a tree, as had come the wound.
Therefore in the fullness of the sacred time the Creator of the world, sent from the Father's home, was born and came forth clothed

in flesh from the Virgin's womb.
A child he lay in the narrow cradle, and the virgin mother bound
his limbs in swaddling clothes; such bands held the hands and feet of
God.
Eternal glory be to the blessed Trinity, to the Father and Son; the
same honor to the Paraclete. Let all the world praise the name of the
one and three.

Text: Pange Lingua Gloriosi by Venantius Fortunatus, Bishop of
Poitiers (France); died c. 600 a.d. Translator: Adrian Fortescue

THEOPHILUS, PATRIARCH OF ALEXANDRIA
IN EGYPT, died c. 412 a.d.

Theophilus was ill equipped to be a bishop, much less the Patriarch of the great Diocese of Alexandria in Egypt. Although his intentions were good in fighting some errors of Origen, his belligerent nature carried him to excess. He even helped to exile the great St. Chrysostom of Constantinople and engaged in a quarrel with St. Jerome. He was eventually rebuked by the Pope himself. Nevertheless he maintained clear, orthodox doctrine regarding the Eucharist, as we shall see now in quotations from some of his works.

He wrote: "Those of you who seek the delights of the ineffable gift ... wear the wedding garment of a sincere faith; and let us together hasten to the mystical banquet. Today Christ invites us; today Christ serves us. Christ, the lover of mankind, renews our strength. Tremendous are the words (of Consecration at Mass) that are pronounced; tremendous is that which is performed. The fatted calf is sacrificed. The Lamb of God, who takes away the sins of the world, is immolated. [As explained before, at Mass Christ does not suffer or die. It would be better to say that the fatted calf (Christ) that was sacrificed is present, offering his same sacrifice in a glorious manner; that the immolated Lamb is doing the same thing.] The Father rejoices; the Son is offered in sacrifice spontaneously. Today he is sacrificed not by the work of God's enemies, but by his own hand, to make us understand that his saving Passion was voluntary."

"The Son of God distributes his body like bread, and gives his life-giving blood to drink like wine. O tremendous mystery! The Creator gives himself for the enjoyment of the work of his hands; his very life he gives to mortals to eat and drink. 'Come,' he exhorts us; 'eat my bread and drink the wine I have mixed for you. I myself have disposed myself to be food; I myself have mixed myself for those who desire me. Being life itself, I made myself flesh voluntarily; by my own choice I took flesh and blood, while being the Word and the substantial image of the Father, in order to save you.' "

† † †

Father, help us to find a life of peace after these days of trouble.

The Patriarch continues: "Eat me, the life, so that you may live (says Christ). This is what I want. Eat the life that never fails, because that is why I came — that you may have life and have it in abundance. Eat my bread, because I am the grain of wheat that gives life. I am the bread of life. Drink the wine I have mixed for you, because I am the drink of immortality ... Receive me like yeast in your dough, so that you partake of that undying life that is in me."

Some Egyptian hermit-monks, infected with some of Origen's errors concerning the divinity of Christ, came to Alexandria and created a popular uproar. Theophilus rails against them in the following quotations. "Now where are those deniers of God, those solitary wolves? Clothed with the false vestiture of piety, they weaken the strength of piety itself. They themselves are pseudo Christians who, because of the Incarnation, deny the consubstantiality of Christ with the omnipotent Father. Let those charlatans, the most absurd of all people, tell us if they can, whose is the body with which the sheep of the Church are fed? In what font (baptism) are they remade sons of truth? Now really, if it is the body of God that is distributed, then Christ the Lord is truly God and not only a man or an angel (as they say) or a servant or one of the incorporeal beings. And if it is the blood of God that is drunk, Christ is not therefore only God, one Person of the adorable Trinity, the Son of God, but also the Word of God made man. And if the body of Christ is food and the blood of Christ is drink, and if Christ (as they say) is only a man, then how is it preached to those who approach the sacred table, that he will lead them to eternal life?"

"And so let us receive the body of Life itself, as St. John the Apostle says: 'Because Life was made manifest'; and in another place, 'The Word was made flesh and dwelled among us.' And that Word is Christ, the Son of the living God, one of the most holy Trinity. Let us drink his most holy blood for the remission of all our sins. Let us partake of the immortality that is in him, while we believe that he is at the same time, priest and victim, offerer and oblation ... Let us not divide in two his divine and indivisible Person, nor the unity of the Trinity." [TEP]

ST. JEROME, PRIEST AND BIBLICAL SCHOLAR, 347-420

St. Jerome, who has been called "God's angry man" because of his tendency to express his anger in dealing with heretics, was born in Dalmatia, on the border of what is now the nation of Bosnia. He was baptized by the Pope at the age of 18. He studied in Rome and Syria. For a while he served as secretary to Pope Damasus, who asked him to translate the books of the Bible from their original Hebrew and Greek into Latin. This he did while living as a hermit in Bethlehem. His version was eventually called the Vulgate (Popular) Bible because of its widespread use in the Church. For centuries it has been the Church's only official Bible. The Church has declared it free from error in matters of faith and morals. St. Jerome's extensive commentaries on the books of the Bible are still in use today. The quotations that follow are from what St. Jerome wrote concerning the Eucharist, something he did only in passing, and only in relation to the Bible.

St. Jerome was totally immersed in the Bible. He saw not only its beauty but also what he deemed its necessity. "Ignorance of the Scriptures," he wrote, "is ignorance of Christ." His understanding and love of the Bible is seen in the bold expressions he used to describe it; expressions, which the Second Vatican Council would use more than 1500 years later in our own day. Both St. Jerome and the Council saw Christ himself in the Scriptures preparing a table of spiritual nourishment for our souls. Vatican II said: "Christ is present in his word, since it is he himself who speaks when the Scriptures are read in the Church." Also, at Mass "the treasures of the Bible are to be opened up more lavishly, so that a richer nourishment may be provided for the faithful at the table of God's word." Taken in isolation, such a daring expression would seem to weaken or deny the doctrine of the Real Presence of Christ in the Eucharist; but when such an expression is seen in conjunction with St. Jerome's several clear references to the Real Presence, it is clear that he is merely enhancing the value and importance of the Bible.

† † †

Out of love place yourselves at one another's service.

St. Jerome writes: "Since the flesh of the Lord is real food, and his blood real drink, spiritually speaking, we have in this present life only one good thing, namely, to eat his flesh and drink his blood not only in the Eucharist, but also in the reading of the Scriptures. For the knowledge of the Scriptures is true food and drink taken from God's word."

He speaks of the institution of the Mass at the Last Supper: "The Savior of the human race celebrated the Pasch in an upper room, and in an upper room that was large and spacious, cleansed of every impurity, furnished and prepared for the spiritual banquet, where he (Christ) entrusted the mystery of the body and blood to his disciples, and left us the eternal feast of the spotless Lamb."

"The heretics immolate many victims and eat their flesh, while they abandon the one victim, Christ, and do not eat his flesh that is the food of the believers" ... St. Jerome makes Christ say: "And they think that my light yoke is very heavy. And I descended to them, leaving the kingdom of heaven to eat with them. Having taken the form of man, I gave them the food of my body, I myself, food and guest!"

Malachi the Prophet says: "You will offer on my altar polluted bread." Jerome says: "We pollute the bread, that is, the body of Christ, when we approach the altar unworthily, and being unclean, we drink the clean blood."

Commenting on Matthew 15:32, where Jesus said he did not want to dismiss the crowd who had been with him for three days without eating, St. Jerome says: "Jesus did not want to dismiss them without eating for fear they might faint on the way. Therefore one puts himself in danger, when he hastens to arrive at his desired mansion (heaven) without eating the heavenly food (Communion)."

† † †

Lord, call men to serve at your altar and to follow you more closely in chastity, poverty and obedience.
Lord, take care of your handmaidens (nuns) vowed to virginity, that they may follow you, the divine Lamb, wherever you go.

Our Scripture scholar comments on St. Paul's Letter to Titus: "The difference between the Loaves of Proposition (in the Old Testament) and the body of Christ is like that between the shadow and the bodies, the image and the truth, the models of things to come and what is prefigured by those models. And so, as a bishop must possess in a great degree, more than any layman, meekness, patience, sobriety, moderation, freedom from lucre, hospitality and kindness, so must he maintain his chastity and, so to speak, his priestly shame, so that he abstains not only from unclean conduct, but also that the mind of one who is to confect the body of Christ be free of sinful looks and thoughts ... The Bread of benediction and the chalice of the Lord do not benefit the infidel and the impure, for he who eats unworthily of this bread and drinks this chalice, eats and drinks his own condemnation."

184

Commenting on the Our Father in St. Matthew, St. Jerome understands the "daily bread" to be the Eucharist and not ordinary bread. He mentions the difference in his day of the way the Latin speaking people spoke of "daily" bread, while the Greek speaking people spoke of "supersubstantial" bread. "That which is written in the Gospel of Matthew (6:11)according to the Latin interpreters is 'Give us this day our daily bread.' But it is better in Greek: 'our supersubstantial bread'; that is, the principal, special or singular bread. When Christ descended from heaven, he said: 'I am the bread that descended from heaven.' Far be it for us, who are forbidden to be concerned about tomorrow, to be ordered to ask in the Lord's prayer for that bread which, soon after it is digested, goes into the sewer ... Some think that the bread has been called 'supersubstantial' because it is above all substances. If it is understood in this way, it does not differ much from what we have explained; for what is special and singular is beside everything and above everything."

† † †

Lord, show the faithful departed the vision of your face, and let them rejoice in the contemplation of your presence.
May we face all life's difficulties with confidence and faith.

"God's angry man" continues his commentary on the Our Father. He insists that "our daily bread" refers to the Eucharist. "Scripture says, 'He gives food to the hungry.' This, according to the letter (of Scripture). We may speak of this in another way. Let us be hungry for Christ, and he will give us bread from heaven. 'Give us this day our daily bread.' Those who say this are hungry; those who want bread are hungry. He who says, 'Give us this day our daily bread' surely speaks with hunger. 'He gives food to the hungry.' Some think he speaks of the heavenly food with reference to the Eucharist. And we accept that thought, because the Eucharist is truly the flesh of Christ and truly the blood of Christ."

On Psalm 116 he says: 'I shall take the chalice of salvation and call upon the name of the Lord.' "Our food and drink is our Savior, for with his flesh we are fed, and we drink his blood."

St. Jerome ends a sermon on Psalm 88 at Mass thus: "If we wanted to comment on the entire Psalm, it appears that we would be making a delay; for the time compels us to approach the flesh of the Savior, the true Lamb, with a pure and unstained conscience in the unity of peace, so that we can fill ourselves worthily with the heavenly bread through our Lord Jesus Christ, to whom be glory forever. Amen."

St. Jerome comments on Luke 15:23 on the return of the Prodigal Son: 'Bring the fatted calf and kill it. Let us eat and feast, for this son of mine was dead and lives again; he was lost and has been found.' "The fatted calf that is immolated for the salvation of penitents is the Savior himself, whose flesh we eat daily and whose blood we drink daily. Faithful reader, you will understand with me that, filled with such richness, we break forth in his praise, saying: 'My heart overflows with beautiful speech; I dedicate my words to the king.' 'And they began to banquet.' "This banquet is celebrated every day; daily the Father receives his Son; Christ is always immolated for the faithful."

† † †

Let your wisdom lead us today, Lord, that we may walk in the newness of life.
O Lord, may we bear hardships with courage for your sake.

We conclude our quotations from St. Jerome on the Eucharist. "We understand that the bread which the Lord broke and gave to the disciples is the body of the Lord, our Savior; since he himself said to them: 'Take and eat, this is my body.' And we understand that is the chalice he spoke of again, saying: 'Drink you all of this, for this is my blood of the new testament, which will be shed for many for the remission of sins...' This is the chalice that we read about in the Prophet: 'I shall take the chalice of salvation and call upon the name of the Lord.' And again: 'How excellent is my inebriating chalice.' Now if the bread that came down from heaven is the body of the Lord, and the wine he gave to his disciples is his blood of the new testament, which was poured out for the remission of all sins, let us reject the Jewish fables and go up with the Lord to the huge, furnished and clean upper room. Let us again receive from him the chalice of the New Testament; and there celebrating the Pasch with him, let us become inebriated with the wine of sobriety ... Moses did not give us the true bread, but the Lord Jesus did. He himself is the guest and the banquet. He himself is the one who eats and is eaten." (We see here that St. Jerome believed that Christ received Holy Communion at the Last Supper. Others believe he did not... The Church does not teach anything officially about this matter. The Apostles surely received Communion. Compiler)

† † †

VICTIMAE PASCHALI *(Easter hymn by Wipo, died 1048)*

Sing to Christ, your Paschal Victim;
Christians, sing your Easter hymn.
The sinless Lord for sinners, Christ God's Son for creatures died. The sheep who strayed, the Lamb of God redeemed.
Then death and life their battle wonderfully fought; and now the King of life, once dead, for ever lives. Tell us, Mary, we pray, what you saw on Easter day. Empty was the grave; and looking, I saw there the glory of his rising. The angel witnesses I saw and folded linen. Christ, my hope, is risen truly; in Galilee he goes before you. We know he rose from death indeed. And so to him we pray, great King and Lord of life, bless us this day.

Translator: Adrian Fortescue

THEODORE, BISHOP OF MOPSUESTIA, 350-428

Theodore was born in Antioch in Syria in the year 350. During the ten years that he served as a priest in that city he became known as a forceful controversialist and an untiring fighter against heresy. He was made Bishop of Mopsuestia, which was situated in today's southern Turkey. He supported his not too distant neighbor, St. John Chrysostom, Patriarch of Constantinople in Greece. Unfortunately he did not possess the humility of mind of that great saint. His pride finally led him into heresy concerning the natures and person of Christ. Theodore spawned a heresy which his disciple, Nestorius, developed into full bloom, when the latter became Patriarch of Constantinople. Nestorianism holds that Christ was two persons, a human person and a divine person joined in some kind of moral union. Accordingly, Mary gave birth to the human person of Christ, not the divine person. She is, therefore, not the mother of God. Nestorianism claims that God cannot suffer and die and consequently that it was the human person of Christ that suffered and died, not God. That heresy still exists today, mainly in Asia, despite the fact that many Nestorians have returned to the Church.

Although Theodore of Mopsuestia did fall into heresy, he was like all the heretics before him in that his faith in the Real Presence of Christ-God in the Eucharist remained orthodox. This was true also in most other aspects of the Eucharist, as we shall see in the following quotations from his works.

"Christ did not say, 'This is a symbol of my body, and this is a symbol of my blood,' but 'This is my body and my blood.' Thus he taught us not to look at the nature of what appears present, but to consider that, through the action of the Eucharist, it is changed into body and blood."

†††

Lord, teach us goodness, discipline, and wisdom, lest we become hardened by evil, weakened by laziness, or ignorant by foolishness. Direct our thoughts, feelings and actions this day, O Lord. Help us to

follow your providential guidance.
May the dead rest in peace; and may their union with us be
strengthened through the sharing of spiritual goods.

In commenting on Christ's first announcement of the Eucharist the day after the first multiplication of the loaves Theodore writes: "With reference to the spiritual food Christ explained it to them in such a way, that what appeared incredible was made credible by the miracle of the multiplication of the loaves."

Theodore understands correctly that the sacrifice of the Mass and the sacrifice of Christ on Calvary are one and the same sacrifice. "All the priests of the New Covenant offer the same sacrifice continually, in every place, and at all times, because the sacrifice of Christ our Lord, which was offered for all, is but one sacrifice."

"From the awesome altar, too sublime to be put into words, we receive an immortal and holy food. If indeed those (priests) who remain near the altar and have been put in front of the divine liturgy, approach the altar to receive the divine food, the others (laity) receive it apart from the altar. However not because of that is there any difference in the same food; for the bread is but one, and but one is the body of Christ, into which the bread that had been presented (at the offertory) is transformed. The bread, solely by the coming of the Holy Spirit, receives such transformation." [The prayer at Mass calling upon the Holy Spirit to sanctify the bread and wine is called the "epiklesis." Theodore wrongly believed that it alone changed the bread into the body and blood of Christ. The words of Consecration — "This is my body; this is my blood" — make the change. Compiler]

One of Theodore's favorite themes is that by receiving the Eucharistic body of Christ we are made members of his mystical body, the Church, with Christ as its head. While St. Paul develops this idea, it was Christ himself who announced this doctrine in his farewell address to the Apostles at the Last Supper: "I am the vine; you are the branches." Just as the same life that courses through the vine courses through the branches, so too one who eats Christ in Holy Communion bears the life of Christ in his soul.

† † †

Deliver us from all harm, Lord, and pour your blessings on our homes.

The Bishop reinforces the doctrine of the Real Presence. "It is to be noted that, when giving the bread to his Apostles Christ did not say: 'This is the symbol or figure of my body,' but 'This is my body.' Likewise with the chalice he did not say: 'This is the symbol or figure of my blood,' but 'This is my blood.' For after the bread and wine had received the grace and coming of the Holy Spirit, he did not want us still to look at their nature, but to take them as the body and blood of the Lord, which they are." [And it is sad to note that 1100 years later during the so-called Reformation most of the founders of the Protestant religions taught that the Eucharistic bread and wine are but symbols or figures of the body and blood of Christ. Compiler]

"It is for everyone to receive Holy Communion. But he receives more who, by his love and faith and actions, shows that he is worthy to receive it, in so far as that is possible for a man. It is evident that no one is really worthy to receive Communion. Indeed, how can a man, who is subject to corruption and sin, show himself to be worthy to take and receive that body which has become immortal and incorruptible, which is in heaven at the right hand of God, and which by title of Lord and King receives honor from the whole world? In a word, we have confidence through the mercy of our Lord, who made these gifts for us. And we approach with all the fervor and care that we are capable of, in order to approach worthily according to the capability of human nature. With such hope we all approach Christ our Lord."

"In holy baptism Christ has given us a new birth, and with the love of a natural mother he has taken care to feed us with his own body ... He placed before us two things, the bread and the chalice; and these are his body and blood, from which we eat the food of immortality, and from which the grace of the Holy Spirit is poured out in us and nourishes us for the purpose of giving us the hope of one day being immortal and incorruptible. In a way that no one can explain, through the bread and the chalice Christ leads us on to partake of the good things to come."

† † †

A humble, contrite heart, O God, you will not spurn.

Theodore on the manner of receiving Communion: "Each of us approaches with eyes downcast and both hands extended. Downcast eyes pay, as it were, a debt of adoration ... And by the fact that both hands are extended equally, one recognizes truly the greatness of the gift he is about to receive. The right hand is extended to receive the oblation that is given; but underneath the right hand there is placed the left hand; and thus great reverence is shown. Now if the extended right hand has a greater rank in receiving the body of Christ, the left hand sustains the right and leads its sister and companion hand without considering it an injustice to carry out the roll of servant for the right hand, even though both have the same dignity, the dignity being the fact that it is the real body of Christ that is being carried."

"When the bishop gives you Communion, he says, 'The body of Christ.' He teaches you with these words not to look at the appearances, but to keep in your mind's eye what has become of that which had been offered at Mass, and that through the coming of the Holy Spirit is now the body of Christ. And so, it is proper that you present yourself for Communion with great fear and much love, keeping in mind the greatness of what is given to you. He merits your fear because of the greatness of his dignity, and your love because of his grace. For that reason, indeed, you say after the bishop, 'Amen.' With that reply you confirm the words of the bishop and put your seal on them. And the same thing is done in taking the chalice ... After having received Communion, with good reason you will make to rise to God an act of thanksgiving and blessing on your account, so as not to be ungrateful for this divine gift. And you will remain in company of all the others to pay your debt of thanksgiving and blessing according to the rule of the Church. For it

191

is proper that all those who have received the spiritual nourishment give thanks together and in common for this great gift." [TEP]

† † †

Lord, enlighten all legislators to enact laws in the spirit of wisdom and justice.
Christ died for our sins to make us an offering to God.

ST. AUGUSTINE, BISHOP OF HIPPO
IN AFRICA, 354-430

St. Augustine was a rare product of the early Church. He was outstanding in several ways. He is considered one of the greatest doctors or teachers of the Church. Despite his brilliant mind, or perhaps because of it, Augustine is one of the most human, down-to-earth Saints. In some of his many writings that are still extant one can feel the warmth of his character. He had a most extraordinary life.

He was born in 354 in the town of Tagaste in what is now the northeastern part of Algiers near the coast of the Mediterranean Sea. His pagan father, Patricius, was an official in the civil government. His saintly mother, Monica, followed the then current custom (which has long been rejected by the Church) of deferring the baptism of children until early manhood. Augustine studied in Tagaste and in the great city of Carthage, which was not far distant. His mind was driven by a restless desire for truth. Unfortunately the lessons by his pagan professors lead him to follow an immoral, sensual life. The tears of his mother, St. Monica, could not move him to desist.

Augustine went to Rome seeking a teaching position, but he found little success. However a Roman official told him of an opening for a professorship in Milan in northern Italy. His move to Milan was providential, not only for him and his career of teaching rhetoric, but also for the entire Church from then until now. His mother prevailed upon him to meet the great Bishop of Milan, St. Ambrose. The teachings of St. Ambrose precipitated a crisis in the life of St. Augustine. Augustine perceived the love that Ambrose had for him, but Augustine disdained his teachings. Taking stock of his own life and his desperate search for truth, Augustine was in virtual panic for not being able to find truth that could satisfy him.

† † †

Father, your Son, our Lord, knew no sin, but was treated as a sinner for us, to save us and restore us to your friendship. Look upon my contrite heart and afflicted spirit, and heal my troubled conscience by your
loving gift of sacramental Confession.
Christ died for our sins to make us an offering to God.

While in a feverish state of mind in his search for truth, Augustine heard a little boy singing a song in a near-by house. The song's refrain was: "Tolle, lege; tolle, lege" (Take and read; take and read.) Wiping the tears from his eyes, he went to his room, picked up St. Paul's Letter to the Romans, and his eyes fell randomly upon the words: "Let us live decently, as people do in daytime: no drunken orgies, no promiscuity, no licentiousness, no wrangling and jealousy. Let your armor be the Lord Jesus Christ. Forget about satisfying your bodies with all their cravings." (Rom 13:13-14) St. Augustine wrote later in his Confessions: "I had neither desire nor need to read further. The miracle of grace was worked in calm and silence." As a catechumen, Augustine received instructions from St. Ambrose and was baptized at the age of 33. After the grace of God it was his mother's tears and prayers that set Augustine on the road to sanctity.

Soon after his baptism St. Augustine was on his way home to Africa with his mother and brother. While resting in Ostia outside of Rome for the sea journey to Africa, St. Monica died. She had but one dying wish, that Augustine and his brother remember her at Mass.

On his return to Africa St. Augustine began to lead the life of a recluse. Soon others joined him in their pursuit of holiness. The bishop of the city of Hippo near-by prevailed upon Augustine to be ordained a priest. When the bishop died, Augustine was elected to succeed him in that post, in which he remained until his death.

In reviewing his life St. Augustine wrote the famous words: "Thou hast made us for thyself, O Lord, and our hearts are restless until they rest in thee." Also, in reference to God: "Late have I loved thee." But he used well the years that God granted him as a Christian and a bishop. He fought heresy tooth and nail, but always with calm and charity; and he begged the civil authorities not to put the heretics to death. His brilliant victory over Pelagianism, which taught that God's grace is not required to lead a morally good life, gained him the title of "Doctor of Grace." From his own experience he understood the necessity of grace.

St. Augustine established an Order of priests known as Augustinians. In his school or seminary he prepared a number of priests and bishops that served the Church in northern Africa.

St. Augustine died on August 18, 430. On his death bed he could hear the Vandals, a barbaric tribe, besieging the city of Hippo. Shortly after his death the Vandals entered the city and burned it. Cardinal Newman writes in The Church of the Fathers, page 137: "The desolation, which at that era swept over the face of [northern] Africa, was completed by the subsequent invasion of the Saracens [Muslims]. Hippo has ceased to be an episcopal city; but its great teacher [Augustine], though dead, yet speaks; his voice is gone out into all lands, and his word unto the end of the world." We are very fortunate that, despite the work of the Vandals, many of St. Augustine's works are extant; and we shall be quoting from some of his works on the Eucharist.

In his many writings on the Eucharist St. Augustine makes it abundantly clear that he maintains the orthodox doctrine concerning Christ's Real Presence, which the Lord announced for the first time in the synagogue in Capernaum. Just like those of other early Fathers of the Church, some of

194

Augustine's expressions, when taken out of their historical context, can and have been misunderstood as denials of the Real Presence. For instance Augustine writes that the Eucharist is a symbol of the unity of the Church, made up of many members, just as the bread and wine are made from many grains of wheat and many grapes. This is a correct and valid expression of the unity of the Church. It is wrong to claim that he denied the Real Presence because he wrote that "the Eucharist is a symbol." Such a claim does violence to the literary and historical context. He said it was a symbol of unity, not a symbol of Christ or of his body and blood. Moreover it should be remembered that for a thousand years after Christ's announcement of the Real Presence, history shows that no one denied that doctrine, although other doctrines like the divinity of Christ were denied. Some founders of Protestant Churches were the first to claim that the Eucharist is but a symbol or figure of Christ or his body. Augustine never had such an idea.

We begin our quotations from St. Augustine on the Eucharist. On the Eucharistic fast: "It is very clear that, when the disciples (at the Last Supper) received the body and blood of the Lord for the first time, they did not receive it fasting. But, for that reason are we to make a calumnious accusation against the Church, because the Eucharist is now received fasting? It has pleased the Holy Spirit that, in honor of so great a sacrament, the body of Christ enter the mouth of a Christian before other foods. This is the reason that this custom is observed throughout the whole world." [We see that Augustine believed that the Holy Spirit guides the Church.]

On Christ's being offered at Mass: "Was not Christ offered but once in person? Nevertheless, is he not offered, not only on the solemnities of the Pasch, but even daily for the people? Therefore one does not lie, when he is asked and replies that Christ is offered now."

On the discussion among the disciples when Christ first announced the Eucharist: "The disciples argued among themselves how the Lord could give his flesh as food, but paid no attention to what he then said to them: 'Truly, truly I say to you that, if you do not eat the flesh of the Son of Man and do not drink his blood, you will not have life in you.' You do not know how this bread is to be eaten, and the manner in which it is to be eaten;

nevertheless, 'If you do not eat the flesh of the Son of man and do not drink his blood, you will not have life in you.' This was not said to cadavers, but to those who were living. And so that they would not understand that he was speaking about this temporal life and argue about that, Christ adds: 'He who eats my flesh and drinks my blood has life eternal.' One does not have life eternal, if he does not eat this bread and drink this blood. Men can have temporal life without this, but in no way can they have eternal life without it." [TEP]

† † †

Eye has not seen, ear has not heard, nor has it so much as dawned on man what God has prepared for those who love him.
Lord, give us courage when evil seems to triumph, and help us never to forget that you are with us to the end of time.

We continue St. Augustine's remarks on the discussion and argument that Christ's disciples had, when he first announced the Eucharist in John 6, and told them that they would not have life in themselves, if they did not eat his flesh and drink his blood. "Men can have temporal life without this, but in no way can they have eternal life without it. Therefore one who does not eat his flesh and drink his blood does not have life in himself; while one who eats his flesh and drinks his blood does have life. To both of these Christ refers when he says 'eternal.' It is not that way with the food that we take to sustain temporal life. One who does not eat common food does not live; nevertheless one may eat it and not live. For many who do eat common food die of old age or disease or some other cause. But it is not that way with the true food and drink, that is, with the body and blood of the Lord. For he who does not eat it does not have life; and he who eats it has life and indeed eternal life."

"From the table of the Lord this sacrament is eaten by some for life; by others, for death. But the sacrament itself is ordained for the life, not death, of those who receive it."

"So that the disciples would not think that with this food and drink eternal life was promised in such a way that those who eat would not die physically, Christ added this thought. Having said, 'He who eats my flesh and drinks my blood has life eternal,' Christ adds: 'And I shall raise him up [resurrect him] on the last day.' Meanwhile one has eternal life in the soul with that rest which the souls of the saints receive. Even what pertains to the body is not deprived of eternal life, which it receives on the last day in the resurrection of the dead." [TEP]

† † †

Father, you did not forget the broken body of your Christ, nor the mockery his love received. We, your children, are weighed down with sin. Do not abandon us, Lord; but give us the fullness of your mercy, for you are our Savior.
My eyes keep watch for your saving help, while I await the word that will sanctify me.
Let us listen to the voice of God.

"Christ said: 'My flesh really is food, and my blood really is drink.' Men seek food and drink, so as not to be hungry and thirsty. But common food and drink does not really accomplish that. However this food and drink (the Eucharist), which makes those who receive it immortal and incorruptible, accomplishes it, because it makes them the society of the saints, where there will be peace with full and perfect unity. That is the reason, which saints before us already saw, that the Lord left us his body and blood under the appearances of bread and wine, because the bread is made one from many grains of wheat and the wine, from many grapes."

"Finally Christ explains how what he says is to come about, and what it is to eat his body and drink his blood: 'He who eats my flesh and drinks my blood remains in me and I in him.' Therefore, this is to eat that food and drink that drink, namely, to remain in Christ and have him remaining in one's self. Consequently, one who does not remain in Christ and in whom

Christ does not remain, does not eat his flesh and drink his blood spiritually, although he touches with his teeth the body and blood of Christ materially and visibly. Rather for his own condemnation he eats and drinks so great a sacrament; while being impure he dares to approach the sacrament of Christ, which only the pure may receive worthily. Of them it is said: 'Blessed are the pure of heart, for they shall see God.' "

"Christ says: 'Just as my living Father sent me, and I live because of my Father, so also he who eats me will live because of me.' He does not say: 'Just as I eat the Father and live because of the Father, so also he who eats me will live because of me.' For the Son is not greater because of his participation from the Father; the Son was born equal to the Father. But we are made greater by partaking of the Son through union with his body and blood, which that eating and drinking signifies. Therefore, in eating him we will live because of him, that is, in receiving him we receive eternal life, which we do not have of ourselves ... In truth, those who eat Christ die in time; but they live eternally, because Christ is life eternal." [TEP]

† † †

Lord, make the peace we pray for a reality.

Commenting on Proverbs 23:1 in the Septuagint Version of the Old Testament, St. Augustine writes: "It is written in a certain place: 'If you sit down to dine at the table of a great person, notice well the things that are placed before you. Extend your hand, knowing that it is proper that you prepare the same things.' You already know what the table is of the Great One. There is the body and blood of Christ. Let one who approaches such a table prepare similar things. And what does it mean to prepare similar things? 'Just as Christ gave his life for us, we too must give our lives for our brothers to edify the people and make a solemn affirmation of the faith.' "

"What a mother eats, her infant eats. Now since an infant is little adapted to eating bread, the mother changes the bread into flesh [in her womb]. Then with the milk from her breast she feeds her infant bread [that is, milk that came from changing the bread she had eaten]. How does the Wisdom of God [Christ] feed us with bread? Because 'the Word was made flesh and dwelled among us.' Consider his humility. 'Man ate the bread of angels' (Psalm 78:25). That is to say that man ate the eternal Word (God the Son), by whom the angels are nourished, and who is equal to the Father. 'His state was divine, yet he did not cling to this equality with God' (Philippians 2:6). The angels are nourished by him. 'But he emptied himself to assume the condition of a slave, and became as men are; and being as all men are, he humbled himself by being obedient in accepting death, even death on a cross.' All this he did, so that from the cross there would be commended to us the flesh and blood of the Lord, the new sacrifice." [TEP]

† † †

Lord Jesus, love of the Father and truth of the Father, you came to earth to relieve the pain of our exile. You took our weakness as your own. Uphold us when our hearts grow faint, until we stand with you before God the Father.
When evil seems to triumph, Lord, and our hope begins to fail, give us courage and perseverance in doing your will.
Day by day I shall bless you, Lord.

In 1 Samuel, Chapter 21, we read how David played an insane person to escape King Saul: "When he fell into their hands, he feigned lunacy." But St. Augustine's copy of the Bible contained a scribe's error, which read: "He was carried in his own hands." In Augustine's commentary on this faulty reading we have a forceful affirmation of the Real Presence: "The Bible says: 'And he was carried in his own hands.' Who can understand how a man can be carried in his own hands? A man can be carried in the hands of others; but no one is carried in his own hands. We do not find how to understand that this happened to David literally; but with Christ we do understand this. For Christ was being

199

carried in his own hands when, commending his body, he said: 'This is my body.' Indeed, he carried that body in his own hands."

"Now you know your worth; now you know whom you approach (in Communion). You know what you eat, what you drink — indeed, whom you eat, whom you drink."

As to the petition, "Give us this day our daily bread," we have seen that some Church Fathers understand it to refer only to ordinary food for the body. Others believe it refers only to the Eucharist, the food of the soul. Still others think it refers to both types of food. St. Augustine added a new idea. His love for Scripture and his understanding of its necessity led him to believe that "daily bread" referred also to the daily reading of the Bible at Mass. He writes: "It is well understood that 'Give us this day our daily bread' refers to the Eucharist, our daily food. The faithful know what they receive; and it is good for them to receive this bread daily, because it is necessary for our (spiritual) life on earth. They pray for themselves, that they become good, that they persevere in goodness and faith and a holy life. This they desire; this they pray for; because if they do not persevere in a holy life, they shall be barred from this bread (Communion). Therefore, what does 'Give us this day our daily bread' mean? Let us live in such a way as not to be barred from the altar. And the word of God, which is opened for you daily, and in a certain way broken (explained), is daily bread."

We continue with Augustine's comments on the Our Father. "What does 'Give us this day our daily bread' mean? Let us live in such a way as not to be barred from the altar. And the word of God, which is opened for you daily, and in a certain way broken (explained), is daily bread. Just as the stomach longs for common bread, so the mind longs for this (Bible) bread. This, therefore, is what we pray for in one petition, and for whatever is necessary for our soul; and our body in this life is included in 'daily bread.'"

From an Easter sermon to the newly baptized adults: "Christ our Lord, who, when he suffered, offered for us what he had taken from us when he was born (his human body). Having been made the prince of priests forever, he established the way of offering sacrifice which you see, the sacrifice of his body and blood. From his body, wounded by the lance, there flowed out

200

water and blood, by which he forgave our sins. Mindful of this grace, and working out your salvation —It is God who works in you — with fear and trembling approach to partake of this altar. Recognize in this bread what hung upon the cross; recognize in this chalice what flowed from his side. All those ancient sacrifices of God's people in the Old Testament prefigured in their great variety this one future sacrifice. Christ himself is the sheep of the old sacrifices because of the innocence of his soul; and he is the goat because of the likeness of his body to our sinful body. And whatever else was prefigured in many and diverse ways in the sacrifices of the Old Testament refers to this one sacrifice, which was revealed in the New Testament." [TEP]

† † †

Now that you are freed from sin and have become slaves of God, your benefit is sanctification, as you tend toward eternal life. Rom.6:22 Lord Jesus, in times of persecution defend and revive your Church by the power and comfort of the Holy Spirit, so that we can be freed from our enemies and praise your saving help. Grant that all who seek the truth may find it; and in finding it may they desire it all the more.

St. Augustine continues his sermon to the newly baptized adults: "Therefore, newly baptized, take and eat the body of Christ, now that you have become members of Christ in the body of Christ (the Church). Take and drink the blood of Christ. Do not become separated; eat the bond that unites you. Do not consider yourselves cheap; drink the price of your salvation. Just as this food is changed into you when you eat and drink it, so also you must be changed into the body of Christ (good members of the Church), when you live with obedience and piety."

"When his Passion was approaching, Christ ate the Pasch with his disciples, took bread and blessed it and said: 'This is my body, which will be given up for you.' Likewise he blessed the chalice and gave it to them saying:

201

'This is my blood of the New Testament, which will be poured out for many for the remission of sins.' [As a catechumen] you either read or heard this in the Gospel, but you did not know that this Eucharist of ours is the Son of God. But now, with your heart sprinkled clean in a pure conscience, and with your body washed with clean water [Baptism], 'Come to him and be enlightened, and your faces will not blush' (Psalm 34:5). Now if you receive worthily this mystery of the New Testament, through which you hope for an eternal inheritance; and if you fulfill the new commandment to love one another, you will have life in you. For you are eating that flesh of whom Life itself says: 'The bread that I shall give is my flesh for the life of the world. If you do not eat my flesh and drink my blood, you shall not have life in you.' "

Explaining the ceremonies of the Mass to the newly baptized adults on Easter, Augustine speaks of the Consecration: "And then, among the holy prayers that you are about to hear, the body and blood of Christ become present, when the word is pronounced. For, take away the word, it is bread and wine; add the word, and it is something else. And this something else, what is it? The body of Christ and the blood of Christ. Therefore take away the word, it is bread and wine; add the word, and it becomes the sacrament. To this you say, "Amen." To say "Amen" is to subscribe to something. "Amen" is translated into Latin 'truly.' " [TEP]

After a slight misquotation of the Bible St. Augustine, in a sermon in the Basilica of St. Cyprian in the great city of Carthage, gives a clear exposition of the Real Presence. He quotes Luke 13:27: "What does it mean: 'We have eaten and drunk (in your name)?' Surely they do not offer as a great reason (for entering heaven) having eaten what he (Christ) ate and drank. Another food is eaten and drunk, namely, Christ himself. And Christ is eaten and drunk by his enemies. The faithful know the immaculate Lamb on which they feed; and would that they eat in such a way as not to be subject to punishment. For the Apostle (Paul) says: 'Whoever eats and drinks unworthily, eats and drinks judgment for himself.' "

From a sermon on St. John, Chapter 6 on the Eucharist: "What word of the Lord inviting you have you heard? Who has invited; whom has he invited; and what has he prepared? The Lord invited slaves, and prepared himself for them as their food. Who dares to eat his own master? Nevertheless he says: 'He who eats me will live because of me.' When Christ is eaten, life is eaten. Nor is he killed so that he can be eaten, but he brings the dead to life. When he is eaten, he nourishes; but he is never depleted. Therefore, brothers, let us not hesitate to eat this bread for fear that we might finish it off and later not find anything to eat. Let Christ be eaten. The one who is eaten lives, because the one who was killed has risen. Nor when we eat him do we make pieces of him ... He remains whole and entire in heaven and in your heart. He remained whole (in heaven) with the Father, when he came into the Virgin. He filled her, but he did not leave the Father. He came to take on flesh, so that men might eat him; and he remained whole and entire with the Father, so that he might feed the angels." [TEP]

† † †

May we live our days in quiet joy and, with the help of the Virgin Mary's prayers, safely reach our home in heaven.
From the rising of the sun to its setting may the name of the Lord be praised,
Listen, my people, and I will speak. I am the Lord, your God.

St. Augustine continues his sermon on the Eucharist: "What you may know, brothers — both those of you who do know, and those who do not know should know — is that when Christ was made man, 'Man ate the bread of angels.' Where, how, in what way, by whose merits and dignity could man eat the bread of angels, if the Creator of the angels had not become man? Therefore let us eat with confidence. What we eat will not be terminated; and let us eat so that we ourselves are not terminated. What does it mean to eat Christ? It is not only to receive his body in the sacrament, for many who are unworthy receive it. Of these the Apostle (Paul) says: 'He who eats the bread and drinks the chalice of the Lord unworthily eats and drinks judgment for himself.' "

"But how is Christ to be eaten? As he himself says: 'He who eats my flesh and drinks my blood remains in me and I in him.' So if one remains in me and I in him, then he eats, then he drinks. But if one does not remain in me nor I in him, although he receives the sacrament, he brings upon himself great torment. He who said: 'He remains in me,' also said: 'He who keeps my commandments remains in me and I in him.' Behold, brothers, if you who are faithful are separated from the body of the Lord, it is to be feared that you may die of hunger. For he said: 'He who does not eat my flesh nor drink my blood will not have life in himself.' If therefore you are separated, so that you do not eat the body and blood of the Lord, it is to be feared that you may die; but if you receive unworthily and drink unworthily, it is to be feared that you will eat and drink judgment. So you find yourselves in great distress. Live rightly and the distress will pass." [TEP]

† † †

Jesus, we ask your forgiveness for the sins of our past and your protection from all future evil.
God did not make death, nor does he rejoice in the destruction of the living.
Lord, when we die, may we who confess our sins be brought to you through the gates of heaven.
Christ desires to lead all men to salvation.

The Bishop of Hippo in Africa continues his sermon on the Eucharist. He speaks of the dilemma or distress some find, because if they do not receive the Eucharist they will die spiritually, and if they receive it unworthily, they will be damned. Augustine says: "Live rightly and the distress will pass. Don't promise yourself life, if you live badly. What God himself does not promise, a man will fool himself if he promises that to himself. What a bad witness — you promise yourself what Truth itself denies you! Truth says: 'If you live badly, you will die forever'; and you tell yourself: 'I live badly, and I shall live with Christ forever?' How can it be that Truth lies and you tell the truth? The Bible says: 'Every man is a liar.' Therefore, you cannot live well, unless he helps you, unless he grants it, unless he bestows it. Therefore pray and eat. Pray and you will be freed from this distress. He will generously grant you the ability to act and live well. Look at your conscience. Your mouth will be filled with the praise of God and with joy. And, having been freed from great distress, you will say to him: 'You make wide room under me for my steps, and my feet have never faltered' "(Psalm 18:36).

From a sermon at Mass on Easter Sunday: "You (adults who had been baptized on Holy Saturday) are reborn to a new life, and so you are called infants. You, especially you who now see this (Mass), listen to what these things mean, as I promised to tell you. And also you faithful, listen, you who are accustomed to see these things. It is good to recall these things, lest they be forgotten. Now what you see on the table of the Lord, as regards their appearances, you are used to seeing them on your own tables. Their appearances are the same, but not their value. For example, you are the same persons you were before (baptism); you don't have new faces. Nevertheless you are new; your bodies have the same old appearance; but you are new by the grace of holiness, just as this (on the altar) is new. As you see, it is still bread and wine; but when the consecration comes, the bread will be the body of Christ, and that wine will be the blood of Christ." [TEP]

We conclude the Bishop's Easter Sunday sermon to the newly baptized, in which he is explaining the Consecration of the Mass: "As you see, it is still bread and wine; but when the consecration comes, that bread will be the body of Christ, and that wine will be the blood of Christ. This is what the name of Christ does; this is what the grace of Christ does, namely, that this appears as it did before, but its value is not that of before. For if it had been eaten before, it would have filled the stomach; but when it is eaten now, it benefits the soul."

From a sermon on Easter Monday: "And what do we (ministers of Christ) serve you, Christ's bread or ordinary bread? Whoever hires a worker for his vineyard can give him bread, but not himself. Christ gives himself to his workers; he gives himself as bread; he gives himself as a reward. It is not as if we were to say: 'If we eat him now, what will we finally have?' We eat him, but he is not finished off; he feeds the hungry, but he himself does not cease to exist. Now he feeds the laborers, for whom he remains their eternal reward. What better thing could we receive than him? If there were something better, he would give it; but nothing is better than God, and Christ is God."

Augustine on liturgical sacrifice: "That true mediator, taking the form of a slave, was made mediator between God and men, Jesus Christ the Man. In the form of God he receives sacrifice with the Father, with whom he is one God. Nevertheless in the form of a slave (man) he preferred to be a sacrifice rather than receive one, lest anyone think that sacrifice is to be offered to a creature. He is the priest of his sacrifice, he himself offering the sacrifice; likewise he is the oblation which is offered. He willed that the daily remembrance of his sacrifice be the sacrifice of the Church, which is his (mystical) body with him as its head. And thus the Church learns how to offer herself through him. The ancient sacrifices of holy men (in the Old Testament) were the many and various signs of this true sacrifice ... and before this greatest and true sacrifice all the false sacrifices must give way."[TEP]

The Bishop concludes his sermon on liturgical sacrifice: "The pagans erect temples to their gods, dedicate altars, consecrate priests, and offer sacrifices. But we do not erect temples to our martyrs as if they were gods. We make memorials of the dead, whose spirits live with God. We do not erect altars on which to sacrifice to the martyrs, but to the one God, who is God of the martyrs and our God. At our sacrifice the men of God, who conquered by their profession of faith, are mentioned by name in their proper place and order. But the priest offering the sacrifice does not invoke the martyrs, because the sacrifice is offered to God, not to them, although he offers the sacrifice in their memory. For the priest is a priest of God, not of them. The sacrifice itself is the body of Christ, which is not offered to the martyrs, because they themselves are the (mystical) body of Christ." [Here St. Augustine joins the Eucharistic body of Christ to the Church, which St. Paul calls the mystical body of Christ.]

"Four things are to be considered in every sacrifice: to whom it is offered; by whom it is offered; what is offered; and for whom it is offered. Christ himself is the one true mediator, who reconciles us to God through his sacrifice of peace. He remains one with him (God the Father) to whom the sacrifice is offered. He remains united with those for whom the sacrifice is offered (the Church, the mystical body of Christ). He himself is the one who offers the sacrifice; and he himself is what is offered." [TEP]

† † †

Father, accept us as a sacrifice of praise, so that we may go through life unburdened by grave sin, walking in the way of salvation, and always giving thanks to you.
Father, precious in your sight is the death of the saints; but precious above all is the love with which Christ suffered to redeem us.
Lord, light and salvation of all nations, protect the missionaries you have sent into the world, and enkindle in them the fire of your Spirit.
Lord, grant that man may shape the world in keeping with human dignity and respond generously to the needs of our time.

NICETAS, BISHOP OF REMESIANA, died c. 414

Nicetas was a bishop of a small district called Remesiana in what is today Serbia. The Greek and Latin civilizations met in that area. Nicetas is known mainly as a catechist, a simplifier of doctrine. Not many of his works are extant. Some Church historians attribute to him the Church's solemn hymn of thanksgiving, the Te Deum. We quote here from a little treatise he wrote on the various names or titles given to Christ.

"Christ is called a Lamb because of his singular innocence. He is called a Sheep (used in Old Testament sacrifices) in order to illustrate his Passion. He is called a Priest, either because he offered to God the Father his body as an oblation and victim, or because he deigns to be offered by us daily."

"If some pagan persecution makes you sad, have confidence, because Christ himself was immolated like a sheep; and as a Priest he will receive you to offer you to the Father ... Are you a lost sinner? You must hunger for holiness, and thirst for the Redeemer, who is Christ. He satisfies, because he is Bread." [TEP]

† † †

TE DEUM, *attributed by some to Bishop Nicetas*

We praise thee, O God, we acknowledge thee to be the Lord. All earth doth worship thee, the Father everlasting. To thee all angels cry aloud, the heavens and all the powers therein. To thee Cherubim and Seraphim continually do cry: Holy, holy, holy, Lord God of hosts. Heaven and earth are full of the majesty of thy glory.
The glorious choir of the Apostles praise thee. The admirable company of the Prophets praise thee. The white-robed army of martyrs praise thee. The holy Church throughout all the world doth acknowledge thee, the Father of infinite majesty, the adorable, true, and only Son. And the Holy Ghost, the Comforter.
Thou art the King of glory, O Christ. Thou art the everlasting Son of the Father. Thou, having taken upon thee to deliver man, didst not disdain the Virgin's womb. When thou hadst overcome the sting of death, thou didst open the kingdom of heaven to all believers. Thou sittest at the right hand of God, in the glory of the Father.
We believe that thou (Christ) shalt come to be our Judge. We pray thee, therefore, help thy servants, whom thou has redeemed with thy precious blood. Make them to be numbered with thy saints in glory everlasting.
O Lord, save thy people, and bless thine inheritance. Govern them and lift them up for ever. Day by day we bless thee. And we praise thy name for ever, yea for ever and ever.
Vouchsafe, O Lord, this day to keep us without sin. O Lord, have

mercy upon us, have mercy upon us. O Lord, let thy mercy be upon us, as we have hoped in thee. O Lord, in thee have I hoped; let me not be confounded for ever.
Translator: Adrian Fortescue

Let us bless Christ, the compassionate and merciful Lord, who wipes away the tears of those who weep.
Merciful God, hear the cries of the dying and comfort them with your presence.
Do not abandon me, my God, when I am old.

MAROUTA, BISHOP OF MAIPHERTAT, died c. 420

Marouta, sometimes considered a saint, was bishop of the city of Maiphertat (meaning "City of the Martyrs") in Persia, which at that time comprised both today's Iran and Iraq. He is known especially for his history of the Christian martyrs who died in the previous century under Sapor 11, King of Persia. We quote from one of his works.

"Christ said: 'Do this always in memory of me.' If the perpetual participation of the sacraments had not been given ... the faithful of future times would have been deprived of the communion of the body and blood. But now as often as we approach the body and blood and receive them in our hands, we believe that we thus touch the body and are of his flesh and bone, as it is written (of Adam and Eve). For Christ did not call this a type or figure but: 'Truly this is my body, and this is my blood.' " [TEP]

ST. MAXIMUS, BISHOP OF TURIN, died c. 420.

It is difficult to find definite information on the life of St. Maximus, Bishop of Turin in northern Italy. He probably died around the year 420. Of his extant works we quote from one of his homilies and two of his sermons.

As he was dying on the Cross, Christ was heard praying the first words of Psalm 22: "My God, my God, why have you forsaken me?" The Church attributes this Psalm to the suffering Christ. Verse 6 says: "I am a worm and no man," or "I am more worm than man." The reference is to the pathetic condition our Lord was in on the cross. In a homily St. Maximus comments on these words as follows:

"I believe the words (I am a worm and no man) are to be understood in this sense, namely, because the worm is born solely of pure earth without the admixture of anything else, it is compared to our Lord, since the Savior also was born solely and purely from Mary. I also read in the Book of Moses (Exodus 16:20) that maggots were bred from the manna. This is plainly a worthy and just comparison. The maggot is bred from the manna, and the Lord Christ is born of the Virgin. Like the manna coming down from heaven Mary, as it were, floods all the people of the Church with food that is sweeter than honey. If anyone neglects to eat this food, he cannot have life in himself, as the Lord himself says: 'He who does not eat my flesh and drink my blood will not have life in himself.' But this food will be changed into judgment, as the Apostle says: 'He who eats and drinks unworthily eats his own judgment.' This was subtly prophesied to the children of Israel in the Old Testament. For when they handled the manna contrary to the divine orders, worms were formed. The worms were like vengeful judges of their stubbornness. It is similar with Christ the Lord, whom one will suffer as Judge, who neglects to eat the fine food and sweet drink, as the Lord says: 'The Father judges no one, but has given all judgment to the Son.'"

† † †

Lord, help us to meet this day's responsibilities, and let nothing separate us from your love.

"We call these (holy confessors) blessed and worthy of praise, who merited to be friends of Christ and of one mind with him. We too, brothers, should hasten to the friendship of the Savior and do his will in everything after the example of the Saints. But what shall we say of those, what name before God can we call them who on Sunday hold the heavenly meal in contempt for the sake of some earthly meal and desert the table of Christ, while they delight in the table of man? Now this is the first offense against the friendship of Christ: while he calls everyone to his table on Sunday, each one feeds on the pleasure of his own wickedness, and does not come to where Christ calls him to fulfill a religious obligation. For a Christian must come to church on Sunday."[TEP]

† † †

A FIFTH CENTURY HYMN IN HONOR OF STS. PETER & PAUL

Bright light of eternity with happy radiance shines on the golden (Feast) day which crowns the princes of the Apostles, opening to sinners a clear path to the stars.
Teacher of the world and doorkeeper of heaven, fathers of Rome and judges of nations; conquering, the one by death of the sword, the other by the cross, now crowned they sit in the court of life.
O happy Rome, hallowed by the glorious death of the two princes; purpled by their blood thou alone are fairer than all other cities.
To the Trinity be eternal glory, honor, power and praise, who in unity rules all things for all ages.
Translator: Adrian Fortescue

Lord Jesus, we stood condemned, and you came to be judged in our place. When you come in glory at the end of time, bring your mercy for those for whom you were condemned.
O God, in your hand are the hearts of the powerful. Bestow your wisdom upon government leaders. May they draw from the fountain of your counsel, and please you in thought and deed.

CASSIAN, ABBOT c.360 - c.435

John Cassian was probably born in Palestine around the year 360. As a young man he and his friend, Germanus, entered a monastery in Bethlehem. After a few years the two young men spent ten years in Egypt visiting and learning from the solitary hermits, the masters of the spiritual life. Later Cassian went to southern France, where he established the famous Abbey of St. Victor at Marseilles. His writings on the ascetical and monastic life were used by the great St. Benedict in the formation of his Benedictine Rule. In some places, as in southern France, Cassian is venerated as a Saint. His extant writings are concerned mainly with the spiritual, ascetical and monastic life. Naturally some of them have references to the Eucharist, and we quote them here.

In Cassian's time there were those who believed that Communion should not be given to persons who are obsessed by the devil, that is, visibly attacked by Satan. Cassian believed that such persons should be given Communion to overcome the attacks by Satan. "Regarding Holy Communion, we do not recall that such persons were ever prohibited from receiving it. On the contrary, whenever it was possible, some believed that such persons should be given Communion every day. As regards the Gospels saying: 'Do not give holy things to the dogs,' you make a false application of these words, if you believe that Holy Communion would become food of devils rather than a purification and defense of body and soul. When such a man (obsessed) receives Communion, he puts to flight, in the manner of a consuming conflagration, that spirit which is in his body or tries to remain hidden in it. And in this way we saw recently how Abbot Andronicus and many others have been cured. The enemy will attack all the more, when he sees one deprived of the heavenly medicine; and he will tempt him more frequently, when he sees him lacking the spiritual remedy." [TEP]

It is my joy, O God, to praise you with song, to sing as I ponder your goodness.
As morning breaks we sing of your mercy, O Lord.

Some Biblical scholars believe that St. Paul in 1 Cor. 11:30 was referring to bodily ailments and death, when he wrote that such punishments were the result of some people's receiving Communion unworthily. Cassian believed that St. Paul referred to spiritual illness and spiritual death. St. Paul says: "In fact that is why many of you are weak and ill and some of you have died." Cassian writes that "spiritual illness and death come principally from this presumption (to receive Communion unworthily). Such a person does not discern the difference between that heavenly food and the lowliness of common foods; nor does he judge Communion to be such that only with a pure soul and body may one dare to receive it. Those receiving Communion unworthily grow weak in faith. With their soul debilitated they are subjected to weakness by the passions, and they sleep the sleep of sin without having any salutary care to rise from their lethal stupor." [TEP]

† † †

FROM EUCHARISTIC PREFACE 1

Our Lord Jesus Christ, the true and eternal priest, instituted the rite of this everlasting sacrifice. First he offered himself to his Father as the victim of our salvation; and he commanded us to perpetuate that offering in memory of him. By eating the flesh that he sacrificed for us, we are strengthened; and by drinking the blood he shed for us, we are purified. Father, grant that in this great mystery we may find the fullness of love and of life. (Roman Missal)

Lord Jesus, you were rejected by your people, betrayed by the kiss of a friend, and deserted by your disciples. Give us the confidence that you

had in the Father, and our salvation will be assured.
By your death on the cross you opened the gates of heaven. Admit
into your kingdom all who died hoping in you.

"We must surround our heart with the guard of humility, so that we retain engraved on our mind this teaching, namely, that we can never arrive at such purification ... that we believe ourselves worthy of the Communion of the sacred body. In the first place, because the majesty of that heavenly manna is so great, that no one having flesh of clay receives this food because of his own merits, but because of free largess of the Lord. Moreover, no one can be so careful amid the dangers of this world, that the darts of sin do not strike him at least now and then and lightly."

"Nevertheless, because we recognize that we are sinners, we must not abstain from the Communion of the Lord. Rather, we must hasten to receive Communion always with greater desire for the remedy of our soul and the purification of our spirit. But we do this with such humility of spirit and with such great faith, that, judging ourselves unworthy to receive such a great favor, we go in search for the remedy of our wounds. Nor should we believe that Communion is received worthily simply because it is received only once a year. Some living in monasteries do just that; and they measure the dignity and sanctification and worth of the divine sacraments in such a way, that they judge that only those who are holy and immaculate should receive them. Rather it is the reception of the divine sacraments that makes us holy and pure. Some monks fall into an arrogant presumption greater than that which they seem to avoid, because they judge themselves worthy of the annual reception. It is much more proper for holy persons to receive Holy Communion every Sunday as a remedy for our weakness, and receive it with such humility of soul that we believe and profess that we are never able to approach the most sacred mysteries because of our own merit. That is more proper than, being elated with a vain presumption, we believe ourselves worthy to receive Communion, albeit only annually." [TEP]

† † †

Lord, be merciful to sinners who have fallen away from your love.
Reconcile them to yourself and to your Church.
The Lord, your God, disciplines you even as a man disciplines his son.
Deut 8:5

PALLADIUS, BISHOP OF HELENOPOLIS, TURKEY, c.363-425

Palladius was born in Galatia, in the central part of today's Turkey. He lived as a monk in Jerusalem and then in Egypt, where monasticism was flourishing. He traveled throughout Egypt collecting information on the various types of monastic life. Later he wrote a history on the monks entitled Lusiac History. He was made Bishop of Helenopolis in northwestern Turkey. Palladius was a friend of the great St. John Chrysostom, Patriarch of Constantinople. Palladius was one of the first to mention "the ablution of the mouth" at Mass after Communion. This consisted of the priest-celebrant taking a little water and/or wine with a little bread to prevent the loss of any particles of the Eucharist by spitting. Later the ablution after Communion became a common practice for the priest at Mass. The practice, of course, stems from belief in the Real Presence of Christ in the Eucharist.

In his history of the monks Palladius writes the following: "This holy man, Macarius, told me this story: (Note that he was a priest.) 'When I was distributing Communion, I thought I had not given Communion to the ascetic, Mark, but that an angel gave him Communion after taking the Host from the altar. And all I saw was the skeleton of the hand of the one who gave Communion.' This Mark was very young and recited from memory the Old and New Testaments."

"A monk named Moses had nightmares, which he attributed to the devil, and consequently would not receive Communion. 'Stop fighting with the demons,' someone told him, 'for such things are a necessary measure for even the most manly asceticism.' But Moses said: 'I shall not stop, as long as the demons bring me bad dreams.' Then the Abbot Isidore said to him: 'In

215

the name of Jesus Christ your nightmares have stopped. Therefore receive Communion with confidence. In order that you would not boast that it was you who conquered this evil, you were seen to be tyrannized by it for your own benefit.' Then Moses went to his cell. After about two months the Abbot questioned Moses, who told him that he no longer suffered anything."

† † †

Lord, look kindly on our weakness and hasten to our aid, for without you we can do nothing.

Palladius writes in his history of the monks: "They tell the story that one day the monk Valente was sewing a basket in poor light and lost his needle. When he couldn't find it, the devil, taking on the figure of Christ, lit a lamp, and thus Valente found the needle. Puffed up with pride because of this (supposed) vision of Christ, he had ideas of grandeur. He became so foolish that he finally despised the reception of Holy Communion. One day after another vision he entered a church, and before the assembled community he said: 'I have no need of Communion, because I have seen Christ today.' Then the holy monks, after chaining him for a year, cured him of this foolishness with prayers. They showed him indifference, and made him lead a more inactive life." [TEP]

† † †

HYMN TO THE HOLY SPIRIT

Father, Lord of earth and heaven,
King to whom all gifts belong,
Give your greatest Gift, your Spirit,
God the holy, God the strong.
Son of God, enthroned in glory,

216

send your promised Gift of Grace,
Make your Church your holy Temple,
God the Spirit's dwelling-place.
Spirit, come, in peace descending as at Jordan,
heav'nly Dove,
Seal your Church as God's anointed,
set our hearts on fire with love.
Stay among us, God the Father,
stay among us, God the Son,
Stay among us, Holy Spirit,
dwell within us, make us one.

James Quinn, S.J.'

Help us, O Lord, to learn the truths thy Word imparts;
To study that thy laws may be inscribed upon our hearts.
Help us, O Lord, to live the faith which we proclaim,
That all our thoughts and words and deeds
may glorify your name.
Help us, O Lord, to teach the beauty of your ways,
That yearning souls may find the Christ and sing aloud his praise.

W.W.Reid

PHILOSTORGIUS, died c. 433

Philostorgius was a heretic. As an Arian he did not believe in the divinity of Christ. He wrote a history of Arianism, covering about 100 years from its beginning down to his own day. Most Arians incorrectly considered St. Lucian of Antioch the father of their heresy. In his history Philostorgius tells of a peculiar incident in the life of the priest-martyr, St.

Lucian. It is to be noted that Philostorgius, although a heretic, refers to the Mass as "the immaculate sacrifice" and "the awesome (or tremendous or making-one-shudder) sacrifice."

"When the martyr Lucian was about to die in prison, the tyrant would not give him a place or altar to celebrate Mass. And his chains and beatings prevented him from moving. Lying down he celebrated on his own chest the awesome sacrifice. Thus he participated in the spotless sacrifice and ordered the rest [who were present] to participate. The sacrifice was celebrated in prison, and the sacred choir of Christians surrounded him as one who was about to die. They took the place of a church, and they gave security, so that the things that took place [at Mass} were not seen by wicked persons." [TEP]

† † †

HYMN TO THE TRINITY

Most ancient of all mysteries, before your throne we lie;
Have mercy now, most merciful, most holy Trinity.
When heaven and earth were still unmade,
when time was yet unknown
You in your radiant majesty did live and love alone.
You were not born, there was no source,
from which your Being flowed;
There is no end which you can reach,
for you are simply God.
How wonderful creation is, the work which you did bless;
What then must you be like, dear God, eternal loveliness!

Frederick William Faber

ST. NILUS OF ANCYRA, died c. 430

Although he apparently was a layman, St. Nilus was Superior of a monastery in the city of Ancyra in Galatia in today's Turkey. As was common with monks at that time, St. Nilus dedicated himself to the ascetic life and to study. He was learned in the Scriptures. There exist today over one thousand letters from his huge correspondence. We quote here from some of his letters.

"The sheet used for writing, made of papyrus and glue, is nothing but a sheet before it receives the signature of the king; but when it receives it, it is something notable and is called sacred. You must think that the same thing happens in the divine mysteries (the common term used for the Eucharist, both sacrifice and sacrament). Before the word of the priest and the descent of the Holy Spirit, the offerings are nothing but ordinary bread and wine. But after that awesome invocation and the coming of the adorable Spirit, who is good and vivifies, there is on the sacred altar not simply bread and ordinary wine, but the precious and immaculate body and blood of Christ, the God of all things. His body and blood purify from all uncleanness those who become partakers of them with fear and great desire."

"It is impossible that the faithful acquire in any other way salvation, the forgiveness of sins, and the heavenly kingdom than by partaking with fear and love of the mystical and undefiled body and blood of Christ, God."

"Abstain from all corruption, and every day partake of the mystical supper; for thus the body of Christ becomes our body." [Although biologically false, this last statement gives witness to belief in the Real Presence.]

"Let us not approach the mystical bread as if it were simply bread, since it is the flesh of God, precious flesh that is venerated and gives life. ... Partaking of the flesh and blood of the Word of God with praise and desire, we inherit eternal life. For he who eats and drinks with a right heart acquires blessedness." [TEP]

† † †

219

Lord, always look with favor on us as we begin our daily work. Let us be fellow-workers with you, dear God.

ST. PAULINUS, BISHOP OF NOLA, ITALY (352 - 431)

Prior to the Christian era there were no institutes of mercy to care for the sick and needy. During the first three hundred years of her existence the Church was not able to establish charitable institutions due to the persecutions. Early in the fourth century the Church was granted permission to exist by the world government of Rome. During the fifth century almost every episcopal city had at least one institution of mercy to care for the sick and needy. St. Paulinus made sure that his episcopal city of Nola in Italy was no exception. He was known for his dedication to the poor.

St. Paulinus was a personal friend of some of the great saints and scholars of his time, such as Sts. Ambrose, Augustine and Jerome. Some 50 of his letters to them and to others are still extant. We quote here from some of them. In addition we have some of his poetry, which was not polished but full of his personal warmth of character.

One translation of Psalm 136:25 reads: "He (God) gives food to all flesh." St. Paulinus comments: "This is not the food that perishes, but that which is made for perpetual sustenance, the kind that is prepared either by the soul active in the things of God or by the Catholic Church. It is the body of 'the true bread which came down from heaven' (John 6:33)and which gives life-giving nourishment to those who hunger for justice. ...This food does not fatten the flesh but strengthens the heart of man. This bread is also a fountain, from which the more one eats the more he hungers, and the more he drinks the more he thirsts for it. So that we eat this bread perpetually, let us grind the good wheat in the mill of this world, the good wheat being the faithful observance of obedience and charity in a pure heart with sincere faith."

† † †

Lord, from the rising of the sun to its setting your name is worthy of
all praise. Let our prayers come like incense before you. May the
lifting up of our hands be as an evening sacrifice acceptable to you,
Lord our God.
Like burning incense let my prayer rise up to you; for you are my
refuge, Lord, and all that I desire in life.

St. Paulinus mentions the custom of giving the Eucharist under the form of a few drops of wine to infants who had just been baptized. "After the priest, like a father, takes from the sacred font [of baptism] those infants, white as snow in their bodies, hearts and dress, and places those newly born lambs around the altar, then he places in their tender mouths the saving food."

After Clarus, one of his priest friends died, St. Paulinus sent a letter to his historian friend, Suplicius Severus, containing some poetry for the epitaph of Clarus. St. Martin of Tours, mentioned in the poem, was a mutual friend. A portion of the poem reads as follows: "On the cross is nailed the flesh with which I feed myself. From the cross flows that blood, thanks to which I drink life and cleanse souls. Oh Christ, let these your gifts go together with your Severus. Let him be the carrier and witness of your cross. May he live from your flesh; may your blood be his drink; may he live and work in your word. And by that road, on which he saw your Martin ascend accompanied by Clarus, may he also be carried by your grace." [TEP]

† † †

Joyfully shout, all you on earth,
give praise to the glory of God;
And with a hymn sing out his glorious praise: Alleluia!

Let all the earth kneel in his sight,
extolling his marvelous fame;
Honor his name; in highest heaven give praise: Alleluia!

Come forth and see all the great works
that God has brought forth;
Fall on your knees before his glorious throne: Alleluia!

Glory and thanks be to the Father;
honor and praise to the Son;
And to the Spirit, source of life and of love: Alleluia!

All you nations, sing out your joy to the Lord:
Alleluia, alleluia!

Lucien Deiss, C.S.Sp.

ISIDORE OF PELUSIUM (EGYPT), died c. 440

Isidore was a priest and the abbot of a monastery near the town of Pelusium at the mouth of the Nile River in Egypt. He was both a theologian and philosopher, but he is best known for his explanations of the Bible. His correspondence was immense. Some two thousand of his letters are still extant, and we quote from them.

"That white sheet [altar cloth], spread out to serve the divine gifts, is a reminder of the service of Joseph of Arimathea. He confined to the sepulcher the body of the Lord wrapped in a sheet. From that Lord we all obtained the resurrection . In like manner we, consecrating the Bread of Proposition on a sheet, have without a doubt the body of Christ. From him as from a fountain flows forth that immortality which the Savior Jesus graciously gave us."

"The reception of the divine mysteries was called Communion, precisely because it graciously gives us union with Christ and makes us partakers of his kingdom."

"We partake of the divine mysteries, without which it is impossible to obtain the heavenly reward. This is clear from the words, free of every lie, the words of Truth itself, who once said: 'He who is not born of water and the Holy Spirit will not enter the kingdom of heaven'; and again, 'He who does not eat my flesh and drink my blood has no part with me.' "

"Now then, if it is impossible to obtain the divine inheritance without these mysteries, and since these mysteries can in no way be had without the mediation of the priesthood, how is it possible that one who despises the priesthood does not insult the divine things and does not also despise his own soul? Therefore, so that such things do not happen, let us consider the priesthood as something divine. Let us weep because of those who come to the priesthood unworthily; and let us not attribute their sins to the priesthood." [TEP]

✝ ✝ ✝

Lord, do not desert us when we are old, but help us to follow your will in both good times and bad, so that we may forever praise your faithfulness.

RABULAS, BISHOP OF EDESSA (SYRIA), died c. 436

Rabulas was Bishop of Edessa in Syria from 412 to 435. He is known for his battles against heresy. He was a zealous reformer of both the clergy and the monks. He wrote both prose and poetry, from which we shall quote. In one of his extant works there is a painting of the Last Supper. It is very strange to see Christ standing, while he distributes Holy Communion under the form of bread to the Apostles, who are also standing.

The doctrine of the Real Presence is evident in an instruction that Bishop Rabulas gave to his priests as follows: "Particles of the sacred body that fall to the floor [when Communion is distributed] are to be sought diligently. If they are found, scrape the place in which they fell. If they fall in the dirt, mix the dirt with water ... If a particle is not found, scrape the floor anyway, just as we said. Do the same thing, if some of the sacred blood has been spilled. If the floor is of stone, let live coals be placed on it."

In a letter to a fellow bishop Rabulas writes about abuses committed by monks, who boasted that they did not eat ordinary bread or drink water or wine, while they took excessive amounts of consecrated bread and wine. "Now I tremble to mention what I have heard about their crime with respect to the body and blood of Jesus, the Son of God. But necessity forces me to mention something that those frightful monks do not hesitate to do, when they madly and without discernment offer the body and blood of Christ our Lord. Their monstrous wickedness is incomprehensible to me. For their constant satisfaction they stuff themselves with the sacred body, which sanctifies those who receive it, and with that living blood, which gives life to those who drink it."

"As a consequence of their decision, they are not able to take food without daily celebrating the sacrifice [Mass]; and without stopping they take the Eucharist daily as a big meal. Therefore they also prepare the Host with a lot of yeast. They make it very nourishing and prepare it carefully, so that it serves as a meal, but not as the sacrament of the body of Christ, which is made without leaven."

The Bishop continues to denounce abuses.

"It also happens, that when those monks travel from one place to another, or when they go on a long journey, they satisfy their natural hunger and thirst two or three times a day with the body of the Lord. And when they have arrived at the end of their journey, they offer the sacrifice again in the afternoon; and they partake of it as if they were still fasting. Even on the holy days of fast during Lent they dare to do the same thing, since they neither fear God nor feel shame before men."

"Nor can the Bread of Proposition of the Jewish priests be compared to the majesty of the grand mystery [Eucharist]. If one wants to compare that Bread of Proposition, which was taken from the altar and eaten by David when he was hungry, with the life-giving bread of God the Word [Son], we would have to look upon a person making such a comparison as a man without judgment. For he does not distinguish between the Bread of Proposition and the body and blood of the Lord, and therefore is guilty of the body and blood of the Lord. That bread was able to purify only bodily stains together with various washings and other ceremonies. But the life-giving flesh and blood of the Lord Jesus expiates the guilt not only of body and soul, but also sanctifies those who receive it with faith. Moreover the reception of this flesh and blood of Christ results in God being in us through his Spirit, just as we are in him through our body. For the Son of God says: 'He who eats my body and drinks my blood remains in me and I in him; and I shall raise him up on the last day' " (John 6:54).

† † †

EVENING HYMN (Christe qui Lux)
Translator: Rev. M. Quinn, O.P. et al.

O Christ, you are the light and day
which drives away the night,
The ever shining Sun of God and pledge of future light.
As now the evening shadows fall,
please grant us, Lord, we pray,
A quiet night to rest in you until the break of day.
Remember us, poor mortal men, we humbly ask, O Lord,
And may your presence in our souls be
now our great reward.

In one of his penitential hymns Rabulas says graphically: "Lord, let not the fire [of hell] devour me, whom you have fed with your body and blood."

In a hymn to all the faithful departed the Bishop writes: "You, who rest in the dust, do not be saddened by the destruction of the members of your body. For the living body [of Christ] that you have received, and the blood which wipes away all sins and which you have drunk, have the power to raise you up and vest your bodies with glory." The Bishop offers a beautiful prayer for the deceased: "Author of life and Lord of the dead, remember your servants who have eaten your body and drunk your blood, and who have now gone to their rest with hope in you. When you come in majesty with your glorious armies of angels [at the end of the world], raise them from their graves, remove them from the dust, vest them with the garments of glory, and place them at your right hand, so that they enter with you into the hall of heaven and sing hymns of praise for your grace." [TEP]

† † †

HYMN FOR SUNDAY

On this day, the first of days,
God the Father's name we praise;
Who, creation's Lord and spring,
did the world from darkness bring.
On this day the eternal Son over death his triumph won;
On this day the Spirit came with his gifts of living flame.
Father, who didst fashion man Godlike in thy loving plan,
Fill us with that love divine, and conform our wills to thine.
Word made flesh, all hail to thee!
Thou from sin hast set us free;
And with thee we die and rise unto God in sacrifice.
Holy Spirit, you impart gifts of love to every heart;
Give us light and grace, we pray;
fill our hearts this holy day.
God, the blessed Three in One, may thy holy will be done;
In thy word our souls are free;
and we rest this day with thee.

Text: Le Mans Breviary, 1748
Translator: Henry W. Baker

ST. POSSIDIUS, BISHOP OF CALAMA (AFRICA), died c. 440

St. Possidius, Bishop of Calama in northern Africa, is best known for his biography of St. Augustine, Bishop of Hippo in Africa. For some 40 years St. Possidius was a close friend and companion of St. Augustine. When the savage Vandals overran northern Africa, St. Possidius was forced out of his See of Calama and went to St. Augustine. He was at Augustine's side, when the great saint died.

In his biography of St. Augustine Possidius writes about the destruction by the Vandals, that Augustine had witnessed before his death. "The holy man [St. Augustine] saw the churches silent, which before had resounded with the divine hymns and praises, and which were reduced now to ashes in many places. The solemn sacrifice [Mass], owed to God everywhere, had ceased; and the sacraments, either were not requested by anyone or could not be administered to those requesting them for lack of priests."

St. Possidius describes the last moments of the life of St. Augustine:

"Finally, having retained full use of his bodily faculties and without having lost his sight or hearing, assisted by us who saw him and prayed with him, he fell asleep with his fathers after having attained a ripe old age [of 76]. We offered to God the sacrifice for the burial of his body, and then he was buried." [TEP]

† † †

Let us not grow weary of doing good; if we do not relax our efforts, in due time we shall reap our harvest. While we have the opportunity, let us do good to all men, but especially to those of the household of the faith.

(Galatians 6:9-10)

Praised be God, the Father of our Lord Jesus Christ, the Father of mercies and the God of all consolation! He comforts us in all our afflictions and thus enables us to comfort those who are in trouble, with the same consolation we have received from him. (2 Cor. 1:3-4) I will listen to what the Lord God is saying.

SALVIAN, PRIEST OF MARSEILLE (FRANCE), died c. 480

As regards writers of his day Salvian is considered by some to be second only to the great St. Augustine of Hippo. To help calm the anguish of the Christians during the invasions of the barbarians who would eventually take over Europe and north Africa, St. Augustine wrote his famous work, The City of God. Salvian, who lived to see the end of the Roman Empire in the West, wrote in a similar vein his work entitled, On the Government of God. Both works tried to show that God is in charge of the world, despite the great evils he sometimes permits.

Salvian writes about some of the grossly false rumors that pagans spread about the Christian religion and especially about the Eucharist. Their false notion that at Mass Christians kill and eat babies is a ridiculous distortion of the doctrine of the Real Presence of Christ in the Eucharist. "With what evil and criminal thoughts the pagans always consider the sacred things of the Lord can be seen in the bloody questions the cruel persecutors ask. They believe that in the Christian sacrifices there is nothing but impurities and abominations. They even believe that the very beginnings of our religion have their origin in nothing but two very grave crimes. First, in homicide, in the homicide of innocent babies, whom the pagans believe are not only killed by the Christians, but what is more abominable, that they are also eaten by the Christians."

✝ ✝ ✝

HYMN TO DIVINE TRUTH

O God of truth, prepare our minds
To hear and heed your holy word;
Fill every heart that longs for you
With your mysterious presence, Lord.

Almighty Father, with your Son
And blessed Spirit, hear our prayer;
Teach us to love eternal truth
And seek its freedom everywhere.
Text: Stanbrook Abbey

Salvian explains the superiority of the New Testament over the Old. "Perhaps someone may ask why God, through the Gospel, demands more of the Christians than he did of the Jews before in the Mosaic law. The clear reason for this is that we give our Lord more because we owe him more. The Jews had the shadow of things; we have the reality. They were servants of God; we are his adopted sons. They received the yoke of the Law; we received freedom. They received curses; we, grace. They received the letter of the Law that kills; we, the spirit that gives life. To the Jews God sent his servant Moses as teacher; to us, his Son. The Jews passed through the Red Sea to the desert; we enter the kingdom of God by baptism. The Jews ate the manna; we eat Christ. The Jews ate the flesh of birds; we eat the body of God. The Jews ate the dew (manna) from heaven; we eat the God of heaven, who, as St. Paul says, existing in the form of God, humbled himself even to death, and death on the cross." [TEP]

EVENING HYMN

Lord Jesus Christ abide with us,
Now that the sun has run its course;
Let hope not be obscured by night,
But may faith's darkness be as light.

Lord Jesus Christ, grant us your peace,
And when the trials of earth shall cease,
Grant us the morning light of grace,
The radiant splendor of your face.

Immortal, Holy, Threefold Light,
Yours be the kingdom, pow'r, and might;
All glory be eternally
To you, life-giving Trinity!

Text: St. Joseph's Abbey, 1967/8

ST. CYRIL, BISHOP OF ALEXANDRIA (EGYPT), died 444

In the early years of the Church, when central doctrines of the Christian faith had not yet been clearly defined, we can see how Satan tried to destroy the faith by moving men to deny doctrines that were already generally accepted. We can also see how God the Holy Spirit, the very soul of the Church, raised up humble men to be staunch defenders of the true faith.

In the early 300's the obstinate priest, Arius of Alexandria in Egypt, claimed that Jesus was not God but merely a supercreature, a God-like creature above man and the angels. Although Jesus was God the Son, according to Arius he did not have the homoousios of God the Father, that is, he did not have the same essence or being or substance of the Father. The theological battle lines were drawn around that Greek word, homoousios. St. Athanasius, deacon and later Bishop of Alexandria, was the outstanding defender of the true faith, which the first Ecumenical Council, that of Nicea in today's Turkey, clearly defined in its Creed in the year 325: Jesus Christ is the Son of God, the only-begotten of the Father, consubstantial (homoousios) with the Father, God from God, Light from Light, true God from true God.

† † †

Lord Jesus, once you spoke to men
Upon the mountain, in the plain;
O help us listen now, as then,
And wonder at your words again.

We all have secret fears to face,
Our minds and motives to amend;
We seek your truth, we need your grace,
Our living Lord and present Friend.

The Gospel speaks, and we receive
Your light, your love, your own command,
O help us live what we believe
In daily work of heart and hand.
Text: H.C.A. Gaunt

A century after Arius in Egypt denied the divinity of Christ, Nestorius, the haughty Bishop of Constantinople in Greece, claimed that Jesus Christ was two persons, human and divine. He said that Jesus was born a human person of Mary. Therefore, said Nestorius, he would not adore as God a babe of two months. He thought that sometime after Jesus the man was born, God the Son descended into Jesus, and for a while formed some sort of union with Jesus. Subsequently, Nestorius claimed, God the Son left Jesus before his passion and death on the cross. Therefore, according to

Nestorius, it was not God who suffered and died on the cross, nor was it God who was born of the Virgin Mary. He rejected Mary's commonly accepted title of Theotokos (Mother of God). Again the theological battle lines formed around a single Greek word, theotokos. St. Cyril rose to the defense of the accepted doctrine.

In 431 as legate of the Pope, Cyril presided over the Ecumenical Council of Ephesus, a city in southern Turkey where, according to tradition, the Blessed Mother lived her last days on earth in the company of St. John the Apostle. The Council was held in a church already dedicated to Theotokos, and on the very first day of the Council the Fathers upheld that title of the Blessed Mother. On hearing this the populace demonstrated their joy that night by illuminating the city; and with cries of Theotokos, Theotokos lead the bishops to their lodging with torches and burning incense. [TEP]

† † †

A MEDIEVAL CHRISTMAS CAROL

Of Mary the Virgin
A Child today is born,
Who, God for ever,
Becomes the Son of man.
He lies in the manger
Who came down from heaven
To die on the cross
For sinful man.

Translator: A. Fortescue

With good reason St. Cyril is known as the Doctor of the Incarnation for having staunchly defended the personal unity of Christ. However, here we are concerned with his doctrine on the Eucharist, which we find especially in his commentaries on the New Testament. We quote from his many extant works. "Christ has let us go free, that is, free of our sins. He has made us resplendent with the grace of adoption, and has given himself to us as good viaticum [food for our journey through life]. For our good he was led away as the immaculate Victim, as a sheep to its killer. He has granted us a participation in the life-giving blessing, that is, of his flesh and blood."

Cyril believes that the holier one is, the greater spiritual benefit he receives from Holy Communion. "Those who are still subject to some interior weaknesses [venial sins] can participate in the blessing [Eucharist] of Christ, but not in the same degree that the saints do. The latter partake of an increase of holiness, the strengthening of soul, and the firm perseverance in things that are holy. The others partake in a way that is proper for those who are ill, that is, to eradicate vice, abstain from sin, mortify pleasures, and regain their spiritual health. For, according to Scripture, Christ is a new creation, and so we receive him into our souls, so that by his holy flesh and blood we may be restored by him and to a new life in him."

St. Cyril also uses that graphic expression, which is rendered in English by the archaic word, "concorporate," that is, " united in the same body." "By the mystical benediction [Eucharist] we have been made concorporate with Christ." It should be noted that St. Paul in Ephesians 3:6 also uses the term "concorporate" in the sense of "sharing the same body." [TEP]

✝ ✝ ✝

Creator of all things, your Son, our Lord, desired to work among us with his own hands. Be mindful of all who earn their living by the sweat of their brow.
Lord God, grant that those who labor for you may trust not in their own work but in your help.

On one occasion Christ said: "I have come that they may have life and have it in abundance." The reference, of course, was not to natural life, which his listeners already had, but to supernatural life. We call it Sanctifying Grace, and define it as a sharing in the life of God himself. St. Cyril understands this so very well. For him everything about Christ was "life-giving": his words, his flesh, his blood. Cyril calls Mass and Communion "the life-giving blessing of Christ." We see in the following quotation of his that he believes that the purpose of Christ's instituting the Eucharist was that his flesh and blood could give us life after he had returned to heaven. "After Judas left [at the Last Supper] the Savior gives the saving mystery to the Eleven [Apostles]. He knew that in a little while, having risen from the grave, he would return to the Father in his own flesh. In order that we would have the presence of the Savior, he gave us his own body and blood, so that the power of corruption be destroyed, that he live in our souls through the Holy Spirit, that we become partakers of holiness, that we conduct ourselves as heavenly and spiritual men ... and become sanctified in body and soul."

Regarding the Real Presence of Christ in the Eucharist Cyril is quite clear: "Christ spoke in a demonstrative way, 'This is my body and this is my blood,' so that you do not think that the things that you see are a figure or type; but the offerings are really transformed into the body and blood of Christ through the ineffable action of God the Almighty. When we partake of the body and blood of Christ, we receive his life-giving and sanctifying strength. It is proper that Christ, through the Holy Spirit, penetrate into us in a manner worthy of God with his holy flesh and precious blood in our bodies. We have the flesh and body of Christ in the form of bread and wine as a life-giving blessing, so that we do not remain unmoved when we see his flesh and blood exposed on the sacred altars of the churches. Accommodating himself to our weakness, God gives the force of life to the offerings and changes them into the very life of God. And do not doubt that this is the truth, for he himself clearly said: 'This is my body and this is my blood." Therefore accept the words of the Savior through faith, for being Truth he does not lie." [TEP]

St. Cyril comments on the manger [a container for food for animals] and the shepherds at Christ's birth. 'She laid him in a manger.' Jesus found man changed [by sin] into an animal. Therefore Jesus was laid in a manger as if he were food for animals, so that changing our animal ways we would return to the intelligence worthy of men. We who were like brute animals in our souls, seeing this table of the manger, we do not now see hay, but the bread of heaven, the body of life ... 'Bethlehem' means 'house of bread.' After the announcement of peace [by the angels], where were the shepherds going to come together but in the spiritual house of the bread from heaven, that is, in the church; for every day in the church there is sacrificed mystically the bread that came down from heaven and gives life to the world."

Christ cured some people by placing his hands on them. St. Cyril tells us why he did it that way. "Although Christ could work miracles with only a word or nod of his head, he also placed his hands on the sick in order to teach us something that is necessary for us. It was proper that we learn that that holy flesh, which he made his own by injecting in it a power that befits God, carries in it the power of the Word [Son] of God. Therefore, may Jesus touch us, or rather, may we touch him in the mystical blessing [Eucharist], so that he frees us also from the diseases of our soul and the attacks and tyranny of the devil." [TEP]

† † †

MEDIEVAL CAROL

While shepherds watch,
The heavenly army sings;
It sings: "Glory in the highest
And peace on earth."

On this feast, because
Thou, Christ, art born,
We rejoice and sing
Gladly to thee.

Translator: A. Fortescue

In Cyril's mind the death of the body does not prevent eternal life. "Those who ate the manna [in the Old Testament] died, because they did not receive from it any share in life, since it was not life-giving. It was only a remedy for bodily hunger and a figure or type of the true manna (Eucharist). But those who receive the bread of life will have immortality as a reward. And completely free of all corruption and their sins, they will ascend to that eternal greatness of the Christian life. Nor is this prevented by the fact that those who partake of Christ have to suffer the death of the body; for although they make this final payment to human nature, nevertheless, as St. Paul says, 'those who are to live, live for God' ... Christ says, 'I will raise him up on the last day,'" as if to say, 'Being in him through the medium of my flesh, I will raise up on the last day him who eats me.' For it is entirely impossible that he who is life by nature would not conquer corruption and subjugate death. Consequently, although death invaded us due to the original prevarication and subjects our body necessarily to corruption, nevertheless Christ being in us through his flesh, we shall surely rise. It is incredible, even impossible, that life does not vivify those in whom it dwells. Just as a burning ember is taken from the fire and straw is piled on it to preserve those sparks of fire, so too our Lord Jesus Christ through the medium of his flesh conceals in us his life and, as it were, deposits in us the spark of immortality, which will destroy whatever corruption is in us."

† † †

FIFTH CENTURY EASTER HYMN

Author of man's salvation, Jesus, joy of hearts, maker of a world redeemed, pure light of them who love thee.
What pity moves thee to bear our sins, that thou guiltless shouldst bear death to save us from death!
Thou dost break through the darkness of hell, taking away chains from prisoners; thou conquering in glorious triumph dost sit at the Father's right hand.

*Leader to heaven and way of life, be thou the end of our desire, thou
our joy after tears,
thou the reward of life for ever.*

Tr.: A. Fortescue

Christ said: "He who eats my flesh and drinks my blood remains in me
and I in him." St. Cyril comments: "If one melts a piece of wax with
another, he sees that the one is entirely in the other. So too, I believe, he
who receives the flesh of Christ our Savior and drinks his precious blood,
as he himself said, forms one unit with him. He is commingled with him,
and in a certain way melted with him through that partaking, so that he is
in Christ and Christ in him. ... Christ does not say that he is in us only
with a certain affectionate relationship, but also with a bodily or physical
participation. ... By partaking of the body of Christ and of his precious
blood he unites himself to us, and we unite ourselves to him. That which
is corruptible by nature [human beings] cannot become vivified in any
other way than by uniting itself bodily to the body of him who is life by
nature, that is, the only begotten Son of God."

St. Cyril criticizes those who, first tricked by the devil into vice, are
further fooled into not receiving Communion out of a misguided respect
for the Eucharist. "If we love eternal life, and if we want to have in us the
giver of immortality, let us not refuse to receive the blessing [Eucharist], as
some of the more lazy people do. Let us not let the devil, the clever deceiver
that he is, lay a snare or trap for us by engendering in us a lamentable
respect. When I examine myself, I find myself unworthy. When will you
ever be worthy? If your sins frighten you, and yet you never stop sinning ...
you will find yourself completely deprived of that sanctity which keeps us
to eternal life. Therefore make up your mind to live a good and holy life,
and thus partake of the blessing [Eucharist]. Believe that the Eucharist has
the power not only to destroy death but also our weaknesses. Christ, who is
in us, holds in check the fierce law of the flesh in our members, rekindles
the loving relationship toward God, and quiets the passions." [TEP]

† † †

*Lord God, our strength and salvation, put in us the flame of your love
and make our love for you grow to a perfect love which reaches to our
neighbor.*
The Lord has saved me; he wanted me for his own.

The Greek word that St.Paul uses in Ephesians 3:6 is translated literally "concorporate"; i.e. united in or sharing in the same body; also, members or parts of the same body. St. Paul uses the word to teach that the pagans (non-Jews) are on a par with the Jews because of their faith in the Gospel, which makes them "concorporate" or members of the same mystical body of Christ together with the Jewish Christians. We have seen that some Church Fathers use that same word to teach that those who receive Holy Communion become "concorporate" with the real, physical body of Christ in the Eucharist. In the following passage St. Cyril uses the same word to refer both to the mystical body of Christ (the Church) and to his real body in the Eucharist:

"So that we would strive for a union with God and among ourselves and form a single unit, even though we have different bodies and souls, the Son of God looked for a way in his wisdom and in the counsel of the Father. With one body, that is, his own, Christ makes those who believe in him concorporate with himself and with the others by blessing them in a mystical union (the Church). Now who can divide or separate the natural union that exists among those who have been made one with Christ by that one holy body (in Holy Communion)? For if 'all partake of the same bread,' we all form one body, since Christ cannot be divided. For that reason the Church is called the body of Christ and each of us a member of that body according to the mind of St. Paul [1 Cor 12:27]. Because we are all united to Christ by the medium of his holy body (Communion), since we receive in our bodies him who is one and indivisible, we owe our membership to him rather than to ourselves." [TEP]

† † †

Lord Jesus Christ, to save mankind you stretched out your arms on the cross.
Father, strike down the pride that rules our hearts.
God, whose power is now at work in us, can do immeasurably more than we ask or imagine.
From the depths of my heart I cry to you, O Lord. Hear me. I will do what you desire.)

St. Cyril continues to explain how we are "concorporate" with Christ in the Church through Holy Communion. "We who partake of his holy flesh acquire that corporal union with Christ. So testifies St. Paul speaking of the mystery of (God's) kindness in Ephesians 3: 'This mystery that has been revealed through the Spirit to his holy Apostles and prophets was unknown to any men in past generations; it means that pagans now share in the same inheritance (as the Jews), that thy are concorporate (parts of the same body), and that the same promise has been made to them in Christ Jesus through the Gospel.' And if we are concorporate with Christ and not only among ourselves, because he is obviously in us by his own flesh, how are we now not clearly one among ourselves and with Christ? Christ is the bond of unity, because he is at the same time God and man."

We are united to one another according to the way just indicated; but we are also united with God. Christ himself explained very clearly how this union exists: 'With me in them, Father, and you in me, may they be completely one.' [John 17:23] Because God the Son is in us bodily as Man, commingled and united to us through the mystical blessing (Eucharist); and he is also in us spiritually as God by the power and grace of his own Spirit. Thus he restores our spirit for a new life, and makes us partakers of his divine nature."

"With good reason we celebrate the holy reunions in our churches on Sundays. ... Christ is present to all of us invisibly and visibly: invisibly, as God; but also visibly in his body; and he permits us to touch his holy flesh. By the grace of God we approach to share the mystical blessing (Eucharist), receiving Christ in our hands, so that we also believe that he really raised his temple (body) from the dead."

† † †

Claim me once more as your own, Lord.
Be mindful of those who devote themselves to the service of their
brothers. Do not let them be deterred from their goals by discouraging
results or lack of support.
Help us and we shall be saved, Lord;
leave us and we are doomed.

Some monks in Cyril's time got the peculiar notion (which would be taken up 11 centuries later by the Lutherans) that consecrated Hosts left over after Mass lost the Real Presence. St. Cyril replies: "And I hear that they say that the mystical blessing (Eucharist) will not sanctify, if some of it remains for another day. But those who say such things are wrong. Because Christ does not change, nor will his holy body be changed, because the force of the blessing (Mass) and the life-giving grace are perpetual in him."

The following quotation is from a letter that Cyril wrote to Nestorius, the heretical Bishop of Constantinople, who claimed that God the Son did not become a man but simply dwelt from time to time in the body of Jesus, an ordinary man: "We announce the death according to the flesh of the Son of God, that is, of Jesus Christ; and we confess his resurrection from the dead and his ascension into heaven, when we celebrate in church the unbloody sacrifice (of the Mass). And so we approach the mystical blessings (Eucharist); and we are sanctified by partaking of the sacred flesh and precious blood of Christ, the Savior of us all. And in no way do we receive it as ordinary flesh, not even of a man who was sanctified and associated with the Son of God by union of dignity, nor of a man who was favored with divine indwelling No, we receive Communion as flesh that is truly life-giving and the very own flesh of the Son of God."

"As God Christ is life by nature, so after he was united with his flesh, he made it life-giving. Therefore, when he says: 'Truly, if you do not eat the flesh of the Son of Man and drink his blood," we do not deduce that that flesh is the flesh of a man in our own condition. How could the flesh of man be life-giving by its own nature? We believe that it is truly the very own flesh of him who for us was made man and was called the Son of Man." [TEP]

† † †

Fill our hearts with zeal for serving you,
O God, so that our thoughts
and actions may redound to your glory.
Lord, you alone can heal me,
for I have offended you by my sins.

ST. PETER CHRYSOLOGUS, BISHOP OF RAVENNA (ITALY), 403-450

St. Peter, Bishop of Ravenna in northern Italy, was so outstanding in his oratorical ability that he was given the name "Chrysologus," meaning "Golden Word." Fortunately some of his sermons are still intact, and we quote from them.

Commenting on the incident in our Lord's life, when the woman who suffered from a hemorrhage and was cured when she pushed through the crowd and touched our Lord's cloak from behind, St. Peter says: "The woman touched his clothing, was cured, and was freed from her old illness. We miserable ones daily deal with and eat the body of the Lord, and yet we are not cured of our wounds. Christ is not lacking toward the sick; but it is their faith that is lacking. Remaining in us now, Christ could cure our wounds much better than he cured the unseen woman in passing."

On the Our Father: "After asking for the Father's kingdom to come, who would ask for ordinary bread? But Christ wants us to ask for our daily viaticum (food for our daily journey through life), for our daily bread in the sacrament of his body. Through that food we arrive at the eternal day and the very table of Christ [in heaven], so that from where we receive pleasure here, we will also receive fullness of pleasure and complete satisfaction there." St. Peter clearly believes that "our daily bread" refers only to Holy Communion, and that there is a "table of Christ" also in heaven, from which the fullness of pleasure is received. Similarly, in the Eucharistic Prayer 1 of the Mass we pray: "Almighty God [the Father], we pray that your angel [probably Christ] may take this sacrifice to your altar in heaven." [TEP]

† † †

Out of love for us God made us according to his own image; and out of love for us he made himself according to our image in becoming man.
O Lord, bless the work we have begun, make good its defects, and let us finish it in a way that pleases you.
Eternal Father, you give us life despite our guilt, and even add days and years to our lives in order to bring us your wisdom.
Through the uncertainties of this earthly journey, O Lord, lead us home to everlasting happiness.

SEDULIUS, PRIEST AND POET (ITALY) died 450

Little is known about Sedulius other than he was a priest who flourished as a Latin poet in Italy in the second quarter of the fifth century. Two of his poems are found in the Latin Liturgy of the Hours for Christmas and Epiphany: A solis ortu cardine, and Crudelis Herodes Deum. He is known chiefly for his very long poem entitled "Paschal Hymn." We quote from a prose version, which he himself made of that hymn:

"The treachery prepared (by Judas) was not hidden from the Lord. He, being the very Bread that was to be handed over to death, pointed out the perpetrator of the future crime, the one to whom he was going to give the bread. Then the words of David [Psalm 41:9] appeared clear: 'He who ate my bread betrayed me.' "

"The Lord Jesus Christ consecrated the two gifts of life, his body and his blood. He offered them to his own disciples as spiritual food and drink, so that faithful souls, nourished with these spiritual banquets, will never experience hunger or thirst. Then the cruelty of that horrible spirit [Satan] entered the heart of Judas, where wickedness found the worst of habitations."

Sedulius comments on the scene after Easter on the shore of the Sea of Galilee, where our Lord had prepared breakfast with the fire, bread and fish for the Apostles, who had been fishing all night. "The fish on the burning coals and the bread that the Apostles found in the same place are not without religious and Catholic significance. It seems that by the fish is understood the water by which we are certainly purified and reborn [in baptism]. The bread signifies Christ the Savior, with whose very own body we are nourished to salvation. The fire represents the Holy Spirit, to whom we have been dedicated and are consecrated to the faith [by Confirmation]." [TEP]

† † †

Lord, we recognize that all the favors we have received today come through your generosity. Do not let them return to you empty, but let them bear fruit.
May the faithful departed be numbered among the saints, whose names are in the Book of Life.

ESIQUIUS OF JERUSALEM, PRIEST,   died after 451

We know little about Esiquius, a priest of Jerusalem, who left a commentary on the Book of Leviticus with references to the New Testament. The Church teaches that the one sacrifice of Christ for our salvation was begun at the Last Supper, when he offered himself to the death under the forms of bread and wine, and was completed the following day with his death on the cross. In the following quotation from Esiquius we see that he already comes close to the understanding of that doctrine.

"Christ not only said: 'I have the power to lay down my life and to take it up again'; but he went ahead and offered himself in sacrifice at the supper with the Apostles, as they know who understand the efficacy of the mysteries (Eucharist). The Seventy [the 70 Jews who are said to have translated the Hebrew Bible into Greek before Christ, and whose translation is called the Septuagint] not only said that Christ was anointed, but also consummated by his own hands. For he was first consummated by his own hands in the mystical supper, when he took the bread and distributed it. Afterwards he was consummated on the cross, when he was nailed to it. At that time, when he received the dignity of the priesthood — or better, when he fulfilled that dignity with his deed, for he always had the dignity — he consummated the sacrifice that he was to offer for us."

Commenting on the law of God in the Old Testament concerning those who ate holy food inadvertently, Esiquius writes: "Out of ignorance one receives the Eucharist, who does not know its efficacy and dignity, who does not know that it is really body and blood. He receives the mysteries, yes; but he does not know the efficacy of the mysteries." [TEP]

† † †

Lord, healer of body and spirit, comfort the sick and be present to the dying.
Father, we look forward to praising you in the company of all your saints in our heavenly homeland.
It is the lowly heart that understands.

KORUIN, ARMENIAN HISTORIAN, died c. 460

Koruin of Armenia wrote a history of the life and death of a holy teacher named Mesrop. Wahan, chief of the Armenian army and a fervent Christian, erected a chapel for the burial of Mesrop.

Koruin writes: "In the crypt of the chapel Wahan put the grave of the holy Mesrop. He arranged for appropriate ornamentation, with beautiful, varied and splendid ornaments of gold, silver and precious stones for the banquet of the altar of the life-giving body and blood of Christ."

† † †

CRUDELIS HERODES DEUM
by Sedulius, fifth century

Cruel Herod, why dost thou fear
when the divine king comes?
He will not take away an earthly kingdom
who brings a heavenly one.
The wise men go, following the star which leads them;
By its light they seek the Light,
by his grace they confess God.
The Lamb of God is washed in baptism of water;
So he, himself without sin, cleanses us of sin.
A new kind of miracle, the jars of water are red;
The water commanded to become wine changes its nature
Jesus, to thee glory, who hast shown thyself to Gentiles,
With the Father and the Holy Ghost for all ages.

Translator: Adrian Fortescue

God wants a loving heart more than sacrifice, knowledge of his
ways more than holocausts.
Always speak and act as men destined for judgment under the law
of freedom.

God, who is justice and truth,
does not judge by appearances.

BALAI, BISHOP (SYRIA), died c. 460

Balai was a country-bishop in the district of Aleppo in Syria. He is known for the many poems that he wrote, which contained dogmatic teaching. We quote from one poem that he wrote for the dedication of a new church.

"Your strength, oh carpenter, is less than that of the angels; but your dignity is equal to that of the heavenly spirits. They serve him with trembling; we, full of confidence, receive Him as food. So that He could be found on earth, He has built himself a house among us mortals; and He has raised altars like cribs, so that the Church can enjoy life from them. Let no one be deceived: the King dwells here. Let us go to the church to contemplate Him. Where [spiritual] sickness finds an easy entrance, there is the Doctor guarding the entrance. His body is visible [that is, the appearances of bread], but his fire [divinity] is hidden, so that the hand of man will not withdraw in panic before Him. He is awesome in heaven, but meek on earth, so that no one will fear to approach Him."

"God's residence is adorned, crowned with exultation, because it is a festive day and a solemnity, and there is a new nuptial habitation for Christ, the Groom. The angels rejoice and man exalts and gives thanks. The altar is prepared, covered with truth; before it stands the priest, and he lights the fire [consecrates]. He takes bread and gives the body; he receives wine and distributes the blood ... The people, united, sing the Sanctus. The King hears it, and makes His mercy descend in torrents."

"May the greatness and majesty of God be adored. Here He gives us His body; in heaven, His reward. On earth is the altar that holds His body; and in the kingdom of heaven He offers eternal life and glory. The disciple received the bread that He had blessed. He called it His body; and the wine, His blood. 'Together with you I have tasted this sacrament; again you will taste it with me in the kingdom of Heaven.' " [TEP]

† † †

Lord, do not let this day be a burden to the afflicted,
but a consolation and a joy.
Help us to pass this day joyfully, O Lord, and to spend it in loving
service of you and our fellow men.

In his poem for the dedication of a new church the Bishop writes: "Yours, O Lord, is the kingdom of heaven; and ours is this house [church]. But for their work the builders ask for the kingdom of heaven. The priest offers in your name the bread, from which you distribute your body to the flock. Where are you, O Lord? There, in heaven. And where are we to look for you? Here, in the sanctuary. Since heaven is too high for us to reach, behold we contemplate you in the church, to which we have easy access. Your throne above has foundations of fire, and who would dare approach it? But your living omnipotence dwells here in bread, and one who wishes may approach and taste it." [It should be noted that the Bishop in saying that Christ "dwells in the bread" was using the same expression we use in the Eucharistic acclamation, "We eat this bread and drink this cup." In liturgical language things are often called what they appear to be. We know that after the consecration there is no bread, only its appearances, and that Christ is not in the bread, as Luther would claim over a thousand years after Bishop Balai. Besides the Bishop was writing poetry, in which one has more freedom of expression than in prose.]

Concerning prayers for the dead the Bishop wrote: "In the cenacle [at the Last Supper] our Lord commanded his disciples: 'Come together and do this in memory of me until my second coming at the resurrection [of the dead].' It is clear that for those who understand that the dead receive benefit from the vigils and the sacrifice of the Mass ... when the priest recalls their names before the altar. Then the inhabitants of heaven rejoice, those on earth leap for joy, and the dead also rejoice; for they are today invited to receive relief through the heavenly sacrifice. Glory be to Him who lives, who by his death has awakened the dead and has offered them hope and resurrection. He is also to return and raise them up to praise him." [TEP]

† † †

*The talent of artists reflects your splendor, O Lord. May their work
give the world hope and joy.
May we face all life's difficulties with confidence and faith.*

CAPREOLUS (died c. 437) and
QUODVULTDEUS (died c. 453), BISHOPS

Capreolus ruled the Church of Carthage in northern Africa (in today's Tunisia) from about 430 to 437. He is known mainly for his battle against Nestorianism, which claimed there were two persons in Christ, a divine and a human person. He sent a letter, still extant, to the Ecumenical Council of Ephesus (431 a.d.). That Council definitively condemned Nestorianism. In the following quotation from one of his letters Capreolus, with very few words, defends the doctrine of the Real Presence of Christ in the Eucharist and shows from Scripture that Christ is one person only, a divine person:

"The Savior himself, speaking in mystery about the nourishment of his flesh and the potion of his blood, knew that his disciples were offended by that claim and that they had said: 'This is a hard saying. Who can bear to hear it?' So Christ says: 'Does this scandalize you? If you see the Son of Man ascending to where he was before...?' Look and note here how, because of the unity of the person of God and man, he affirms that the Son of Man is to ascend to where he was before [as God]; and it is clear that he was formed in the womb of the Virgin, and from that womb he took the origin of his human birth [as Man]."

Quodvultdeus [literally, What God wills] succeeded Capreolus as Bishop of Carthage. He too had to fight heresy.

In one of his sermons the Bishop speaks to the Jews [who were probably not present] and invites them to conversion and to partake of the Eucharist: "What will you do, oh Jews, who have killed the Son of God? Where will you flee; where will you hide? What mountains, what rocks are to fall upon you [Luke 23:30]? ... But come, enter, hear my advice and do not despair. You were infuriated, you killed, you shed the blood of Christ, you are in danger, you did not believe the Son of God. So, what must you do now, except believe, be baptized, and drink the blood you shed? Do not be horrified: the blood of the Physician has been shed and has become medicine for those who were furious. Why do you hesitate? 'Taste and see how sweet the Lord is.' "

† † †

Father, do not let us rouse your burning indignation by sin.

Although it is clear that Bishop Quodvultdeus had good will toward the Jews of his day, nevertheless the Jews rightly took offense at being accused of having killed God, since they lived 400 years after the death of Christ. Just what the Bishop (and others) had in mind when making such statements is not clear. Nevertheless the Jews were rightly offended. The Ecumenical Council Vatican 11 in our day set the record straight: "Even though the Jewish authorities and those who followed their lead pressed for the death of Christ, neither all Jews indiscriminately at that time, nor Jews today, can be charged with the crimes committed during Christ's passion. It is true that the Church is the new people of God, yet the Jews should not be spoken of as rejected or accursed, as if this followed from holy Scripture. Consequently, all must take care, lest in catechizing or in preaching the word of God, they teach anything that is not in accord with the truth of the Gospel message of the spirit of Christ." [Nostra Aetate n. 4] We quoted the Bishop because of his graphic affirmation of the Real Presence.

Referring to the instruction God gave for the construction of the Altar of Holocausts in the Old Testament, Bishop Quodvultdeus writes: "The table and altar, which are to receive the sacred flesh and that of the priest, what else are we to understand by these things other than the cross, on which our spotless Lamb was immolated? For he is both priest and victim, confirming that the sanctified bread on his table is his sacred body."

✝ ✝ ✝

CHRISTMAS HYMN by Prudentius, died c. 405

Begotten of the Father's love before the world was made; called Alpha and Omega, he the source and end of all things that are, that were, that shall be; for ever and ever.
O blessed birth, when the Virgin conceiving of the Holy Ghost brought forth our salvation, when the Child, redeemer of the world, lifted his sacred head;
for ever and ever.
Thee old men and young proclaim; choirs of boys, matrons, children, joining their voices, sing hymns to thee;
for ever and ever.
Translator: Adrian Fortescue

THEODORET, BISHOP OF CYRUS IN SYRIA, died c.460

Theodoret is the last outstanding product of the great theological school of Antioch in Syria. He was intellectually competent in various fields. His commentaries on Sacred Scripture show him to be an outstanding exegete. Parts of his history of the Church are still extant. Because of his oratorical ability he was invited several times to preach in Antioch. Although in the beginning of his episcopal career he dragged his feet in combating heresy, later he proved himself to be an exceptional champion of orthodoxy.

The Bishop comments on his copy of Psalm 63:2, which reads: "I have presented myself in your presence in the holy place." He writes: " Let the multitude of the Gentiles who have come to believe always say: 'I have presented myself in your presence in the holy place,' that is, in the church in which You are sacrificed without a [bloody] sacrifice, where You are distributed without being divided, where You give Yourself to be eaten while remaining unconsumed."

Theodoret teaches that the sacrifice of Christ on Calvary and in the Mass is one and the same sacrifice with only the manner of offering being different. "Now if the priesthood of the Mosaic Law ended, and if the high priest [Christ] according to the order of Melquisedech offered sacrifice and made the other sacrifices unnecessary, then why do the priests of the New Testament celebrate the mystic liturgy [Mass]? It is clear to those who are versed in divine matters that we do not offer another, distinct sacrifice, but we celebrate the memory of that one, salutary sacrifice; for the Savior Himself commanded us: 'Do this in memory of me.' " [TEP]

† † †

Lord God, remember your people, the Jews, whom you chose from the beginning.
God, you do not allow us to be tested beyond our ability. Strengthen the weak and raise up the fallen.
Lord, may our prayer rise up to you, and your blessing come down upon us.
I am worn out with crying, for longing for my God.

Bishop Theodoret comments on the Temple veil hanging before the Holy of Holies: "The flesh of the Lord is called 'veil', because through it we acquire entrance into the holy of holies [heaven]. Just as the high priest according to the [Mosaic] Law entered the Holy of Holies through the veil — and it was impossible to enter any other way —so also those who believe in the Lord acquire heavenly citizenship by partaking of his most holy body."

Theodoret addressed a word to the Eastern Roman Emperor residing in Constantinople in Greece. He was, of course, Catholic; but he had caused the death of innocent people. "You, oh Emperor, are prince of men equal to yourself and slaves like you. For one is the Lord and King of everything, the Creator of all things. Now with what eyes will you look at the church of our common Lord? With what feet will you walk its sacred floor? How will you extend those hands, from which the blood of unjust deaths is still dripping? How will you receive with those hands the most holy body of the Lord? How will you lift the precious blood to that mouth of yours, which has unjustly shed so much blood due to the rage of your words? Go back, and do not try to augment with subsequent sins the wickedness of the former ones." [TEP]

† † †

EVENING HYMN,
attributed to St. Ambrose of Milan: died 397)

O blessed light, Trinity and Unity, Source of all,
Now that the bright sun disappears,
pour thy light into our hearts.

We praise thee with our hymns morning and evening.
Humbly we glorify thee through all ages.

To God the Father be glory and to his only Son,
With the Holy Ghost, the Comforter, for all ages.

Translator: Adrian Fortescue

Wisdom of God be with me, always at work in me.

POPE ST. LEO THE GREAT, died 461.

Pope St. Leo I, who ruled the Church for 21 years from 440 to 461 is generally considered the greatest pope of Christian antiquity. He is known in history as a civic leader also. At the time when the Roman Empire in the West was in shambles and about to die, St. Leo was successful in pleading with Attila the Hun and his wild hordes from southern [today's] Russia to spare Rome from plunder. A few years later he convinced the Vandal King Gaiseric to stop plundering Rome.

Leo I is one of two popes that history designates with the title "Great." Pope St. Gregory I is the other.

Due to the spread of the Monophysite heresy, which claimed that Christ had no human nature but only the divine nature, the fourth Ecumenical Council was called in Chalcedon [in today's western Turkey] in the year 451 to settle the matter. In his letter to the Council Leo spelled out clearly both the human and divine natures in the one person of Christ. The Council not only defined that doctrine dogmatically but also professed its belief in the primacy of the pope with the words: "Peter [St. Peter, the first pope] has spoken through Leo."

Some attribute the Leonine Sacramentary [probably the earliest Roman missal] to Leo I. We still use some of its prayers today at Mass. Leo was the first to use the Latin word "missa" [dismissal; Mass] specifically for the Eucharistic celebration.

Although Pope St. Leo the Great was a staunch defender of the faith, especially that of the unity of the Church and the primacy of the pope, his chief gift was that of being a good pastor. This is seen in the many sermons and letters of his that are still extant. What pertains to the Eucharist in these writings is mainly his clear witness to, and defense of, the Real Presence of Christ in the Eucharist.

† † †

Christ nourishes and supports the Church, for which he gave himself up to death.
God, our help and deliverer, do not abandon us among the many temptations of life, but deliver us from evil and turn our tears and struggles into joy.

In a letter to the citizens of Constantinople in Greece, Pope Leo writes against a heresy that was troubling them at the time: "In what darkness of ignorance, in what laziness have they [the heretics] not remained prone even to this day, so that they have not learned by hearing or reading what runs from mouth to mouth with such unanimity in the Church of God? Not even the tongues of children silence the truth of the body and blood of Christ in the sacrament of Communion. This is what is distributed; this is what is received in that mystic distribution of the spiritual food. In receiving the strength of the heavenly food we are transformed into the flesh of Him who became our flesh."

"Jesus [at the Last Supper], firm in his determination and fearless in carrying out the Father's mandate, put an end to the Old Testament and created the new Pasch. The Apostles were seated with him to eat the mystic supper, while in the hall of Caiphas they were discussing how they would be able to kill Christ. He instituted the sacrament of his body and blood and thus taught what victim should be offered to God. Nor did he exclude the traitor [Judas] from this mystery, in order to show that he was not upset by any injustice, even though he knew beforehand the voluntary wickedness [of Judas]. Judas himself was the cause of his own ruin and perfidy by following the devil as his leader and not wanting to follow Christ. The honor of the Apostolic order of priesthood was not denied you, Judas, nor was Holy Communion ... Why did you distrust the goodness of him who did not deny you the communion of his body and blood, and who did not even refuse you the kiss of peace, when you arrived with the crowd and the armed guard to arrest him?"

Christ said in the Garden of Gethsemani: "Father, if it is possible, let this chalice pass from me." St. Leo writes: "From these words of Christ it is not to be thought that the Lord wanted to avoid his passion and death, since he had already given his disciples the sacraments of his passion and death."

✝ ✝ ✝

Naked I came forth from my mother's womb, and naked I shall go back again. Job 1:21.

"Now since the variety of flesh sacrifices [of the Old Testament] have ceased, only the oblation of your body and blood substitutes fully for all the diversity of those victims. Because you are the true 'Lamb of God who takes away the sins of the world.' You bring to perfection all of the mysteries in yourself, so that just as there is but one sacrifice instead of all those victims, so also there is but one kingdom for all the nations."

"The partaking of the body and blood of Christ does nothing else than change us into what we eat, into him with whom we [in Baptism] have died, been buried, and risen, and him whom we bear completely in spirit and flesh."

"Since Christ has said: 'If you do not eat the flesh of the Son of Man and drink his blood, you will not have life in you," you should partake of the sacred table in such a way that you have no doubt whatsoever concerning the truth of the body and blood of Christ. What you believe by faith you take in your mouth. In vain do they say 'Amen' (when receiving Communion), if they question what they receive." [TEP]

† † †

Faith of our fathers! Faith and prayer
Shall win all nations unto thee;
And through the truth that comes from God,
Mankind shall then indeed be free.

Faith of our fathers, holy faith!
We will be true to thee till death.

Faith of our fathers! we will love
Both friend and foe in all our strife:
And preach thee too, as love knows how,
By kindly deeds and virtuous life.

Faith of our fathers, holy faith!
We will be true to thee till death.

Frederick W. Faber, 1814-1863

ISAAC OF ANTIOCH (SYRIA), died c. 461

Little is known about the life of Isaac of Antioch. He was a monk and lived near the city of Antioch in Syria. His writings contain attacks against the then Christological errors of Nestorius and Eutyches, both of whom erred concerning the human nature, and therefore the human body, of Christ. We quote from a homily Isaac wrote in the form of a poem:

"Faith invited me to refresh myself with her provision. She made me sit at her table ... I saw her jar full of blood in place of wine; and in the middle of the table instead of bread there was placed the body which had been sacrificed. I saw the blood, and I felt great fear; I saw the sacrificed body, and trembling seized me."

"Then faith made signs to me: 'Eat and be still; drink, son, and don't speak.' I sat up straight at her banquet, and she gave me an elevated place, while she said to me: 'Stay with me, and work with me for a great salary.' She mixed for me the cup of her love, and my parched palate was refreshed. From her hands I received and took the sacred blood in place of wine."

"Faith embraced me and put her arm under my head and supported me like a child. She offered me the body and the blood, while she said: 'Take and be refreshed.' She whispered in my ear mysterious and wonderful things; she sang me sweet songs to give me joy with her melodies. She comforted me as one does a baby; she cheered me as one does a little child. And she taught me to praise with hymns the precious things she had presented to me."[TEP]

† † †

Prove yourselves innocent and straightforward, children of God beyond reproach, in the midst of a twisted and depraved generation, among whom you shine like the stars in the sky. **Philippians. 2:14-15**
What great nation is there that has gods so close to it as the Lord, our God is to us whenever we call upon him? **Deut 4:7**
Lord, we thank you for guiding us through the course of this day's work. In your compassion forgive the sins we have committed through human weakness.
Lord, you are near to those whose heart is right.

Isaac continues his homily in the form of a poem: "Faith showed me the body that had been killed. She placed part of it on my lips, and with great tenderness said to me: 'Consider what you eat.' Then she offered me the pen of the Holy Spirit and demanded that I take it. I took it; I wrote and professed: 'This is the body of the Lord.' Likewise I took the chalice, and drank it in her banquet of faith. Then I noted that from the chalice came the aroma of that body which I had eaten. And what I had said about the body, namely that it is the body of God, I likewise testified about the chalice, that is, 'This is the blood of our Redeemer.'

All this faith taught me in her banquet, and she sent me forth into the world to preach that truth, which is certain." [TEP]

† † †

The Church's one foundation is Jesus Christ her Lord;
She is his new creation by water and the word:
From heav'n he came and sought her to be his holy bride;
With his own blood he bought her, and for her life he died.

Elect from ev'ry nation, yet one o'er all the earth,
Her charter of salvation, one Lord, one faith, one birth;
One holy name she blesses, partakes one holy food,
And to one hope she presses, with ev'ry grace endued.

Though with a scornful wonder men see her sore opprest,
By schisms rent asunder, by heresies distrest;
"Yet saints their watch are keeping, their cry goes up,
"How long?"
And soon the night of weeping shall be the morn of song. Amen.

Text: Samuel John Stone, 1866

Be glad, Virgin Mary, for you have deserved to bear the Christ, the creator of heaven and earth. You have brought forth the Savior of the world.
Your word is a lamp to my feet and a light to my path.

GELASIUS OF CYZICUS (TURKEY), c. 475

Gelasius, a priest in Cyzicus in Bithynia in today's western Turkey, about the year 475 wrote a history of the Council of Nicea, the first Ecumenical Council, in 325. His work contained the history of the Church during the reign of the first Christian Roman Emperor, Constantine the Great.

About the Eucharist Gelasius writes: "Concerning the divine table and the mystery of the body and blood of Christ, which is on it. Again here let us not drag our feet looking at the bread and chalice placed on the sacred table, but raising our spirit, let us consider with faith that on that sacred table there is 'the Lamb of God who takes away the sin of the world.' He is there sacrificed in an unbloody manner by the priests. When we truly receive his precious body and blood, we believe that these are the symbols of our resurrection. We receive not a great but small amount, so that we understand that we do not receive it to fill us up, but to make us holy." [Holy Communion is a symbol and pledge of our resurrection from the dead, for Christ said in John 6:54: "Anyone who does eat my flesh and drink my blood has eternal life, and I shall raise him up on the last day," that is, the day of the last judgment at the end of the world.] [TEP]

† † †

HYMN TO THE BLESSED MOTHER

The God whom earth and sea and sky adore
and laud and magnify,
Whose might they own, whose praise they tell,
in Mary's body deigned to dwell.
O Mother blest! the chosen shrine
wherein the Architect divine,
Whose hand contains the earth and sky,
vouchsafed in hidden guise to lie.
Blest in the message Gabriel brought;
blest in the work the Spirit wrought;
Most blest to bring to human birth
the long desired of all the earth.
O Lord, the Virgin born, to thee eternal praise and glory be,
Whom with the Father we adore and Holy Ghost for ever more.
Text: Venantius Fortunatus, 530-609. Translator: J.M.Neale

FAUSTUS, BISHOP OF RIEZ (FRANCE), died c.480

Faustus, a native of Great Britain, became the Abbot of the famous monastery of Lerins in France, and was later made Bishop of Riez in southeastern France. He spent much energy opposing the teaching of his compatriot, Pelagius, who denied the necessity of grace in the spiritual life. He is known especially for his writings on predestination. We quote from one of his homilies on the Eucharist:

"Because the body of Christ after the Ascension was to be taken from our sight and raised to the stars, it was necessary, if it was to be adored constantly, that He consecrate on that day (Holy Thursday) the sacrament of his body and blood. With good reason he availed himself of that mystery by which his body was offered in sacrifice as the price of our redemption. Now that the [fruits of the] redemption run every day without stopping for the salvation of men, the oblation of our redemption should be perpetual, and that perennial Victim should always be alive in our memory and always present as a grace. The one true and perfect Victim must be judged by faith, not by appearances; nor must he be considered by the eyes of the exterior man, but rather by the love of the interior man. Therefore, with reason, the heavenly authority confirms: 'My flesh is truly food, and my blood is truly drink.' "

"Let all vacillation of doubt be set aside, when he who is the author of the gift is also the witness to the truth. The visible [human] priest with his word changes visible creatures [bread and wine] into the substance of his body and blood with His secret power, saying: 'Take and eat; this is my body.' And repeating the sanctification , he says: 'Take and drink; this is my blood.' Just as by a sign of God commanding there suddenly appeared out of nothing the height of the heavens, the depth of the waves, and the breadth of the earth, so too does the divine omnipotence give a similar power to the words of the spiritual sacraments; and their effect produces reality."

† † †

Our Eucharistic King, through baptism you made us all share in your royal priesthood, so that we could offer you a continual sacrifice of praise.

The Bishop compares the hidden effects of baptism with those of the Eucharist: "Without perceiving it with the bodily senses and setting aside the old vileness, you were suddenly invested with a new dignity. And just as you were not able to see or feel how God cured your wounds, washed away your infection, and cleansed your filth, so also when you approach the venerable altar to be filled with heavenly food, gaze upon the most holy body and blood of your God, honor them, contemplate them, touch them with your mind, take them with the hand of your heart, and especially receive them with a spiritual swallowing."

260

Bishop Faustus comments on Exodus 16:18 concerning the manna: "He who gathered much, had none too much; and he who gathered little did not go short." "This cannot be taken if said of common food, which, if we offer it to hungry people, no single person will receive all of it but only a part. But when we speak of this Eucharistic bread, one does not receive less than all do together. One alone receives it all; two receive it all; many receive it all without any diminution; because the blessing of this sacrament knows how to be multiplied, but it does not know how to be used up by being multiplied."

"All who come to faith in Christ, before the words of baptism are pronounced, are chained by their old sins. But once those words are pronounced, they are then free of all scum of sin. In the same way when the creatures of bread and wine to be blessed with the heavenly words are placed on the sacred altars, before they are consecrated by the invocation of his name, there is present the substance of bread and wine. But after the words are pronounced, they are the body and blood of Christ. What is there to wonder about, if one is able to change by a word the very things he created by a word? Indeed it seems to be a lesser miracle to change into something better what he had created out of nothing." [TEP]

† † †

Lord, may our young people be concerned
with remaining blameless in your sight,
and may they generously follow your call.
I love you, Lord; you are my strength.

ELISCHE THE DOCTOR, HISTORIAN, died c. 480

Many questions surround the person of the Armenian historian called Elische the Doctor. Some think he was a bishop. Many homilies are attributed to him. We quote from his explanation of the Our Father. The version of the Bible he uses is somewhat different from ours.

"Give us this day our permanent bread" ... How can bread from the earth be so called? Surely it is not permanent. The infant cannot eat it, nor can sick people. Misery forbids our taking bread; and death removes it from our midst. 'Your fathers ate manna in the desert and died. This is the true bread come down from heaven. He who eats this bread will never die.' They heard his words but did not understand it immediately with their spirit. Therefore he repeated the same word two or three times, so that it would easily enter their ears and they would be able to understand with faith the force of his words. He said: 'I am the living bread come down from heaven. He who eats this bread will never taste death.' This is the bread he teaches us to ask God for as permanent in the Our Father."

"If you pay attention, he who eats this bread with purity and prepares himself to receive it, as is proper, has no need of the kingdom of this world. In mortal hands is placed the immortal Bread, and instantly these hands also become immortal. The entire man is spiritualized in spirit, soul, and body; and he becomes a partaker of Christ, when he eats this bread. He need only keep immaculate to the end the principle of strength. Now there is no earthly suffering that can conquer him. Silver is worthless in his eyes, and he looks on gold with hatred. The grandeur of this world is considered pain, because his thoughts have been sanctified toward heavenly freedom; for he has been filled with the immortal Bread." [TEP]

✝ ✝ ✝

Lord God, may this lifting up of our hearts in prayer
be a sacrifice pleasing in your sight.
Jesus, may our children imitate your example
by growing in wisdom and grace.
Lord, show me your ways and teach me
to walk in your paths.

The Armenian historian continues his explanation of the Our Father: "This is a Bread prepared for all. With it the child appears mature in age. For the person weakened by sickness the strength of God resides in this Bread. He who departed the life of his world took with him on his journey to God a life that is immortal."

"This is what our Lord taught us to ask for in his prayer: Give us our daily bread, not the bread of earth, but the Bread of the Lord. It is clear that we are dealing not only with the bread of heaven but also with the Lord himself of all things. For he says: 'This is my body; this is my blood.' Although he cannot be broken, for love of you he was broken. And you, who were broken in your will, he has united with himself in his divinity, which cannot be broken. 'Do not leave my soul in hell nor permit your holy one to see corruption.' (Psalm 16:10) On Friday he was crucified in order to break death. On Sunday he gathered together the broken bones of Adam and joined them together with immortality. And he truly showed himself to many and not just with one appearance. One day he gave himself as bread in the upper chamber [on Holy Thursday]; and from then until now he always gives himself as bread on the holy altar in our churches. First he tasted himself; then he made all of us table companions of the sacrifice of his passion. Now he cannot suffer, but he will be given homage by angels and men in the glory of his Father. And he has taken the sufferings of all of us on his divinity, which does not suffer."[TEP]

† † †

Lord, teach us today to recognize your presence in everyone, especially in the poor and in those who mourn.
Grant that we may live today in peace with everyone and never render evil for evil.
Lord, may our love for you grow into a love that reaches our neighbor.
Incline my heart according to your will, O God; and speed my steps along your path.
Do to no one what you yourself dislike.
Lord, share with us the treasure of your love.

JOHN MANDAKUNI, BISHOP AND PATRIARCH OF THE ARMENIANS, died c. 498

Bishop Mandakuni left a number of sermons and liturgical prayers. As regards the Eucharist he gave forceful instructions especially on the proper and improper dispositions of soul for receiving Holy Communion. He condemned not only the laity who knowingly receive Communion unworthily, when they are in mortal sin, but also the priests who give Communion to persons who they know are living in mortal sin.

"How terrible must be the punishment of those condemned persons, who carry in their heart the goad of enmity toward their neighbors, and yet dare to approach the sacred mysteries. How the fire and darkness of hell will torment them! You receive the body of the Lord, and you try to deceive God by attempting to hide your enmity toward your neighbor ... One who approaches the body of the Lord while living in enmity toward his neighbor, such a one does not receive the body that gives life but the fire that devours: 'He eats and drinks his condemnation.' ... There are also others for whom the desire to receive the holy mysteries does not impel them in any way to reconcile themselves with their neighbors. For many days they remain away from the holy sacrament. To them it seems more difficult to deal with their brother and reconcile themselves with him than to remain away and not receive the holy sacrament of the body and blood of Christ. For fear of appearing humiliated before their enemy they neglect the sacrament of the Lord. They abstain from the sacrament and believe they do an honor to God by not approaching the sacrament."

† † †

Lord, Father of all, strengthen us to work for your blessings of unity and peace in the world.
Act on God's word in the Bible. If all you do is read it, you are deceiving yourself.
Give us strength, O Lord, to imitate you by being patient with those

we meet today.
Lord, do not remember the sins of our youth and our stupidity, but
remember us with your love.
Christ loved us and washed away our sins in his own blood.

Instructions on receiving Communion: "If your conscience does not testify that you have been sanctified [free of mortal sin], it is clear that your reception of the holy sacrament is not according to the will of God, as St. Paul says: 'This is the will of God, the testimony of your conscience.' So if your conscience testifies that you are holy [without mortal sin], then your reception is according to the Will of God. But if you approach in [mortal] sin, know that you go forth with the sentence of condemnation and that you are the worst of sinners. For such a man is more wicked than murderers, who in their depravity shed blood. The man who murders another man is called a man-killer; but one who receives the body of the Lord unworthily is a God-killer, because he crucifies again the Son of God (Hebrews 6:6)." [Here the Bishop refers to that passage of St. Paul in which he speaks of those who would be willing to crucify Christ again. He refers to those whose dispositions of soul are so evil that, were they able to do it, they would put Christ back on the cross.]

"Why do you treat with disrespect the tremendous sacrament? Do you not know that at the moment the holy sacrament comes to the altar, the heavens above open, Christ comes down and arrives, the choirs of angels fly from heaven to earth, and everyone is filled with the Holy Spirit? Therefore those who are tormented by pangs of conscience are unworthy to take part in this sacrament until they are purified through penitence."

"Do not look upon it as simply bread; don't consider it to be wine; for the holy and tremendous mystery is not visible. Its power is spiritual, since Christ did not give us anything visible in the Eucharist or in baptism, but something spiritual. We see the water [in baptism]; but we believe in the divine Word, who says: 'This is my body and my blood. He who eats my body and drinks my blood lives in me and I in him; and I will raise him up on the last day.' We know with true faith that Christ dwells on our altars, that we approach him, that we gaze upon him, that we touch him and kiss him [In some places it was customary to kiss the Host before eating it.] and take and receive him within us, that we become one [mystical] body as members and sons of God."

The Bishop continues his instructions on the Eucharist: "You priests, you ministers and dispensers of the holy sacrament, approach with fear, guard it carefully, administer it in a holy manner, and serve it diligently. You have a real treasure; guard it therefore and keep it with great fear. For you also there await inexorable punishments, if you know the wickedness of someone who dares approach the body of Christ, and you fail in your duty to exhort him to remain away and correct him. Your failure and partiality will make you guilty of giving the body of Christ to the wicked and unworthy, guilty of throwing Christ's body, as it were, to dogs and swine. How will you excuse yourselves, how will you be able to receive pardon? What punishments and torments will fall on you for having become traitors and sinners against the body of the Lord? Look: you have the power of Christ, you live from Christ, and you hand Christ over to the wicked!"

"Let us come with great reverence and examine our hearts with greater diligence. We do not want to be so negligent as to receive Communion only on feast days. It is the same offering that we offer and the same sacrament that we distribute on Fridays, Sundays, Pentecost and Easter. Keep your soul pure for the moment of Communion, and don't put it off from one day to another. In no way is it to be considered something daring to receive Communion many times with a pure heart, for by it you are made to live and your soul is refreshed more and more. But if you are unworthy and have something for which your conscience reproaches you, and you receive Communion just once in your whole life, that would be the death of your soul [mortal sin]."

"If a king heard that a prince wanted to ally himself with him today, but tomorrow deserted him and became a confidant of the king's enemies, would the king reveal his plans to him? Would he not incarcerate him and punish him? And how much more will Christ condemn and punish the one who enters with him to the sacrament of the Lord today and tomorrow abandons the sacrament to do the will of the enemy? Are you free of sin today when you think: Tomorrow I shall leave and do my own will? Before God this would be worse." [TEP]

GENNADIUS, PRIEST & HISTORIAN OF MARSEILLE (FRANCE), died c. 494

Gennadius of Marseille in today's southern France wrote much that has been lost. However his history of the literature of the fifth century is extant and is perhaps his most precious work. We quote here from his Book of Ecclesiastical Dogmas, where he refers to the reception of the Eucharist and the administration of the sacrament of Penance (Reconciliation, Confession). It should be noted that the sacrament of Penance in the history of the Church has been administered in various ways at different times and in different places. Gennadius speaks of how the sacrament was administered publicly in Marseille. In many places public penitential practices were imposed for sins that were both grave and public. Such public penances had to be completed prior to absolution and reception of Holy Communion. It appears that Gennadius refers also to the sacrament being administered privately to individual penitents, as it is commonly done today.

"I neither praise nor censure one who receives Eucharistic Communion every day. However, I exhort people to receive Communion every Sunday, if they have no desire to commit [mortal] sin. I advise him who wants to commit [venial] sin to receive Communion rather than be purified [by the sacrament of Penance]. Even if one feels remorse of conscience but has no desire to sin, before receiving Communion let him make satisfaction [with tears and prayers]. Let him have confidence in the Lord, whose custom it is to forgive sins in view of a pious confession. Then let him approach the Eucharist confidently and without fear. But this I say to him who is not weighed down with sins that are capital and mortal." [TEP]

† † †

*Like the rising sun, O Lord, warm us with your rays, and restrain us
from every evil impulse.*
*Keep guard over our thoughts, words and actions, O Lord, and make
us pleasing in your sight this day.*
*With joy we cry out to you, Lord, and ask you: Open our hearts to sing
your praises.*
Dawn finds me ready to welcome you, my God.

Gennadius continues his instructions on the sacrament of Confession.
"Now he who is burdened with mortal sins committed after baptism I exhort
to make satisfaction first with public penance (penitential practices); then,
after he has been reconciled by the absolution of the priest, let him partake
of Communion. In this way he will not receive Communion for his own
judgment and condemnation. But we do not deny that mortal sins are also
forgiven with a secret satisfaction [probably private Confession]. However
in this case by the mercy of God there is to be a prior change of one's
worldly habits and a manifestation of love of religion by the correction of
one's life and a continual, even perpetual, sorrow for sin. Moreover this is
done only on the condition that the person performs works that are contrary
to those sins for which he is sorry, and that he receive Communion in a
humble and prayerful manner." [TEP]

† † †

When Jesus comes to be baptized,
He leaves the hidden years behind,
The years of safety and of peace,
To bear the sins of all mankind.
The Spirit of the Lord comes down,
Anoints the Christ to suffering,
To preach the word, to free the bound,
And to the mourning, comfort bring.
He will not quench the dying flame,

And what is bruised he will not break,
But heal the wound injustice dealt,
And out of death his triumph make.
Our everlasting Father, praise,
With Christ, his well-beloved Son,
Who with the Spirit reigns serene.
Untroubled Trinity in One.

Text: Stanbrook Abbey, 1971

DIONYSIUS THE PSEUDO-AREOPAGITE
(end of fifth century)

There lived in the last half of the fifth century a man who authored works in philosophy and theology. As an author he chose to use the name Dionysius the Areopagite, the name of the man in Athens, Greece, who was converted through the preaching of St. Paul. Pseudo Dionysius most likely studied philosophy in Athens and later lived in Syria. His works were held in high esteem during the Middle Ages, even to the point of placing them immediately after Sacred Scripture. The great St. Thomas Aquinas often quotes from his works. Dionysius left two descriptions of the Mass liturgy presided over by a bishop and his priests. He usually writes long, involved sentences lacking the clarity we would desire. We have broken up his sentences here for easier reading.

"In the first place let us consider in a holy manner why that which is common to all the sacraments is attributed to the Eucharist in a special way, so that it alone is called communion and synaxis [assembly]. Every one of the other sacraments reunites our separated lives in one uniform manifestation; and with this holy reunion of what is separated it gives us a participation in and union with the One [God]."

"We say that the participation in the rest of the hierarchical symbols [sacraments] reaches its consummation in the divine and perfect gifts of the Eucharist. Another sacrament can hardly be given but what the most divine Eucharist, like a crown of each of the means of sanctification, realizes in a holy manner the union of the baptized person with the One [God] and completes his communion with God ... Let us consider and examine in detail and in conformity with the spirit of the hierarchy the sacred rite and profound meaning of the most holy Sacrament." [TEP]

The author then proceeds to describe the liturgy of the Mass presided over by the bishop and his priests. He refers to the bread and wine on the altar as "sacred symbols through which Christ is signified and partaken of."

† † †

It is easy with the Lord on the day of death to repay man according to his deeds.
Tender and compassionate is the Lord, patient and ready to forgive.

Chapter IX

THE EUCHARIST IN THE SIXTH CENTURY

EUGENE, BISHOP OF CARTHAGE (AFRICA), died 505

In the latter part of the fifth century the barbarian tribe named Vandals conquered north Africa, which at that time was mostly Catholic. The Vandal King, Huneric, tried to force Arianism on all his subjects. Eugene, who became Bishop of Carthage in 480, sent a copy of a creed containing the true Christian faith to the King. For his efforts the Bishop died in exile in Albi in Gaul (France) in 505. We quote from the profession of faith he had sent to the King. The principal point in this profession of faith is, against Arianism, that Christ, the Son of God, is of the same substance or essence of God the Father; that is, that Christ is truly God. The references to the Eucharist interest us:

"Now that the Son is the substance of the Father, the prophetic oracles through the mouth of Solomon pointed this out long ago: 'You demonstrated your substance and your sweetness, which you have in your son.'(Wisdom 16:21) It is clear that the Father poured out his sweetness over the people of Israel in the figure and image of the heavenly bread [manna]. The Lord himself taught this in the Gospel saying: 'It was not Moses who gave you bread come down from heaven; but it is my Father who gives you the bread that comes down from heaven.' He clearly shows himself to be bread when he says: 'I am the living bread come down from heaven.' Concerning him the prophet David says: 'Man ate the bread of angels.' " [TEP]

† † †

CHRISTMAS HYMN (about 6th century)

Jesus , Redeemer of all, born of the high Father
before light was made, equal to him in glory.
Thou light and splendor of the Father, eternal hope of all, hear the
prayers thy servants

throughout the world make to thee.

Remember, maker of all things, thou once didst take our form, born in the holy Virgin's.

This day, as it comes each year, bears witness that thou once didst go forth from the Father to be the world's salvation.

Thee (Christ), author of new redemption, do stars, earth and sea, do all things under heaven with a new song proclaim.

And we, whom thy precious blood has washed, on thy birthday bring the homage of our hymns to thee.

Jesus, born of the Virgin, glory to thee, with the Father and the Holy Ghost, for all ages.

Translator: Adrian Fortescue

VICTOR de VITA, BISHOP OF BYZACENA (AFRICA), died c.500

Victor was bishop in northern Africa toward the close of the fifth century. He is famous mainly for his "History of the persecution of the Province of Africa in the time of Geiseric and Huneric, King of the Vandals." After the barbarian tribe of Vandals had conquered northern Africa, they tried to force the Catholics there to accept Arianism, which denied the divinity of Christ. The persecutions resulted in many Catholic martyrs. We quote from the Bishop's history:

"At the time the sacraments were being distributed to the people of God, the Arians under Geiseric entered the church; and with great fury scattered the body and blood of Christ on the floor, and then trampled on them with their dirty feet."

Bishop Victor writes that one group of martyrs was made up of "bishops, priests, deacons, and other members of the Church." Referring to the group the Bishop says: "An innumerable crowd of faithful came running down to the martyrs. They carried infants in their arms and placed them along the way of the martyrs, while they shouted in these words: 'In whose hands are you leaving us while you go for your crowns? Who are going to baptize these infants with the water of the perennial font ...? Who will perform the usual rite of the divine sacrifice? If we are permitted, we wish to go with you, so that in this way the children would not be separated from their parents.' " [T]

ST. AVITUS, BISHOP OF VIENNE (FRANCE), died 519

Besides being Bishop of Vienne in Gaul (France) St. Avitus was a statesman and poet. On Christmas Day in 496 Clovis, King of the pagan Franks who had invaded Roman Gaul, was baptized along with 3,000 of his warriors. Many Franks followed their king into the Church, so that eventually France became "the eldest daughter of the Church," that is, the first nation to embrace the Church as a nation. St. Avitus congratulated Clovis with the words: "Your faith is our victory." St. Avitus was outstanding in his loyalty to the Holy See of Rome. His famous words were: "If the Pope of the City of Rome is called into doubt, not only the bishop but the episcopacy itself will fail." He was considered the greatest Christian poet of his day, and in his verse he remained a theologian and master of doctrine. As poetry, of course, his words do not read as easily as prose.

"The impiety of the rebellious Jews is punished in that superstitious rite in which they eat with veneration a corruptible animal, a lamb, while they despise with a very dangerous hunger the eating of the true and immaculate Lamb. ... As an eternal and most pious father, our Redeemer, when about to complete the sacrament of the flesh he had taken, gave to the sons he had created and redeemed the hope of adoption. Before the day of his death he assigned to us heavenly goods and made a testament, by which he made us the inheritors of what he was giving us with such generosity. In this he proceeded as men usually do, although not out of necessity as men usually do in making their testament. For he was not going to lose what he destined for his children. Rather he was going to keep his sons along with the inheritance he had destined for them. This testament of his we call the New Testament. For all those who had been disinherited there was instituted one sole inheritor, the Christian people."

† † †

DOXOLOGY *(Apostolic Constitutions of 4th century in Greek and in St. Benedict's Rule in Latin of 6th century)*

To thee praise, to thee a hymn is due; to thee glory, God the Father and Son with the Holy Ghost, for ever and ever. Amen
Tr:Adrian Fortescue

The Bishop of Vienne continues with his poem on the Eucharist: "But this inheritance (the Eucharist given by Christ at the Last Supper) is not divided up in a human way, nor is it reduced by being distributed among many as with a corruptible distribution. It embraces all; it invites all. Nor is anything taken from the portion of those who already have it in order to give it to those who are to be born. Let the desire for children grow and multiply as it will — the inheritance remains intact for all."

"The Old Testament having been fulfilled, this New Testament is realized in its own way and is celebrated with mysteries of absolute firmness. Our ineffable Redeemer himself, using very trustworthy witnesses [the Apostles] wrote this Testament when he was handed over to death, sealed it when he suffered, and opened it when he rose. And since everything was done legitimately, with reason St. Paul says: 'If a will is drawn up in due form, no one is allowed to disregard it or add to it,' that is, change it."

"Let us faithfully now recognize the sum of the inheritance we have received. It is that, while the Apostles were eating, he consecrated the order of the eternal offering. Thus we see that he did not lessen for us the fullness of that substance [humanity], which he assumed for us. Rather he left it all to us. Others give their things to their inheritors — he gave himself, that is, the flesh and blood of his body."

† † †

Lord God and Maker of all things,
creation is upheld by you.
While all must change and know decay,
you are unchanging, always new.
You are man's solace and his shield,
his rock secure on which to build;
You are the spirit's tranquil home;
in you alone is hope fulfilled.
To God the Father and the Son and Holy Spirit
render praise,
Blest Trinity,
from age to age the strength of all our living days.

Text: Stanbrook Abbey

JAMES, BISHOP OF SARUGH (SYRIA), died 521

James, Bishop of Sarugh, on the Euphrates River in eastern Syria was one of the best Syriac writers. He was proficient in both prose and poetry. Like most Syrians of his day James loathed the heresy of Nestorius, who claimed that Christ was two persons, divine and human. And like many Syrians, James fell into the heresy of the Monophysites, who denied Christ a human nature and claimed that Christ's human body was assumed into the divine nature of Christ. In matters pertaining to the Eucharist, however, the Bishop was generally orthodox. We quote from his writings at some length because of their beauty. You will note that his poetic spirit shines through his prose.

"All the other sacrifices [of the Old Testament] were included spiritually in bread and wine, which, in a mysterious way, become flesh and blood. With this sacrifice [Mass] the ancients [Christians] already approached God the Lord; and also to later generations the divine Majesty grants mercy through these sacrifices."

"With bread and wine the high priest Melchisedech exercised before God his office in a mysterious way ... Christ, the eternal high priest in the fullest sense, chooses bread and wine to be offered from among everything that could be offered. As a man full of the Holy Spirit and therefore discerning everything, he knew beforehand that only in his sacrifice was the whole world to obtain mercy..."

"Now the daughter [the Church] of the King [Christ] did not take from the ancients [Jews and pagans] the sensible image [of their sacrifices]; but she consecrates today in truth the mysterious bread. She saw her Lord in the middle of the supper hall how he consecrated his body [at the Last Supper]; and from him she learned how to do the same just as the Lord had done it first. It was not Melchisedech who taught the Church what to do. The Church looked at her Lord; and as he did, so she does every day. She did not take as her model Moses, who was just a man; but Jesus, who is God, taught her the mysteries [of the Eucharist]. And behold, he watches over these mysteries; he honors them; he is proud of them, because he is the great Victim, in whom are included the living and the dead."

Bishop James insisted that Masses be offered for the dead. He says that, just as Moses wrote the names of the twelve tribes of the Jews on the ephod that the priest wore during the sacrifices, "So you also write on the bread of sacrifice the memorial of yourself and your deceased friends, as you give the priest gifts that he offers to God. Prepare a banquet (bread and wine for Mass) and invite your deceased to come to the sacrifice, which helps to strengthen and fortify all souls. Have compassion on the deceased person and show your love for him, not by preparing huge solemnities for mourning, which are of no value to him. Before God present the name and memorial of the deceased together with an offering. Then your faith will not be disillusioned. Place the memorial of the deceased on the altar in the house of reconciliation (church) in the form of bread and wine, which serve for the mysteries of the body and blood."

The Bishop reprimands those who do not go to church to offer Mass for their dead, but instead go to the cemetery to weep and talk to the dead. The Bishop believed that the souls of the deceased were present at the Masses offered for them. "Do not call out to the dead person in the grave, for he does not hear you, since he is not there. Rather seek him in the house of mercy (the church); there all the souls of the dead assemble, for that is the place where that Life is found which strengthens them. Here there is kept their memorial and their names in the great Book of God, in which all are inscribed. The blood of the Crucified distills resurrection drop by drop over their souls, and grants them the strength to come to him."

† † †

Lord, when we die, may we who confess our sins be brought to you through the gates of heaven..
Lord Jesus Christ, by your death you opened the gates of our death in triumph.
Our lives are surrounded with passing things; set our hearts on things of heaven.

The Bishop continues his rather poetical explanation of the Mass:
"Then (after the Offertory of the Mass) the Holy Spirit arises and descends upon the sacrifice, and takes form in the mysterious bread, and it becomes the body. And with the flapping of his wings he soars around the wine and changes it into the blood. Now the body and the blood form the sacrifice that sanctifies everyone. With this sacrifice the priest makes expiation for all the deceased, because the sacrifice has in itself a force to conquer death and destroy death's seat. At the fragrance of life that exhales from the sublime sacrifice all the souls assemble and approach to be expiated. And in the resurrection, which is poured out of the body of the Son of God, the deceased breathe life day after day and thus are purified. Therefore take care to remember your dear deceased persons, and be preoccupied with the sacrifice that can bring pardon to your deceased."

"In the glorious mysteries [of the Eucharist] the Church serves its Lord in a spiritual way; at her divine offices the angels marvel with holy admiration. The faith of the Church, oh intelligent man, is such that bread and wine are changed into the body and blood. When the Church breaks the bread, she sees there only the body; and when she mixes the wine with water, she fills the chalice with blood. Then she mentions the names of all the deceased and unites them intimately with herself by means of the spiritual offerings. The Church assembles them for a taste of the body and blood; and the deceased rejoice with her spiritually in the banquet."

† † †

At the hour of death, O Lord, let your merciful presence be with us;
may we be found faithful
and leave this world in your peace.
Lead the departed into the light of your dwelling-place, so that they
may gaze upon you for all eternity.
Tender and compassionate is the Lord,
patient and ready to forgive.
Lord, you promised your kingdom to those
who are humble like little children.
Lord, shine on those who dwell in spiritual darkness.

The Bishop reprimands those, especially the wealthy, who do not bring offerings of bread for Mass or send them by another person. "What rich man brings to the house of God bread for the Eucharist, or brings it with his own hands, if indeed he brings it at all to the church? Either he does not bring it at all; or if he brings it, he gives it to some insignificant person in his house to bring it, while he does not come. Happy the widow who brings her offering with her own hands; happy the poor woman who herself brings it and is proud to do so! She does not offer the bread for the Eucharist the way the rich man does. She herself brings it and prays with a sincere heart to the Lord that he deign to receive it from her hand. In a similar way the priest presents to the Lord her mourning together with her sacrifice and her prayers, when he makes a memento of the dead. She understands well how to choose offerings for the Lord and present them, but not the rich man who arranges that they be brought to the Lord as if he were a poor man."

"Welcome is the sacrifice of the poor, when it is offered covered with tears and accompanied by faith and charity: the bread of the sacrifice in the hands, tears in the eyes, praise of God in the mouth, and a sacrifice of faith in the offering! Only a sacrifice presented with love is accepted. Praise be to the Lord, who in his love has given his only Son as a sacrifice for many!" [TEP]

† † †

Send the fire of your Holy Spirit within us, O Lord, so that we can serve you with chaste bodies and please you with pure minds.
Come, let us worship God who holds the world and its wonders in his creating hand.
With simplicity of heart I have joyfully offered everything to you, my God.
Do not allow us to be overcome by evil today, but grant that we may overcome evil by doing good.
Show us your goodness in every creature, that we may contemplate your glory everywhere.

ST. FULGENTIUS, BISHOP OF RUSPE (TUNISIA), 468 - 533

The kingdom of the Vandals in northern Africa was founded the year the great St. Augustine died, 430 a.d.; and it came to an end in the year that St. Fulgentius died, 533. But during those 100 years the Church suffered persecution not only from the Vandals, but also from the Arians. One of the great defenders of the Church in north Africa was a learned follower of St. Augustine, St. Fulgentius, the Bishop of Ruspe in northern Tunisia. He was exiled along with 60 other bishops to Sardinia for his steadfastness in defending the faith. During those troublesome years St. Fulgentius was outstanding both for his learning and his virtue.

St. Fulgentius, against the heretics that wanted to divide the Church, insists on the Christian charity that makes the Church one. "The spiritual edifice of the body of Christ [the Church] is made in charity according to the words of Blessed Peter: 'The living stones [the baptized] are built into a spiritual house, into a holy priesthood to offer spiritual sacrifices that are acceptable to God through Jesus Christ.' This spiritual edifice, I say, is never asked for more appropriately than when that same body of Christ, which is the Church, offers in the sacrament of bread and chalice the very body of Christ and his blood: 'Now the chalice which we drink is the communion with the blood of Christ, and the bread which we break is a partaking of the body of the Lord. And because the bread is one, we are many in one single body and all partake of one single bread.' " [1 Co 10:16-18] [TEP]

† † †

O Holy Spirit, Soul of my soul, I adore thee.
Enlighten, guide, strengthen and console me.
Tell me what I ought to do, and command me to do it.
I promise to be submissive in everything
Thou permittest to happen to me.
Only show me what is thy holy will.
Cardinal Mercier
Father, do not allow greed to possess us, but give us understanding
to know your law and direct us according to your will.

At the Last Supper our Lord celebrated the Jewish Passover or Paschal Feast with his Apostles. That Feast commemorated the Jewish liberation from Egyptian slavery. During the celebration at the Last Supper Christ instituted the new Passover or Paschal Feast commemorating our liberation from sin though his death on the cross. During the Jewish Passover a communal cup of wine was passed around to those present probably four times: at the opening of the ceremony, just before the meal began, at the end of the meal, and at the end of the ceremony. Most likely during the meal itself our Lord instituted the New Passover by consecrating the bread; then at the third communal libation immediately after the meal he probably consecrated the wine and ordered the Apostles to perform the same dual consecration in memory of him until he would return at the end of time. Once Jesus had offered himself to the death during the dual consecration, he most likely skipped the fourth and last communal libation after singing the customary hymn.

Apparently St. Fulgentius was not aware of how the Jews celebrated their Passover. When he was asked why St. Luke in his Gospel, and St. Luke alone, mentions a communal cup of wine (probably the second in the ceremony) prior to the cup of consecration, the Bishop gives a rather unique explanation. "In other passages of the Bible the word 'cup' [chalice] can be understood in different ways according to the true faith. But in this passage of the Gospel it is not permitted to understand anything other than what the words of the Savior himself and our Teacher teach us. He says: 'This chalice is the New Testament in my blood.' Now since this chalice is called the New Testament, not without reason is the Old Testament understood in that chalice which he gave first. Thus the Lord himself gave two chalices, the Lord who gives his faithful people both Testaments." Although the dear Saint's explanation cannot be considered correct from a liturgical point of view, his conclusion is theologically sound, as is also his will to defend the truth of Scripture. May God help us all to follow the Saint's example.

On the Eucharist: "In the sacrifice itself of the body of Christ we begin by giving thanks in order to show that Christ is not to be given [in death] to us, but that he has already been given to us. In giving thanks to God in the offering of the body and blood of Christ, let us recognize that

Christ is not to die for our sins, but that he has already died, and that we are not to be redeemed by that blood, but that we have already been redeemed."

"Christ is the one 'bread come down from heaven and which gives life to the world.' And the bread that he gives is his flesh for the life of the world. That flesh is surely the flesh of the just and immortal God; and by receiving it holiness and life is given to that flesh [of ours], which is born with the penalty of death and the stain of [Original] sin."

"Now the very partaking of the body and blood of the Lord, when we eat his bread and drink his chalice, shows that we die to the world and have our life hidden with Christ in God. Likewise it shows that we crucify our flesh with its vices and concupiscences. As a result all of the faithful who love God and neighbor, although they do not drink of the chalice of physical suffering, nevertheless drink the chalice of the love of the Lord. Inebriated with the Lord, let them mortify their earthly members; and clothed with the Lord Jesus Christ, let them not indulge the flesh with its appetites; and let them not muse on what is seen but on what is not seen."

"Holy Church, when asking in the sacrifice of the body and blood of Christ that the Holy Spirit be sent to her, surely asks for the gift of charity, with which she is able to keep 'the unity of the spirit in the bond of peace.' And since it is written that 'love is as strong as death', the Church asks for the charity not only to mortify the earthly members, but also to remember our Redeemer who freely died for her." [TEP]

† † †

At daybreak be merciful to me, O God,
and make known to me the path that I must walk.
May the sick feel their companionship
with the suffering Christ.

PROCOPIUS OF GAZA (Palestine), died c. 538

Procopius of Gaza in Palestine was an outstanding representative of the School of Gaza, which was famous for its teachers of rhetoric. However, Procopius occupied himself with the study of Sacred Scripture. We quote from one of his commentaries on the Bible.

Commenting on Christ's sacrifice, which began with the Last Supper, Procopius writes: "Our High Priest Jesus, when evening began, offered in sacrifice the lamb [his body] which he had taken. With his disciples he celebrated the Paschal banquet and distributed the sacred mysteries [the Eucharist]. When the end of the Mosaic Law [Old Testament] arrived, then were established the beginnings of the Gospel [New Testament]. And he who was really a priest, but exteriorly was a Lamb, offered himself in sacrifice. If we make the sacrifice of Christ to begin at the Last Supper, the number of three days and three nights will be maintained. Like Jonah he remained sleeping in the bowels of the earth for that amount of time. Following this way of counting, we include the day of the resurrection."

"Sometimes when we hear others, we understand greater and more profound things than we would have been able to understand on our own. For example, when the eunuch heard Philip commenting on the mystery of 'Christ, after he had received Philip as a neighbor, he was helped greatly to understand that passage of the prophecy (Acts 8:32-33). Now we are all relatives and neighbors, if we attend to the sincere meaning of our faith. The Bible says [the Jews were to take a Paschal lamb] 'according to the number of persons present.' Now the heavenly and divine Lamb is accustomed to be food for souls." [TEP]

† † †

Come, worship the Lord, for we are his people,
the flock he shepherds.
From the rising of the sun to its setting
may the Lord be praised.
Holy, holy, holy! Lord God Almighty!

ST. CAESARIUS, BISHOP OF ARLES
(FRANCE), 470 - 543

St. Caesarius, a native of Gaul (France), was one of the bright lights of France in the early sixth century. The Diocese of Arles in southeastern France was granted a certain primacy in the Church of Gaul; and as a result St. Caesarius, its Bishop, had an outstanding role in the development of the Church. He had a large part in numerous local Councils. He helped destroy the last vestiges of Arianism in Gaul. As an ardent follower of St. Augustine, he not only made his own the great Doctor's teaching on grace, but he also imitated St. Augustine's easy and familiar style of speech. Indeed, St. Caesarius' greatest gift was his preaching ability; and we quote here from some of his extant sermons.

"As often as sickness strikes, let the sick person receive the body and blood of Christ."

At the time of St. Caesarius it was the custom in some places for married people to refrain from sexual contact for various days as a preparation for receiving Holy Communion. "He is a good Christian who, whenever the holy feasts arrive, maintains chastity with his own wife for various days before. He does this in order to dare approach with a free and secure conscience to the altar of the Lord with chaste body and pure heart."

"Advise the members of your families not to let spring from their lips indecent and lustful songs contrary to chastity and purity, for it is not right that there come a lustful and amorous song from that mouth into which enters the Eucharist of Christ."

The Saint has harsh words for those who leave Mass before it is finished. "I plead with you, dearest brothers, and I admonish you that no one leave the church before the divine mysteries are ended ... We rejoice at the faith and devotion of many of you. Yet there is a good number of you who are less attentive to the health of your souls; and after the reading of the divine lessons they promptly leave the church. Others, while the lessons are being read, engage in idle chatter with the result that they themselves do not hear the readings, nor do they let others hear them. We would hold such people less guilty, if they did not come to church."

The Bishop continues his instructions: "If you consider it properly, you will understand that Masses are not celebrated in the church when the divine readings are recited, but when the gifts are offered and the body and blood of the Lord are consecrated. The readings, be they from the Prophets, the Apostles or the Gospels, you yourselves can read in your homes or hear them read to others; but the consecration of the body and blood of the Lord you cannot hear or see in any other place than in the house of the Lord. Therefore, anyone wanting to hear Mass entirely and with profit to his soul must remain in church with his body in a humble position and with a contrite heart until the Lord's Prayer has been recited and the blessing has been given to the people."

Through a holy exaggeration the Bishop enhances the written word of God in one of his sermons: "I ask you, brothers and sisters, tell me: what seems greater to you, the word of God or the body of Christ? If you want to answer with the truth, you have to say that the word of God is not less than the body of Christ. Therefore the same care that we take, when the body of Christ is administered to us so that nothing falls to the floor from our hands — that same care we must take, when the word of God is preached to us, lest any of it be lost from our hearts by thinking about other things or by talking. For one will not be less guilty who hears the word of God with negligence, than one who through negligence lets the body of Christ fall to the floor."

† † †

Lord, protect and defend those who are discriminated against because of race, color, class, language or religion, that they may be accorded the rights and dignity which are theirs. Watch over your people, Lord, as the treasure of your heart, and guide their steps along safe paths that they may see your face. Lead me, Lord, in the path of your commandments.

The Bishop told his listeners how to prepare for receiving Holy Communion. "Let us clean the dwelling of our heart with great brilliance and all diligence, with fastings, vigils, almsgiving and principally with the brilliance of chastity. Let us not keep hatred in our heart toward anyone, and let us love not only our friends but also our enemies and those who are against us. Then let us recite with safe confidence the Lord's Prayer: Forgive us our trespasses, as we forgive those who trespass against us."

St. Caesarius exhorts his listeners to receive Communion at Christmas, but to receive it worthily. "By God's favor, most beloved brothers, the day is near on which we celebrate the birth of the Lord and Savior. Therefore I plead with you and admonish you, let us work as best we can with God's help, so that on that day we can approach the altar of the Lord with a pure and sincere conscience, with a clean heart and chaste body. Thus may we merit to receive his body and blood, not for our condemnation but as a remedy for our soul. For our [spiritual] life consists in the body of Christ, as the Lord himself said: 'If you do not eat the flesh of the Son of man and drink his blood, you will not have life in you.' Therefore, let anyone wishing to receive Life [Christ] change his life; because if he does not change his life, he will receive Life for his condemnation. As a result of receiving Life, such a one will be sicker rather than healed, deader than before rather than enlivened. For so said the Apostle: 'He who eats the body of the Lord and drinks his blood unworthily, eats and drinks his own condemnation.' "

"We have been invited to a wedding where we ourselves, if we do what is right, are the bride. Let us think about what kind of a wedding it is; let us consider who the groom is, and to what banquet we have been invited. We have been invited to a table on which is found not the food of men, but on which is placed the bread of angels."

† † †

On Sunday, as we celebrate the resurrection of Christ, help us, Lord, to spend the day in the spirit of joy.

"If no one would presume to approach the table of any powerful person with clothing that is torn and dirty, with how much more reverence and humility should a person withdraw from the banquet of the eternal King, that is, from the altar of the Lord, anyone who is found to be wounded with the poison of envy or hatred or filled with the fury of anger?"

The Bishop speaks of the women receiving Communion not in their hands, as the men do, but on a clean cloth they hold in their hands. "All of the men, when they approach the altar, wash their hands with water; and all the women present immaculate cloths, on which they are to receive the body of Christ. Brothers, I am not telling you something hard to understand, namely, just as the men wash their hands with water, in the same way let them wash their souls with almsgiving. Likewise the women, namely, just as they present an immaculate cloth on which to receive the body of Christ, let them also present a chaste body and a clean heart, in order to receive the sacrament of Christ with a good conscience."

"All the Christians, as I have said, who are grave sinners, the more they come to church and receive Communion at the altar, the more they are seen blessing themselves frequently; if they do not amend their lives through penitence, it is clear they do not serve Christ but the devil."

† † †

You have been told, O man, what is good, and what the Lord requires of you: Only to do what is right and to love goodness, and to walk humbly with your God. Micah 6:8

Lord, may all who died in your love share in your happiness with Mary, our Mother, and all your holy ones.

Lord Jesus, dispel the terrors of death and the darkness of error. Lead your people along safe paths, that they may rest securely in you and live forever in your Father's house.

More on receiving Communion: "And so, brothers, with the help of God let us flee mortal sins. And insisting on daily almsgiving, and with assiduous prayers, let us also make up for small sins, from which we can never be free..."

"And whenever some Feast arrives, let us come to church not only with a chaste body, but also with a pure heart. Above all, let us not keep rancor in our hearts toward anyone, for he who hates even one person let him hear what Scripture says: 'He who hates his brother is a murderer!' And if one is a murderer who hates his brother, with what conscience can he dare receive Communion at the altar of the Lord? And so, he who committed an injury, let him ask pardon promptly; and he who received the injury, let him grant pardon promptly, so that with security we can say to God in the Lord's Prayer: 'Forgive us our trespasses, as we forgive those who trespass against us.'" [TEP]

† † †

The setting sun now dies away,
And darkness comes at close of day;
Your brightest beams, dear Lord, impart,
And let them shine within our heart.

We praise your name with joy this night:
Please watch and guide us till the light;
Joining the music of the blest,
O Lord, we sing ourselves to rest.

To God the Father, God the Son,
And Holy Spirit, Three in One,
Trinity blest, whom we adore
Be praise and glory evermore.

Translator: Geoffrey Laycock
Lord, attend the dying with great mercy.

JOHN MAXENTIUS, MONK, died early 6th. century

A group of monks from Scythia in today's southern Russia and southwestern Siberia tried to win over the heretical Monophysites at the beginning of the sixth century. The most outstanding among the monks was John Maxentius, some of whose writings are still extant. We quote from a dialogue he recorded between a Nestorian and a Catholic. Both clearly believe in the Real Presence. The Catholic believes in the presence of God's body in the Eucharist, while the Nestorian believes in the presence of a man who was united to Christ from time to time. As we see, the Nestorian believes that Christ abandoned the man at the time of the Passion, so that the man suffered and died, not God. In announcing the Eucharist Christ used the title he was most fond of, "Son of Man": "If you do not eat the flesh of the Son of Man and drink his blood, you will not have life in you." (John 6:53)

"Nestorian: 'If the body of Christ is the body of God and not of the man assumed by him, then why is it not said: 'If you do not eat the flesh of God' instead of 'the flesh of the Son of Man.?'

Catholic: 'Although it be the flesh of the Son of Man, nevertheless the very flesh of the Son of Man is the flesh of God. For if it is not the flesh of God, then how can it give eternal life to those who believe?'

Nestorian: 'Because that has been given by God, who is united to that flesh.'

Catholic: 'If the flesh is united to God, how is it not the flesh of God?'

Nestorian: 'Now since you argue shamelessly against the clear words of the Gospel, I ask you, who is he who, when he approaches the Passion, says to his disciples: 'Take and eat, all of you, for this is my body, which will be broken for you for the remission of sins?' ' (Mt 26:26)

Catholic: 'The same one who said: 'I am the way, the truth, and the life.' " (John 14:6)

† † †

God's word is alive; it strikes to the heart. It pierces more surely than a two-edged sword.

CASSIODORUS, ROMAN SENATOR AND MONK, 480-570

Cassiodorus was from a noble Roman family. His family ancestors had worked in the government of Rome. While serving in the Senate in Rome he wrote works on history, morality and philosophy. At the age of 60 he left public life and established a monastery, where he lived as a lay monk. He wanted only monks who demonstrated superior intellectual abilities. As a result many fine works were produced in his monastery. However, by limiting entrance to the intellectuals he caused the collapse of his monastery, which hardly outlived him. St. Benedict took up where Cassiodorus left off and established the famous monasteries at Subiaco and Mount Cassino. The religious works of Cassiodorus, however, caused him to be declared one of the first theological Doctors of the Middle Ages.

Cassiodorus associates the Mass with Psalm 16:4, which says: "Their idols are multiplied, and they run after them." The monk writes: "Christ speaks to them who are not to assemble with the blood of animals, nor with the custom of immolating [animal] victims. Rather they are to assemble for the immolation of his body and blood, which, having been celebrated throughout the world, has saved the human race."

St. Paul writes in 1Co 11:28: "Let a man examine himself and so eat that bread and drink the chalice." The monk writes: "If [the Eucharist] cannot be placed on a dirty cloth or in a dirty vase — no one dares to do that — how much less must it be received with a dirty heart? That kind of dirt God abhors above all other things, and that dirt alone does injury to his body. Joseph [of Arimathea], that just man, buried the body of the Lord wrapped in a clean sheet and in a clean sepulcher." St. Paul continues: "For he who eats and drinks unworthily eats and drinks his own condemnation." The monk says: "He who approaches unworthily is doubly guilty. He is guilty of sin and of usurpation. "He does not make proper discernment of the body of the Lord." "He receives it as if it were ordinary food." [TEP]

† † †

Praise the Lord for his infinite greatness.

VERECUNDUS, BISHOP OF JUNCA
(Tunisia) died 552.

Verecundus was Bishop of Junca in modern Tunisia on the northern coast of Africa. He is known as a Biblical exegete and has left us numerous commentaries on Sacred Scripture. We quote from his commentary on the Song of Moses in Deut.32, where it says that God gives the Jews rich food of the pastures and blood of the fermenting grape for drink.

"The blood of the grape is the blood of the martyrs or, surely, the blood shed in the very Passion of the Lord, blood with which we fill ourselves daily at the sacred altars, blood that inebriates the mind, so that we lay aside earthly things and take up the heavenly ones. Therefore, one who has been filled with such a drink says [with the Psalmist]: 'How noble is the chalice that inebriates.' "

Verecundus comments on Bible passages stating that God feeds his people, such as in Deut 33:19: "He keeps them alive in famine," and Psalm 23:1: "The Lord is my shepherd; I shall not want." The Bishop comments: "The Lord feeds us not only with bodily food, but also with spiritual food ... Without doubt he feeds us with the words of Scripture, with the knowledge of those words, with the provisions of the body of Christ, and with the drink of his blood that is offered on the sacred altars." [TEP]

† † †

Guide us as we work; and teach us to live in the spirit that has made us your sons and daughters, in the love that has made us brothers and sisters.
Watch over the priests and deacons of your Church, so that after they

293

have preached to others they themselves may remain faithful in your
service.
How happy are we who have the Lord for our God. We are the people
he chose as his inheritance.
Help us to meet this day's responsibilities, and let nothing separate
us from your love.
How good is God to the pure of heart!
I long to be in God's holy dwelling-place.

PRIMASIUS, BISHOP OF HADRUMETUM (AFRICA), died c. 552

Hadrumetum in northern Africa. His only extant work is a commentary on the Book of Revelations, from which we quote:

"Now if the grace [of martyrdom] is given to all the faithful in general, one should aspire to the highest degree of that grace, for one is aided in this aspiration if he is washed in the font of his Lord [baptism], eats the flesh of the Lamb [Eucharist], and is inflamed with spiritual fire [Confirmation]. There are some who, although they are not seen to undergo martyrdom by a public act, nevertheless in God's eyes they undergo martyrdom habitually by serving God day and night, that is, in good times and in bad."

Revelations 2:17 says: "If anyone has ears to hear, let him listen to what the Spirit is saying to the churches: to those who prove victorious I will give the hidden manna." The Bishop comments: "The hidden manna, that is, the invisible bread come down from heaven [Jn 6:51], who became man precisely so that man might eat the bread of angels."

"The Church has received 'all power in heaven and on earth,' while she makes present the sacrifice of God, with the Lord offering himself in the first place and with the saints offering their bodies as a living and holy victim."

Primasius writes: "St. Paul says: 'All these things [in the history of the Old Testament] were figures [warnings] for us,' 'and just as God fed the

Jews with visible manna, so now he feeds the Church with food from heaven." [TEP]

† † †

Jesus, Mary, Joseph, I give you my heart and my soul.
What joy to see a family united in love!
The blessing of God rest upon it.
Shed upon your Church the rays of your glory, that it may be seen as
the gate of salvation open to all nations.
When your heart is torn with grief, the Lord is near you.
Help us to spend this day for your glory
and our neighbor's good.

FACUNDUS, BISHOP OF HERMIANE (TUNISIA), died c. 571

Facundus, Bishop of Hermiane in modern Tunisia on Africa's northern coast, was an ardent admirer of St. Augustine of neighboring Hippo, whom, he called "the principal preacher of the Catholic faith." Facundus was a vigorous fighter for what he believed to be true, but unfortunately he did not have the intellectual humility of St. Augustine. While he maintained belief in all of Catholic doctrine, he refused to submit to the authority of the Pope in a current dogmatic controversy.

Regarding the Eucharist Bishop Facundus insisted that it is indeed proper to speak of receiving the body and blood of Christ: "The faithful of Christ, who receive his body and blood, with reason are said to receive the body and blood of Christ."

Facundus quotes St. John, Chapter 6, containing the promise of the Eucharist by Christ. The Bishop makes little comment, because he believes the words are so clear that they need no comment. But he does comment of verse 66, in which St. John speaks of the disciples who did not believe in Christ's promise and left him: "After this many of his disciples left him and stopped going with him." The Bishop says: "Here is the impatient spirit of reason [that is, the spirit of one who rejects as false whatever he does not understand] and the spirit that defies authority. That is the spirit by which the heretics are carried about, when they are more eager to be scandalized and march away than they are to learn." Unfortunately the Bishop himself succumbed to that spirit, when he defied the authority of the Pope and died in schism. [TEP]

† † †

What does the Lord, your God, ask of you but to fear the Lord, your God, and follow his ways exactly, to love and serve the Lord, your God, with all your heart and all your soul? We praise you because you are rich in mercy and for the abundant love with which you have loved us. It is by way of admonition that the Lord chastises those who are close to him. Judith 8:27

Sing for joy, God's chosen ones; give him the praise that is due.

ST. GREGORY OF TOURS (FRANCE), died c. 593

St. Gregory was born in Claremont-Ferrand, France, of a noble Gallo-Roman family of the senatorial class. He received the best literary and religious education available at that time. When he fell ill, he made a pilgrimage to the tomb of St. Martin of Tours, where he was cured. Ten years later the people of Tours chose him for their bishop.

St. Gregory is important not only as a literary figure but also as a politician and bishop. His literary works were extensive and principally in history, especially the history of the Franks, one of the invading tribes that settled mostly in today's France. He wrote in a form of Latin that some call "rustic," but which was common among the elite of his day. Gregory gives witness to the dawn of the Romance languages, which have Latin as their root. Latin had prevailed throughout the Roman Empire extending in the West to Britain. It was only natural that, after the invading tribes of Franks in Gaul and Goths in Spain and Italy had settled down for some 200 years, they adopted the Latin language and made some changes in it by way of additions and subtractions from their native languages with modifications that reflected their patterns of thought.

In St. Gregory's day there was political turmoil throughout Europe, including Gaul, where the Frankish chieftains were quarreling among themselves and unable to maintain social stability. As more pagans embraced Christianity they looked to the bishops to fill the political vacuum. Thus it was that the bishops grew in importance politically. They maintained that importance throughout Europe through the Middle Ages, even after the various nations were born. Several Frankish kings and chieftains recognized Gregory's influence and importance in the political field.

† † †

I love you, Lord; you are my strength. You keep me safe; your mighty power protects me.
Blessed are they who hunger and thirst for holiness, for they shall be satisfied.
Let the word of Christ, rich as it is, dwell in you.

As an historian St. Gregory wrote on the lives of various Saints and the many miracles (true or alleged) that people of that time liked to read about. We quote from one of his books on miracles:

"We weep for our crimes and lament them without knowing if we are clean. When we are stained with sin and approach the very altar of the

Lord, we daringly take his holy body and blood more for our condemnation than to receive pardon. I recall an incident, which as a youth I heard had taken place. It happened on the day of the commemoration of the passion of the great martyr, St. Polycarp. In the village of Rigomage near Arvernia they were celebrating the Saint's Feast. After the reading of the passion of the martyr and the other readings that introduce the priestly canon, the time arrived for the offering of the sacrifice. The deacon took the tower [tabernacle in circular form], in which was kept the mystery of the body of the Lord, and began to carry it to the door. When he entered the church to put it on the altar, it slipped out of his hands and was carried through the air. In this way it came to rest on the altar without the hand of the deacon being able to reach it. We believe that this happened for no other reason than that the deacon's conscience was stained ... Only one priest and three women, one of whom was my mother, were permitted to see this. The rest of the people did not see it. I confess that I too was present at that Feast, but I did not merit to see it." [TEP]

✝ ✝ ✝

Lord, help married couples with an abundance of your grace, so that they may better symbolize the mystery of your Church.
For the aged: Stay with us, Lord Jesus, for evening draws near. Be our companion on our way to set our hearts on fire with new hope.
Father, help us to work generously for the salvation of the world, so that your Church may bring us and all mankind into your presence.
Lord, do not let us be drawn into the current of this passing world, but free us from every evil and raise our thoughts to our heavenly home.
Heal our hearts wounded by hatred and jealousy.

Chapter X

THE EUCHARIST IN THE 6th & 7th CENTURIES

ESIQUIUS, ABBOT, 6th & 7th Century

Little is known about Esiquius, other than that he was Abbot of a monastery in the Sinai peninsula, south of Israel and east of Egypt, where God had appeared to Moses and given him the Ten Commandments. It is not certain when Esiquius lived, although it was surely in the sixth or seventh century.

In an article on temperance and virtue Abbot Esiquius refers to the Eucharist in a way that is beautiful but open to misinterpretation by us. Just what the Abbot had in mind cannot be determined from the few words of his that we have on the subject of Holy Communion. His words can be understood exactly what we know today after centuries of development of doctrine under the guidance of the Holy Spirit and the magisterium of the Church. However, his words can be understood in a way that would be false to Catholic teaching. In order to understand the Abbot's beautiful words correctly, let us briefly review what we know today regarding the disposition of soul required for the fruitful reception of Holy Communion.

We recall that St. Paul said that to receive Communion unworthily is to eat and drink one's own condemnation. Surely to receive Holy Communion when one is conscious of being in mortal sin is to receive it unworthily. The recent Catechism of the Catholic Church, n.1385, confirmed what we have long been taught, namely: "Anyone conscious of a grave [mortal] sin must receive the sacrament of Reconciliation [Confession] before coming to Communion." The reason, of course, is obvious. Since the principal sacramental grace of Holy Communion is a feeding grace, one that nourishes the life of God (sanctifying grace) in the soul, obviously it cannot nourish a life that has been destroyed by mortal sin. Therefore one conscious of mortal sin must not approach for Communion.

† † †

Bring to a harvest worthy of heaven the praise
we offer you this day.
Let us love in deed and in truth
and not merely talk about it. (1Jn3:18)
Listen, my people, to my teaching;
give ear to the words I speak.

Although it is widely known that one who is conscious of mortal sin may not receive Holy Communion, what about a person who has committed mortal sin and, due to a lack of memory or a sincere belief that the sin has been forgiven in sacramental Confession, he is no longer conscious of being in the state of mortal sin? If he is no longer attached to the sin because he has attrition or sorrow for the sin for some supernatural motive (e.g. loss of heaven or fear of hell), when he receives Communion, his mortal sin is forgiven and he enjoys God's friendship. Since attrition (in the meaning just mentioned) is sufficient to receive forgiveness of mortal sin by the absolution of the priest in Confession, surely the same disposition of soul is sufficient to receive that forgiveness by the entry of Christ in Communion. Although this conclusion is not a definitive teaching of the Church, it is nevertheless the common opinion of theologians who are accepted by the Church. St. Thomas Aquinas (Summa T., P.3,Q.79, A 3) says: "This sacrament [Eucharist] can effect the forgiveness of sin...when received by one in mortal sin of which he is not conscious, and for which he has no attachment...By approaching this sacrament devoutly and reverently he obtains the grace of charity, which will perfect his contrition and bring forgiveness of sin."

After these preliminary remarks we can read the Abbot's words with more understanding: "When we, unworthy as we are, are admitted, not without fear and trembling, to the divine and immaculate mysteries of Christ, our God and King, we should should demonstrate temperance and perfect watch over our mind. This, so that the divine fire, that is, the body of our Lord Jesus Christ, consumes our sins, dispels from our hearts the wicked spirits of evil, forgives the sins we have committed, and the soul is free of the disturbances of evil thoughts. And if after Communion we watch our soul diligently and monitor the doors of our heart, when we are admitted again to Communion, the divine body fills the soul more and more with splendor and makes it like a star." [TEP]

Dawn finds me watching, crying out to you, O Lord.

Chapter XI

THE EUCHARIST IN THE SEVENTH CENTURY

EVAGRIUS SCHOLASTICUS, died c. 601

Evagrius was a lawyer in Antioch of Syria. He enjoyed the esteem of the Patriarch of Antioch, whom he defended several times before the Eastern Roman Emperor at Constantinople. Evagrius himself was in favor at the imperial court. His great accomplishment was being an outstanding historian of his period. His Ecclesiastical History treated the Christological controversies for nearly 200 years up to his own day. He records what he calls "the ancient custom in Constantinople" of having little children of grammar school age consume the Hosts left over after Mass, if there were too many to keep in the tabernacle. "It is an ancient custom in Constantinople that when a great quantity of sacred parts [Hosts] of the immaculate body of Christ our God remain [after Mass], they call little children of those in grammar schools to eat them."

Evagrius, whom the historian Altaner accuses of being credulous regarding miracles, writes: "On one of these occasions [when little children were called to consume the Hosts] the son of a Jewish glass maker was among the children called. That boy, when asked by his parents why he was late from school, told them what had happened and what he had eaten with the the children. The father, inflamed with anger, took the child and threw him into the burning furnace, in which he baked glass. The mother, looking for her child and not being able to find him, ran through the city crying and shouting."

"On the third day the mother, standing at the door of her husband's office...began to call her son by name. The child, recognizing the voice of his mother, answered from the furnace. She broke open the doors and entered. She saw her son standing among the burning wood without the fire ever touching him. When asked how he had remained unharmed, he said a lady in a purple dress had come to him frequently, given him water, extinguished the burning wood near him, and given him something to eat."

"When notice of these things came to the knowledge of Emperor Justinian, he made the boy a lector and his mother a deaconess, after they were baptized. But he ordered the father, who refused to become a Christian, to be crucified as a killer of his son. This is true." [TEP]

POPE ST. GREGORY THE GREAT, died 604

Pope St. Gregory I is known in history as Gregory the Great, due to his outstanding character and achievements. He was born in Rome of the nobility and for a while dedicated himself to political affairs. Soon he felt the call to the religious life. He sold his many possessions, donated much to charity, and built seven monasteries. He lived in the last one as a monk.

He was the first monk to become pope. He naturally nourished the religious life in the Church and favored the Benedictines, who acted as a conquering army of the Roman Church for the conversion of the barbarians who had invaded Europe. St. Gregory made their conversion one of his priorities. To convert England he sent St. Augustine and forty Benedictines.

Pope Gregory initiated and extended the temporal power of the popes, who used their resources to assist the Roman populace, who had been practically abandoned by the Eastern Roman Emperor residing in Constantinople in Greece. By his many interventions Gregory made the primacy of the pope felt universally throughout the Church, while he applied to himself the now famous title of "Servant of the Servants of God."

Many of St. Gregory's oratorical, moral and liturgical writings are still extant. His work in the liturgy is of particular interest to us. Our Kyrie Eleison in its present form is from him. The Gregorian Sacramentary [Mass book] was issued by Gregory. He developed the existing Roman liturgical melody into Gregorian chant. From his insistence that Mass be said with some solemnity comes our expression that Mass is "celebrated." He continued the custom of Mass in private homes, and he introduced the responsorial chants at Mass.

✝ ✝ ✝

Your word, O Lord, guides my steps as a lantern and lights up my pathway before me.
Lord, do not let us be drawn into the current of this passing world, but free us from every evil and raise our thoughts to our heavenly home.

In commenting on the Parable of the Good Shepherd, who left the ninety-nine sheep in the desert to look for the lost one, St. Gregory refers the ninety-nine to the angels in heaven that Christ left to come to earth in search of man. With reference to the Good Shepherd who gives his life for the sheep the Pope says: "He did what he recommended; he demonstrated what he commanded. The Good Shepherd gave his life for the sheep even to the point of putting his body and blood in our sacrament and filling the sheep he had redeemed with the food of his own flesh."

In one of his Dialogues St. Gregory writes:

"Peter: What can be done to benefit the souls of the dead?

Gregory: If after death one's sins are not unpardonable, that is, if one does not die in mortal sin, it is usual that the sacred offering of the saving Host helps souls a great deal also after death. Indeed, it seems that sometimes even the souls themselves of the deceased ask for that offering [Mass]."

Regarding the custom of Gregorian Masses [Masses said on thirty consecutive days for the deceased], which take their name from Pope Gregory, he writes the following: "Thirty days after the death of the monk Justus my soul began to feel sorry for the deceased brother, to ponder his pains with great sorrow, and to search for a remedy to free him, if indeed one existed. Then I called Precious, the Superior of our monastery, and with sorrow I said to him: 'It has been a long time that our dead brother has been tormented by fire. We must do something for him out of charity and help him as much as we can to be free of punishment. Go, therefore, and see to it that beginning today the sacrifice is offered for him for thirty consecutive days. By no means let a day pass without the Host of salvation being offered for his forgiveness.' The Superior left immediately and did what I said."

307

"... Justus appeared one night in a vision to his carnal brother, Copius, who asked : 'How are you brother?' Justus replied: 'Until today I had been feeling bad, but today I feel good, because I have reached union with God in heaven.' ..It was on that very day that the thirtieth offering [Mass] had been made for Justus."

The Pope warns not to depend too much on Masses for one's self after death. "Among other things it must be considered that it is safer to do for one's self during life that good which everyone hopes others will do for one after death. For it is better to exit this life free of punishment than to seek such freedom after it has been lost. And so it is that we must dispose the present time with all our soul, because we see how it passes, and offer to God daily sacrifices of tears and daily Hosts of his flesh and blood.'

"For only this Victim saves the soul from eternal death. In mystery he makes present for us the death of the Only-begotten Son. Although 'rising from he dead he dies no more, and death has no more dominion over him,' nevertheless living immortal and incorruptible he is immolated again for us in this mystery of the sacred oblation [Mass]. For there his body is received; his flesh is distributed for the salvation of the people; his blood is poured out now, not in the hands of unbelievers, but in the mouths of the faithful." [TEP]

✝ ✝ ✝

EVENING HYMN BY POPE ST. GREGORY I

Blessed Creator of light who sendest forth the light of day,
Who didst begin creation by making the first light,
Who ordainest morn and even to be called day;
The dark night falls, hear the prayers we make with tears.
Let not our souls heavy with sin lose the gift of life,
Lest forgetting eternal things they bind themselves in sin.
But let them knock at the door of heaven,
let them gain the prize of life.

May we flee from crime and cleanse ourselves of evil.
Help us, most loving Father, and thou the only-begotten equal to the
Father
With the Holy Ghost, reigning for all ages.

Translator: A. Fortescue

Lord, do not direct world leaders to give attention only to the
needs of their own nations, but give them respect and deep concern for
all peoples.

More on the Mass: "Now with these things in mind let us ponder what this sacrifice is for us, this sacrifice which always re-presents the passion of the Only-begotten Son for our forgiveness. For who among the faithful can doubt that at the very hour of the sacrifice the heavens are opened at the voice of the priest, that in that mystery of Jesus Christ the choirs of angels are present, that the things of earth are united to the things of heaven, and that things visible and invisible are made one?"

"It is necessary, when we offer Mass, that we immolate ourselves to God with heartfelt sorrow; for we who celebrate the mysteries of the passion of our Lord, must imitate what we do. For then indeed it will be an offering to God for us, when we make ourselves the offering."

"We say the Lord's Prayer immediately after the Canon [Eucharistic Prayer], for it was the custom of the Apostles to consecrate the Host of the offering with the Canon only. And it seems improper to me that we say over the oblation of the body and blood of the Lord a prayer composed by learned men and not the one composed by our Redeemer. Moreover the Lord's Prayer is said by the entire congregation among the Greeks but among us by the priest alone." [TEP]

† † †

309

OLDEST KNOWN LATIN EUCHARISTIC HYMN

Come, all ye holy, take the body of your Lord,
Drink of his chalice, take the blood for you outpoured.
Saved by his body, by his sacred blood, we raise
Grateful our voices unto God in hymns of praise.
Giver of life, he, Christ our Savior, Son of God,
Bought our redemption by his cross and precious blood.
Dying for all men, he, the Lord, prepared this feast,
Offered as victim, offering himself as priest.
God to our fathers ordered sacrifice of old;
So he in symbols Christ the victim true foretold.
Giver of light, the one Redeemer of our race,
He to his holy servants gives abundant grace.
Come, who with pure hearts in the Savior's words believe;
Come, and partaking saving grace from him receive
God our defender, guardian sure in this our strife,
Gives to his faithful after death eternal life.
He to the hungry gives as food this heavenly bread,
Fountain of life, he gives to drink the blood he shed.
Christ, source of all things, who here feeds us sinful men,
When his great day dawns, judge of all, will come again.

Text: from 7th. century Bangor antiphonary. Tr. A. Fortescue

The way we can be sure of our knowledge of Christ is to keep his
commandments. 1Jn.

ST. ISIDORE OF SEVILLE (SPAIN), c.560-636

After following the religious life in a monastery for some time, St. Isidore succeeded his brother, St. Leander, as Archbishop of Seville in Spain. Because of his efforts in restoring studies in Spain after the invasion of the Goths, and especially because of his innumerable literary works, the Church has declared him a Doctor of the Church. Just as Pope St. Gregory the Great witnessed the beginnings of the Italian language with his "rustic" Latin, so too St. Isidore witnessed the beginnings of the Spanish language with his Latin "corrupted" by so many foreign words. Both men were educators of the early Middle Ages.

St. Isidore: "The Greeks call the sacrament of the bread and wine 'Eucharist', which in Latin means 'good grace.' And what better thing is there than the body and blood of Christ?"

On sacramental grace: "The sacraments are performed with benefit in the Church, because the Holy Spirit, who is in the Church, in a hidden manner produces the very effect of the sacraments. For this reason, whether the sacraments be administered in the Church of God by good or bad ministers, the benefits of the sacraments are not increased by the merits of the good ministers, nor are they decreased by the merits of the bad ministers. The reason is that it is the Holy Spirit, who in Apostolic times manifested himself by visible works, now gives the sacraments life in a mystical way ... For this reason the sacraments are called 'mysteries' in Greek, because they contain something secret and hidden."

On disposition for Communion: "Those in the Church who lead bad lives and do not stop receiving Communion, because they believe that with Communion they will be purified, let them know that Communion does nothing for their purification. As the Prophet Jeremiah says: 'What is this, that my beloved has committed many evils in my house? Can consecrated meat rid you of your guilt?' (Jr 11:15) And St. Paul says: 'Let a man examine himself, and so eat of that bread and drink from the chalice.' " (1Co 11:28).

St. Isidore believes that "daily bread" in the Our Father refers to both material and spiritual food: "Here [in the Our Father] daily bread is asked for, bread that is given for the soul and the body."

On the institution of the Eucharist: "Now the sacrifice, which is offered to God by Christians, Christ our Lord and Teacher first instituted, when he entrusted to the Apostles his body and blood before he was handed over. As it is read in the Gospel: 'Jesus took bread and the chalice and, blessing them, gave them to the Apostles.' "

On the Eucharistic fast: "There is mystery in the fact that the first time the Apostles received the body and blood of the Lord, they did not receive them fasting. But throughout the entire Church now they are always received by those who are fasting. For thus it pleased the Holy Spirit through the Apostles that, in honor of so great a sacrament the Lord's body enter the mouth of a Christian before the other food; and therefore this custom is observed throughout the whole world. For the bread that we break is the body of Christ, who said: 'I am the living bread come down from heaven.' And the wine is his blood, and this is what is written: ' I am the true vine.' But the bread, because it strengthens the body, therefore it is called the body of Christ; and the wine, because it produces blood in the flesh, therefore it refers to his blood."

These words of St. Isidore need a little explanation. For him bread and wine are "the truest sacrament" or truest sign of the body and blood of Christ. In a word, Christ "very properly" chose bread to be changed into his body, because bread strengthens the body. Likewise he "very properly" chose wine to be changed into his blood, because [it was thought] wine produces blood in one's body. Therefore bread and wine are "the truest sacrament" or truest sign of what is present, namely, the body and blood of Christ.

† † †

HYMN TO THE BLESSED MOTHER (7th. century)

Hail, star of the sea, blessed Mother of God and ever virgin, happy gate of heaven.
Receiving that Ave from the mouth of Gabriel, establish us in peace, changing the name of Eve (Eva).
Loosen the chains of sinners, give light to the blind, drive away our ills, obtain for us all good things.

Show thyself a mother; may he hear thy prayers who, born for us, was willing to be thy Son.
Virgin above all others, meeker than all, make us free from sin, meek and pure.

Translator: Adrian Fortescue

On dispositions for Communion: "Some say that, if there is no sin to prohibit one, the Eucharist should be received daily, for by the Lord's command we ask that this bread be given us daily: 'Give us this day our daily bread.' This is well said, if they receive it with reverence, devotion and humility and not because, out of a presumption due to pride, they trust in their own holiness. As to the rest, if there are sins that separate one, as if dead, from the altar, he must first do penance; only then must this saving medication be received. For one who eats unworthily, eats and drinks his own judgment. And this is to receive unworthily, when one receives when one should be doing penance [for his mortal sin]."

On the necessity of Communion: "Now if there be no sins great enough that one be judged separated from Communion, he should not remain away from the medicine of the Lord's body; lest perhaps if he abstain from Communion for a long time, he be separated from the body of Christ. It is manifest that they live who receive his body. Therefore it is to be feared that, while one is separated from the body of Christ for a long time, he remain alien to salvation. For Christ himself says: 'If you do not eat the flesh of the Son of Man and drink his blood, you have no life in you.' Let him who has stopped sinning not stop receiving Communion."

On Mass for the dead: "Since it is observed throughout the whole world, we believe that to offer a sacrifice for the faithful departed and to pray for them is a custom handed down from the Apostles themselves. For the Catholic Church has this custom everywhere; and if she did not believe that the sins of the faithful departed are forgiven, she would not offer for their souls alms and sacrifice to God.... Furthermore, when the Lord says: 'He who sins against the Holy Spirit will not be forgiven in this world or in the next' [Mt 12:32], he shows that sins are to be forgiven there for some people, and that they are to be purified with some purging fire." [TEP]

† † †

Bless the work we have begun, Lord, make good its defects, and let us finish it in a way that pleases you.

ST. SOPHRONIUS, PATRIARCH OF JERUSALEM, c.550-638

St. Sophronius was born about 550 in Damascus, the Capital of Syria. He made several journeys throughout the Middle East and lived for a while as a monk in Alexandria in Egypt, before he was elected Patriarch of Jerusalem in 634. He was the first to denounce the new heresy, called Monothelitism, which held that Christ did not have a human will, but only a divine one. Much of his tenure as Patriarch was taken up fighting that heresy, which denied Christ a true human nature. That heresy was condemned by the seventh ecumenical council, the Third of Constantinople, in 680-681. The Council solemnly declared that the one Person, Christ, has two complete natures, divine and human, and consequently two wills.

The Muslims date the beginning of their era in the year 622 with Mohammed's flight (Hegira) from Mecca to Medina in Arabia. He united all the tribes of Arabia into a politico-religious system that he called Islam [surrender, that is, to God]. With an army of 40,000 men Islam spread throughout the Middle East to Constantinople, all along the northern coast of Africa, and throughout Spain. Jerusalem was attacked about 635. The Patriarch Sophronius helped to defend the Holy City and finally negotiated a surrender. In exchange for an annual tribute the Patriarch obtained civil and religious liberty for the Christians. In most of the territory conquered by Islam the Christian communities were obliterated or reduced to insignificance.

✝ ✝ ✝

HYMN TO THE BLESSED MOTHER (c. 600 a.d.)

Glorious among virgins, high above the stars,
thou didst nourish at thy breast
as a child him who created thee.
What unhappy Eve lost thou
dost restore by thy holy Child;
thou dost open the gates of heaven
that sinners may rise to the stars.
Thou art queen of the gates on high
and of the shining halls of light.
People redeemed,
praise the life given through the Virgin.
Jesus, to thee be glory
who art born of the Virgin,
with the Father and the Holy Ghost for ever and ever.

Text: Venantius Fortunatus   Translator: Adrian Fortescue

The Patriarch of Jerusalem wrote a long work on the Egyptian martyrs, Cyrus and John, who were venerated greatly in Alexandria. St. Sophronius believed he owed the preservation of his sight to those martyrs. We quote from his long work containing accounts of many miracles attributed to the two martyrs.

The Patriarch writes of a curious custom with reference to an olive oil lamp that burned in honor of the two martyrs in a church dedicated to them: "Instead of receiving the body and blood of Christ, the Lord and God of us all, many take some oil from the lamp of the Saints without knowing, I believe, what they are doing and without realizing the magnitude of their offense. Yes, I too say that the oil of the lamp has been sanctified. But what is that in comparison to the One Who sanctifies the Saints themselves?"

315

St. Cyrus, the Martyr, says to a non-Catholic: "Truly, brother, I have ardently wished that you would accept our faith, and that I would hear you say those words: 'Amen, Amen, O Lord.' " The non-Catholic then understood that Cyrus was speaking of the reception of the mysteries of Christ [Holy Communion]. Sophronius continues: "At the moment of reception of Holy Communion is when we give that response to the priests distributing the vivifying and salvation-laden body and blood of Jesus Christ, our God. Thus we give testimony with our own words as to what the priests distribute, namely, that it is really, and is said to be, for our spiritual nourishment and for the remission of sins."

† † †

We thank you then, dear Father,
For all things bright and good:
The seedtime and the harvest,
Our life, our health, our food.
And all that we can offer
Your boundless love imparts;
The gifts to you most pleasing
Are humble, thankful hearts.

Text: M. Claudius. Tr.: Jane M. Campbell

St. Sophronius relates the conversion of one Peter, a paralytic, to the true faith. "The most fervent martyrs [Cyprus and John] presented themselves to Peter, the paralytic, in a dream and spoke to him kindly and sweetly: 'Do you want to enjoy good health and overcome this disease, which is the worst of all ailments?' Peter immediately accepted the proposition and said 'Yes' with his lips and indicated the same with his head. He moved his hands as best he could and expressed his desires in that way. The martyrs, seeing his ardent desire for health, by way of an option said: 'If you want to be free of this disease, get up and enter the precious Jordan.' (By that name, says Sophronius, the people of Alexandria in Egypt designate the font of holy baptism, because our Lord Jesus Christ was baptized in the river Jordan for our purification.) Bathing yourself there, receive in your hands the mysteries of Christ [Communion] which are there. Show with your hands the life-giving and happy reception of the body and blood of Christ.' When Peter heard this, he said it as a wicked proposition, and he cursed the Council of Chalcedon, even though he knew well who they were that formed that Council. [In the year 451 the Council of Chalcedon in western Turkey was the third Ecumenical Council. It reaffirmed that in Christ there is only one person but two complete natures, divine and human. It condemned the Monophysite heresy, that held there was only the divine nature in Christ. That heresy was favored by many in Egypt.] The Egyptians have a great hatred for that Council with an irrational and incredible sentiment, just as their fathers and forefathers had against the Jewish people at an earlier time. For this reason Peter said he did not want to obtain health nor conform his faith to the Council of Chalcedon." Sophronius writes that later, as his pain grew more severe, Peter accepted the faith of the holy martyrs.

From the Patriarch's poetry about the Last Supper: "When He, who is the Lamb of God the Father, ate the lamb of Moses, in place of the lamb of the Old Law He put himself—marvel of marvels...Oh love, oh charity, with which Christ gave to men his own flesh as food." [TEP]

ST. MAXIMUS THE CONFESSOR,
c.580-662 (Middle East)

St. Maximus, born of a noble Greek family, was for a time the chief secretary of one of the Eastern Roman Emperors residing in Constantinople. After renouncing all earthly honors, Maximus entered a monastery, where he made his religious profession. When he opposed an Emperor who dabbled in theology and liked to play bishop and pope, the Emperor exiled him, subjected him to torture, and finally executed him for his adherence to the true faith. Thus Maximus died a martyr after earning the title of Confessor for his staunch defense of the faith.

St. Maximus traveled throughout the Middle East and north Africa opposing the new heresy of Monothelitism, which claimed that Christ had only a divine will. It denied Christ a human will and, consequently, a complete human nature. From his extant works on religion we see that St. Maximus was also a theologian. We quote here from his commentaries on the very important theological works of one calling himself Dionysius the Areopagite:

"For what reason is the Church accustomed to use an uneven number of breads and chalices when presenting the precious body and blood of the Lord? All of those things which are done in the Church have a sublime reason. Now, since mainly these symbols [bread and chalice] are mysteries and images of the divine substance, which is simple; and since every creature is composite and the divine substance alone is simple and without composition, therefore the Church sets forth the breads and chalices in an uneven number, thus signifying with them the Divinity."

† † †

Lord Jesus Christ, be present now,
And let your Holy Spirit bow
All hearts in love and truth today
To hear your word and keep your way.

Text: Anonymous   Tr.: Catherine Winkworth

Lord, may this day's work be pleasing to you.

In giving a brief description of the Mass ceremonies St. Maximus begins thus: "The blessed elder [Dionysius the Areopagite] judged that it was proper—and never stopped exhorting every Christian—to frequent the holy church of God and never leave off the sacred Mass, which takes place there. And this, not only because of the holy angels that assist at Mass, and who always note each one who enters, give an account of it to God, and finally pray for them. But another reason for assisting at Mass is the grace of the Holy Spirit, who in an invisible way is surely always present but in a special and particular way during the time of Mass. He is there changing and transforming each of those present, truly molding them to be more divine according to their abilities... In the sacred partaking of the immaculate and life-giving mysteries [Holy Communion] there is a certain communion and identity with God, which we receive by way of a likeness to him and by which man is judged worthy to come from being a man to be God." [TEP] In this regard it should be noted that some Church Fathers speak of our becoming God or like God or divinized in the sense that through Sanctifying Grace, which the Eucharist gives us in abundance, we share God's life and his very nature in so far as human beings can do that. In the parable of the vine and the branches Christ taught that we share his life: "I am the vine; you are the branches." And St. Peter in 2Peter 1:4 speaks of our sharing in the divine nature.

† † †

O Father, whose creating hand
Brings harvest from the fruitful land,
Your providence we gladly own,
And bring our hymns before your throne
To praise you for the living Bread
On which our lives are daily fed.

Donald Hughes

*May this day bring us closer to salvation.**

ANASTASIUS SINAITA, ABBOT (PALESTINE) 630-700

Anastasius was abbot of one of the monasteries on the Holy Mountain, Mt. Sinai, where God had given Moses the Ten Commandments. The Abbot spent much of his life fighting the Monophysite heresy, which denied Christ a true human nature. Only a few of his extensive writings remain:

"It is wrong for Timothy [a Monophysite heretic] to say: 'In Christ, even after the Incarnation, there is no more than one nature, the divine one.' Now if Christ is only divinity, and the divinity cannot be seen, nor touched, nor sacrificed, nor does it have members nor can it be eaten, it is evident that Timothy, along with the Jews, denies the sacrifice and communion of the sacred mysteries [Eucharist]. Nor does he believe or really confess that the body and blood of Christ are something visible, created and earthly, which the priest gives to the people with these words: 'Body and blood of our Lord, God and Savior, Jesus Christ.' ... Timothy should say to the communicant: 'Only the divinity of our Lord Jesus Christ.' ... For Timothy, the Incarnation is a fable."

In one of his works the Abbot answers questions. "Question. What sins are forgiven after death by the liturgical celebrations, prayers, and alms, all of which are offered for those who have died? Answer. If the sins [of the deceased] are light and of little gravity, the deceased receives some benefit from those things which are done for him. But if his sins are great and grave, God excludes him from Himself. Therefore we must look after our own souls and not hope that after death we will be pardoned through the offerings of others."

† † †

We turn to you that we may be forgiven
For crucifying Christ on earth again.
We know that we have never wholly striven,

Forgetting self, to love the other man.

Fred Kaan

Heal our hearts wounded by hatred and jealousy.

The Abbot continues answering questions. "Question. If while washing one's mouth or bathing one drinks water without wanting to, may he receive Communion or not? [Obviously the Eucharistic fast from midnight was observed at that time in that place.] Answer. Yes. Because if the devil finds an occasion to bar one from Communion, he will see to it continually that one drinks involuntarily. For this same reason the Fathers do not forbid one to receive Communion in such circumstances, nor one who has suffered nocturnal fantasies. Nevertheless when approaching the divine mysteries [Communion] let us do so with fear, as the woman with a hemorrhage approached Christ." [Luke 8:47]

"Question. Is it better to receive Communion every day, or from time to time, or only on Sundays? Answer. To this question there are various answers. For some it is proper to receive Communion daily; for others this would not be proper; and for others Communion would never be proper."

"Question. "Is it good to carry Holy Communion in a pyx, when one is going on a journey; or is it better to receive Communion wherever one finds Communion? Answer. The most holy body of Christ suffers no injury, when it is carried in that way and taken about from place to place. Christ himself [in his earthly life] was brought to everyone; and, as I said, he receives no injury from that, but only from an impure heart. But it is not proper to receive Communion outside the Catholic Church, as the Apostle Paul teaches, saying: 'One Lord' that is, the true Lord; 'one faith' [Eph 4:5], that is, the pious faith, because the others are not faith but death. If we separate from our own wife and unite with another, that is not marriage but adultery. With much more reason must we guard ourselves from separating from our holy and immaculate spouse, the Church of Christ."

321

† † †

Lord, direct our civic leaders according to your will and help them to keep us in peace.

In a sermon on the Mass the Abbot speaks of abuses at Mass: "And there are many who do not take care to consider with what purity and with what sorrow for their sins they are to approach the sacred table, but think only about what clothes they are to wear. Others come, but do not remain until the end of Mass. Others inquire as to how far the Mass is on and if the time for Communion has arrived. Then, like dogs, they rush forward, grab the mystical bread, and leave. Others, while in the temple of God are not quiet even for a moment, but starting a conversation among themselves, they pay more attention to the gossip than to the prayers. Others, neglecting the sacred liturgical functions, give themselves over to pleasures of the flesh. Others pay no attention whatever to their conscience, nor do they bother to cleanse the stains of their sins by penance. Instead they pile up sins upon sins, while they contemplate the beauty and shapes of the women. Thus, because of their unbridled desires they make the house of God a house of immorality. Others talk about their business and possessions, thus making a market out of that place and during the most awesome hour. Others during the Mass occupy themselves with speaking bad of the rest and even of the very priests who are offering the sacrifice."

"Now what is more horrible than that way of conducting oneself? And while guilty of many robberies, of vice, and of every type of crime we wash our hands with a little water [as was customary in some places] and thus, unclean and dirty we receive that holy body and divine blood, which was poured out for the salvation of the world."

† † †

**God, whose almighty word
Chaos and darkness heard**

And took their flight:
Hear us, we humbly pray,
And where the Gospel day
Sheds not its glorious ray
Let there be light.

John Marriott

The Abbot continues his sermon on the Mass: "To enter the church and venerate the holy images and venerable crosses is not sufficient in itself to please God, nor does the washing of one's hands produce a complete purification. But what is truly pleasing to God is that a man flee from sin, cleanse his stains by a confession and with tears, and break the chains of his sins with humility of heart; and in this way let him approach the immaculate mysteries [Communion] . . . Stand before God with peace and sorrow; confess your sins to God through the medium of the priests . . . Beg mercy, beg pardon, beg the forgiveness of your past sins and to be free of future sins, so that you can approach worthily to such great mysteries and partake with a pure conscience of the body and blood, and so that they will be for your purification and not your condemnation."

At least in some places in the early Church, when time for Holy Communion arrived, the priest or deacon would call out in Latin "Sancta sanctis" (in Greek "Ta Hagia tois hagios") meaning "Holy things for holy people." The purpose was to give a last minute reminder of the sanctity of Communion and the proper dispositions required for a fruitful reception. In his sermon on the Mass the Abbot comments on this custom:

"The priest continues, saying: 'The holy things for the holy people.' What does this mean? Take care, dearly beloved, how you approach for the reception of the divine mysteries, lest some of you hear these words as you approach for Communion: 'Do not touch Me; depart from Me, you who foment rancor and do works of evil. Go far away, you who do not deign to forgive your brother.' Then [after you forgive him] come and offer your gift and you will be worthy of Communion. Cast from yourself all the uncleanness of evil, and then approach and receive the purifying burning coal [Is 6:6]. Say to Him [the Lord]: 'I recognize, O Lord, my many sins and debts; but because of your command I have pardoned my brothers, so that I will be able to obtain pardon from you, O Lord.' Something like this the priest means to say with the short exclamation, "Hagia, hagios.' " [TEP]

Chapter XII

THE EUCHARIST IN THE EIGHTH CENTURY

ST. ANDREW OF CRETE, BISHOP 660 - 740

St. Andrew was born in Damascus, the Capital of Syria. After spending some time as a monk in Jerusalem, he served as a deacon in the famous church of St. Sophia in Constantinople, Greece. Finally he was made bishop of a diocese on the island of Crete off the coast of today's Turkey. He is noted principally for his sacred poetry. Some of his work is still found today in the liturgical books of the Byzantine Catholic liturgy. We quote here a few "Canons" (verses) that he composed for Holy Week:

"Oh Lover of mankind! Reclining at the Supper with your disciples, you unveiled for them the great mystery of your Incarnation, saying: 'Eat the bread that gives life; drink with faith the blood that has been emptied from the wound in the side of God.' "

"Christ is the Pasch, the great and holy Pasch. Eaten as bread and sacrificed as a lamb, he has been offered as a victim for us. In a mysterious manner we all receive his body and his blood with piety."

"You [Judas] stretched out your hands, in which you had received the bread of incorruptibility, in order to receive the coins of silver. With treachery you offered a kiss with that mouth with which you had received the body and the blood of Christ."

"Christ, the heavenly, and divine bread, gave a banquet to the world. Lovers of Christ, in mouths of clay but in pure hearts, let us receive with faith him who, sacrificing himself, now offers the Pasch among us."

"Oh Mother of God, your womb became a holy altar which contained the heavenly bread. Whoever eats of this bread does not die, as he, who nourishes everything, has said." [TEP]

† † †

EIGHTH CENTURY HYMN TO ST. JOHN THE BAPTIST

Thy father, doubting the message from on high, lost the gift of speech;
but thou when born
didst heal the organs of his voice.
Hidden before birth thou knewest the coming of the King; so did both
mothers through their sons declare secret things.
Text: Paul the Deacon, O.S.B. (died 799)
Tr.: Adrian Fortescue

ST. JOHN DAMASCENE, MONK AND PRIEST, c.675 - c.749

Church historians usually consider the Patristic Period closed with the death of St. John Damascene about the year 749. St. John was born in Damascus (hence "Damascene"), the capital of Syria, about 675. His father was a ranking officer to the Caliphs (Muslim rulers). He represented the Christians before the Caliphs and collected taxes from the Christians to ensure their freedom. John's grandfather had negotiated the surrender of Damascus to the Muslim Arabs in 634, just two years before the death of Mohammed, the founder of the Islamic (Muslim) religion. Before he was called to the religious life and the priesthood, St. John apparently followed in his father's footsteps as an officer to the Caliphs in Damascus.

Leaving his high-ranking political office in Damascus, St. John entered the monastery of St. Sabas in Palestine, where he devoted himself to prayer and study. His literary and philosophical background was of immense help to him both in his study of theology and in his endeavors to defend the faith against the Christian heretics and the non-Christian sects, including Islam. He is best known as a defender of sacred images during the Iconoclast (image-breaking) heresy, which raged mainly in the East during the eighth and ninth centuries. (The roots of the heresy apparently stem from a faulty understanding of several Old Testament passages concerning images.)

† † †

FROM EIGHTH CENTURY HYMN FOR DEDICATION OF A CHURCH

Blessed City Jerusalem, called vision of peace, built in heaven of living stones, encircled with angels as a bride with her maids.
Coming down new from heaven, adorned like a spouse for marriage, let her be wedded to the Lord. And all her streets and walls gleam with purest gold.
Her gates shine with pearls, standing ever open. For his reward each one may enter there, who for Christ's name has suffered here on earth.
Her stones, polished by hammer-strokes and sharp blows, are fitted by the Builder's hands, each in its place, to stay firm in the holy house of God.
Translator: Adrian Fortescue

St. John is the last of the Eastern Doctors of the Church. Pope Leo X111 conferred that title upon him in 1890. His most important writings are in dogmatic theology. Our interest, of course, is in his writings on the Eucharist. He gives a strong exposition of the doctrines of the Real Presence and transubstantiation. He teaches that the Mass is the unbloody and universal sacrifice foretold by the Prophet Malachy in the Old Testament. Holy Communion, he says, gives us a share in the divine nature by way of participation and communion with Christ and the brethren.

St. John follows the teaching, commonly held in the East, that the consecration of the bread and wine at Mass is brought about by the epiclesis, that is, the invocation and coming of the Holy Spirit. "God said: 'This is my body' and 'This is my blood' and 'Do this in memory of me'; and by virtue of this omnipotent command this is realized until he comes. Now that is what St. Paul says: 'Until he comes.' And the rain comes down for this new harvest by means of the epiclesis, which is the fructifying force of the Holy Spirit. Just as everything God did, He did by the operation of the Holy Spirit, so now also the operation of the Holy Spirit does things which go beyond nature and which nature cannot comprehend. Only faith can comprehend them. The most holy Virgin said [to the angel Gabriel]: 'How can this [my having a son] be, since I do not know man?' The Archangel answers: 'The Holy Spirit will descend upon you, and the power of the Most High will cover you with his shadow.' And now you ask how does bread become the body of Christ, and wine and water, the blood of Christ. Likewise I say to you: 'The Holy Spirit comes and does this, which is beyond all word and thought.' "

† † †

You have compassion for the sinner, Lord, as a father has compassion for his children.
Shine the brightness of your light on us, that we may love you always with a pure heart.
May the fire of your word consume our sins and its brightness illumine our hearts.

On transubstantiation St. John writes: "The body of Christ is truly united to the Divinity, that body that was born of the holy Virgin. It is united to the Divinity not because it ascended into heaven and comes down from heaven, but because the bread and wine themselves are changed into the body and blood of God. If you ask about the manner in which this is realized, be satisfied in hearing that it is realized by means of the Holy Spirit. In the same way the Lord, by means of the Holy Spirit, took flesh for himself and in himself from the holy Mother of God. And we cannot know any more about that except that the word of God is true and efficacious and omnipotent; but the manner in which this is realized is not possible to know. Nevertheless it is not less intelligent to say the following. By nature the bread by being eaten, and the water and wine by being drunk, are changed into the body and blood of the one who eats and drinks them;

but they do not result in a body different from that of the eater and drinker. Likewise, the bread at Mass and the water and wine, by means of the epiclesis [invocation] and the coming of the Holy Spirit, are changed in a supernatural way into the body and blood of Christ; and there are not two bodies, but one and the same body of Christ."

St. John on the Real Presence: "The bread and wine are not a figure of the body and blood of Christ. (Let such a notion be far from us.); but they are the very divinized body of the Lord. Now the Lord himself said: 'This is my body, not a figure of my body; and this is my blood, not a figure of my blood.' And before that he had said to the Jews: 'If you do not eat the flesh of the Son of man and drink his blood, you will not have life in you, because my flesh is real food and my blood is real drink.' And again: 'He who eats me will live.' "

"The Eucharistic oblation is called participation, because by means of it we participate in the Divinity of Jesus. It is called communion, and it really is, because by it we communicate with Christ and receive his flesh and his divinity. Also by it we are united with one another and we communicate with one another, because by partaking of the one same bread we are all the one same body of Christ . . . and we become members of one another, since we are concorporate with Christ." [TEP]

PRAYERS BY ST. JOHN DAMASCENE FOR BEFORE COMMUNION

1. Lord Jesus Christ, our God, You alone have the power to forgive the sins of men. Being good and the Lover of men, do not take into account my errors, whether conscious or not. Make me worthy to receive without condemnation your divine, glorious, immaculate and life-giving mysteries. Let my reception of Communion not be for my punishment or for addition to my sins, but for my purification and sanctification. Let it be a pledge of life and of a place in your future kingdom. Let it be a rampart and defense against my spiritual enemies; and may they be destroyed. Finally, let my

Communion blot out my many faults. For You are a God of mercy, of compassion, and of love for men; and we sing to your glory together with the Father and the Holy Spirit now and always and forever. Amen.

2. I stand before the doors of your church, and yet I am not free from having bad thoughts. But you, Oh Christ God, justified the publican and had compassion on the Canaanite woman. And as you opened the gates of Paradise to the thief, open to me the heart of your goodness. Now that I approach and touch You, receive me as you did the sinful woman, and the woman with a hemorrhage. The latter, having touched the fringe of your garment, promptly recovered her health; and the sinful woman, having embraced your immaculate feet, obtained forgiveness of her sins. But I, poor as I am, who dare to receive your entire body, let me not be cast into the fire, but receive me as you did those women. Enlighten my soul, and burn away the atonement due to my sins. I beg this through the prayers of the Virgin that gave you birth and through the prayers of the heavenly powers; for You are blessed forever. Amen.

3. My heart is wounded; my zeal for you is dissolving me; my love for you, O Lord, has transformed me. I am shackled to you by love. Let me be filled with your flesh; let me be sated with your life-giving and divinizing blood; let me enjoy your goodness. Submerge me in the delights of your Divinity. Let me be made worthy, so that when you return in your glory, I may go out to meet you, as I am taken up above the clouds in the air. In the company of your chosen ones let me praise you, adore you, and glorify you, while I give you thanks and praise you together with the Father, Who has no beginning, and with your most holy and good and life-giving Spirit, now and always and forever. [End of TEP]

Chapter XIII

THE EUCHARIST IN THE 8th & 9th CENTURIES

END OF PATRISTIC PERIOD

Divine, public Revelation, by which God makes known to men his mind and his will in order to lead them to eternal salvation with him in heaven, began with Adam and Eve and ended with the death of the last Apostle, St. John the Evangelist, around the year 100 a.d. The history of the Catholic Church that followed for some 700 years is known as the Patristic Period. During that period the Fathers of the Church, both clergy and laity known for their virtuous lives and orthodox doctrine, are witnesses to the faith of the Church during that period. Many of their writings are still extant. We have quoted from some of their writings throughout that entire period and from everywhere in the known, civilized world at that time: from Ireland to Arabia and Iran, from Russia to Spain and northern Africa.

In the extant writings of the Fathers that deal with the Eucharist, which is our only concern, we saw that the interest of the Fathers was mainly pastoral. They stressed the doctrine of the Real Presence of Christ in the Eucharist with a view to preparing their listeners and readers for the proper reception of Holy Communion.

INTRODUCTION TO THE MIDDLE AGES

During the Middle Ages, which lasted some 800 years from the end of the Patristic Period until around the year 1550 a.d. at the time of the Protestant Reformation, the emphasis of Eucharistic doctrine shifted from the fact of the Real Presence to the manner in which the Real Presence takes place. In short, during the Middle Ages the theologians were concerned with what would come to be called "transubstantiation." Before St. Thomas refined the doctrine of transubstantiation in the 13th. century, the term (substance) was used in a general way to describe the inner reality of things. To use a clumsy example let us look at putty. When taken from a new can, putty is soft, moist and gray. After it is applied to a window pane, it becomes hard, dry and white—yet we know that it is the same putty.

Continuing to use our example of the putty, we know that after it dries and hardens, it is still the same putty that was moist and soft. Something remains the same; something changes. What remains the same is its inner reality, namely, putty. The inner reality is called "substance," what the thing really is, namely, putty. What changes is the outer reality, the appearances (also called "species" or "accidents"). The appearances are what is perceived by our external senses; the inner reality or substance is perceived only by our mind.

The philosophical concepts of "substance" and "appearances" were gradually refined during the Middle Ages through Eucharistic debates concerning the manner of Christ's presence in the consecrated Host. There was disagreement as to the manner in which Christ becomes present and the manner in which he remains present. Most of the Eucharistic debates were conducted in monasteries of religious Orders, beginning with the Benedictines and later with the Franciscans and Dominicans. At that time the religious monasteries were the chief institutions of learning. During the thirteenth century St. Thomas Aquinas, an Italian Dominican and chief exponent of the Scholastic intellectual movement, had refined the concepts of "substance" and "accidents" (appearances). The X11 Ecumenical Council in the year 1215 and the Ecumenical Council of Trent (1545-1563) both solemnly defined the doctrine of transubstantiation.

Church historians usually consider the Period of the Middle Ages to have ended about the middle of the sixteenth century with the Protestant Revolt (so-called Reformation) and the the Council of Trent, which was called to counteract Protestantism and initiate the counter-Reformation. The Modern Period is usually reckoned from the end of the Middle Ages to the present day.

After bidding farewell to St. John Damascene, the last of the Patristic witnesses to the Catholic faith, let us turn to St. Paschasius Radbertus, the deacon who was chosen Abbot of the Benedictine monastery of Corbie in the northwestern region of Picardy in France. His treatise on the Body and Blood of our Lord, as we shall see, occasioned the first Eucharistic controversy of the Middle Ages.

Chapter XIV

THE EUCHARIST IN THE NINTH CENTURY

ST. PASCHASIUS RADBERTUS,
ABBOT 786 - 860

St. Paschasius Radbertus, Abbot of the Benedictine monastery of Corbie in France, published a treatise in the year 844 entitled "On the Body and the Blood of the Lord." The purpose of the treatise was to correct some false ideas that were current among some of the monks. One of the monks, Ratramnus, even entered into a literary controversy with his Abbot. However, the monk's ideas were so vague, that everyone was free to interpret them to his own liking. Not so with the Abbot, whose ideas were precise, even when crudely expressed, and were faithful to the teachings of the Church Fathers during the preceding Patristic Period. The Abbot's main point is the identity of the historic body of Christ and of his Eucharistic body.

The Abbot writes: "I ask myself what is the main idea of those who affirm that the true flesh and the true blood of Christ are really not in the Eucharist. The sacrament would then contain a certain power of the flesh but not the flesh itself, a certain power of the blood but not the blood itself. It would be, therefore, a figure and not a reality, a shadow and not the body itself."

"You ask me for the solution of this question, which many believe doubtful. Since they do not understand well, let them at least believe the words of the Savior, who, being true God, cannot lie. Therefore, when Christ says: 'This is my body, or my flesh, and this is my blood,' as I see it, he does not mean to speak of another flesh that is not his very own, which was born of the Virgin Mary and nailed to the cross; nor of some other blood different from that which was poured out on the cross and until then circulated through his veins. In addition, if the Eucharistic mystery would contain some other flesh and some other blood, distinct from those of Christ when on earth, it would not bring us the remission of sins. And if it did not have life in itself, it would not be able to diffuse life in our souls."

† † †

*Whatever you do, work at it with your whole being, and do it for the
Lord rather than for men. Col 3:23
If you love me, says the Lord, keep my commandments.*

The Abbot continues his treatise on the Real Presence and
transubstantiation: "Truly, this is the same flesh of Christ that was crucified
and buried. And this is true of the sacrament of this flesh which is realized
and consecrated by the priest at the altar with the words of Christ and the
power of the Holy Spirit. ... Don't be shocked, poor mortal, and don't look
here for the ordinary course of nature. But if you truly believe that this
flesh was formed in the virginal womb of Mary by the power of the Holy
Spirit, then also believe that what is realized on the altar by the word of
Christ and the power of the Holy Spirit is the body of Christ who was born
of the Virgin."

"This sacrament is at the same time reality and figure ... It is reality
because the body and blood of Christ by the power of the Holy Spirit and
the words of consecration are produced from the substance of the bread
and wine ... It is also figure, because in one visible species the mind perceives
something very different from what our eyes see and our taste senses." [E]

† † †

NINTH CENTURY EASTER HYMN

*Called to the Lamb's royal banquet, clothed in white robes, after
crossing the Red Sea, let us sing to Christ the Prince;
Whose divine love gives us his sacred blood; he, our high Priest, offers
his sacred body.
Now is Christ our Passover; he our paschal sacrifice, pure unleavened
bread of sincerity to pure minds.
Our true heavenly sacrifice by which hell is defeated, the chains of
death are broken, the reward of life is obtained.*

Christ conquering unfolds his standard;
hell is driven back and heaven opened,
while he overcomes the king of darkness.
That thou, Jesu, be the eternal Easter joy of our hearts,
set us free from the dread death of sin,
who has given us new life.

Latin: Ad regias agni dapes.
Translator: Adrian Fortescue

[EUCHARISTIA, abbreviated by "E," is the authorized Spanish translation of the original encyclopedia by twenty-eight French scholars.]

Chapter XV

THE EUCHARIST IN THE ELEVENTH CENTURY

BERENGARIUS, ARCHDEACON & HERETIC, 998-1088

It is worth noting that for 1000 years after Christ the Catholic Church taught the doctrine of the Real Presence of Christ in the Eucharist, and during that time no Christian is known to have denied that doctrine formally and intentionally. In the tenth century some had misunderstandings concerning transubstantiation and the Real Presence; and in their efforts to explain the true doctrine they unintentionally and implicitly denied the truth. But then came the deacon Berengarius, the first to deny the Real Presence and transubstantiation explicitly and intentionally.

Berengarius was born in Tours, France, in the year 998. He showed some talent and was chosen Archdeacon by the Bishop of Angers. (At that time the archdeacon was the most important administrator of the diocesan bishop and the second-in-command of the diocese.) One of Berengarius's contemporaries wrote: "He assumed a theatrical manner and was able to deceive undiscerning minds in such a way as to win a reputation for learning without being learned." In the History of the Catholic Church, Vol. 4, page 148, Mourret-Thompson writes: "He gathered about his person and won to his teaching a mass of restless souls who were intolerant of any yoke and eager for every novelty; such persons form the nucleus of every heresy in every period of history."

Berengarius had a vacillating mind and a versatile character. One of his first teachers, Fulbert of Chartres, considered him an unsound and dangerous spirit. The Archdeacon adopted an attitude of haughty independence toward the pope, whom he ridiculed. He hired poor students and sent them throughout France to spread his popularity and his heresy. Berengarius stubbornly insisted on his false theory that, in the pursuit of all knowledge, reason and the testimony of the five bodily senses hold the first place. Obviously in the field of theology, which deals with divine Revelation, such a theory is false. Three hundred years later John Wyclif, forerunner of the Protestant Revolt, relied on the same false theory. [E]

† † †

The Lord knows how fleeting are the thoughts of men.

In eleventh century France, the eldest daughter of the Church, the Eucharist was the center not only of Catholic piety, but also of social life. In honor of the Eucharist many masterpieces of architecture were built, and religious music was revived. If agreements for the peace of families or society were made in the presence of the Eucharist, they took on a sacred character. Persons accused of crimes made appeal to the judgment of God present in the Eucharist. Consequently, when Berengarius openly attacked the Eucharist, the King of France stepped in to prevent social disorder. The Pope sent a representative to conduct the Council of Tours, to which Berengarius was summoned. He subscribed under oath, and "from the bottom of my heart," to the following proposition: "After the consecration [of the Mass] the bread and wine on the altar are the body and blood of Jesus Christ." However, soon afterwards he retracted his oath and resumed teaching his heresy.

At a Roman Council Berengarius took the following oath: "I, Berengarius, in my heart believe and with my mouth profess that through the mystery of the sacred prayer and the words of our Redeemer the bread and wine which are placed on the altar are substantially changed into the true and proper and living flesh and blood of Jesus Christ, our Lord. And I profess that after the consecration it is the true body of Christ, which was born of the Virgin, and which, offered for the salvation of the world, was suspended on the cross and which sits at the right hand of the Father. And I profess that it is the true blood of Christ, which was poured out from his side, his true blood, not only through the sign and power of the sacrament, but also in its proper nature and true substance. As the faith is contained in this Brief, and as I read it, and as you understand it, so do I believe it;

and I shall no longer teach contrary to this faith. So help me God and these holy Gospels of God." [E]

✝ ✝ ✝

Lord Jesus, remember that when our sins plowed long furrows on your back, your death broke the bonds of sin and Satan forever.
Heal hearts that are broken; gather together those who have been scattered, and enrich us all from the fullness of your eternal wisdom.

Throughout the rest of his life Berengarius, due to his volatile mind, repeatedly professed and denied the true faith. Church historians believe that he finally died reconciled to the Church. He died on the Feast of the Epiphany (manifestation) of our Lord to the Gentiles (non-Jews, in the persons of the Magi). On his death bed he is reported to have said: "Today, being the day of his manifestation, my Lord Jesus Christ will appear to me, either, as I hope, to raise me to glory for my repentance, or, as I fear, to punish me for the heresy which I have been instrumental in spreading." [E]

✝ ✝ ✝

NINTH CENTURY HYMN FOR PENTECOST
(Veni Creator Spiritus)

Come, Creator Spirit, visit the souls of thy people, fill with grace from on high the hearts which thou hast created.
Thou who art called the Comforter, gift of the most high God, living fount, fire, love and unction of souls.
Sevenfold in thy gifts, finger of the Father's right hand, thou promised truly by the Father giving speech to tongues.
Inflame our senses with thy light, pour thy love into our hearts, strengthen our weak bodies with lasting power.
Drive far away the enemy, grant peace at all times; so under thy

guidance may we avoid all evil.
Grant us by thee to know the Father and to know the Son; and thee,
Spirit of both, may we always believe.
To God the Father be glory, to the Son who rose from the dead and to
the Comforter, for all ages.

Text: Rabanus Maurus, Archbishop of Mainz,
Germany (d. 856)
Tr.: A. Fortescue

† † †

EVENING HYMN
by Alcuin of York, England (d. 804)

Now that evening brings the end of labor, Lord, who has kept us safe
in thy protection, gratefully we offer thee our thanks and worship now
and at all times.
From all the sins which we this day committed cleanse our
conscience, Christ our Lord and Savior.

Tr.: Adrian Fortescue

Chapter XVI

THE EUCHARIST IN THE TWELFTH CENTURY

EUCHARISTIC DOCTRINE
BEGINS TO BE CLARIFIED

Like all other heresies, that of the French deacon Berengarius, resembled a monster which, when one head is cut off, it grows one or two more heads. The heresy continued for years in different forms. Thus a challenge was forced upon the orthodox theologians, those who pursue the noble task of applying their minds to the truths that God has revealed, in order to understand them better, to clarify them, and thus to help us understand them better. In this way dogmatic progress in Eucharistic doctrine began, not by adding to the truth that God had revealed but by explaining and clarifying it.

Among the first questions that the theologians took up was: What happens to the substance of the bread and wine at Mass? They taught correctly that the substance of bread and wine does not coexist with the body and blood of Christ. However, they erred in believing that the substance of the bread and wine simply ceased to exist, and that in its place there was substituted the body and blood of Christ. Later the Church would clarify that the substance of the bread and wine is changed into the substance of the body and blood of Christ. Thus, Christ does not enter the bread and wine; but the bread and wine are changed into Christ.

† † †

ELEVENTH CENTURY HYMN TO MARY (SALVE REGINA)

Hail, holy queen, mother of mercy,
hail our life, our sweetness & our hope.
To thee do we cry, poor banished children of Eve.
To thee do we send up our sighs,
mourning and weeping in this vale of tears.
Turn then, most gracious advocate,

> *thine eyes of mercy toward us.*
> *And after this exile show unto us*
> *the blessed fruit of thy womb, Jesus.*
> *O clement, O loving, O sweet Virgin Mary.*

> *Text: Hermann the Lame of Reinachau,*
> *Germany (d. 1054)*
> *Translator: Adrian Fortescue*

The theologians continue to clarify Eucharistic doctrine. When asked HOW the bread and wine are changed into the body and blood of Christ, they answered correctly by stating that the nature of this change is one of the greater mysteries of the Christian faith. It simply cannot be understood completely by the human mind.

There was much discussion as to the MANNER in which Christ is present in the Eucharist. If Mass is said in a thousand places at the same time, does Christ have a thousand bodies? Or if the Host is broken into ten pieces, are there ten bodies of Christ present? Guitmond, a French Benedictine and Bishop of Aversa in southern Italy, answered correctly: "In the thousand Masses celebrated simultaneously there is present the same body of Christ, whole and entire and without any division ... In each of the parts of the broken Host there is present the entire body of Christ. Nevertheless, the sum of the parts of the broken Host is not many bodies, but the one, sole body of Christ ... just as the soul is present whole and entire in the thousand parts of the human body. And even when the soul is present whole and entire in each of those parts, there are nevertheless not many souls, but one soul."

Some questions were left to be solved later, such as: What happens to the body of Christ after Communion? What if the Host was accidentally eaten by animals? Some thought that after Communion the body of Christ ascended to heaven, or that it remained in one's stomach until the day of his burial, or that it evaporated into thin air, or that it came out with the blood when one was bleeding. Even the best theologians at that time thought that God would not permit the consecrated Host to become corrupt (spoiled, moldy) in the tabernacle, nor permit it to be eaten by animals. Later it would be discovered that those theologians were wrong in this matter. [E]

✝ ✝ ✝

Father, you ordained your priests to be ministers of Christ and stewards of your marvelous gifts, so fill them with fidelity, wisdom and love.

During the twelfth century the first theological summas appeared. ("Summa" is Latin for "sum" or "total.") The theological summa was an effort to present the whole of Catholic doctrine in a systematic manner while adding greater precision to the doctrines. The most famous of the summas, that of St. Thomas Aquinas, would not appear until the following century.

During the Patristic Period the Fathers of the Church often mentioned that the Mass is a sacrifice. They made no effort to understand how it is a sacrifice or precisely in what the sacrifice consists. Likewise during the Eucharistic controversies of the tenth and eleventh centuries much was written about the sacrifice of the Mass, but again, without precision regarding the essence of the sacrifice.

Peter Lombard, a native of Lombardy in northern Italy, the most outstanding theologian of the twelfth century, was Bishop of Paris. He made a large collection of opinions (called "Sentences" in Latin) of the Fathers and earlier theologians concerning divine Revelation. This work became the standard textbook for theology, until it was replaced by St. Thomas's Summa Theologica in the following century. Peter believed the Mass to be a true sacrifice, because it is the memorial and representation of the true sacrifice and immolation of Christ on the cross. Christ was immolated once on the cross, Peter said; but he is immolated every day in the Eucharist, because every day the memorial of his own immolation on

Calvary is renewed. He thought the passion and death of Christ are represented in the Mass by the breaking of the Sacred Host.

† † †

ELEVENTH CENTURY HYMN TO MARY
(Alma Redemptoris Mater)

Holy Mother of our Redeemer, thou gate leading to heaven and star of the sea; help the falling people who seek to rise, thou who, all nature wondering, didst give birth to thy holy Creator. Virgin always, hearing that greeting from Gabriel's lips, take pity on sinners.
Text: Herman the Lame, monk of Reichenau, Germany. Translator: Adrian Fortescue

During the twelfth century much attention was paid to the doctrine of transubstantiation and, consequently, to the substance and accidents (species, appearances) of the Eucharist. Peter Lombard came to the correct conclusion that the accidents exist by themselves and are not inherent in the body and blood of Christ. Their purpose, according to Peter, is to cover and encircle Christ, to put our faith to the test, to be the sacramental sign of the Eucharist, to enable us to experience no repugnance in receiving the body and blood of Christ, which is offered to us in Communion under the species of bread and wine.

The theologians of this century correctly explained that the Eucharistic body of Christ is his immortal and glorious body, as it is in heaven. The Eucharistic body, therefore, has the power of multilocation, of being in different places at the same time. Moreover, the body is present whole and entire in each of the two sacramental species (of bread and wine). Incidentally the theologians correctly solved the peculiar question of what happens if an animal eats a consecrated Host, or if one receives Communion in the state of mortal sin. In both cases the true body of Christ would be eaten, but it would not suffer in any way. His body would be like a ray of light, they said, that passes through dirty places without experiencing any harm or impropriety. Peter Lombard said that Christ can be received in two ways: sacramentally only and both sacramentally and spiritually. Those who knowingly receive Christ unworthily receive him sacramentally only, that is, they are fed with the body of Christ without being united to him by charity and thus commit a very grave sin. The faithful who are well disposed and united to Christ and the Church receive Christ also spiritually, with the fruit of the sacrament.

The cult of the Eucharist that began in the eleventh century developed rapidly during the next century, until it climaxed in the thirteenth with grand and popular celebrations.

✝ ✝ ✝

Father, you called men and women to chastity for the sake of the kingdom here and hereafter, so let them faithfully follow your Son.

Chapter XVII

THE EUCHARIST IN THE THIRTEENTH CENTURY

MARKED DEVELOPMENT OF EUCHARISTIC DOCTRINE

Two giant steps were taken in the development of Eucharistic doctrine during the thirteenth century. The new developments, of course, were already contained implicitly in the Eucharistic doctrine of the New Testament and were mentioned in passing by many of the Fathers during the Patristic Period. Now, however, came greater confirmation and clarification.

In 1215 at the Ecumenical Lateran Council IV the Church officially sanctioned the word, "transubstantiation," to describe the change of substances that takes place at the Consecration of the Mass. The Church never uses that word in the sense of Aristotelian or Scholastic philosophy, but in the ordinary and general meaning that that word had previously, namely, that the "substance" is the hidden reality of an object, while the "accidents" or "species" are its appearances. The Council declared: In the universal Church of the faithful "Jesus Christ is the priest himself and the sacrifice. His body and blood are truly contained in the sacrament of the altar under the species of bread and wine. By divine power the bread is transubstantiated into his body and the wine into his blood, so that to accomplish the mystery of unity, we ourselves receive from him what he took from us [our human nature]. And surely no one can perform this sacrament except a priest who has been rightly ordained and according to the keys of the Church, which Jesus Christ himself gave to the Apostles and their successors."

✝ ✝ ✝

EASTER SEQUENCE
(Victimae Paschali Laudes of 11th century)

Sing to Christ, your paschal Victim; Christians sing your Easter hymn.
The sinless Lord for sinners, Christ, God's Son, for creatures died; the sheep who strayed, the Lamb of God redeemed.
Then death and life their battle wonderfully fought; and now the King of life, once dead, for ever lives.
Tell us, Mary, we pray, what you saw on Easter day. Empty was the grave, and looking I saw there the glory of his rising.
The angel witnesses I saw, and folded linen. Christ, my hope, is risen truly. In Galilee he goes before you.
We know he rose from death indeed; and so to him we pray, great King and Lord of Life, bless us this day.
Text: Wipo (died 1048), chaplain to Emperor Conrad II of Germany
Translator: Adrian Fortescue

The second giant step in the study of theology and in the understanding of the Eucharist was the introduction of reason. Prior to this century theology was based primarily on authority, the authority of the official Church pronouncements and especially the authority of the Fathers of the Church, who had been outstanding for their holiness and orthodoxy. Now, in addition to theology based on authority, there was added theology based on reason. To assist in this new endeavor the works of the ancient Greek philosopher Aristotle were found to be very valuable. To be sure, his works had to be "baptized" by deleting his pagan errors, but his thought as a whole proved useful to the theologians, especially St. Thomas Aquinas. Obviously none of Aristotle's teaching was ever incorporated into Catholic dogma, but it was found helpful in explaining Catholic teaching.

St. Thomas believed that the act of God in the transubstantiation of the Eucharist to be greater and more mysterious than the divine act of creation. He explained that transubstantiation is not like the

356

transformation of food into one's own flesh; nor does it consist in the annihilation of the bread and wine but in changing them into the body and blood of Christ. All of the substance of the bread and wine is changed into all of the substance of the body and blood of Christ. No such change is found in nature.

St. Thomas taught that Christ is present in the Eucharist in the same way that a substance is present in anything. Therefore, Christ is present whole and entire in the whole Host and whole and entire in each of its parts, even before it is broken. Similarly, theologians before St. Thomas taught that Christ is present in the same way that a soul is present in a body, namely, whole and entire in the whole body and whole and entire in each of its parts.

St. Thomas joined other theologians in the belief that the species (appearances) of bread and wine do not inhere in the body of Christ, but exist by themselves. The species signify that Christ is present in the Host; and he is so dependent upon the species that, if they become corrupt or disappear, then Christ ceases to be present. In no other way is Christ affected by the elements, such as heat or cold or the breaking of the Host.

Many times St. Thomas mentions the Mass and its sacrificial character, but only in passing. He treats well the symbolism of sacrifice in general, but years would pass before the essence of the Mass was treated directly and formally. He comes close, however, when he mentions the Secret Prayer of the former Tridentine liturgy of the Ninth Sunday after Pentecost, which states that every time the Mass is celebrated "the work of our redemption is carried out (renewed, made present)." [E]

† † †

HYMN FOR A MARTYR
(11th. century Milan, Italy)

God, of thy soldiers the lot, crown and reward, free from bonds of sin those who sing the martyr's praise.

For he, deeming the joys of the world and the tempting pleasures of
sin full of bitterness, so came to heaven.
Bravely he went to his torment, manfully he bore it; so shedding his
blood for thee he now possesses eternal joy.
In humble prayer we beg thee, most merciful, on this triumph of the
martyr, to wash away thy servants' guilt.

Text: Author unknown
Translator: Adrian Fortescue

Chapter XVIII

THE EUCHARIST IN THE 14th & 15th CENTURIES

THE GREAT HERESY LOOMS ON THE HORIZON

Following the thirteenth century, the century of St. Thomas Aquinas, which some consider the greatest century of the Church, there followed some 200 years of religious controversy and moral decay leading up to the so-called Protestant Reformation.

Over the centuries the Church in Europe had acquired immense material wealth from the gifts that the faithful had offered her for noble and spiritual reasons. True, she used her wealth to care for the poor and the sick; but there was much wealth remaining. At that time all Europe was Catholic; but all the members of the Church remained quite human. Immense wealth presents many temptations. The less fortunate members of the Church saw some of the hierarchy living a life of ease and pleasure. Many men entered the priesthood for financial gain rather than for service to God and the people. The faithful saw many priests and bishops leading immoral lives. A good number of bishops were civil princes and occupied mainly with civil affairs. Many bishops got the notion that the authority of bishops in a local or ecumenical council was equal to or greater than that of the pope. Great scandal was caused when, besides the true pope in Rome, there was an antipope in Avignon, France, and another in Pisa, Italy. All three, of course, claimed to be the true pope.

In that spiritual chaos it was natural for the civil rulers to try to wean the faithful away from some of their allegiance to the Church and to give it to the rulers. Moreover the rulers had their eyes on the Church's wealth and favored any priest who defended their false claims to the patrimony of the Church.

† † †

14th. CENTURY HYMN TO THE SORROWFUL MOTHER
(Stabat Mater Dolorosa)

Sorrowful, weeping stood the mother
by the cross on which hung her Son.
Whose soul, mournful, sad, lamenting,
was pierced by a sword.
Oh how sad, how afflicted was
that blessed mother of the Only-begotten.
How did she mourn and lament, loving mother,
while she saw the torment of her divine Son.
What man would not weep if he saw
the mother of Christ in such sorrow?
Who would not mourn with her,
seeing Christ's mother mourning with her Son?
For the sins of his race she sees Jesus
scourged and in torment.
She sees her dear Son dying in anguish,
as he gives up the ghost.
O mother, fount of love,
make me feel the strength of thy sorrow,
that I may mourn with thee.
Make my heart burn with love for Christ my God,
that I may please him.
Holy Mother, do this:
fix the wounds of the Crucified firmly in my heart.
Share with me the pain of thy wounded Son,
who deigns to bear so much for me.
While I live let me mourn with thee,
suffering with him who bore the cross.
I wish to stand with thee by the cross
and to share thy woe.
Blessed Virgin of all virgins,
be not hard to me; let me weep with thee.

Reform! Reform! In the midst of such dreadful conditions as described above good men cried out for reform. Priests preached reform. Some bishops called for reform. A few popes tried to reform the Church. Christ himself through his Church was crying out for reform, but for the most part worldly concerns smothered the cries for reform. However, reform would come — late, but surely, and in a way that few expected.

The spiritual chaos during the 14th and 15th centuries in Europe offered a fertile field for rebellion against the leaders of the Church, priests and bishops and popes, many or most of whom were openly failing in their duty to God and to the faithful. In such sad circumstances the most formidable rebel is the heretic. How easy to get a following of sincere, confused, scandalized laity by claiming that widespread spiritual poverty is due to the fact that the Church has abandoned the teachings of Christ for those of Satan. And, of course, the heretic always claims that he is the one whom Christ has sent to reform the Church and bring it back to its former sanctity by reforming its doctrines. And now enter the heretic.

WYCLIFFE AND HUS, FORERUNNERS OF PROTESTANT REFORMATION

Father John Wycliffe (1324-1384), an English priest and professor at Oxford, sounded the trumpet that would call forth the Protestant Reformers about 200 years later. He rightly saw that the Church was in need of a giant reform; but he wrongly set about reforming Church doctrine. There was nothing wrong with Church doctrine. Reform was needed in the field of moral conduct, the moral conduct of popes, bishops, priests and also much of the laity.

Among other doctrines Wycliffe took up the doctrine of the Eucharist with the hope of defeating priests of the religious Orders, who were his most ardent adversaries. He expressed his admiration for Berenguer, the French deacon, who 300 years earlier was the first to make a formal denial of the Real Presence. He also made his own the false theory of Berenguer that in the pursuit of all knowledge, including that of religion, human reason and the testimony of the five bodily senses are paramount.

Wycliffe denied transubstantiation and insisted that the bread and wine remain after the Consecration. He claimed that Christ was somehow present in the bread and wine, but in a state different from that in which he is in heaven. When it was pointed out to him that, by denying transubstantiation, he was denying a doctrine that had been defined by an ecumenical council, that of Lateran 1V, a hundred years earlier. He knew that he would be branded and treated as a heretic for denying doctrine defined by an ecumenical council. Therefore he tried to escape his dilemma by appealing to another of his heresies. He claimed that only those predestined to heaven belong to the Church; and since it was unknown if the bishops at that council were predestined, the value of their doctrine is in doubt.

During these turbulent times an alliance was formed between England and Bohemia (Czechoslovakia) through marriage between the two royal families. As a result of increased communication between the two countries Wycliffe's heretical ideas entered Bohemia. Father John Hus (1369?-1415), a Bohemian professor at the University of Prague, translated some of Wycliffe's works and accepted all of the latter's heretical doctrine except that on the Eucharist. Hus held to transubstantiation but insisted on Communion under both forms. (His followers were called "Utraquists," from the Latin "uterque," meaning "both").

The Ecumenical Council of Constance (1414-1418) in Germany condemned the errors of both Wycliffe and Hus. Because some of Hus's errors were revolutionary and causing civil disturbances, and because he refused to recant, the civil authorities had him burned alive at the stake. It was thought that such horrible punishment would deter any further civil disturbance; but the spirit of the times was such, that the very opposite result came about in the form of the Hussite Wars for twenty years between the followers of Hus and Catholic Germany.

The efforts of Wycliffe and Hus resulted in no reform of the Church whatsoever. Moral decay, especially among the clergy, continued. The laity were growing fond of some of the revolutionary ideas of the two heretics regarding civil authority. For another hundred years this situation would continue, until the stage was set for the entrance of the Protestant Reformers.

Chapter XIX

THE EUCHARIST IN THE SIXTEENTH CENTURY

THE PROTESTANT REFORMATION: MULTIPLE CHURCHES

As was outlined before, by the sixteenth century the moral reform of the Church had been postponed for some 250 years by the popes and bishops. A calamity was waiting to happen. It started in the person of a German priest, Father Martin Luther, who is generally considered the founder of Protestantism. It appears that in the beginning Luther had intended to reform the Church; but he attacked doctrine more than morals. Soon his "reform" turned into a religious revolution with the backing of some civil authorities, who saw political and financial gain in some of Luther's ideas. The conditions of the times were such that his heretical ideas found eager acceptance not only in Germany, but also in the Scandinavian countries to the north.

Luther lived to see other "reformers," like Father Zwingli and Father Oecolampadius in Switzerland, and Calvin in both France and Switzerland. All three contradicted not only Luther but also one another; and each established his own Church, something Luther never intended at the beginning of his revolt. The Protestant Movement was already out of control, and has since broken up into more than 200 different Churches in our country alone.

† † †

STABAT MATER DOLOROSA
Let me remember the death of Christ,
give me a share in his passion, thinking of his pain.
Let me be wounded with his wounds,
be filled with the cross and precious blood of thy Son.
That I may not burn in flames, may I be protected by thee, holy Virgin,

at the day of judgment.
Christ, when I leave this world,
grant me to come by thy mother to the palm of victory.
When the body dies, grant that my soul
may enter the glory of paradise.

Latin text: Jacopone da Todi (died 1306),
Italian poet and Franciscan tertiary.
Translator: Adrian Fortescu

THE PROTESTANT REFORMATION: THE RULE OF FAITH

The reason for the multiplication of Churches or sects was seen in Luther's own day to be his novel idea concerning the rule of faith, that is, the way one can know what one should believe. From the very beginning of Christianity the Catholic Church, in the persons of the Apostles, understood the rule of faith to be God's Revelation as contained both in his written word (Bible) and in his unwritten word (Sacred Tradition). The bishops, the successors of the Apostles, relied on the teachings of the Apostles and understood that they themselves possessed that teaching office (called the magisterium), which Christ had established and given to the Apostles. As Christian theology developed over the centuries in the Church, the theologians found the rule of faith not only in divine Revelation (Bible and Sacred Tradition) and the official teaching of the Church by the magisterium, but also in the writings of the Church Fathers as witnesses to Catholic belief in their respective times and places. To help one understand what divine Revelation, the Church and the Fathers taught, theologians applied human reason to doctrine in order to clarify it.

Luther proposed a new idea regarding the rule of faith, that is, how one knows what to believe. He claimed that the rule of faith is not found in Sacred Tradition, nor in the teaching of the magisterium, nor in the teachings of the Fathers, but in the Bible only and as the Bible is interpreted by the individual. In effect, he denied the authority of the pope and made every man his own pope. As a result new Churches came, and still come, into being constantly.

To understand conditions in our own day, it should be noted that in the 18th. century, the period called the "Enlightenment," human reason became the sole rule of faith for many. We see that still today; and in Protestant circles it is often used in conjunction with "the Bible only" as the sole rule of faith. For Catholics the rule of faith is divine Revelation as proposed by the magisterium of the Church. But our interest is in the Eucharist.

† † †

If you love me, says the Lord, keep my commandments.

THE EUCHARIST IN PROTESTANTISM

Following Luther's rule of faith (the Bible only and individually interpreted), the various "Reformers" naturally taught different ideas concerning the Eucharist. Luther himself insisted on the Real Presence of Christ in the Eucharist because, he said, he found that in the Bible. However, he rejected transubstantiation, which he said is not in the Bible. Instead, he taught impanation, that is, Christ is really present in the bread and wine. Luther is quoted as saying: "My conscience is effectively firm in the opinion that in the Eucharist there is true bread and true wine together with the true flesh and true blood of Christ."

Luther tried to retain the Mass, and for a while he continued to say Mass daily. However, he got the novel idea that Christ is present at Mass only from the Consecration to the time of Communion. Consequently he considered it idolatry to adore Christ in the tabernacle or at Benediction of the Blessed Sacrament. He said he did not hate any liturgical Feast as much as he hated Corpus Christi.

When Luther heard that Father Zwingli and Father Oecolampadius in Switzerland were teaching that the Eucharist was only a symbol or figure of Christ's body, he said those priests were possessed by the devil and beyond salvation. The Catholic cleric Calvin, the founder of Presbyterianism, said that the bread and wine contain a power or virtue of the body of Christ, but not the real body of Christ. Henry VIII, King of England, meanwhile wrote a treatise on the sacraments of the Church, for which the Pope conferred on him the title of "Defender of the Faith," a title still coveted by the monarchs of England who defend a Protestant faith. But when the Pope would not give Henry a Declaration of Nullity of his first marriage, the King denied the supremacy of the pope and declared himself head of the new Church of England (Anglican Church). He retained most of Catholic doctrine, including that of the Eucharist, but his successors did not.

† † †

> *Whether you eat or drink — whatever you do — you should do all for the glory of God. (1Co 10:31)*

As the original Protestant Churches kept breaking up into many different Churches or sects, most of them adopted the ideas of Zwingli and Oecolampadius regarding the Eucharist, namely, that it is simply a mere symbol or figure or memorial of Christ or of his body and blood. And following Luther's rule of faith most believe, they say, only what is in the Bible, which they consider themselves free to interpret privately.

Lutheranism broke up into various branches or Synods. The Church of England (Anglicanism) spawned the various Episcopal Churches and Methodism, from which was born the Salvation Army. Calvanism produced not only Presbyterianism but also various Reformed Churches. The Anabaptists, who insisted on re-baptizing those baptized as infants, gave birth to the Baptists, who in turn gave birth to the Disciples of Christ and the Churches of Christ. And so it went, and is still going on, with everyone free to believe what he sees fit concerning the Eucharist.

The Protestant Reformation reformed nothing in the Catholic Church, and therefore was not a true reform but a revolt against the Catholic Church.

However, the Reformation, as it is called, occasioned the Counter-Reformation, which is still in progress in the Catholic Church.

† † †

10th CENTURY HYMN FOR A CONFESSOR
(ISTE CONFESSOR)

*This confessor of the Lord, whom people throughout the world praise
with due honor, on this day deserves joyfully to receive honor of praise.
Who faithful, wise, humble, pure, while breath filled his mortal frame
led a holy life without blame.
For whose great merit, often those who lay sick, conquering the power
of disease, were restored to health.
So our choir sings his praise, that we may be helped by his prayers at
all times.*

Text: Author unknown
Translator: Adrian Fortescue

THE COUNTER REFORMATION

The Protestant so-called Reformation was so revolutionary in its doctrine that it shocked the popes and bishops into embarking on the long-overdue reform of the Church. Said reform is called the Counter Reformation. This reform was so deep that, even to this day, we see the effects of it, especially in the way the Church bends over backwards to avoid those things that led up to the Protestant revolt. The nineteenth ecumenical council met in the city of Trento in northern Italy to spearhead the true reform. Before the Council of Trent the Church had found need to convene an ecumenical council, which possess all the teaching authority Christ left to his Church, on average every 100 years. But the Council of

371

Trent was so thorough that no ecumenical council was convoked until Vatican I, three hundred years later in 1869.

The countless heretical teachings of the Protestant Reformation was the occasion of a giant leap forward in the development of Catholic doctrine in the Council of Trent, which convened on and off from 1545 to 1563. Among other matters the Council took up the many errors that the Protestant Reformers had introduced regarding the Eucharist. This resulted in greater clarification of Eucharistic doctrine, much of which we shall present in this work for our edification and spiritual nourishment.

† † †

HYMN FOR PASSIONTIDE (Pange Lingua)

Sing, my tongue, the victory of the glorious battle; sing the triumph of the cross; how the Redeemer of the world being sacrificed yet conquered.

The Creator, pitying Adam's race, when it fell by the taste of the forbidden fruit, then noted the tree; that by a tree the loss from a tree should be repaired.

So was the work of our salvation ordered, that art should destroy the art of the deceiver, that healing should come from a tree, as had come the wound.

Therefore in the fullness of the sacred time the Creator of the world, sent from the Father's home, was born and came forth clothed in flesh from the Virgin's womb.

A child he lay in the narrow cradle, and the virgin mother bound his limbs in swaddling clothes; such bands held the hands and feet of God.

Eternal glory be to the blessed Trinity, to the Father and Son; the same honor to the Paraclete. Let all the world praise the name of the one and three.

† † †

*Father, you sent Jesus Christ into the world to absolve the sins of
men, so free all the dead from their sins.
From the beginning of mankind, Lord, you intended husband and wife
to be one, so keep all families
united in sincere love.*

*Text: Venantius Fortunatus (died c. 601),
Bishop of Poitiers, France
Translator: Adrian Fortescue*

THE COUNCIL OF TRENT ON THE EUCHARIST

The Council of Trent's decree on the Most Holy Eucharist was published
on Oct. 11, 1551. It begins by stating that the Council was convened with
the "special guidance and direction of the Holy Spirit to provide remedy
for all the heresies and other very serious troubles by which the Church of
God is at present wretchedly agitated and torn into many different factions."
However, the decree says that from the very beginning of the Council it
had a special desire "to uproot the 'cockle' of accursed errors and schisms,
which the enemy (Satan) in these troubled times of ours has sown in the
doctrine of the faith and in the use and worship of the sacred Eucharist,
which our Savior left in his church as a symbol of that unity and charity
with which he wished all Christians to be mutually bound and united."
The Council declares that it is transmitting that sound and genuine doctrine
about the Eucharist that the Catholic Church, "instructed by our Lord
Jesus Christ himself and by his Apostles, and taught by the Holy Spirit
who day by day brings her to all truth [John 14:26], has always held and
will preserve even to the end of time."

The first definition of the Council concerning the Eucharist was
logically that of the Real Presence, which forms the basis of the rest of the
doctrine on the Eucharist. "In the nourishing sacrament of the Holy
Eucharist after the consecration of the bread and wine our Lord Jesus Christ,

true God and true man, is truly, really, and substantially contained under the species of those sensible things." Christ is present "truly, really and substantially." "Truly" present, that is, against those who claimed he is not present. "Really" present, that is, in reality and not simply in sign or figure or power. "Substantially" present, that is, in his real body as it is in heaven and not in some ephemeral manner. The Council left no doubt as to the reality of Christ's presence in the Eucharist. And it added that "the whole Christ" is present, with his body, blood, soul and divinity. Therefore Christ, true God and true man, whole and entire, is living in the Eucharist, just as he is living in heaven.

The Council recalled that Christ instituted the Eucharist at the Last Supper, and then it offered reasons for its institution. "He wished that this sacrament be received as the spiritual food of souls [Mt 26:26], by which they may be nourished and strengthened, living the life of him who said: 'He who eats me, the same shall also live by me.' [Jn 6:57] The Eucharist is clearly a nourishing sacrament to nourish Sanctifying Grace, that participation of Christ's life in the soul. Obviously if one is without that life because of mortal sin, one must not approach to receive Communion. That would be horrible, repugnant, like stuffing food into the mouth of a corpse.

† † †

HYMN FOR LENT (prior to 10th century)

Hear, merciful Creator, the prayers which we make with tears in this holy Lenten fast.
Reader of hearts, thou knowest how weak is our strength; show mercy to us who turn to thee.
Much have we sinned, but spare us repentant. For the glory of thy name heal our sick souls.
Let our bodies be subdued by abstinence; so may our souls, fasting from all evil, leave the food of sin.

Tr.: A. Fortscue

374

The second reason for the institution of the Eucharist, the Council said, was to give us "an antidote, whereby we may be freed from daily faults and be preserved from mortal sins." The Bible says that even the holy man sins many times a day. The reference, of course, is to venial sin and a less than generous response to what we believe would please God even without his commanding it. But most important for us Holy Communion gives us the wherewith to avoid mortal sin by increasing Actual Grace, which enlightens our mind and moves our will to avoid sin.

The Council mentions a third reason for Christ's having instituted the Eucharist. "Christ wished that this sacrament be a pledge of future glory and of everlasting happiness." This recalls Christ's words: "Anyone who eats my flesh and drinks my blood has eternal life, and I shall raise him up on the last day." When one receives Holy Communion with the proper disposition of soul, he receives a promise or pawn or pledge that Christ will raise his body from the grave and transfigure it gloriously upon his entrance into heaven.

The last reason the Council offered for instituting the Eucharistic sacrament was that it "be a symbol of that one body [the Church] of which he himself is the head, and to which he wished us to be united, as members, by the closest bond of faith, hope and charity, that we might 'all speak the same thing and that there might be no schisms among us.' " Holy Communion represents and produces unity in the Church.

† † †

HYMN TO CHRIST'S CHURCH (Jerusalem Et Sion)

Daughters of Jerusalem and Sion, all the company of faithful people, sing a hymn of lasting joy. Alleluia.
For Christ, King of justice, this day has espoused our mother, the Church, whom he saved from the depth of woe.
He, God and man, hanging on the tree of the cross founded her with blood and water from his side.

Eve was a cruel mother to her children; the Church is the true mother
of the chosen people, giver of life, refuge & guardian of unhappy man.
She is the ship in which we are borne safely,
the fold in which we are at peace,
the column of truth by which we stand firm.
So may Christ, joining us to his wedding feast, give us true
happiness, inviting us to the joy of his elect.

Text: Ascribed to Adam (d. 1192),
monk of St. Victor's Monastery (Paris)
Translator: Adrian Fortescue

The Council pointed out the excellence of the sacrament of the Eucharist over the other sacraments. "The other sacraments first have the power of sanctifying, when one uses them; but in the Eucharist there is the Author of sanctity himself before it is used."

The Council described the Eucharistic presence of Christ in this way: "Immediately after the consecration the true body of our Lord and his true blood together with his soul and divinity exist under the species of bread and wine. But the body indeed under the species of bread, and the blood under the species of wine by the force of the words [of consecration]; but the body itself under both species by the force of that natural connection and concomitance by which the parts of Christ the Lord, 'who has now risen from the dead to die no more,' are mutually united. The divinity also is present because of that admirable hypostatic union with his body and soul. Therefore, it is very true that as much is contained under either species as under both. For Christ whole and entire exists under the species of bread and under any part whatsoever of that species; likewise the whole Christ is present under the species of wine and under its parts." Christ is present in the Eucharist in a manner similar to that in which the human soul is present in the human body. We have but one soul, and it is indivisible. Therefore it is present whole and entire in our whole body and whole and entire in each part of our body. Otherwise the various parts of our body could not function.

The Council of Trent saw fit to repeat the doctrine of transubstantiation, which had been defined by the Ecumenical Council, Lateran IV, 300 years before and which the Protestant Reformers denied. "By the consecration of the bread and wine a conversion takes place of the whole substance of bread into the substance of the body of Christ our Lord, and of the whole substance of the wine into the substance of his blood. This conversion is appropriately and properly called 'transubstantiation' by the Catholic Church." Again it must be remembered that the Church did not "canonize" Thomistic and Aristotelian teaching regarding "substance and accidents." The Church used the word, "substance," in its older and common meaning , namely, to designate that reality which underlies the appearances of things. For example, the substance remains the same in water, snow and ice, while the appearances change. This is the opposite of transubstantiation, in which the substances change and the appearances remain the same.

Because some of the Reformers wrongly claimed that Christ is present in the Host only at the time of Communion, and that it is idolatry to adore the Host outside of Communion, the Council reinforced the ancient custom of the Church of adoring the Host outside of Communion with the adoration which is due only to God. "It is not less to be adored because it was instituted by Christ our Lord to be received [in Communion]. For we believe that same God to be present [in the sacrament], of whom the eternal Father when introducing him to the world says: 'And let all the angels of God adore him,' whom the Magi 'falling down adored,' who finally as the Scriptures testify was adored by the Apostles in Galilee." And the Council goes on to defend the Feast of Corpus Christi with all its external display and including public procession with the Blessed Sacrament.

† † †

Let the light of your light shine on me,
O Lord; teach me your way of holiness.
May we face life's difficulties with confidence and faith.

The Council of Trent recalled that as early as the Council of Nicea I in 325 a.d. the custom of reserving the Blessed Sacrament was already recognized and should be continued, along with the custom of carrying the Eucharist to the sick.

In Canon 11 of the Council it declares that proper dispositions of soul are required to receive Communion worthily. "If anyone says that faith alone is sufficient preparation for receiving the sacrament of the most Holy Eucharist, let him be anathema (condemned). And that so great a sacrament may not be unworthily received, and therefore unto death and condemnation, this holy Council ordains and declares that sacramental Confession must necessarily be made beforehand by those whose conscience is burdened by mortal sin, however contrite they may consider themselves." The recent Catechism of the Catholic Church repeats this demand in #1385: "Anyone conscious of a grave sin must receive the sacrament of Reconciliation before coming to Communion."

After speaking of "spiritual Communion," that is, an ardent desire for receiving Communion without actually receiving the sacrament, the Council begs the Protestants to come back into the Church and receive sacramental Communion. "And finally this holy Synod with paternal affection admonishes, exhorts, entreats and beseeches, 'through the bowels of the mercy of God', that each and all who are called under the Christian name will now finally agree and be of the same opinion in this 'sign of unity', in this 'bond of charity'... Mindful of so great a majesty and such boundless love of our Lord Jesus Christ, who gave his own beloved soul as the price of our salvation, and gave his 'own flesh to eat', may they believe and venerate these mysteries of his body and blood with that constancy and firmness of faith, with that devotion of soul, that piety and worship, as to be able to receive frequently that 'supersubstantial bread' (Mt 6:11). And may it be for them truly the life of the soul and the perpetual health of mind, that being invigorated by the strength thereof, after the journey of this miserable pilgrimage, they may be able to arrive in their heavenly country to eat without any veil that same bread of angels, which they now eat under the sacred veils."

COUNCIL OF TRENT ON THE MASS

Because of the errors that the Protestant Reformers were spreading regarding the sacrifice of the Mass, the greatest treasure Christ left to the Church, the Council of Trent decreed "that in the holy Catholic Church there should be maintained complete and perfect in every way the faith and doctrine concerning the great mystery of the Eucharist." The Council then issued several decrees on the Mass.

At the Last Supper Jesus Christ, our God and Lord, was about to offer himself once to God the Father upon the altar of the cross by the mediation of death, so that he might accomplish the eternal redemption for all who were to be sanctified. But in order that his priestly office might not come to an end with his death, he offered to God the Father his own body and blood under the species of bread and wine, so that he might leave to his beloved spouse, the Church, a visible sacrifice whereby that bloody sacrifice once to be completed on the cross might be made present again, and its memory remain even to the end of the world, and its saving grace be applied to the remission of those sins which we daily commit [i.e. venial sins]. Declaring himself constituted "a priest forever according to the order of Melchisedech," he constituted the Apostles priests of the New Testament and commanded them and their successors in the priesthood in these words to offer sacrifice: 'Do this in memory of me.' This the Catholic Church has always understood and taught ... He instituted a new Passover, in which he himself would be immolated under visible signs [species of bread and wine] by the Church through the priests in memory of his own passage from this world to the Father."

† † †

HYMN IN HONOR OF HEAVEN

What, how great is that day of rest which the heavenly court ever keeps; what rest to the weary, what a reward to the strong, when God shall be all in all.

True Jerusalem is that city whose eternal peace is highest joy, where every wish is satisfied, where no wish can exceed what we shall possess.

There all troubles shall be over and we shall sing the songs of Zion in safety; there the blessed people will give eternal thanks for thy gifts to thee, O Lord.

There day of rest succeeds day of rest in the unchanging joy of them who keep unbroken rest; nor will the hymns ever cease which we with the angels shall sing.

Meanwhile we must lift our hearts, looking eagerly towards our fatherland, hoping at last to come to Jerusalem after long exile in Babylon.

To the eternal Lord be glory for ever, from whom and through whom and in whom are all things.

All things from the Father, through the Son, in the Spirit of the Father and Son.

Text: Peter Abelard, monk and professor at University of Paris (d.1142)
Translator: Adrian Fortescue

The Council declared the further grandeur of the Mass in 1) that it is the "clean oblation" which the Prophet Malachi [1:1,11] foretold must be offered in every place, and 2) that it is the sacrifice of which, St. Paul says, they cannot partake who practice devil worship, and 3) that it is the sacrifice that was prefigured by all the sacrifices from the beginning of time. The good things signified in all those sacrifices are contained in the Mass, which is the consummation and perfection of them all. Moreover this clean and perfect sacrifice of the Mass cannot be defiled by any unworthiness on the part of those who offer it.

The Council makes it clear that the priesthood which men possess today is simply a sharing in Christ's own priesthood. Therefore, it is the power of Christ the Priest that the human priest uses to change bread and wine into Christ at Mass and to forgive sins in the sacrament of Confession.

With clarity the Council pointed out the identity of Christ's sacrifice on the cross and the sacrifice of the Mass. They are one and the same sacrifice; only the manner of offering is different: on the cross the sacrifice was offered in a cruel and bloody manner; at Mass that same sacrifice is offered in a glorious, unbloody manner. "In this divine sacrifice, which is celebrated in the Mass, that same Christ is contained and immolated in an unbloody manner, who on the altar of the cross once offered himself in a bloody manner ... It is one and the same Victim, the same one now offering by the ministry of the priests as he who then offered himself on the cross, the manner of offering alone being different." We shall note later that from the close of the Council of Trent until our own day theologians have offered various explanations of this doctrine of the identity of the sacrifice of Christ and the sacrifice of the Mass.

Because the Mass is the sacrifice of Christ, only the manner of offering being different, the Council goes on to explain some of the benefits of the Mass. "The holy Synod teaches that Mass is truly propitiatory and has this effect, namely, if contrite and penitent we approach God with a sincere heart and right faith, with fear and reverence, we obtain mercy and find grace in seasonable aid. For, appeased by this oblation, the Lord grants the grace and gift of penitence, pardons crimes and even great sins ... The fruits of Christ's bloody oblation on the cross are received most abundantly through the unbloody oblation of the Mass." In this way the Mass in no way derogates from the bloody sacrifice of Christ on Calvary. "Mass is offered rightly according to the tradition of the Apostles not only for the sins of the faithful living and for their punishments and other necessities, but also for the dead in Christ who are not yet fully purged."

"And though the Church has been accustomed to celebrate some Masses now and then in honor and in memory of the Saints, yet she does not teach that the sacrifice is offered to them, but to God alone who has crowned them. ... The priest gives thanks to God for their victories and implores their patronage, so that they themselves may deign to intercede for us in heaven, whose memory we celebtrate on earth."

The Council states: "Holy Mother Church has instituted certain rites ... and makes use of ceremonies such as mystical blessings, lights, incense, vestments, and many other things of this kind in accordance with Apostolic teaching and tradition, whereby both the majesty of so great a sacrifice might be commended, and the minds of the faithful roused by these visible signs of religion and piety to the contemplation of the most sublime matters which lie hidden in this sacrifice."

"Lest the sheep of Christ suffer hunger, and little ones ask for bread and there be no one to break it for them, the holy Synod commands pastors and everyone who has the care of souls to explain frequently during the celebration of Masses, either themselves or through others, some of the things which are read in the Mass, and among other things to expound some mystery of this most holy sacrifice, especially on Sundays and Feast days."

Canon 2 on the Eucharist reads: "If anyone says that by these words, 'Do this in memory of me', Christ did not make the Apostles priests, or did not ordain that they and other priests might offer his own body and blood, let him be anathema [condemned]."

† † †

ANTHEM TO MARY *(Ave Regina Caelorum)*
*Hail, queen of heaven; hail lady of the angels. Hail root and gate
from which the Light of the world was born. Rejoice, glorious Virgin,
fairest of all. Farewell, most beautiful; and pray for us to Christ.*
V. Grant that I may praise thee, O holy Virgin.
R. Give me strength against thine enemies.
Let us pray.
*Grant, O merciful God, help to our weakness, that we who
commemorate the holy mother of God, may by the help of her
intercession rise from our sins. Through the same Christ our Lord.*
Amen.

Text: first known in 12th. century.
Translator: Adrian Fortescue

Do not be conquered by evil, but conquer evil with good.

CATECHISM OF THE COUNCIL OF TRENT

The nineteenth Ecumenical Council of Trent (1545-1563) condemned Protestantism and enacted reforms. To aid in the true reformation of the Church the Council authorized what is apparently the first universal catechism, a summary of the Christian faith for the entire Church. It was published in September 1566 by the authority of Pope St. Pius V. Our quotations from this Catechsim, often called the "Roman Catechism," are taken from the English translation by Maynooth College in Ireland, dated June 10, 1829.

The Preface to the Catechism points out its purpose and authority. "The Fathers of the general Council of Trent, anxious to apply some healing remedy to an evil of such magnitude [the Reformation], were not satisfied with having decided the more important points of Catholic doctrine against the heresies of our times, but deeming it further necessary to deliver some fixed form of instructing the faithful in the truths of religion from the very rudiments of Christian knowledge; a form to be followed by those to whom are lawfully entrusted the duties of pastor and teacher... The Fathers deemed it of the first importance that a work should appear, sanctioned by the authority of the holy Synod, from which pastors and all others on whom the duty of imparting instruction devolves, may draw with security precepts for the edification of the faithful; that as there is 'one Lord, one faith' there may also be one standard and prescribed form of propounding the dogmas of faith, and instructing Christians in all the duties of piety."

† † †

EASTER HYMN TO MARY *(Regina Caeli)*

*Queen of heaven, rejoice, alleluia; for he whom thou wast chosen to
bear, alleluia; has risen as he said, alleluia; pray for us to God,
alleluia.*
V. Rejoice and be glad, O Virgin Mary, alleluia.
R. For the Lord has risen indeed, alleluia.
*Let us pray. O God, who didst vouchsafe to give joy to the world
through the resurrection of thy Son, our Lord Jesus Christ; grant, we
beseech thee, that, through his mother, the Virgin Mary, we may
obtain the joys of everlasting life. Text: first known c. 1200.*

Tr.:Adrian Fortescue

In its Preface the Catechism makes it clear to whom it was principally
directed, namely, the pastors of parishes. "The Holy Synod intended that
such things only should be treated of as might assist the pious zeal of pastors
in discharging the duty of instruction... All the doctrines of Christianity,
in which the faithful are to be instructed, are derived from the word of
God, which includes Scripture and Tradition..."

"We, therefore, deem it proper to acquaint pastors that, whenever they
have occasion, in the ordinary discharge of their duty, to expound any
passage of the Gospel, or any other part of Scripture, they will find its
substance [in the Catechism], to which they will recur, as the source from
which their exposition is to be drawn."

The Catechism explains what it means by the word, "faith." "Here we
speak of that faith by which we yield our entire assent to whatever has
been revealed by Almighty God. That faith thus understood is necessary
to salvation no man can reasonably doubt; particularly as the Sacred
Scriptures declare that: 'Without faith it is impossible to please God."
[Hebr 11:6] For as the end proposed for man as his ultimate happiness
[heaven] is far above the reach of the human understanding, it was,
therefore, necessary that it should be made known to him by Almighty

God. This knowledge is nothing else than faith, by which we yield our unhesitating assent to whatever the authority of our Holy Mother the Church teaches us to have been revealed by Almighty God."

† † †

HYMN FOR EASTER (Ad Regias Agni Dapes)

Called to the Lamb's royal banquet, clothed in white robes, after crossing the Red Sea, let us sing to Christ the Prince;
Whose divine love gives us his sacred blood; he our high Priest offers his sacred body.
Now is Christ our Passover; he our paschal sacrifice, pure unleavened bread of sincerity to pure minds.
O true heavenly sacrifice by which hell is defeated, the chains of death are broken, the reward of life is obtained.

Text: early 9th century; modified by Pope Urban V111 in l7th century.

Tr.: A. Fortescue

Continuing to use the English translation by Maynooth College, Ireland, we quote from Catechism material on the Eucharist:

"Of all the sacred mysteries bequeathed to us by our Lord as unfailing sources of grace, there is none that can compare to the most holy Sacrament of the Eucharist; for no crime, therefore, is there reserved by God a more terrible vengeance than for the sacrilegious abuse of this adorable Sacrament, which is replete with holiness itself... That the faithful, therefore, deeply impressed with the divine honor due to this heavenly Sacrament, may derive from its participation abundant fruit of grace, and escape the just anger of God, the pastor will explain with indefatigable diligence all those things which seem best calculated to display its majesty."

385

"This sacrament is significant of three things: the passion of Christ, a thing past; divine grace, a thing present; and eternal glory, a thing future. It is significant of the passion of Christ: 'As often as you shall eat this bread and drink the chalice, you shall show the death of the Lord until he comes" [ICo 11:26]. It is significant of divine grace, which is infused on receiving this Sacrament to nurture and preserve the soul...By the Sacrament of the Eucharist we are spiritually nurtured and supported. It is also significant of eternal glory, which according to the divine promises, is reserved for us in our celestial country ['Anyone who eats my flesh and drinks my blood has eternal life, and I shall raise him up on the last day' " (Jn 6:54).

† † †

HYMN FOR FEAST OF ALL SAINTS
*Have pity, Christ, on thy servants, for whom at thy mercy seat the
Virgin asks the Father's grace.
And you, blessed army of heaven ordered in nine choirs, drive away
past evil with those present and to come.   Apostles and Prophets,
pray the great Judge to forgive us, who truly mourn our sins.
Ye martyrs purple-stained, and you white-robed in glorious confession
of faith, call us exiles to our home.
Pure choir of virgins, hermits whom
the desert sent to heaven,
place us on thrones above.*

*Text: unknown author of 14th century.
Tr.: Adrian Fortescue*

The Catechism offers reasons for adding a little water to the wine used at Mass. "That our Lord made use of wine in the institution of this Sacrament has been at all times the doctrine of the Catholic Church... With the wine used in the sacred mysteries the Church of God, however, has always mingled water, because, as we know on the authority of councils and the testimony of St. Cyprian, our Lord himself did so; and also because this mixture renews the recollection of the blood and water that issued from his sacred side. The word 'water' we also find used in the Apocalypse to signify the people [Rev 17:1,5], and therefore water mixed with wine signifies the union of the faithful with Christ their head. This rite, derived from apostolic tradition, the Catholic Church has at all times observed. But care must be taken not only to mingle water with wine, but also to mingle it in small quantity; for in the opinion of ecclesiastical writers the water is changed into wine." [Therefore the water made wine becomes the blood of Christ]

† † †

HYMN TO THE HOLY TRINITY

Praise to thee, God the Father, and to thy Son who became our brother in this exile. From both proceeds the holy Comforter, together with the Father and the Son God and Lord. Lord have mercy. Join all souls in the bond of union and fasten close the ties of love. Let not our sins provoke thee to vengeance, but grant forgiveness while we repent of them.
Lord have mercy.
Grant that we may receive worthily the holy viaticum, that we may be defended by this shield at the end of life. Grant that we may be joined in joy to thy heavenly court, there to see thy mysteries. Lord have mercy.

Text: J. Mohr: Canciones Sacrae, Pustet, 1891.
Translator: A. Fortescue

Trust firmly in the Lord and do his will; and you will dwell secure in the land of promise.

The Catechism took up the matter of the propriety of Christ's having chosen bread and wine to be used for the Eucharist. "We come now to consider the aptitude of these two elements to declare those things of which they are the sensible signs. In the first place, they signify Christ, the true life of the world; for our Lord himself has said: 'My flesh is meat indeed, and my blood is drink indeed.'[Jn 6:55] As, therefore, the body of our Lord Jesus Christ nourishes to eternal life those who receive it with purity and holiness, with great propriety is this Sacrament composed principally of those elements which sustain life; thus giving the faithful to understand that the soul is nurtured with grace by a participation of the precious body and blood of Christ."

"These elements [bread and wine] also prove the dogma of the Real Presence. Seeing, as we do, that bread and wine are every day changed by the power of nature into human flesh and blood, we are, by the obvious analogy of the fact, the more readily induced to believe that the substance of bread and wine is changed by the celestial benediction into the real body and blood of Christ. This admirable change also contributes to illustrate what takes place in the soul. As the bread and wine, though invisibly, are really and substantially changed into the body and blood of Christ, so are we, although interiorly and invisibly, yet really, renewed to life, receiving in the Sacrament of the Eucharist the true life."

"Moreover, the body of the Church, although one and undivided, consists of the union of many members, and of this mysterious union nothing is more strikingly illustrative than bread and wine. Bread is made from many grains, wine is pressed from many grapes, and thus are we too, although many, closely united by this mysterious bond of union, and made as it were one body."

† † †

Lord, clothe us with the weapons of light and unite us under the one banner of love, that we may receive our eternal reward after the battle of earthly life.
I put my trust in the Lord; his promise bears me up.

The sublime mystery of the Eucharist is to be judged not by the senses but by faith. "To return to those things of which the faithful are on no account to be suffered to remain ignorant, the pastor, aware of the awful denunciation of the Apostle [Paul] against those who discern not the body of the Lord [1Co 11:29], will first of all impress on the minds of the faithful the necessity of detaching as much as possible their minds and understandings from the dominion of the senses; for were they with regard to this sublime mystery to constitute the senses the only tribunal to which they are to appeal, the awful consequence must be their precipitation into the extreme of impiety. Consulting the sight, the touch, the smell, the taste, and finding nothing but the appearances of bread and wine, the senses must naturally lead them to think that this Sacrament contains nothing more than bread and wine. Their minds, therefore, are as much as possible to be withdrawn from subjection to the senses, and excited to the contemplation of the stupendous power of God."

"The Catholic Church then firmly believes and openly professes that in this sacrament the words of consecration accomplish three things: first, that the true and real body of Christ, the same that was born of the Virgin and is now seated at the right hand of the Father in heaven, is rendered present in the Holy Eucharist; secondly, that however repugnant it may appear to the dictate of the senses, no substance of the elements [bread and wine] remains in the Sacrament; and thirdly, a natural consequence of the two preceeding and one which the words of consecration also express, that the accidents [appearances] which present themselves to the eyes or other senses exist in a wonderful and ineffable manner without a subject. The accidents of bread and wine we see; but they inhere in no substance, and exist independently of any. The substance of the bread and wine is so changed into the body and blood of our Lord, that they altogether cease to be the substance of bread and wine."

† † †

Create in me a clean heart, O God;
renew in me a steadfast spirit.

The Real Presence is proved from the Bible. "The pastor...will give his best attention to show how clear and explicit are the words of our Savior, which establish the real presence of his body in the Sacrament of the Eucharist. When our Lord says: 'This is my body, this is my blood,' no man however ignorant, unless he labors under some obliquity of intellect, can mistake his meaning; particularly if he recollect that the words 'body' and 'blood' refer to his human nature, the real assumption of which by the Son of God no Catholic can doubt. To use the admirable words of St. Hilary, a man not less eminent for piety than learning: 'When our Lord himself declares, as our faith teaches us, that his flesh is meat indeed, what room can remain for doubt?' "

"The pastor will also adduce another passage from Scripture in proof of this sublime truth: having recorded the consecration of the bread and wine by our Lord and also the administration of the sacred mysteries to the Apostles by the hands of the Savior, the Apostle [Paul] adds: 'But let a man prove himself, and so eat of that bread and drink of the chalice, for he that eateth and drinketh unworthily, eateth and drinketh judgment to himself, not discerning the body of the Lord.' If, as heresy asserts, the Sacrament presents nothing to our veneration but a memorial and sign of the passion of Christ, why exhort the faithful in language so energetic to prove themselves? The answer is obvious: by the heavy denunciation contained in the word 'judgment' the Apostle marks the enormity of his guilt, who receives unworthily and distinguishes not from common food the body of the Lord concealed beneath the eucharistic veil. The preceding words of the Apostle develop more fully his meaning: 'The chalice of benediction,' he says, 'which we bless, is it not the communion of the blood of Christ? and the bread which we break, is it not the participation of the body of the Lord?' Words which prove to demonstration the real presence of Jesus Christ in the holy Sacrament of the Eucharist."

† † †

If God has loved us so, we must have
the same love for one another.

The dogma of the Real Presence is proved also by Sacred Tradition, as it is found in the Fathers of the Church and the Councils of the Church.

"These passages of Scripture [pertaining to the Eucharist and just cited] are to be expounded by the pastor; and he will emphatically impress upon the attention of the faithful that their meaning, in itself obvious, is placed beyond all doubt by the uniform interpretation and authority of the Holy Catholic Church. That such has been at all times the doctrine of the Church may be ascertained in a two-fold manner: by consulting the Fathers who flourished in the early ages of the Church and in each succeeding century, who are the most unexceptionable witnesses of her doctrine, and all of whom teach in the clearest terms, and with the most entire unanimity, the dogma of the real presence... To adduce the individual testimony of each Father would prove an endless task." [In the previous pages of this work we quoted testimony from over one hundred Fathers.]

The second proof of the dogma of the Real Presence is found in the local and ecumenical Councils of the Church. "Another means of ascertaining the belief of the Church on matters of faith is the condemnation of the contrary doctrine. That the belief of the real presence was that of the universal Church of God, unanimously professed by all her children, is demonstrated by a well authenticated fact. When in the eleventh century Berengarius presumed to deny this dogma, asserting that the Eucharist was only a sign, the innovation was immediately condemned by the unanimous voice of the Christian world. The Council of Vercelli, convened by authority of Leo 1X, denounced the heresy, and Berengarius himself retracted and anathematized his error. Relapsing, however, into the same infatuation and impiety, he was condemned by three different Councils, convened, one at Tours, the other two at Rome... The general Council of Lateran held under Innocent III further ratified the sentence [of condemnation]; and the faith of the Catholic Church on this point of doctrine was more fully declared and more firmly established in the [ecumenical] Councils of Florence and Trent.

The Catechism points out the dignity conferred on the Church by the institution of the Eucharist. "Nothing contributes more to light up in the pious soul spiritual joy; nothing is more fertile of spiritual fruit, than the contemplation of the exalted dignity of this most august Sacrament. From it we learn how great must be the perfection of the Gospel dispensation [the New Testament], under which we enjoy the reality of that, which under the Mosaic Law was only shadowed by types and figures. Hence St. Denis, with a wisdom more than human, says that our Church is a mean between the synagogue and the heavenly Jerusalem, and participates of the nature of both."

"The perfection of the Holy Catholic Church and her exalted glory, removed only by one degree from heaven, the faithful cannot sufficiently admire. In common with the inhabitants of heaven we too possess Christ, God and man, present with us; but they — and in this they are raised a degree above us — are admitted to the actual enjoyment of the beatific vision; whilst we, with a firm and unwavering faith offer the tribute of our homage to the Divine Majesty present with us not, it is true, in a manner visible to mortal eye, but hidden by a miracle of power under the veil of the sacred mysteries."

Why is the bread and wine consecrated separately? "Wisely was it ordained that two distinct consecrations should take place. They represent in a more lively manner the passion of our Lord, in which his blood was separated from his body; and hence, in the form of consecration we commemorate the effusion of his blood. The sacrament is to be used by us as the food and nourishment of our souls; and it was most accordant with this that it should be instituted as meat and drink, which obviously constitute the proper food of man."

† † †

Lord, you open the way and no one can close it. Lead into your light
those who have fallen asleep
in the hope of resurrection.
If you hunger for holiness, God will satisfy your longing with good
measure and flowing over.

Why is the Eucharist sometimes called bread after the consecration? "Here the pastor will not omit to observe to the faithful that we should not at all be surprised, if even after consecration the Eucharist is sometimes called bread. It is so called because it has the appearance and still retains the natural quality of bread, which is to support and nourish the body. That such phraseology is in perfect accordance with the style of the Holy Scriptures, which call things by what they appear to be, is evident from the words of Genesis (18:2), which say that Abraham saw three men, when in reality he saw three angels. And the two angels who appeared to the Apostles after the ascension of our Lord are called, not angels, but men.'" (Acts 1:10)

Regarding transubstantiation: "This admirable change, as the Council of Trent teaches, the Catholic Church most appropriately expresses by the word 'transubstantiation.' When in the natural order the form of a being is changed, that change may be properly termed 'a transformation.' In like manner, when in the Sacrament of the Eucharist the whole substance of one thing passes into the whole substance of another, the change our predecessors in the faith wisely and appropriately called 'transubstantiation.'"

"But according to the admonition so frequently repeated by the Holy Fathers, the faithful are to be admonished against the danger of satisfying a prurient curiosity by searching into the manner in which this change is effected. It mocks the powers of conception, nor can we find any example of it in natural transmutations, nor even in the wide range of creation. The change itself is the object not of our comprehension, but of our humble faith; and the manner of that change forbids the temerity of a too curious inquiry."(Eccus.3:22)

† † †

If you hunger for holiness, God will satisfy your longing, good
measure, and flowing over.
Left to itself, our nature is inclined to sin; let your love, O Lord,
always strengthen us by your grace.

"The pastor will next teach that our Lord is not in the Sacrament as in a place: place regards things only in as much as they have magnitude; and we do not say that Christ is in the Sacrament in as much as he is great or small, terms which belong to quantity, by in as much as he is a substance. The substance of bread is changed into the substance of Christ, not into magnitude or quantity; and substance, it will be acknowledged, is contained in a small as well as in a large space. The substance of air, for instance, whether in a large or small quantity, and that of water whether confined in a vessel or flowing in a river, must necessarily be the same. As then the body of our Lord succeeds to the substance of the bread, we must confess it to be in the Sacrament after the same manner as the bread was before consecration. Whether the substance of the bread was present in greater or less quantity is a matter of entire indifference."

"It is becoming to the piety of the faithful, omitting subtle disquisitions, to revere and adore in the simplicity of faith the majesty of this august Sacrament; and with sentiments of gratitude and admiration to recognize the wisdom of God in the institution of the holy mysteries under the species of bread and wine. To eat human flesh or to drink human blood is most revolting to human nature, and therefore God in his infinite wisdom has established the administration of the body and blood of Christ under the forms of bread and wine, the ordinary and agreeable food of man. From its administration under these forms also flow two other important advantages: it obviates the calumnious reproaches of the unbeliever, to which a manducation of the body and blood of our Lord under human form must be exposed; and [secondly] by receiving him under a form in which he is impervious to the senses, our faith is augmented."

† † †

Children, says the Lord, listen to my words of wisdom;
pay attention to my counsel.
If God has loved us so, we must have
the same love for one another.

The Catechism lists five salutary effects of the sacrament of the Eucharist. First, it imparts grace. "With great truth is the Holy Eucharist called the fountain of all grace, containing as it does after an admirable manner, the source of all gifts and graces, the author of all the Sacraments, Christ our Lord, from whom as from their source, they derive all their goodness and perfection."

"It will also be found expedient to consider attentively the nature of bread and wine, the symbols of this sacrament: what bread and wine are to the body, the Eucharist is in a superior order to the health and joy of the soul. It is not, like bread and wine, changed into our substance; but in some measure changes us into its own nature, and to it we apply these words of St. Augustine: 'I am the food of the grown; grow and thou shalt partake of this food; nor shalt thou change me into thee as thou dost thy corporal food, but thou shalt be changed into me.' "

"If then 'grace and truth come by Jesus Christ [Jn 1:17] , these spiritual treasures must be poured into that soul which receives with purity and holiness him who says of himself: 'He that eateth my flesh and drinketh my blood abideth in me and I in him.' Those who piously and religiously receive this Sacrament receive, no doubt, the Son of God into their souls, and are united as living members to his body; for it is written: 'He that eateth me the same shall also live by me'; and also: 'The bread that I shall give is my flesh for the life of the world.' Explaining these words of the Savior St. Cyril says: 'The Eternal Word, uniting himself to his own flesh, imparted to it a vivifying power; it became him therefore to unite himself to us in a wonderful manner through his sacred flesh and precious blood.' "

But one must be in the state of grace to receive the grace of the Eucharist. "Natural food can be of no use to one already dead; and likewise the sacred mysteries can avail him nothing who lives not in Spirit. Hence this Sacrament has been instituted under the forms of bread and wine to signify that the object of its institution is not to recall to life a dead soul [in mortal sin], but to preserve life to a living one."

In continuing its comparison between natural food and the spiritual food of the Eucharist the Catechism says: "As the body is not only supported but increased by natural food, from which we derive new pleasure every day, so also the life of the soul is not only sustained but also invigorated by feasting on the Eucharistic banquet, which imparts to it an increasing zest for heavenly things. With strictest truth and propriety therefore, do we say that this Sacrament, which may be well compared to manna 'having in it all that is delicious and the sweetness of every taste' (Wisd 16:20), imparts grace to the soul."

The second effect of this sacrament is that it remits venial sin. "That the Holy Eucharist remits lighter offenses or, as they are commonly called, venial sins, cannot be a matter of doubt. Whatever losses the soul sustains by falling into some slight offenses through the violence of passion, these the Eucharist, which cancels lesser sins, repairs in the same manner, not to depart from the illustration already adduced, that natural food, as we know from experience, gradually repairs the daily waste caused by the vital heat of the system. Of this heavenly Sacrament justly, therefore, has St. Ambrose said: 'This daily bread is taken as a remedy for daily infirmity.' This, however, is to be understood of venial imperfections only."

The third effect is that "the Holy Eucharist is also an antidote against the contagion of sin and a shield against the violent assaults of temptation. It is, as it were, a heavenly medicine, which secures the soul against the easy approach of virulent and deadly infection."

The fourth effect is that the Eucharist "also represses the licentious desires of the flesh and keeps them in due subjection to the spirit. In proportion as it inflames the soul with the fire of charity, in the same proportion does it necessarily extinguish the fire of concupiscence."

† † †

You forgave the penitent woman and placed the wandering sheep on your shoulders.
Do not deprive us of your mercy, O Lord.

The fifth and last salutary effect of the sacrament is, according to the Catechism, that "the Holy Eucharist facilitates to an extraordinary degree the attainment of eternal life: 'He that eateth my flesh and drinketh my blood,' says the Redeemer, hath everlasting life, and I will raise him up on the last day'(Jn 6:54). The grace which it imparts brings peace and tranquility to the soul; and when the hour shall have arrived in which he is to take his departure from this mortal life, like another Elias, who in the strength of his miraculous repast, walked to Horeb, the Mount of God, the Christian, invigorated by the strengthening influence of this heavenly food, shall wing his way to the mansions of everlasting glory and never-ending bliss."

To receive the salutary effects of Holy Communion the Catechism points out that proper preparation is required. In the first place, of course, one must be in the state of Sanctifying Grace, that is, not conscious of having committed any mortal sin since his last good Confession. "It is the property of the best and most salutary medicine, if seasonably applied, to be productive of the greatest benefit; but if unseasonably, to prove most pernicious and destructive... Food when received into a healthy stomach nourishes and supports the body; but the same food, when received into a stomach replete with peccant humors, generates malignant disease.."

Second, faith in the Real Presence is required. The faithful are "to distinguish table from table, this sacred table from profane tables (1Co 11:29), this celestial bread from common bread. This we do when we firmly believe that the Eucharist really and truly contains the body and blood of the Lord."

"Another very necessary preparation is to ask ourselves, if we are at peace with our neighbor, if we sincerely and from the heart love him." 'If thou offerest thy gift at the altar and there rememberest that thy brother has aught against thee, leave there thy offering before the altar, and go first to be reconciled to thy brother, and then coming thou shalt offer thy gift.' "

The Catechism mentions other things we can do to prepare ourselves properly to receive Communion. "We should also reflect in the silence of our own hearts how unworthy we are that God should bestow on us this divine gift; and with the Centurion, of whom our Lord declared that he had not found 'so great faith in Israel,' we should exclaim: 'Lord, I am not worthy that thou shouldst enter under my roof.'(Mt8:8)

"We should also put the question to ourselves whether we can truly say with Peter: 'Lord, thou knowest that I love thee.' "

"Our preparation should not, however, be confined to the soul; it should also extend to the body. We are to approach the Holy Eucharist fasting. "Finally the Catechism adds that we should make "whatever other preparations piety will suggest to the devout communicant."

Regarding the frequency of Communion we read: "Let not the faithful imagine that it is enough to receive the body of the Lord once a year only, in obedience to the decree of the Church. They should approach oftener: but whether monthly, weekly, or daily cannot be decided by any fixed universal rule. St. Augustine, however, lays down a most certain rule applicable to all: 'Live,' he says, 'in such a manner as to be able to receive every day.' It will therefore be the duty of the pastor frequently to admonish the faithful, that as they deem it necessary to afford daily nutriment to the body, they should also feel solicitous to feed and nourish the soul every day with this heavenly food The soul stands not less in need of spiritual, than the body of corporal, food. The words, 'thou sinnest daily, receive daily,' convey the sentiments not only of St. Augustine, but of all the Fathers who have written on the subject."

† † †

We adore you, O Christ, and we bless you; because by your holy Cross
you have redeemed the world.
May the Holy Trinity be blessed.
Christ conquers! Christ reigns! Christ commands!
Grant that I may praise you, O sacred Virgin; give me strength
against your enemies.

As to Communion under only one form the Catechism says: "The Church, no doubt, was influenced by numerous and cogent reasons, not only to approve but to confirm by solemn decree, the general practice of communicating under one species. In the first place the greatest caution was necessary to avoid accident or indignity, which must become almost inevitable if the chalice were administered in a crowded assemblage. In the next place the Holy Eucharist should at all times be ready for the sick; and if the species of wine remained long unconsumed, it were to be apprehended that it may become vapid. Besides, there are many who cannot bear the taste or smell of wine. Lest therefore what is intended for the nutriment of the soul should prove noxious to the health of the body, the Church in her wisdom has sanctioned its administration under the species of bread alone. We may also observe that in many places wine is extremely scarce; nor can it be brought from distant countries without incurring very heavy expense and encountering very tedious and difficult journeys."

"Finally, a circumstance which principally influenced the Church in establishing this practice, means were to be devised to crush the heresy, which denied that Christ, whole and entire, is contained under either species, and asserted that the body is contained under the species of bread without the blood, and the blood under the species of wine without the body. This object was attained by Communion under the species of bread alone, which places, as it were, sensibly before our eyes the truth of the Catholic faith."

† † †

Direct, we beg you, O Lord, our actions by your holy inspirations, and carry them on by your gracious assistance, that every prayer and work of ours may begin always with you, and through you be happily ended. (Roman Ritual) (Partial indulgence)

O my God, because you are infinite goodness and worthy of infinite love, I love you with my whole heart above all things, and for love of you I love my fellow-men as myself. (Partial indulgence)

The Catechism will naturally have some things to say about the Mass. "The nature of the Eucharist as a sacrifice we now come to explain, that pastors may know what are the principal instructions to be communicated to the faithful regarding this mystery on Sundays and holidays in compliance with the decree of the Council of Trent. Not only is this sacrament a treasure of heavenly riches, which if we turn to good account will purchase for us the favor and friendship of heaven; but it also possesses the peculiar and extraordinary value, that in it we are enabled to make some suitable return to God for the inestimable benefits bestowed on us by his bounty. If duly and legitimately offered, this Victim is most grateful and most acceptable to God. If the sacrifices of the Old Law, of which it is written: 'Sacrifices and oblations thou wouldst not... were so acceptable in his sight... what have we not to hope from the efficacy of a sacrifice in which is immolated no less a Victim than He, of whom a voice from heaven twice proclaimed: 'This is my beloved Son, in whom I am well pleased.' "

"The pastor will teach in the first place that the Eucharist was instituted by our Lord for two great purposes, to be the celestial food of the soul, preserving and supporting spiritual life, and to give to the Church a perpetual sacrifice, by which sin may be expiated, and our heavenly Father, whom our crimes have often grievously offended, may be turned from wrath to mercy, from the severity of just vengeance to the exercise of benignant clemency... Nor could our divine Lord, when about to offer himself to his eternal Father on the altar of the cross, have given a more illustrious proof of his unbounded love for us, than by bequeathing to us a visible sacrifice, by which the bloody sacrifice, which a little while after was to be offered once on the cross, was to be renewed, and its memory celebrated daily throughout the universal Church even to the consummation of time, to the great advantage of her children."

✝ ✝ ✝

Most Sacred Heart of Jesus, have mercy on us.

"We therefore confess that the sacrifice of the Mass is one and the same sacrifice with that of the cross: the victim is one and the same, Christ Jesus, who offered himself, once only, a bloody sacrifice on the altar of the cross. The bloody and unbloody victim is still one and the same, and the oblation of the cross is daily renewed in the Eucharistic sacrifice, in obedience to the command of the Lord: 'This do, for a commemoration of me.' The priest is also the same, Christ our Lord; the ministers who offer this sacrifice consecrate the holy mysteries not in their own but in the person of Christ. This the words of consecration declare: the priest does not say, 'This is the body of Christ,' but 'This is my body'; and thus invested with the character of Christ, he changes the substance of the bread and wine into the substance of his real body and blood."

"That the holy sacrifice of the Mass, therefore, is not only a sacrifice of praise and thanksgiving, or a commemoration of the sacrifice of the cross; but also a sacrifice of propitiation, the pastor will teach as a dogma defined by the unerring authority of a general Council of the Church."

"If, therefore, with pure hearts and a lively faith, and with a sincere sorrow for past transgressions, we immolate and offer in sacrifice this most holy victim, we shall, no doubt, receive from the Lord 'mercy and grace in seasonable aid.' So acceptable to God is the sweet odor of this sacrifice, that through its oblation he pardons our sins, bestowing on us the gifts of grace and repentance. This is the solemn prayer of the Church: as often as the commemoration of this victim is celebrated, so often is the work of our salvation promoted, and the plenteous fruits of that bloody victim flow in upon us abundantly, through this unbloody sacrifice."

"The pastor will also teach that such is the efficacy of this sacrifice, that its benefits extend not only to the celebrant and communicant, but also to all the faithful whether living or numbered amongst those who have died in the Lord, but whose sins have not yet been fully expiated."

Chapter XX

THE EUCHARIST FROM TRENT TO OUR DAY

The Protestant Revolt of the sixteenth century had one very happy and very beneficial result, namely, the Council of Trent, which met on and off from 1545 to 1563. In order to combat the many errors proposed by the Protestant Reformers, the Council, under the inspiration of the Holy Spirit, saw fit to define a huge volume of Catholic doctrine taken from divine Revelation in the Bible and in Sacred Tradition. This was necessary to prevent Catholics from falling into religious error. Included in the Council's doctrinal definitions was, as we saw, considerable material on the Eucharist.

In its long history the Church had found it necessary to convene a General or Ecumenical Council about every 100 years. The Council of Trent was so thorough, that no Ecumenical Council was held until Vatican I some 300 years later.

During the four centuries since the close of the Council of Trent there have been no major developments in doctrine concerning the Eucharist. For the most part the Protestants have maintained the Eucharistic errors of their founders, while the hundreds of different sects that were born from the original Protestant Churches have usually followed the errors of the parent Churches. Since the devil never sleeps, the Church has had to correct some relatively minor errors to protect the faith of Catholics. However, both officially and through the work of her theologians, the Church has sought to deepen our understanding and appreciation of the Eucharistic doctrine defined by the Council of Trent.

† † †

O Mary, of all women
Thou art the chosen one,
Who ancient prophets promised
Would bear God's only Son;
All Hebrew generations

Prepared the way to thee,
That in your womb the God-man
Might come to set man free.
Text: Michael Gannon

After the Council of Trent some bishops and priests were limiting the frequency with which both adults and children could receive Holy Communion. This prompted the Sacred Congregation of the Council to issue the following decree in 1679.

"Although the daily and frequent use of the most holy Eucharist has always been approved by the holy Fathers of the Church, yet never have they appointed certain days either for receiving it more often or certain days of the weeks and months for abstaining from it, which the Council of Trent did not prescribe; but as it considered the frailty of human nature, although making no command, it merely indicated what it would prefer when it said: 'The Holy Council would indeed wish that at every Mass the faithful present would communicate by the sacramental reception of the Eucharist.'" [And the Decree applied its words to both adults and children.]

"...the diligence of pastors will be especially alert, not that some may not be deterred from frequent or daily partaking of Holy Communion by a single formula of precept, or that days for partaking be established generally, but rather let it be decided what should be permitted to each, or should be decided for themselves by themselves, or by the priests or confessors. And let this be prohibited entirely, namely, if one approach the sacred banquet frequently or daily, let him not be repelled. And yet, let the pastor see to it that everyone taste of the sweetness of the body of the Lord more rarely or more frequently according to his measure of devotion and preparation."

The Decree mentions the proper preparation required for receiving Communion frequently or daily, as people should receive it. "They ought to understand their own weakness, so that because of the dignity of the Sacrament and the fear of the divine punishment they may learn to revere the celestial table on which is Christ; and if at any time they should feel themselves not prepared, to abstain from it and to gird themselves for a greater preparation."

† † †

Be still and know that I am God.

In March of 1743 Pope Benedict X1V prescribed a Profession of Faith for Oriental Catholics (Maronites), which simply repeated the Profession of Faith of the Council of Trent. Regarding the Eucharist it states the following:

"I revere and accept the Council of Trent; and I profess what was defined and declared in it, and especially that there is offered to God in the Mass a true, proper and propitiatory sacrifice, for the living and the dead; and that in the Most Holy Sacrament of the Eucharist, in accordance with the faith that had always been in the Church of God, there is contained truly, really and substantially the body and blood together with the soul and divinity of our Lord Jesus Christ, and hence the whole Christ; and that there is made a change of the whole substance of the bread into the body, and of the whole substance of the wine into the blood, which change the Catholic Church most fittingly calls transubstantiation; and that under each species and in each single part of each species, when a division is made, the whole Christ is contained."

Pope Pius VI in 1794 had to condemn many errors that were made in the local Synod of Pistoia in northern Italy six years previous. Regarding the Eucharist the Pope condemned the proposition that Mass is illicit if only the priest receives Holy Communion. He also condemned the Synod's failure to mention transubstantiation in its explanation of the Eucharist, and that the priest celebrant cannot apply the special fruit of the Mass according to his wishes, and that there be no more than one altar in any church.

† † †

O God, our help in ages past,
Our hope for years to come,
Be now our guide while life shall last,

And our eternal home.
Text: Isaac Watts

Accept one another as Christ accepted you.

Pope Pius VII in May of 1822, as well as Pope Pius X in December of 1910, had to repeat the former correction of the error by Oriental Catholics that held the "epiclesis" (invocation of the Holy Spirit) to be necessary for "the perfect and complete" consecration of the gifts at Mass. The Church teaches that the words of Christ at the consecration are sufficient to change "the entire substance of the bread into the body of Christ, and the entire substance of the wine into the blood of Christ."

In his encyclical on the Eucharist of May 1902, entitled "Mirae caritatis," Pope Leo X111 saw fit to correct the error of those who contended that the reception of Holy Communion is intended only for a certain class or type of persons. "Away then with that widespread and most pernicious error on the part of those who express the opinion that the reception of the Eucharist is for the most part assigned to those who, free of cares and narrow in mind, decide to rest at ease in some kind of a more religious life. For this sacrament (and there is certainly none more excellent or more conducive to salvation than this) pertains to absolutely all, of whatever office or pre-eminence they are, as many as wish (and no one ought not to wish this) to foster within themselves that life of divine grace, whose final end is the attainment of the blessed life with God." D.S.3361 [Sources]

In that same encyclical Pope Leo repeats what the Council of Trent had declared concerning the connection of the Eucharist to the Church, namely, that Christ left the Eucharist to the Church "as a symbol of its unity and love, by which he willed that all Christians be joined and united to one another ... a symbol of that body, of which he is the head." D.S.3362

Likewise the Pope explains that the Eucharist benefits all those belonging to the Communion of Saints. "The Communion of Saints is nothing more than the mutual communication of help, expiation, prayers, and benefits among the faithful, whether they enjoy the heavenly homeland or are consigned to the cleansing fire or are still wayfarers on earth. They are all united together to form the city, of which Christ is the head and love is the soul." D.S.3363

✝ ✝ ✝

It is my joy, O God, to praise you with song.

POPE ST. PIUS X 1903-1914

Due to lingering effects of the rigoristic heresy of Jansenism, there arose in Belgium at the end of the last century and the beginning of the twentieth heated debate concerning the frequency with which Holy Communion is to be received and the essential requirements for receiving it. The debate became so acrimonious that the Pope was asked to settle it. This he did by a Decree in December of 1905, which included a Decree by the Sacred Congregation of the Council.

"The desire of Jesus Christ and of the Church, that all the faithful of Christ approach the sacred banquet daily, is especially important in this, that the faithful of Christ being joined with God through the sacrament may receive strength from it to restrain wantonness, to wash away the little faults that occur daily, and to guard against more grievous sins to which human frailty is subject; but not principally that consideration be given to the honor and veneration of God, nor that this be for those who partake of it a reward or recompense for their virtues. Therefore, the Sacred Council of Trent calls the Eucharist 'an antidote, by which we are freed from daily faults and are preserved from mortal sins.' "

"Because of the plague of Jansenism, which raged on all sides, disputes began to arise regarding the dispositions with which frequent and daily Communion should be approached; and some more than others demanded greater and more difficult dispositions as necessary. Such discussions brought it about that very few were held worthy to partake daily of the most blessed Eucharist, and to draw the fuller effects from so saving a sacrament, the rest being content to being renewed either once a year or every month or at most once a week. Such a point of severity was reached that entire groups were excluded from frequenting the heavenly table, for example, merchants or those who had been joined in matrimony."

† † †

Lord, grant that we should always
offer you the Psalms you have made.
Then we will live to praise you
and never forget your commands.

By order of the Pope the Congregation of the Sacred Council published the following Decree.

1. "Let frequent and daily Communion ... be available to all Christians of every order or condition, so that no one who is in the state of grace and approaches the sacred table with a right and pious mind, may be prevented from this.

2. Moreover, right mind is in this, that he who approaches the sacred table indulges not through habit or vanity or human reasonings, but wishes to satisfy the pleasure of God, to be joined to Him more closely in charity and to oppose his infirmities and defects with that divine remedy.

3. Although it is especially expedient that those who practice frequent and daily Communion be free from venial sins, at least those completely deliberate, and of their effect, it is enough, nevertheless, that they be free from mortal sins, with the resolution that they will never sin in the future...

4. Care must be taken that careful preparation for Holy Communion precede, and that actions befitting the graces follow thereafter according to the strength, condition and duties of each one.

5. Let the counsel of the confessor intercede. Yet let confessors beware lest they turn away anyone from frequent or daily Communion, who is found in the state of grace and approaches with a right mind...

6. ...Finally, after the promulgation of this Decree let all ecclesiastical writers abstain from any contentious disputation about dispositions for frequent and daily Communion." D.S.3375-3383 ["Sources"]

† † †

May your people, Lord, offer themselves to you as a living sacrifice and be filled with the abundance of your love.
O God, make the peace we pray for a reality.
May we live our days in quiet joy and, with the help of the Virgin Mary's prayers safely reach our heavenly home.

PIUS X ON AGE FOR FIRST COMMUNION

Pope Pius X had the Sacred Congregation of the Sacraments issue its Decree, Quam singulari, on Aug. 8, 1910.

I. "The age of discretion both for Confession and for Holy Communion is that at which the child begins to reason, that is, at about the seventh year, more or less. The obligation of satisfying both precepts of Confession and Communion begins from that time.

II. For first Confession and for First Communion a full and perfect knowledge of Christian doctrine is not necessary. But the child will be obliged afterwards to learn gradually the whole catechism in accord with his intelligence.

III. The knowledge of religion which is required in a child, that he may prepare himself fittingly for his First Communion, is that by which in accord with his capacity he perceives the mysteries of faith by a necessity of means [mysteries of faith necessary for salvation; that is, that God rewards the good and punishes the evil, and, if possible, the mysteries of the Trinity and Incarnation], and by which he distinguishes Eucharistic bread from the common or corporeal, in order that he may approach the most blessed Eucharist with that devotion which his age carries.

IV. The obligation of the precept of Confession and Communion which rests upon a child, falls especially on those who should have care of him, that is, upon parents, confessor, teachers and pastor. But to the father, or those who take his place, and to the confessor, it pertains, according to the Roman Catechism, to admit the child to First Communion.

VI. Those who have charge over children must make every effort to see that these same children after First Communion approach the holy table often, and, if it can be done, daily, just as Jesus Christ and Mother Church desire; and that they do this with that devotion of mind which is appropriate to such an age. Let those who have this responsibility remember besides the very serious obligation by which they are bound, see to it that the children themselves continue to be present at the public instructions in catechism, or otherwise in some manner supply the same with religious instruction. The practice of never admitting children to Confession, or of never absolving them when they have arrived at the use of reason, is to be disapproved entirely." D.S.3530-3535 [Sources]

POPE PIUS XII 1939-1958

The Pope was aware of the work being done in liturgical circles, not only concerning the history of the liturgy, but also of movements to make changes in the Latin liturgy, as well as some errors that were being proposed. This liturgical movement by the scholars culminated in the renewal of the liturgy after Vatican Council II by Pope Paul VI.

To guide the scholars in their work Pope Pius addressed an encyclical to all Catholic bishops on Nov. 20, 1947. We quote here from that encyclical, entitled "Mediator Dei":

66. "The mystery of the Most Holy Eucharist which Christ, the High priest instituted, and which he commands to be continually renewed in the Church by His Ministers, is the culmination and center, as it were, of the Christian religion."

67. "Christ the Lord, 'Eternal priest according to the order of Melchisedech,' 'loving His own who were in the world,' at the last supper, on the night He was betrayed, wishing to leave His beloved Spouse, the Church, a visible sacrifice, such as the nature of men requires, that would represent the bloody Sacrifice offered once on the cross, and perpetuate its memory to the end of time, and whose salutary virtue must be applied in remitting those sins which we daily commit, ... offered His Body and Blood under the species of bread and wine to God the Father, and under the same species allowed the Apostles, whom He at that time constituted the priests of the New Testament, to partake thereof, commanding them and their successors in the priesthood to make the same offering.' "

68. "The august Sacrifice of the altar, then, is no mere empty commemoration of the passion and death of Jesus Christ, but a true and proper act of sacrifice, whereby the High Priest by an unbloody immolation offers Himself a most acceptable Victim to the Eternal Father, as He did upon the Cross. 'It is one and the same Victim; the same Person who offers it by the ministry of His priests, Who then offered Himself on the Cross, the manner of offering alone being different.' "

76. "Christ suffered death as Head of the human race: 'See how we were bought: Christ hangs upon the cross, see at what price he makes His purchase ... He sheds His Blood, He buys with His Blood, He buys with the Blood of the Spotless Lamb, He buys with the Blood of God's only Son. He who buys is Christ; the price is His Blood; the possession bought is the world.' " [St. Augustine]

77. "This purchase, however, does not immediately have its full effect; since Christ after redeeming the world at the lavish cost of His own Blood, still must come into complete possession of the souls of men. Wherefore, that the redemption and salvation of each person and of future generations unto the end of time may be effectively accomplished and be acceptable to God, it is necessary that men should individually come into vital contact with the Sacrifice of the Cross, so that the merits, which flow from it, should be imparted to them."

79. "The august Sacrifice of the altar is, as it were, the supreme instrument whereby the merits won by the Divine Redeemer upon the Cross are distributed to the faithful; 'as often as this commemorative Sacrifice is offered, there is wrought the work of our Redemption.' [Secret of IX Sunday after Pentecost]. This, however, so far from lessening the dignity of the actual Sacrifice on Calvary, rather proclaims and renders more manifest its greatness and its necessity, as the Council of Trent declares. Its daily immolation reminds us that there is no salvation except in the Cross of Our Lord Jesus Christ, and that God Himself wishes that there should be a continuation of this Sacrifice 'from the rising of the sun till the going down thereof,' [Mal 1:11] so that there may be no cessation of the hymn of praise and thanksgiving which man owes to God, seeing that he requires His help continually and has need of the Blood of the Redeemer to remit sin which challenges God's justice."

† † †

By your death on the cross you opened the gates of heaven, O Lord. Admit into your kingdom all the dead who hoped in you.

The Pope explains that at Mass both the priest-celebrant and the faithful offer Christ the Victim, but in different ways. 85. "It must also be said that the faithful do offer the Divine Victim, though in a different sense."

86. "This has already been stated in the clearest terms by some of Our Predecessors and some Doctors of the Church. 'Not only,' says Innocent III of immortal memory, 'do the priests offer the Sacrifice, but also all the faithful: for what the priest does personally by virtue of his ministry, the faithful do collectively by virtue of their intention.' We are happy to recall one of St. Robert Bellarmine's many statements on this subject. 'The Sacrifice,' he says, 'is principally offered in the person of Christ. Thus the oblation that follows the Consecration, is a sort of attestation that the whole Church consents in the oblation made by Christ, and offers it along with Him.' "

87. "Moreover the rites and prayers of the Eucharistic Sacrifice signify and show no less clearly that the oblation of the Victim is made by the priests in company with the people." ...

90. "The faithful offer to the ministers at the altar bread and wine to be changed into the Body and Blood of Christ, and by their alms they get the priest to offer the divine Victim for their intentions."

91. "But there is also a more profound reason why all Christians, especially those who are present at Mass, are said to offer the Sacrifice."

92. "In this most important subject it is necessary, in order to avoid giving rise to a dangerous error, that we define the exact meaning of the word 'offer.' The unbloody immolation at the words of consecration, when Christ is made present on the altar in the state of a victim, is performed by the priest and by him alone, as the representative of Christ and not as the representative of the faithful. It is because the priest places the divine Victim upon the altar that he offers it to God the Father as an oblation for the glory of the Blessed Trinity and for the good of the whole Church."

† † †

"Lord God, you are God, and your words are truth." (St. Bernard)

The Pope continues to explain how the faithful, along with the priest, offer the Mass.

92. "Now the faithful participate in the oblation, understood in this limited sense, after their own fashion and in a twofold manner, namely, because they not only offer the Sacrifice by the hands of the priest, but also, to a certain extent, in union with him. It is by reason of this participation, that the offering made by the people is also included in liturgical worship."

94. "We are very pleased to learn that this teaching, thanks to a more intense study of the Liturgy on the part of many, especially in recent years, has been given full recognition. We must, however, deeply deplore certain exaggerations and over-statements which are not in agreement with the true teaching of the Church."

98. "In order that the oblation by which the faithful offer the divine Victim in this Sacrifice to the heavenly Father may have its full effect, it is necessary that the people add something else, namely the offering of themselves as a victim. ... It is then [at Mass], with the High priest and through Him they offer themselves as a spiritual sacrifice, that each one's faith ought to become more ready to work through charity, his piety more real and fervent, and each should consecrate himself to the furthering of the divine glory, desiring to become as like as possible to Christ in His most grievous sufferings."

The Pope exhorts communicants to remain after Mass to make a suitable thanksgiving.

123. "When the Mass, which is subject to special rules of the Liturgy, is over, the person who has received Holy Communion is not thereby freed from his duty of thanksgiving; rather, it is most becoming that, when the Mass is finished, the person who has received the Eucharist should recollect himself, and in intimate union with the Divine Master hold loving and fruitful converse with Him. Hence they have departed from the straight way of truth, who, adhering to the letter rather than the sense, assert and teach that when Mass has ended, no such thanksgiving should be added, not only because the Mass is itself a thanksgiving, but also because this pertains to a private and personal act of piety and not to the good of the community."

After pointing out that the personal colloquies between the communicant and Christ after Mass are necessary to enjoy more fully the supernatural treasures of the Eucharist both for ourselves and others, the Pope quotes the words of The Imitation of Christ to the communicant: 'Remain on in secret and take delight in your God; for He is yours Whom the whole world cannot take away from you.' Following this the Pope speaks of adoration due to the Eucharist.

129. "The Eucharistic Food contains, as all are aware, 'truly, really and substantially the Body and Blood together with the Soul and Divinity of Our Lord Jesus Christ.' [In 1947, when the Pope wrote this encyclical, one could say that all Catholics "are aware" of the Real Presence; but, sadly, that is not the case today, fifty years later.] "It is no wonder, then, that the Church, even from the beginning, adored the Body of Christ under the appearance of bread; that is evident from the very rites of the august Sacrifice, which prescribe that the sacred ministers should adore the most Holy Sacrament by genuflecting or by profoundly bowing their heads."

130. "The Sacred Councils teach us that it is the Church's tradition right from the beginning, to worship 'with the same adoration the Word Incarnate as well as His own flesh,' and St. Augustine asserts that: 'No one eats that flesh, without first adoring it,' while he adds that 'not only do we not commit a sin by adoring it, but that we do sin by not adoring it.' "

131. "The reservation of the Sacred Species for the sick and those in danger of death introduced the praiseworthy custom of adoring the Blessed Sacrament which is reserved in our churches. This practice of adoration, in fact, is based on strong and solid reasons. For the Eucharist is at once a Sacrifice and a Sacrament: but it differs from the other Sacraments in this, that it not only produces grace, but contains in a permanent manner the Author of grace Himself." ... The Pope says that in adoring Christ hidden behind the Eucharistic veils and praying to Him, the Church not only manifests her faith in the Real Presence but also professes her gratitude to Christ and enjoys the intimacy of His friendship.`

Since the devil is always on the prowl, as St. Peter says in 1Pet5:8,the Pope corrected some current errors concerning the Eucharist, errors which unfortunately are still with us to some extent. There were those who claimed that the historical Christ was was not the same as the Eucharistic Christ.

134. "Nor is it to be admitted that by this Eucharistic Cult men falsely confound the Historical Christ, as they say, Who once lived on earth, with the Christ Who is present in the august Sacrament of the altar, and Who reigns glorious and triumphant in heaven and bestows supernatural favors. On the contrary, it can be claimed that by this devotion the faithful bear witness to and solemnly avow the faith of the Church that the Word of God is identical with the Son of the Virgin Mary, Who suffered on the Cross, Who is present in a hidden manner in the Eucharist and Who reigns upon His heavenly throne. Thus St. John Chrysostom states: 'When you see It (the Body of Christ) exposed, say to yourself: thanks to this Body, I am no longer dust and ashes, I am no more a captive but a free man: Hence I hope to obtain Heaven and the good things that are there in store for me, eternal life, the heritage of the Angels, companionship with Christ; death has not destroyed this Body which was pierced by nails and scourged, ... this is that Body which was once covered with blood, pierced by a lance, from which issued saving fountains upon the world, one of blood and the other of water ... This Body He gave to us to keep and eat, as a mark of His intense love.' "

176. The Pope lamented the neglect of visits to our Lord in the tabernacle, of Confession of devotion, and of devotion to Mary, which holy men have called a sign of "predestination."

In his monumental work entitled "Missarum Solemnia" (The Mass of the Roman Rite: Its Origins and Development), published about four months after the publishing of Mediator Dei, Father Joseph A. Jungmann, S.J., in his Forward, quotes one of the closing statements of Pope Pius XII in this encyclical:

201. "The Mass is the chief act of divine worship; it should also be the source and center of Christian piety."

† † †

Do not give the devil a chance to work on you. (Eph.4:27)

VATICAN COUNCIL II (1962-1965)

Less than four months after the death of Pope Pius XII his successor, John XXIII, surprised the Catholic world by announcing an upcoming Ecumenical Council, that of Vatican II, the twenty-first such council in the history of the Church. The Council covered a wide range with its sixteen official documents.

Since "the Church believes as it prays," it was natural that the Council's first promulgation was The Constitution on the Sacred Liturgy, which interests us here, because it deals with the Eucharist.

The guidance of God the Holy Spirit is equally present in all Ecumenical Councils, which, together with the Pope alone, wield all of the divine authority Christ left to his Church. Even prior to the first Ecumenical Council of Nicaea 1 in 325 a.d. the Church was well aware of its divine assistance, as we see in the letter written by the Apostles themselves at the Council of Jerusalem in 50 a.d. The letter begins: "It has been decided by the Holy Spirit and by ourselves, etc."(Acts 15:22-29)

At Vatican II the Holy spirit guided the Fathers of the Council to avail themselves of much of the work done in the field of liturgy prior to the Council. While Pope Pius XII had to correct some errors in liturgical movements before the Council, he rejoiced at the vast amount of knowledge that was being gleaned from ancient documents that were being discovered. He himself had prepared the way for many of the liturgical statements of the Council in his encyclical, Mediator Dei, as well as in his address to the participants in the International Conference on Pastoral Liturgy held in Assisi in September 1956. In addition Pius anticipated the Council in his reform of the liturgy of Holy Week.

Many of us were accustomed to the liturgy authorized by the Council of Trent four hundred years earlier. Thanks to the discoveries in rather recent years ancient liturgies have come to light. The "new" liturgy, authorized by Vatican II, embodies some of the beautiful elements of ancient liturgies. What the Council itself declared and authorized was not only beautiful, but would also have led immediately to a greater understanding and appreciation of the liturgy, and consequently to greater holiness, had the Church not been thwarted in its implementation.

As is the case with all ecumenical councils, neither the Council Fathers nor the Holy Spirit Himself were able to satisfy all the theological parties, factions, and cliques that were represented at Vatican II. So great was the pride and arrogance of some who did not get their way at the Council, that with help from the mass media (through which the devil seems to be working overtime), they set about frustrating the implementation of the

Council's decisions. Some dissenters were so bold as to claim that they were acting "in the name of the Council," or "in the spirit of Vatican II," while they hindered the Council from bearing fruit. That same evil spirit of dissension is still with us today, just as it was three years after the Council when Pope Paul VI issued the encyclical, Humanae Vitae, on marriage, including the regulation of birth. Dissension over the doctrine contained in that encyclical has caused a serious rift in the Church up to our day.

Despite the good work of the Council Fathers, as shown in The Constitution on the Sacred Liturgy, we are all aware of the sad state in which we find the liturgy, and even Eucharistic doctrine, today. There is hardly a proper word to describe what passes for a Mass in some churches, while a good percentage of Catholics apparently have lost their faith in the Real Presence. Open dissenters and pseudo liturgists, acting "in the spirit of the Council," have stolen the fruit of the Council, deprived us of our necessary spiritual nourishment, and fed us straw instead. At this writing Cardinal Ratzinger, Secretary of the Congregation for the Doctrine of the Faith, at the Holy Father's request is seeking ways to restore to the liturgy and to the Church in general a sense of the sacred. Some claim that the reform of the liturgy by the Council needs to be reformed. No, the actual liturgy we have today needs to be reformed. The reform by Vatican II needs no reform, only true implementation.

† † †

Protect us, Lord, as we stay awake; watch over us
as we sleep, that awake, we may keep watch with Christ, and asleep,
rest in His peace.

The reform of the official, public prayer of the Church (that is, the liturgy) by the Council of Trent in the sixteenth century sparked an interest in liturgical studies that lasted four hundred years and culminated in the reform ordered by Vatican Council II in its Constitution on the Sacred Liturgy. We want to consider some highlights of that first document of the

Council. And it should be noted that after that document was published some 25 other documents on the liturgy were issued by, or in connection with, the Council. Among them were three Instructions by the Council on the Proper Implementation of the new liturgy. In those places where these Instructions were not implemented properly we see the liturgical chaos that passes for liturgy today.

What results have followed the opening words of the first document of the Second Vatican Council? "1. The sacred Council has set out to impart an ever-increasing vigor to the Christian life of the faithful; to adapt more closely to the needs of our age those institutions which are subject to change; to foster whatever can promote union among all who believe in Christ; to strengthen whatever can help to call all mankind into the Church's fold. Accordingly it sees particularly cogent reasons for undertaking the reform and promotion of the liturgy.

"7. Christ is always present in his Church, especially in her liturgical celebrations. He is present in the Sacrifice of the Mass not only in the person of his minister, 'the same now offering, through the ministry of priests, who formerly offered himself on the cross,' but especially in the eucharistic species. By his power he is present in the sacraments so that when anybody baptizes it is really Christ himself who baptizes. He is present in his word since it is he himself who speaks when the holy scriptures are read in the Church. Lastly, he is present when the Church prays and sings, for he has promised 'where two or three are gathered together in my name there am I in the midst of them.' " (Mt 18:20)

✝ ✝ ✝

Into your hands, Lord, I commend my spirit.

The Constitution on the Liturgy continues.

11. "In order that the liturgy may be able to produce its full effects it is necessary that the faithful come to it with proper dispositions, that their minds be attuned to their voices, and that they cooperate with heavenly

grace lest they receive it in vain. Pastors of souls must, therefore, realize that, when the liturgy is celebrated, something more is required than the laws governing valid and lawful celebration. It is their duty also to ensure that the faithful take part fully aware of what they are doing, actively engaged in the rite and enriched by it."

12. "The spiritual life, however, is not limited solely to participation in the liturgy. The Christian is indeed called to pray with others, but he must also enter into his bedroom to pray to his Father in secret." [Mt. 6:6]

13. "Popular devotions of the Christian people, provided they conform to the laws and norms of the Church, are to be highly recommended, especially when they are ordered by the Apostolc See."

14. "Mother Church earnestly desires that all the faithful should be led to that full, conscious, and active participation in liturgical celebrations which is demanded by the very nature of the liturgy, and to which the Christian people, 'a chosen race, a royal priesthood, a holy nation, a redeemed people' (1 Pet 2:9, 4-5) have a right and obligation by reason of their baptism... pastors of souls should energetically set about achieving it through the requisite pedagogy."

22. "No other person, not even a priest, may add, remove, or change anything in the liturgy on his own authority."

34. "The rites should be distinguished by noble simplicity. They should be short, clear and free from useless repetitions. They should be within the people's powers of comprehension, and normally not require much explanation."

† † †

Lord, help us to be faithful to your word and endure our exile bravely,
until we are called to our heavenly home,
to which the Virgin Mary,
Mother of your Church, has preceded us.

The Constitution on the liturgy continues.

48. "The Church ... earnestly desires that Christ's faithful, when present at this mystery of faith [Mass], should not be there as strangers or silent spectators. On the contrary, through a good understanding of the rites and prayers they should take part in the sacred action, conscious of what they are doing, with devotion and full collaboration. ... Offering the immaculate victim, not only through the hands of the priest but also together with him, they should learn to offer themselves."

During the Council and for some ten years afterwards the liturgy of the Mass was revised according to the following principles laid down by the Council.

50. "The rite of the Mass is to be revised in such a way that the intrinsic nature and purpose of its several parts, as well as the connection between them, may be more clearly manifested, and that devout and active participation by the faithful may be more easily achieved. ... Parts [of the Mass] which suffered loss through accidents of history are to be restored to the vigor they had in the days of the holy Fathers, as may seem useful or necessary."

51. "The treasures of the Bible are to be opened up more lavishly so that a richer fare may be provided for the faithful at the table of God's word. ...

52. "By means of the homily the mysteries of the faith and the guiding principles of the Christian life are expounded from the sacred text during the course of the liturgical year. The homily, therefore, is to be highly esteemed as part of the liturgy itself. In fact at those Masses which are celebrated on Sundays and holidays of obligation, with the people assisting, it should not be omitted except for a serious reason.

53. "The 'common prayer' or 'prayer of the faithful' is to be restored after the gospel and homily, especially on Sundays and holidays of obligation."

54. "A suitable place may be allotted to the vernacular in Masses which are celebrated with the people. ... Nevertheless care must be taken to ensure that the faithful may also be able to say or sing together in Latin those parts of the Ordinary of the Mass which pertain to them."

The Constitution on the liturgy continues its directives for revising the rite of the Mass.

55. "The more perfect form of participation in the Mass whereby the faithful, after the priest's communion, receive the Lord's Body from the same sacrifice, is warmly recommended. The dogmatic principles laid down by the Council of Trent remaining intact, communion under both kinds may be granted when the bishops think fit, not only to clerics and religious but also to the laity, in cases to be determined by the Apostolic See."

56. "The two parts, which in a sense go to make up the Mass, viz. the liturgy of the word and the eucharistic liturgy, are so closely connected with each other that they form but one single act of worship. Accordingly this sacred Synod strongly urges pastors of souls that, when instructing the faithful, they insistently teach them to take their part in the entire Mass, especially on Sundays and holidays of obligation."

57. "Concelebration whereby the unity of the priesthood is appropriately manifested has remained in use to this day in the Church both in the East and in the West. For this reason it has seemed good to the Council to extend permission for concelebration. ... The regulation, however, of the discipline of concelebration in the diocese pertains to the bishop. ... Each priest shall always retain his right to celebrate Mass individually."

The Constitution has the following on the other sacraments and the sacramentals.

59. "The purpose of the sacraments is to sanctify men, to build up the Body of Christ, and, finally, to give worship to God. Because they are signs they also instruct. They not only presuppose faith, but by words and objects they also nourish, strengthen, and express it. That is why they are called 'sacraments of faith.' They do, indeed, confer grace, but, in addition, the very act of celebrating them most effectively disposes the faithful to receive this grace to their profit, to worship God duly, and to practice charity. It is, therefore, of the greatest importance that the faithful should easily understand the sacramental signs, and should eagerly frequent those sacraments which were instituted to nourish the Christian life."

The Constitution on the liturgy laid down directives for revising the sacramentals also.

60. "Holy Mother Church has, moreover, instituted sacramentals. These are sacred signs which bear a resemblance to the sacraments. They signify effects, particularly of a spiritual nature, which are obtained through the Church's intercession. By them men are disposed to receive the chief effect of the sacraments, and various occasions of life are rendered holy."

61. "Thus, for well-disposed members of the faithful the liturgy of the sacraments and sacramentals sanctifies almost every event of their lives with the divine grace which flows from the paschal mystery of the Passion, Death, and Resurrection of Christ. From this source all sacraments and sacramentals draw their power. There is scarcely any proper use of material things which cannot thus be directed toward the sanctification of men and the praise of God."

62. "With the passage of time, however, there have crept into the rites of the sacraments and sacramentals certain features that have rendered their nature and purpose far from clear to the people of today. Hence changes are necessary to adapt them to present-day needs."

79. "The sacramentals are to be revised, account being taken of the primary principle of enabling the faithful to participate intelligently, actively, and easily. The circumstances of our times must also be considered. ... Provision should be made for the administration of some sacramentals, at least in special circumstances and at the discretion of the Ordinary (bishop), by qualified lay persons."

81. "Funeral rites should express more clearly the paschal character of Christian death, and should correspond more closely to the circumstances and traditions found in various regions."

77. "The Marriage rite ... is to be revised and enriched so that it will more clearly signify the grace of the sacrament and will emphasize the spouses' duties. 'If any regions use other praiseworthy customs and ceremonies when celebrating the sacrament of Matrimony, the sacred Synod earnestly desires that these by all means be retained' [from Council of Trent]."

The Constitution on the liturgy ordered the revision of The Divine Office, sometimes called simply "The Office" or "The Breviary" or "The Liturgy of the Hours."

83. "Jesus Christ, High Priest of the New and Eternal Covenant, taking human nature, introduced into this earthly exile that hymn which is sung throughout all ages in the halls of heaven. He attaches to himself the entire community of mankind and has them join him in singing his divine song of praise. For he continues his priestly work through his Church. The Church, by celebrating the Eucharist and by other means, especially the celebration of the divine office, is ceaselessly engaged in praising the Lord and interceding for the salvation of the entire world."

84. "The divine office, in keeping with ancient Christian tradition, is so devised that the whole course of the day and night is made holy by the praise of God. Therefore, when this wonderful song of praise is correctly celebrated by priests and others deputed to it by the Church, or by the faithful praying together with a priest in the approved form, then it is truly the voice of the Bride [the Church] herself addressed to her Bridegroom [Christ]. It is the very prayer which Christ himself together with his Body addresses to the Father."

85. "Hence all who partake in the divine office are not only performing a duty for the Church, they are also sharing in what is the greatest honor for Christ's Bride; for by offering these praises to God they are standing before God's throne in the name of the Church, their Mother."

Regarding the Liturgical Year:

102. ... "Once a week, on the day she [the Church] has called the Lord's Day, she keeps the memory of the Lord's resurrection. .. In the course of the year, moreover, she unfolds the whole mystery of Christ from the incarnation and the nativity to the ascension, to Pentecost and the expectation of the blessed hope of the coming of the Lord. Thus recalling the mysteries of the redemption, she opens up to the faithful the riches of her Lord's powers and merits, so that these are in some way made present for all time; the faithful lay hold of them and are filled with saving grace." She honors with a special love Blessed Mary, who is inseparably linked with her Son's saving work.

The Constitution on the liturgy turned its attention to sacred music. **112.** "The musical tradition of the universal Church is a treasure of inestimable value, greater even of that of any other art. The main reason for this pre-eminence is that, as a combination of sacred music and words, it forms a necessary or integral part of the solemn liturgy. Sacred scripture, indeed, has bestowed praise on sacred song. So have the Fathers of the Church and the Roman Pontiffs, who in more recent times, led by St. Pius X, have explained more precisely the ministerial function exercised by sacred music in the service of the Lord. Therefore, sacred music is to be considered the more holy, the more closely connected it is with the liturgical action, whether making prayer more pleasing, promoting unity of minds, or conferring greater solemnity upon the sacred rites. The Church, indeed, approves of all forms of true art which have the requisite qualities, and admits them into divine worship.... the purpose of sacred music is the glory of God and the sanctification of the faithful."

114. ... "Bishops and pastors of souls must take great care to ensure that whenever the sacred action is to be accompanied by chant, the whole body of the faithful may be able to contribute that active participation which is rightly theirs."

116. "The Church recognizes Gregorian chant as being specially suited to the Roman liturgy. Therefore, other things being equal, it should be given pride of place in liturgical services. Other kinds of sacred music, especially polyphony, are by no means excluded from liturgical celebrations so long as they accord with the spirit of the liturgical action [that is, permitting active participation of the laity]."

120. "The pipe organ is to be held in high esteem in the Latin Church... Other instruments also may be admitted for use in divine worship, in the judgment and with the consent of the competent territorial authority."

121. "The texts intended to be sung must always be in conformity with Catholic doctrine. Indeed, they should be drawn chiefly from the sacred scripture and from liturgical sources."

POPE PAUL VI (1963-1978)

Even before the Second Vatican Council closed, the Pope had "serious pastoral concern and anxiety" about those "who, with reference to Masses which are celebrated in private, or to the dogma of transubtantiation, or to devotion to the Eucharist, spread opinions which disturb the faithful and fill their minds with no little confusion about matters of faith. It is as if everyone were permitted to consign to oblivion doctrine already defined by the Church, or else interpret it in such a way as to weaken the genuine meaning of the words or the recognized force of the concepts involved." This is surely a fair description of what we see today, some thirty years later, which may have been envisioned by the Pope through the influence of the Holy Spirit. To combat errors regarding the Eucharist Pope Paul VI issued an encyclical, entitled Mysterium Fidei [Mystery of Faith], on Sept. 3, 1965.

First, the Pope reiterates the doctrine of the Real Presence of Christ in the Eucharist, a true mystery, which the human mind cannot fully comprehend. To repel "every virus of rationalism" he recalls that "the Eucharist is a very great mystery," the very mystery of faith, in which, as Pope Leo XIII said, "are contained in a remarkable richness and variety of miracles, all supernatural realities." Referring to a common Protestant denial of the Real Presence, the Pope quotes St.Bonaventure: "There is no difficulty about Christ's presence in the Eucharist as a sign, but that He is truly present in the Eucharist as He is in heaven, this is most difficult. Therefore to believe this is especially meritorious."

The Pope continues: "It is logical, then, that we should follow a guiding star in our investigations of this mystery, the magisterium of the Church, to which the Divine Redeemer entrusted for protection and for explanation the revelation which he has communicated to us through Scripture or Tradition. For we are convinced [as St. Augustine says] that 'what since the days of antiquity was preached and believed throughout the whole Church with true Catholic Faith is true, even if it is not submitted to rational investigation, even if it is not explained by means of words.' "

POPE PAUL VI (Mysterium Fidei)

The Pope continues regarding false expressions of the truth. "Having safeguarded the integrity of the faith, it is necessary also to safeguard also its proper mode of expression, lest by the careless use of words, we occasion (God forbid) the rise of false opinions regarding faith in the most sublime of mysteries."

"It cannot be tolerated that any individual should on his own authority modify the formulas which were used by the Council of Trent to express belief in the Eucharistic Mystery. ... It must be admitted that these formulas can sometimes be more clearly and accurately explained. In fact, the achievement of this goal is highly beneficial. But it would be wrong to give to these expressions a meaning other than the original. Thus the understanding of the faith should be advanced without threats to its unchangeable truth. It is, in fact, the teaching of the First Vatican Council that 'the same signification [of sacred dogmas] is to be forever retained once our Holy Mother the Church has defined it, and under no pretext of deeper penetration may that meaning be weakened.' "

The Pope corrects errors regarding the Mass . "We desire to recall at the very outset what may be termed the very essence of the dogma, namely, that by means of the Mystery of the Eucharist, the Sacrifice of the Cross, which was once offered on Calvary, is remarkably re-enacted and constantly recalled and its saving power exerted for the forgiveness of those sins which we daily commit..."

"To shed further light on the mystery of the Church, it helps to realize that it is nothing less than the whole Church which, in union with Christ in His role as Priest and Victim, offers the Sacrifice of the Mass and is offered in it. ... For even though a priest should offer Mass in private, that Mass is not something private; it is an act of Christ and of the Church. In offering this Sacrifice, the Church learns to offer herself as a sacrifice for all. Moreover, for the salvation of the entire world she applies the single, boundless, redemptive power of the Sacrifice of the Cross. For every Mass is offered not for the salvation of ourselves alone, but also for that of the whole world."

Pope Paul continues correcting the errors by some Catholics regarding the Real Presence. After mentioning various ways in which Christ is present in His Church, he says: "But there is another manner in which Christ is present in His Church, a manner which surpasses all the others; it is His presence in the Sacrament of the Eucharist, which is for this reason [as Aegidius Romanus writes] 'a more consoling source of devotion, a more lovely object of contemplation, a more effective means of sanctification than all the other sacraments.' The reason is clear; it contains Christ Himself and it is [as St. Thomas Aquinas writes] 'a kind of perfection of the spiritual life; in a way it is the goal of all the sacraments.' " After quoting several Fathers of the Church on the Real Presence, the Pope repeats the words of the Council of Trent, which "openly and sincerely professes that within the Holy Sacrament of the Eucharist, after the Consecration of the bread and wine, our Lord Jesus Christ, true God and true Man, is really, truly and substantially contained under those outward appearances." The Pope continues: "In this way, the Savior in His humanity is present not only at the right hand of the Father according to the natural manner of existence, but also in the Sacrament of the Eucharist [as Trent says] 'by a mode of existence which we cannot express in words, but which, with a mind illuminated by faith, we can conceive, and must most firmly believe, to be possible to God.' "

The Pope corrected those Catholic theologians who preferred the words and ideas of "transignification" and "transfiguration" to "transubstantiation." He writes: "To avoid misunderstanding this sacramental presence which surpasses the laws of nature and constitutes the greatest miracle of its kind we must listen with docility to the voice of the teaching and praying Church. This voice, which constantly echoes the voice of Christ, assures us that the way Christ is made present in this Sacrament is none other than by the change of the whole substance of the bread into His Body, and of the whole substance of the wine into His Blood, and that this unique and truly wonderful change the Catholic Church rightly calls transubstantiation."

The Pope continues correcting the views of some Catholic theologians concerning Christ's presence in the Eucharist. "As a result of transubstantiation, the species of bread and wine undoubtedly take on a new meaning and a new finality, for they no longer remain ordinary bread and wine, but become the sign of something sacred, the sign of a spiritual food. However, the reason they take on this new significance and this new finality is simply because they contain a new 'reality' which we may justly term ontological. Not that there lies under those species what was already there before, but something quite different; and that not only because of the faith of the Church, but in objective reality, since after the change of the substance of the bread and wine into the Body and Blood of Christ, nothing remains of the bread and wine but the appearances, under which Christ, whole and entire, in His physical 'reality' is bodily present, although not in the same way that bodies are present in a given place."

On the worship to be offered to the sacrament of the Eucharist: "The Catholic Church has always offered and still offers the cult of latria [which is offered to God alone] to the Sacrament of the Eucharist, not only during Mass, but also outside of it, reserving consecrated Hosts with the utmost care, exposing them to solemn veneration, and carrying them processionally to the joy of great crowds of the faithful."

Finally Pope Paul exhorts all, clergy and laity, to "tirelessly promote the cult of the Eucharist, the focus where all other forms of piety must ultimately emerge." He quotes St. Augustine probably for the benefit especially of erring theologians: "He who desires life finds here a place to live in and the means to live by. Let him approach, let him believe, let him be incorporated so that he may receive life. Let him not refuse union with the members, let him not be a corrupt member, deserving to be cut off, nor a disfigured member to be ashamed of. Let him be a grateful and healthy member. Let him cleave to the body, let him live by God and for God. Let him now labor here on earth, that he may afterwards reign in heaven."

POPE JOHN PAUL II (Dominicae Cenae)

On February 24, 1980 Pope John Paul II sent a letter addressed principally to all the bishops of the Church on matters pertaining to the Eucharist.

In his opening lines (Article 2) the Pope reminded the bishops that the Council of Trent had declared that the Eucharist is the principal and central "raison d'etre" of the sacrament of the priesthood, which effectively came into being at the moment of the institution of the Eucharist at the Last Supper. "We are united in a singular and exceptional way to the Eucharist. In a certain way we derive from it and exist for it. We are also, and in a special way, responsible for it."

Regarding worship of the Eucharist, the Pope says in **3**: "The encouragement and the deepening of Eucharistic worship are proofs of that authentic renewal which the [Vatican II] Council set itself as an aim and of which they are the central point. And this, venerable and dear brothers, deserves separate reflection. The Church and the world have a great need of Eucharistic worship. Jesus waits for us in this sacrament of love. Let us be generous with our time in going to meet him in adoration and in contemplation that is full of faith and ready to make reparation for the great faults and crimes of the world. May our adoration never cease."

On the link between the Eucharist and the Church:

"**4**. From that moment [the Last Supper] until the end of time, the Church is being built up through that same communion [Mass and Holy Communion] with the Son of God, a communion which is a pledge of the eternal Passover." The Pope goes on to speak of "that close relationship between the Church's spiritual and apostolic vitality and the Eucharist, understood in its profound significance and from all points of view."

† † †

A partial indulgence is granted to the faithful, who visit the Most Blessed Sacrament to adore it; a plenary indulgence is granted, if the visit lasts for at least one half an hour.

[Enchiridion of Indulgences by the Sacred Apostolic Penitentiary, 1968]

The Pope writes on the link between the Eucharist and charity.

"**5**. Christian life is expressed in the fulfilling of the greatest commandment, that is to say, in the love of God and neighbor, and this love finds its source in the Blessed Sacrament, which is commonly called the sacrament of love. The Eucharist signifies this charity, and therefore recalls it, makes it present and at the same time brings it about. ...Eucharistic worship is therefore precisely the expression of that love which is the authentic and deepest characteristic of the Christian vocation. This worship springs from the love, and serves the love, to which we are called in Jesus Christ."

"**6**. The authentic sense of the Eucharist becomes of itself the school of active love for neighbor. ... The Eucharist educates us to this love in a deeper way; it shows us, in fact, what value each person, our brother or sister, has in God's eyes, if Christ offers Himself equally to each one, under the species of bread and wine. If our Eucharistic worship is authentic, it must make us grow in awareness of the dignity of each person. The awareness of that dignity becomes the deepest motive of our relationship with our neighbor. ...The sense of the Eucharistic mystery leads us to a love for our neighbor, to a love for every human being."

On the sacred character of the Eucharist. "**8**. There is a close link between this element [liturgy] of the Eucharist and its sacredness, that is to say, its being a holy and sacred action. Holy and sacred, because in it are the continual presence and action of Christ, 'the Holy One' of God, 'anointed with the Holy Spirit', 'consecrated by the Father' to lay down His life of His own accord and to take it up again, and the High Priest of the New Covenant. For it is He who, represented by the celebrant, makes His entrance into the sanctuary and proclaims His Gospel. It is He who is 'the offerer and the offered, the consecrator and the consecrated.' The Eucharist is a holy and sacred action, because it constitutes the sacred species, the 'Sancta sanctis', that is to say, the 'holy things (Christ, the Holy One) given to the holy', as all the Eastern liturgies sing at the moment when the Eucharistic Bread is raised in order to invite the faithful to the Lord's Supper."

The Pope continues on the sacred character of the Eucharist.

"8. The sacredness of the Mass, therefore, is not a 'sacralization', that is to say, something that man adds to Christ's action in the Upper Room, for the Holy Thursday supper was a sacred rite, a primary and constitutive liturgy, through which Christ, by pledging to give His life for us, Himself celebrated sacramentally the mystery of His passion and resurrection, the heart of every Mass. Our Masses, being derived from this liturgy, possess of themselves a complete liturgical form, which, in spite of its variations in line with the families of rites, remains substantially the same. The sacred character of the Mass is a sacredness instituted by Christ. The words and actions of every priest, answered by the conscious active participation of the whole Eucharistic assembly, echo the words and actions of Holy Thursday."

"The priest offers the holy sacrifice 'in persona Christi'; this means more than offering 'in the name of' or 'in the place of' Christ. 'In persona' means in specific sacramental identification with 'the eternal High Priest' who is the author and principal subject of this sacrifice of His, a sacrifice in which, in truth, nobody can take His place. Only He - only Christ - was able and is able to be the true and effective 'expiation for our sins and ... for the sins of the whole world.' Only His sacrifice - and no one else's - was able and is able to have 'a propitiatory power' before God, the Trinity, and the transcendent holiness. Awareness of this reality throws a certain light on the character and significance of the priest celebrant who, by confecting the holy sacrifice and acting 'in persona Christi', is sacramentally (and ineffably) brought into that most profound sacredness, and made part of it, spiritually linking with it in turn all those participating in the Eucharistic assembly. ... The Church has a special duty to safeguard and strengthen the sacredness of the Eucharist."

† † †

Hidden God, devoutly I adore you,
Truly present underneath these veils.

We see in the Pope's letter to the bishops of the Church that he is combating errors that were current then and unfortunately are still current. One such error would reduce the Eucharist to a holy meal only. The Pope, therefore points out that it is also, and especially, a sacrifice.

"**9**. The Eucharist is above all else a sacrifice. It is the sacrifice of the Redemption and also the sacrifice of the New Covenant. 'Today's sacrifice', the Greek Church stated centuries ago, 'is like that offered once by the Only-begotten Incarnate Word: it is offered by Him (now as then), since it is one and the same sacrifice.' Accordingly, precisely by making this single sacrifice of our salvation present, man and the world are restored to God through the paschal newness of Redemption. This restoration cannot cease to be: it is the foundation of the "new and eternal covenant" of God with man and of man with God. If it were missing, one would have to question both the excellence of the sacrifice of Redemption, which in fact was perfect and definitive, and also the sacrificial value of the Mass. In fact, the Eucharist, being a true sacrifice, brings about this restoration to God."

"Consequently, the celebrant, as minister of this sacrifice, is the authentic priest, performing - in virtue of the specific power of sacred ordination - a true sacrificial act that brings creation back to God. Although all those who participate in the Eucharist do not confect the sacrifice as he does, they offer with him, by virtue of the common priesthood, their own spiritual sacrifices represented by the bread and wine from the moment of their presentation at the altar."

"By virtue of the consecration, the species of bread and wine represent in a sacramental, unbloody manner the bloody propitiatory sacrifice offered by Him on the cross to His Father for the salvation of the world. Indeed, he alone, giving Himself as a propitiatory Victim in an act of supreme surrender and immolation, has reconciled humanity with the Father, solely through His sacrifice, 'having canceled the bond which stood against us' " (Col 2:14).

☩ ☩ ☩

O memorial of my dying Savior!

The Pope continues on the sacrificial aspect of the Eucharist.

"**9**. To this sacrifice [on Calvary], which is renewed in a sacramental form on the altar, the offerings of bread and wine, united with the devotion of the faithful, nevertheless bring their unique contribution, since by means of the consecration by the priest they become sacred species.

"All this [the new liturgy] should fill us with joy, but we should also remember that these changes demand new spiritual awareness and maturity, both on the part of the celebrant - especially now that he celebrates 'facing the people' - and by the faithful. Eucharistic worship matures and grows when the words of the Eucharistic Prayer, especially the words of consecration, are spoken with great humility and simplicity, in a worthy and fitting way, which is understandable and in keeping with their holiness; when this essential act of the Eucharistic Liturgy is performed unhurriedly; and when it brings about in us such recollection and devotion that the participants become aware of the greatness of the mystery being accomplished and show it by their attitude."

In reference to the Liturgy of the Word the Pope writes: "**10**. Complete renewal makes yet other demands. These demands consist in a new sense of responsibility towards the Word of God. ... The same sense of responsibility also involves the performance of the corresponding liturgical actions (reading or singing), which must accord with the principles of art. To preserve these actions from all artificiality, they should express such capacity, simplicity and dignity as to highlight the special character of the sacred text, even by the manner of reading or singing...Only the Word of God can be used for Mass readings. The reading of Scripture cannot be replaced by the reading of other texts, however much they may be endowed with undoubted religious and moral values. On the other hand such texts can be used very profitably in the homily."

† † †

As the rain and snow come down from the heavens and do not return without watering the earth, so the word that goes from My mouth

does not return to Me empty,
says the Lord.

Besides being a sacrifice the Eucharistic mystery has two tables, that of the Word of God and that of the Bread of the Lord (Holy Communion).

"**11**. In Eucharistic Communion [Christ] entrusts Himself to each one of us, to our hearts, our consciences, our lips and our mouths, in the form of food. Therefore there is a special need, with regard to this question, for the watchfulness spoken of by the Gospel, on the part of pastors who have charge of Eucharistic worship and on the part of the People of God, whose 'sense of faith' must be very alert and acute particularly in this area."

"With the help of your brothers in the priesthood do all you can to safeguard the sacred dignity of the Eucharistic ministry and that deep spirit of Eucharistic communion which belongs in a special way to the Church as the People of God."

The Pope speaks of those who could receive Holy Communion, but do not, even though they are not conscious of mortal sin. They neglect Communion not so much out of a sense of unworthiness as out of a lack of hunger and thirst for the Eucharist due to inadequate sensitivity toward the great sacrament of love and a lack of understanding of its nature.

The Pope noted also the opposite phenomenon of recent years. "Sometimes, indeed quite frequently, everybody participating in the Eucharistic assembly goes to Communion; and on some occasions, as experienced pastors confirm, there has not been due care to approach the sacrament of Penance so as to purify one's conscience. This can of course mean that those approaching the Lord's table find nothing on their conscience, according to the objective law of God, to keep them from this sublime and joyful act of being sacramentally united with Christ. But there can also be, at least at times, another idea behind this: the idea of the Mass as only a banquet in which one shares by receiving the body of Christ in order to manifest, above all else, fraternal communion. It is not hard to add to these reasons a certain human respect and mere 'conformity.' "

The Pope continues commenting on the fact that so many receive Communion and so few go to Confession. "**11.** This phenomenon demands from us watchful attention and a theological and pastoral analysis guided by a sense of great responsibility. We cannot allow the life of our communities to lose the good quality of sensitiveness of Christian conscience, guided solely by respect for Christ, who, when He is received in the Eucharist, should find in the heart of each of us a worthy abode. This question is closely linked not only with the practice of the sacrament of Penance but also with a correct sense of responsibility for the whole deposit of moral teaching and for the precise distinction between good and evil, a distinction which then becomes for each person sharing in the Eucharist the basis for a correct judgment of self to be made in the depths of the personal conscience. St. Paul's words, 'Let a man examine himself' [I Co 11:28] are well known; this judgment is an indispensable condition for a personal decision whether to approach Eucharistic Communion or to abstain..."

"It is necessary for all of us who are ministers of the Eucharist to examine carefully our actions at the altar, in particular the way in which we handle that food and drink which are the body and blood of the Lord our God in our hands: the way in which we distribute Holy Communion; the way in which we perform the purification ... God preserve us from acting in a way that lacks respect, from undue hurry, from an impatience that causes scandal. Over and above our commitment to the evangelical mission, our greatest commitment consists in exercising this mysterious power over the body of the Redeemer, and all that is within us should be decisevely ordered to this. We should also remember that to this ministerial power we have been sacramentally consecrated, that we have been chosen from among men 'for the good of men.' We especially, the priests of the Latin Church, whose ordination rite added in the course of the centuries the custom of anointing the priest's hands, should think about this."

† † †

*O Jesus, Pelican of heaven, wash me, a sinner,
in your Blood.*

On Communion in the hand: "11. In some countries the practice of receiving Communion in the hand has been introduced. This practice has been requested by individual episcopal conferences and has received approval from the Apostolic See. However, cases of deplorable lack of respect towards the Eucharistic species have been reported, cases which are imputable not only to the individuals guilty of such behavior but also to the pastors of the Church who have not been vigilant enough regarding the attitude of the faithful towards the Eucharist. It also happens, on occasion, that the free choice of those who prefer to continue the practice of receiving the Eucharist on the tongue is not taken into account in those places where the distribution of Communion in the hand has been authorized. It is therefore difficult in the context of this present letter not to mention the sad phenomena previously referred to. This is in no way meant to refer to those who, receiving the Lord Jesus in the hand, do so with profound reverence and devotion, in those countries where this practice has been authorized ...

"As ministers of the Holy Eucharist, they [priests] have a primary responsibility for the sacred species, because it is a total responsibility: they offer the bread and wine, they consecrate it, and then distribute the sacred species to the participants in the assembly who wish to receive them."

Regarding lay people as Eucharistic ministers, the Pope requires that there be a just need and an adequate preparation: "11. To touch the sacred species and to distribute them with their own hands is a privilege of the ordained, one which indicates an active participation in the ministry of the Eucharist." The Church grants this faculty to "lay people who are chosen for this to meet a just need, but always after an adequate preparation."

✝ ✝ ✝

On the cross was veiled your Godhead's splendor,
Here your manhood lies hidden too;
Unto both alike my faith I render,
And, as sued the contrite thief, I sue.

The Pope points out why it is necessary for the priest celebrating Mass to carry out the liturgical requirements set by the Church. "**12.** The priest as minister, as celebrant, as the one who presides over the Eucharistic assembly of the faithful, should have a special sense of the common good of the Church, which he represents through his ministry, but to which he must also be subordinate, according to a correct discipline of faith. He cannot consider himself a 'proprietor' who can make free use of the liturgical text and of the sacred rite as if it were his own property, in such a way as to stamp it with his own arbitrary personal style. At times this latter might seem more effective, and it may better correspond to subjective piety; nevertheless, objectively it is always a betrayal of that union which should find its proper expression in the sacrament of unity.

"Every priest who offers the holy Sacrifice should recall that during this Sacrifice it is not only he with his community that is praying but the whole Church, which is thus expressing in this sacrament her spiritual unity, among other ways by the use of the approved liturgical text. To call this position 'mere insistence on uniformity' would only show ignorance of the objective requirement of authentic unity, and would be a symptom of harmful individualism.

"This subordination of the minister, of the celebrant, to the Mysterium which has been entrusted to him by the Church for the good of the whole people of God, should also find expression in the observance of the liturgical requirements concerning the celebration of the holy Sacrifice. These refer, for example, to dress, and in particular to the vestments worn by the celebrant." After praising the priest prisoners who celebrated Mass under extraordinary conditions in death camps, the Pope continues: "Although in those conditions this was proof of heroism and deserved profound admiration, nevertheless in normal conditions to ignore the liturgical directives can be interpreted as a lack of respect towards the Eucharist, dictated perhaps by individualism or by an absence of a critical sense concerning current opinions, or by a certain lack of a spirit of faith."

The Pope continues explaining why it is incumbent upon priests, with reference to the veneration of the Eucharist, to avoid scandal and maintain the people's sense of faith in this sacrament. "**12.** Upon all of us who, through the grace of God, are ministers of the Eucharist, there weighs a particular responsibility for the ideas and attitudes of our brothers and sisters who have been entrusted to our pastoral care. It is our vocation to nurture, above all by personal example, every healthy manifestation of worship towards Christ present and operative in that sacrament of love. May God preserve us from acting otherwise and weakening that worship by "becoming unaccustomed' to various manifestations and forms of Eucharistic worship which express perhaps 'traditional' but healthy piety, and which express above all that 'sense of the faith' possessed by the whole People of God, as the Second Vatican Council recalled."

The Pope asks forgiveness "in my own name and in the name of all of you, venerable and dear brothers in the episcopate, for everything which, for whatever reason, through whatever human weakness, impatience or negligence, and also through the at times partial, one-sided and erroneous application of the directives of the Second Vatican Council, may have caused scandal and disturbance concerning the interpretation of the doctrine and the veneration due to this great sacrament. And I pray the Lord Jesus that in the future we may avoid in our manner of dealing with this sacred mystery anything which could weaken or disorient in any way the sense of reverence and love that exists in our faithful people."

On the close and necessary connection between the liturgy and the whole life of the Church: "**13.** A very close and organic bond exists between the renewal of the liturgy and the renewal of the whole life of the Church. The Church not only acts but also expresses herself in the liturgy, lives by the liturgy, and draws from the liturgy the strength for her life." (cont'd.)

The Pope says that, since the Church draws from the liturgy the strength for her life: "**13.** liturgical renewal carried out correctly in the spirit of the Second Vatican Council is, in a certain sense, the measure and the condition for putting into effect the teaching of that Council which we wish to accept with profound faith, convinced as we are that by means of this Council the Holy Spirit 'has spoken to the Church' the truths and given the indications for carrying our her mission among the people of today and tomorrow.

"We shall continue in the future to take special care to promote and follow the renewal of the Church according to the teaching of the Second Vatican Council, in the spirit of an ever living Tradition." In carrying out the renewal of the liturgy the Council had "recourse to what is ancient, what comes from the heritage of the Fathers and is the expression of the faith and doctrine of a Church which has remained united for so many centuries."

"Above all I wish to emphasize that the problems of the liturgy, and in particular of the Eucharistic Liturgy, must not be an occasion for dividing Catholics and for threatening the unity of the Church. This is demanded by an elementary understanding of that sacrament which Christ has left us as the source of spiritual unity. And how could the Eucharist, which in the Church is the 'sacramentum pietatis, signum unitatis, vinculum caritatis' [St. Augustine: "sacrament of piety, sign of unity, bond of love"], form between us at this time a point of division and a source of distortion of thought and of behavior, instead of being the focal point and constitutive center, which it truly is in its essence, of the unity of the Church herself?" (Dated February 24, 1980)

† † †

Soul of Christ, sanctify me.
Body of Christ, save me.
Blood of Christ, inebriate me.
Water from the side of Christ, wash me.
Passion of Christ, strengthen me.
Within your wounds, hide me.

PROMINENT WORKS OF THE TWENTIETH CENTURY

Due to the outstanding development of Eucharistic doctrine that was offered by the Council of Trent, no major advance in official doctrine concerning the Eucharist has been made since then. For the last 400 years theologians have been absorbing and explaining what Trent defined. In this century a few works among several others deserve special mention.

In 1915 Maurice de la Taille, S. J., a Canadian lector of theology at the Gregorian University in Rome, published in Latin a huge tome entitled Mysterium Fidei (Mystery of Faith). In 50 "Elucidationes" (Explanations) he explains and defends the dogmatic doctrine of Trent on the Eucharist with abundant quotations from the ancient Fathers of the Church. Several subsequent editions of that work have been made as well as an English translation.

In 1948 Joseph A. Jungmann, S. J., professor of theology at the University of Innsbruck in Austria, published in German a two volume work with the Latin title Missarum Sollemnia (Mass Ceremonies; The Mass of the Roman Rite: Its Origins and Development). Apparently it is the most authoritative and complete history of the liturgy of the Roman Mass. Father Jungmann lectured on liturgy at the University of Notre Dame and was a "peritus" (expert), available for consultation by the Fathers of the Second Vatican Council. His masterpiece has been translated into English.

A two volume work was published in 1978 by La B. A. C. (La Biblioteca de Autores Cristianos), under the direction of the University of Salamanca in Spain. The author, Jesus Solano, S. J., collected all that could be found of the writings of the Fathers of the Church pertaining to the Eucharist, from the very beginning down to St. John Damascene (died 749 a.d.) He published Textos Eucaristicos Primitivos in a bilingual edition, with the original languages and his Spanish translation on each page. Most of our quotations of the Fathers are our translations of his Spanish text.

† † †

O good Jesus, hear me.

In Argentina in the year 1950 under the title EUCARISTIA there appeared the sole authorized translation of the huge Eucharistic Encyclopedia in French, published under the direction of Maurice Brilliant with the collaboration of twenty-eight French theologians and scholars. In some respects this is an exhaustive work, which treats the Eucharist from practically every aspect from its origin to our day.

The latest prominent work is, of course, the CATECHISM OF THE CATHOLIC CHURCH. The original French edition appeared in 1992 after six years of labor by experts in the various pertinent fields and the collaboration of the entire episcopate of the Catholic Church. It is the first universal catechism since that of the Council of Trent, over 400 years ago. In publishing the catechism Pope John Paul II said that it "is a statement of the Church's faith and of Catholic doctrine, attested to or illumined by Sacred Scripture, the Apostolic Tradition, and the Church's magisterium. I declare it to be a sure norm for teaching the faith. ... It is meant to encourage and assist in the writing of new local catechisms, which take into account various situations and cultures, while carefully preserving the unity of faith and fidelity to Catholic doctrine."

The official English translation of the Catechism was delayed for two years due to difficulties with the so-called inclusive language, which did not reflect properly the doctrine contained in the French edition.

We are happy to close our Eucharistic meditations by quoting from this latest official compendium of the fundamental teachings of the Catholic Church on faith and morals in the field of the Eucharist, and by offering a few explanations.

† † †

Down in adoration falling,
Lo! the sacred Host we hail;
Lo! o'er ancient forms departing,
Newer rites of grace prevail;
Faith for all defects supplying,
Where the feeble senses fail.

CATECHISM OF THE CATHOLIC CHURCH

In closing our meditations on the Eucharist we can do no better than to quote from the recent Catechism and offer a few explanations that seem appropriate. The numbers are from the articles in the Catechism itself.

INTRODUCTION

In the opening article, 1322, we are told that we, "who have been raised to the dignity of the royal priesthood (of the faithful) by Baptism, ... participate with the whole community in the Lord's own sacrifice by means of the Eucharist." We are reminded, therefore, that the Mass makes present Christ's one sacrifice of Calvary, in which we participate by uniting ourselves with Christ in offering that sacrifice now in a glorious manner and by joining our sacrifices to his.

Also in 1323 it says that Christ instituted the Mass at the Last Supper "in order to perpetuate the sacrifice of the cross throughout the ages until he should come again, and so to entrust to his beloved Spouse, the Church, a memorial of his death and resurrection: a sacrament of love, a sign of unity, a bond of charity, a Paschal banquet 'in which Christ is consumed, the mind is filled with grace, and a pledge of future glory is given to us.' "

At its very institution Christ intended that the Mass be offered until his return to earth at the end of the world. Some of the fruits of Holy Communion are mentioned. Its fruitful reception requires love of God and neighbor and increases that love. As a sign of unity, Communion cannot be received fruitfully by those who do not hold to the Catholic faith, whether they have been baptized in the Catholic Church or not. When Christ promised the Eucharist (John 6), he said that those receiving him he would "raise up on the last day." When receiving Communion we do well to remind ourselves that the Host we receive is a pawn or pledge that we can redeem at our death to receive eternal life in heaven, if we continue to live in the spirit of what we receive.

THE EUCHARIST - SOURCE AND SUMMIT OF ECCLESIAL LIFE

1324. "The Eucharist is 'the source and summit of the Christian life.' The other sacraments, and indeed all ecclesiastical ministries and works of the apostolate, are bound up with the Eucharist and are oriented to it. For in the blessed Eucharist is contained the whole spiritual good of the Church, namely Christ himself, our Pasch."

Just as the central event in the history of salvation and of the world was Christ's redemptive sacrifice on Calvary, so too all the spiritual life and activity of the Church come from and are bound up with the Mass, which perpetuates that one sacrifice of Christ.

1325. "The Eucharist is the efficacious sign and sublime cause of that communion in the divine life and that unity of the People of God by which the Church is kept in being. It is the culmination both of God's action sanctifying the world in Christ and of the worship men offer to Christ and through him to the Father in the Holy Spirit."

By saying "that communion in the divine life" the Catechism refers to Sanctifying Grace, which is a participation in God's own life. Holy Communion, under the appearances of bread and wine, is obviously a sign or symbol of food or feeding. It is also an "efficacious sign," that is, it produces what it signifies. Therefore, it nourishes God's life in our soul or, as the text says, it signifies and causes "that communion in the divine life."

And since we all share in the one life of God, the Eucharist thus produces that unity among us necessary to form the Church.

Because the Mass makes Christ's sacrifice present again, there can be no greater work of sanctification than the Mass and no greater act of worship.

† † †

We adore you, O Christ, and we bless you; because by your Holy Cross you have redeemed the world.
May the Most Blessed Sacrament be praised and adored forever.

1326. "By the Eucharistic celebration we already unite ourselves with the heavenly liturgy and anticipate eternal life, when God will be all in all" (1Co 15:28).

In the Book of Revelation we read about the heavenly liturgy that is offered on the golden altar standing before the throne of God. On the altar are the prayers of the Saints. And in Hebrews we read that Christ Himself, the glorious Victim of Calvary, intercedes for us. He stands, as it were, before God the Father, showing Him His glorious wounds and thus continues to offer his one and only sacrifice of Calvary. The prayers of the Saints were heard through the merits of Christ's sacrifice, which is perpetuated in the Mass, as it is in heaven. The Eucharist thus unites us with the worship of the Saints in heaven; and in this way it anticipates eternal life, where all the redeemed are gloriously subjected to God. Thus God will be "all in all," that is, everything to every one.

1327. "In brief, the Eucharist is the sum and summary of our faith."

Because the Eucharist contains God the Sanctifier, it is the sum and summary of our faith or religion, which comes from God and leads us to God in heaven.

VARIOUS NAMES OF THE EUCHARIST

1328. "The inexhaustible richness of this sacrament is expressed in the different names we give it. Each name evokes certain aspects of it.

EUCHARIST (Greek for "thanksgiving), because it is an action of thanksgiving to God. Before consecrating the bread and wine at the Last Supper, Christ "gave thanks" and He "blessed" those elements. This was in keeping with the customary Jewish blessings, especially during meals. Such blessings proclaimed God's works of creation, redemption, and sanctification.

† † †

The way we can be sure that we are in union with God is to conduct ourselves just as Christ did. (1Jn 2:6)

1329. THE LORD'S SUPPER. This name is given to the Eucharist, "because of its connection with the supper which the Lord took with his disciples on the eve of his Passion and because it anticipates the wedding feast of the Lamb in the heavenly Jerusalem."

In the Book of Revelations the Messianic kingdom of heaven begins with the marriage of Christ the Lamb (Victim of Calvary) with his bride, the Church (those redeemed, the Saints). "Alleluia! The reign of the Lord our God Almighty has begun; let us be glad and joyful and give praise to God, because this is the time for the marriage of the Lamb. His bride is ready, and she has been able to dress herself in dazzling white linen, because her linen is made of the good deeds of the saints." (Rev. 19:7-9) The dazzling white linen of the Saints represents their victorious purity, a gift of God through the divine grace given them and enabling them to perform their good works. All grace, of course, comes from Christ's sacrifice on Calvary, which is perpetuated in the Mass. The Mass, in turn, applies grace to our souls.

THE BREAKING OF BREAD, "because Jesus used this rite, part of a Jewish meal, when as master of the table he blessed and distributed the bread, above all at the Last Supper. It is by this action that the disciples will recognize him (at Emmaus) after his Resurrection, and it is this expression the first Christians will use to designate their Eucharistic assemblies (Mass); by doing so they signified that all who eat the one broken bread, Christ, enter into communion with him and form but one body with him."

At Masses with the early Christians who were few in number, one large Host or loaf could be consecrated and then broken to distribute Holy Communion. In this way the spiritual union binding Christians together through mutual charity was signified in a vivid manner and produced by receiving Communion. "The fact that there is only one loaf means that, though there are many of us, we form a single body because we all have a share in this one loaf." (1Co 10:17) In the same way the doctrine of the Mystical Body of Christ was easily signified, with Christ as the head and all the baptized united to Him as various members of His body.

† † †

There is a jealous ear that overhears everything. (*Wisdom 1:10*)

SYNAXIS (Greek for "assembly") is also used for the Eucharist, because "the Eucharist is celebrated amid the assembly of the faithful, the visible expression of the Church," as is clear from 1Co 11:17-34.

1330. "The MEMORIAL of the Lord's passion and Resurrection.

THE HOLY SACRIFICE, "because it makes present the one sacrifice of Christ the Savior and includes the Church's offering. The terms 'holy sacrifice of the Mass', and the biblical terms "sacrifice of praise', 'spiritual sacrifice', 'pure and holy sacrifice' are also used, since the Eucharist completes and surpasses all the sacrifices of the Old Covenant."

The HOLY AND DIVINE LITURGY, "because the Church's whole liturgy finds its center and most intense expression in the celebration of this sacrament; in the same sense we also call its celebration the SACRED MYSTERIES. We speak of the MOST BLESSED SACRAMENT because it is the Sacrament of sacraments. The Eucharistic species reserved in the tabernacle are designated by this same name.

1331. HOLY COMMUNION, because by this sacrament we unite ourselves to Christ, who makes us sharers in his Body and Blood to form a single body. We also call it: "THE HOLY THINGS" ("ta hagia" in Greek; "sancta" in Latin). In all oriental liturgies, at the time of Communion, the priest would issue an invitation together with a reminder or instruction: "Ta hagia tois hagios" (Holy things for holy persons). The same invitation and reminder was issued in some Latin liturgies: "Sancta sanctis," a reminder of the proper dispositions required for the fruitful reception of Holy Communion, namely, that one be in the state of sanctifying grace and have a proper intention. "The holy things" was also the first meaning of the phrase "'communion of saints" in the Apostles' Creed. As we use the phrase to mean the communion of saints (holy persons), it was originally used to mean the communion of holy things, that is, the holy things resulting from the Redemption and which we on earth and the souls in Purgatory and the Saints in heaven all hold in common: sanctifying grace and, for us, the means to produce it, namely the sacraments, especially the Eucharist. Also included in "the holy things" are the mutual prayers that are offered: we, the Church Militant, for the Church Suffering in Purgatory and to the Church Triumphant in heaven, and both those phases of the Church for us.

1331. The Eucharist is also called THE BREAD OF ANGELS, BREAD FROM HEAVEN. These terms are taken from the Bible. St. Ignatius of Antioch (died c. 110), the first to use the term "Catholic Church," called the Eucharist MEDICINE OF IMMORTALITY, "antidote to avoid death, to live forever in Christ Jesus." The Fathers of the Church also gave the name VIATICUM to the Eucharist. The viaticum was the ration of food that the Roman soldier would receive daily in the morning to provide him with sustenance for the day's march or journey ("via" in Latin). The Fathers used the term for our daily spiritual journey to heaven. The Church uses the word today especially when referring to the Eucharist when administered to a dying person to assist him on his way to heaven.

1332. Finally the Eucharist is called "HOLY MASS (Missa), because the liturgy (Mass) in which the mystery of salvation is accomplished concludes with the sending forth (missio) of the faithful, so that they may fulfill God's will in their daily lives." Note that the Catechism states that in the Mass "the mystery of salvation is accomplished." This is another way of stating that what was accomplished on Calvary, namely our salvation, is made present in the Mass, the only difference being the manner in which that one sacrifice of Christ is offered: on Calvary in a bloody manner, at Mass in an unbloody and glorious manner.

THE EUCHARIST IN THE ECONOMY OF SALVATION

THE SIGNS OF BREAD AND WINE

1333. "At the heart of the Eucharistic celebration are the bread and wine that, by the words of Christ and the invocation of the Holy Spirit, become Christ's Body and Blood. Faithful to the Lord's command the Church continues to do, in his memory and until his glorious return [at the end of time], what he did on the eve of his Passion: 'He took bread...' 'He took the cup filled with wine...' The signs of bread and wine become, in a way surpassing understanding, the Body and Blood of Christ; they continue also to signify the goodness of creation. Thus in the Offertory we give thanks to the Creator for bread and wine, fruit of the 'work of human hands,' but above all as 'fruit of the earth' and 'of the vine'-gifts of the Creator." Melchizedek, offering these, prefigured the Mass.

1334. "In the Old Covenant bread and wine were offered in sacrifice among the first fruits of the earth as a sign of grateful acknowledgment to the Creator. But they also received a new significance in the context of the Exodus: the unleavened bread that Israel eats every year at Passover commemorates the haste of the departure that liberated them from Egypt; the remembrance of the manna in the desert will always recall to Israel that it lives by the bread of the Word of God ["He fed you with manna, which you did not know, nor did your fathers know, that he might make you know that man does not live by bread alone, but that man lives by everything that proceeds out of the mouth of the Lord." [Deut. 8:3]; their daily bread is the fruit of the promised land, the pledge of God's faithfulness to his promises. The 'cup of blessing' at the end of the Jewish Passover meal adds to the festive joy of wine an eschatological dimension: the messianic expectation of the rebuilding of Jerusalem. When Jesus instituted the Eucharist, he gave a new and definitive meaning to the blessing of the bread and the cup."

1335. "The miracles of the multiplication of the loaves, when the Lord says the blessing, breaks and distributes the loaves through his disciples to feed the multitude, prefigures the superabundance of this unique bread of his Eucharist. The sign of water turned into wine at Cana already announces the Hour of Jesus ' glorification. It makes manifest the fulfillment of the wedding feast in the Father's kingdom, where the faithful will drink the new wine that has become the Blood of Christ." [Thus the Eucharist not only gives us hope to partake of the Father's feast in heaven, but also anticipates it by uniting us to His Son here on earth.]

1336. "The first announcement of the Eucharist divided the disciples, just as the announcement of the Passion scandalized them: 'This is a hard saying; who can listen to it?' The Eucharist and the Cross are stumbling blocks. It is the same mystery and it never ceases to be an occasion of division. 'Will you also go away?' The Lord's question echoes through the ages, as a loving invitation to discover that only he has 'the words of eternal life' and that to receive in faith the gift of the Eucharist is to receive the Lord himself."

THE INSTITUTION OF THE EUCHARIST

1337. "The Lord, having loved those who were his own, loved them to the end. Knowing that the hour had come to leave this world and return to the Father, in the course of a meal he washed their feet and gave them the commandment of love." 'A new commandment I give to you, that you love one another; even as I have loved you, that you also love one another. By this all men will know that you are my disciples, if you have love for one another.' (John 13:34-35) Although the commandment of mutual love is found in the Old Testament, Jesus calls it "new" because of the great emphasis He places on it. He offers it as the only badge by which Christians can be recognized as Christians.

"In order to leave them a pledge of his love, in order never to depart from his own and to make them sharers in his Passover, he instituted the Eucharist as a memorial of his death and Resurrection, and commanded the apostles to celebrate it until his return [at the end of the world]; 'thereby he constituted them priests of the new Testament.' " The Council of Trent defined that at the Last Supper, after consecrating the bread and wine, with his words, "Do this in memory of me," Christ constituted the Apostles priests of the new Testament and also instituted the sacrament of Holy Orders, by which others become priests through sharing Christ's own priesthood. (D.S. 1740, 1752)

1338. In their Gospels Matthew, Mark, and Luke record the institution of the Eucharist at the Last Supper, as does also St. Paul in 1Corinthians, Chapter 11. St. John, who wrote his Gospel later, does not repeat the account of the institution, but in Chapter 6 records Christ's words in announcing the doctrine of the Eucharist and how He had prepared the minds of the people to receive this new doctrine by working two miracles the previous day. He multiplied the five loaves of bread to feed five thousand men, not counting women and children, and then that night He walked on the water of the Sea of Galilee to meet the Apostles struggling with their boat in a storm. With these miracles He showed that both bread and his body are mere creatures in his hands, and that he can do with them as he chooses. In the Eucharist, He said, He chooses to change bread and wine into His body and blood to make them "real food and real drink." He calls Himself the bread of life, come from heaven.

1339. "Jesus chose the time of Passover to fulfill what he had announced at Capernaum (namely): giving his disciples his Body and Blood: 'Then came the day of Unleavened Bread, on which the Passover lamb had to be sacrificed. So Jesus sent Peter and John, saying, "Go and prepare the Passover meal for us, that we may eat it...." 'They went.... and prepared the Passover. And when the hour came, he sat at table, and the apostles with him. And he said to them, "I have earnestly desired to eat this Passover with you before I suffer; for I tell you I shall not eat it again until it is fulfilled in the kingdom of God." ... And he took bread, and when he had given thanks he broke it and gave it to them, saying, "This is my body which is given up for you. Do this in remembrance of me." And likewise the cup after supper, saying, "This cup which is poured out for you is the New Covenant in my blood." [Luke 22:7-20]

1340. "By celebrating the Last Supper with his apostles in the course of the Passover meal, Jesus gave the Jewish Passover its definitive meaning. Jesus' passing over to his Father by his death and Resurrection, the new Passover, is anticipated in the Supper and celebrated in the Eucharist, which fulfills the Jewish Passover and anticipates the final Passover of the Church in the glory of the kingdom."

'DO THIS IN MEMORY OF ME'

1341. "The command of Jesus to repeat his actions and words "until he comes" does not only ask us to remember Jesus and what he did. It is directed at the liturgical celebration, by the apostles and their successors, of their memorial of Christ, of his life, of his death, of his Resurrection, and of his intercession in the presence of the Father."

St. Paul in 1 Cor 11:26 writes: "For as often as you eat this bread and drink the cup, you proclaim the Lord's death until he comes."

About Christ's intercession with God the Father St. Paul writes in Heb 7:25: "His power to save is utterly certain, since he is living to intercede for all who come to God through him." And in Rom 8:34: "He not only died for us—he rose from the dead, and there at God's right hand he stands and pleads for us," as it were, showing His Father His glorified wounds. And 1 John 2:1 "We have our advocate with the Father, Jesus Christ."

1342. "From the beginning the Church has been faithful to the Lord's command ['Do this in memory of me.']. Of the Church in Jerusalem it is written: 'They devoted themselves to the apostles' teaching and fellowship, to the breaking of bread and the prayers.....Day by day, attending the temple together and breaking bread in their homes, they partook of food with glad and generous hearts." (Acts 2:42,46)

These words contain a very brief summary of the religious practices of the very first Christians. They were Jewish converts. They would gather in the Jewish Temple [There were no churches yet.] where they had gathered for Jewish worship. There the Apostles would explain the Christian event as it is found in the prophecies of the Old Testament. The New Testament had not yet been written.] The Apostles would lead them in community prayers. In the evening they would gather in their homes for Mass ["breaking of bread"], which was offered in conjunction with the evening meal, just as Christ had done at the Last Supper. The joy they experienced was that which comes from faith. Since they were few in number, the sense of fellowship or brotherhood was strong, so strong that they shared their material goods to help one another. As congregations grew in size, obviously the sense of brotherhood lessened; and later, when churches could be built, Mass was transferred to early morning before daily work and naturally the meal in conjunction with Mass was dropped.

1343. "It was above all on 'the first day of the week,' Sunday, the day of Jesus' resurrection, that the Christians met 'to break bread.' (Acts 20:7) From that time on down to our own day the celebration of the Eucharist has been continued so that today we encounter it everywhere in the Church with the same fundamental structure. It remains the center of the Church's life."

1344. "Thus from celebrator to celebration, as they proclaim the Paschal mystery of Jesus 'until he comes,' the pilgrim People of God advances, 'following the narrow way of the cross' (1 Cor 11:26), toward the heavenly banquet, when all the elect will be seated at the table of the kingdom."

THE LITURGICAL CELEBRATION OF THE EUCHARIST

THE MASS OF ALL AGES

About the year 155 St. Justin, a layman and philosopher in Rome, wrote to the pagan Emperor to explain what the Christians did at their meetings for Mass. They had been accused of practicing evil things, including the killing and eating of babies (a reference to the Real Presence). Justin's letter contains the earliest known full account of Mass in Rome at that time. It is clear that the basic outline of the order of Mass has remained the same down to our day for all the great liturgical families, including those of the East. In number 1345 of the Catechism there is a quotation from Justin's letter, but we have a more complete quotation on our pages 51 and 52.

1346. The Mass is one single act of worship consisting of the liturgy of the Word (Bible readings and homily) and the liturgy of the Eucharist consisting of the presentation of the bread and wine, the consecratory thanksgiving, and communion. Throughout the centuries the Eucharistic table has been the table of the Word of God and of the Body of the Lord. "The Church has always regarded, and continues to regard the Scriptures, taken together with sacred Tradition, as the supreme rule of her faith....All the preaching of the Church, as indeed the entire Christian religion, should be nourished and ruled by sacred Scripture. In the sacred books the Father who is in heaven comes lovingly to meet his children, and talks with them." [Dei Verbum 21] In number 1347 the Catechism suggests that Christ Himself may have followed this order of Mass on the first Easter evening, when he walked with the disciples of Emmaus explaining the Scriptures to them and then, sitting with them at table, "He took bread, blessed and broke it, and gave it to them."

Death was not God's doing, he takes no pleasure in the extinction of the living. To be - for this he created all; the world's created things have health in them, in them no fatal poison can be found.
(Wis 1:13-14)

THE MOVEMENT OF THE CELEBRATION

1348. All gather together. "Christians come together in one place for the Eucharistic assembly. At its head is Christ himself, the principal agent of the Eucharist. He is High priest of the New Covenant; it is he himself who presides invisibly over every Eucharistic celebration. It is in representing him that the bishop or priest acting in the person of Christ the head presides over the assembly, speaks after the readings, receives the offerings, and says the Eucharistic Prayer. ALL have their own active parts to play in the celebration, each in his own way: readers, those who bring up the offerings, those who give communion, and the whole people whose 'Amen' manifests their participation."

1349. The Liturgy of the Word includes writings from the Old Testament, letters of the Apostles, and the Gospels. The homily is an exhortation to accept the Word as what it truly is, namely, the Word of God, and to put it into practice. The General Intercessions or Prayer of the Faithful is according to St. Paul's words: "I urge that supplications, prayers, intercessions, and thanksgivings be made for all men, for kings, and all who are in high positions."

1350. There follows the presentation of the offerings (the Offertory), in which bread and wine are brought to the altar. They will be offered by the priest in the name of Christ in the Eucharistic sacrifice, in which they will become his body and blood. St. Irenaeus: "The Church alone offers this pure oblation to the Creator, when she offers what comes forth from his creation with thanksgiving." The presentation of the offerings commits the Creator's gifts into the hands of Christ who, in his sacrifice, brings to perfection all human attempts to offer sacrifice.

1351. "From the very beginning Christians have brought, along with the bread and wine for the Eucharist, gifts to share with those in need. This custom of the collection, ever appropriate, is inspired by the example of Christ who became poor to make us rich."

1352. The anaphora: "With the Eucharistic Prayer - the prayer of thanksgiving and consecration - we come to the heart and summit of the celebration:

In the PREFACE the Church gives thanks to the Father, through Christ, in the Holy Spirit, for all his works: creation, redemption, and sanctification. The whole community thus joins in the unending praise that the Church in heaven, the angels and all the saints, sing to the thrice-holy God.

In the 'EPICLESIS,' the Church asks the Father to send his Holy Spirit (or the power of his blessing) on the bread and wine, so that by his power they may become the body and blood of Jesus Christ, and so that those who take part of the Eucharist be one body and one spirit. Some liturgical traditions put the "epiclesis" after the anamnesis.

In the INSTITUTION NARRATIVE, the power of the words and the action of Christ, and the power of the Holy Spirit, make sacramentally present under the species of bread and wine Christ's body and blood, his sacrifice, which was offered on the cross once for all."

1354. "In the ANAMNESIS that follows, the Church calls to mind the Passion, resurrection, and glorious return of Christ Jesus; she presents to the Father the offering of his Son, which reconciles us with him.

In the INTERCESSIONS the Church indicates that the Eucharist is celebrated in communion with the whole Church in heaven and on earth, the living and the dead, and in communion with the pastors of the Church, the Pope, the diocesan bishop, his presbyterium and his deacons, and all the bishops of the whole world together with their Churches."

1355. "In the COMMUNION, preceded by the Lord's prayer and the breaking of the bread, the faithful receive 'the bread of heaven' and 'the cup of salvation', the body and blood of Christ who offered himself 'for the life of the world.' " St. Justin wrote, "Because this bread and wine have been made Eucharist ('eucharisted', according to an ancient expression), we call this food 'Eucharist'; and no one may partake of it unless he believes that what we teach is true, has received baptism for the forgiveness of sins and new birth, and lives in keeping with what Christ taught."

SACRAMENTAL SACRIFICE: THANKSGIVING, MEMORIAL, PRESENCE

1356. "If from the beginning Christians have celebrated the Eucharist, and celebrated it in a form whose substance has not changed despite the great diversity of times and liturgies, it is because we know ourselves to be bound by the command the Lord gave on the eve of his Passion: "Do this in memory of me."

1357. "We carry out this command of the Lord by celebrating the memorial of his sacrifice . In so doing, we offer to the Father what he has himself given us: namely, the gifts of his creation, bread and wine which, by the power of the Holy Spirit and by the words of Christ, have become the body and blood of Christ. Christ is thus really and mysteriously made present."

1358. We must therefore consider the Eucharist under these three aspects, which have reference to the three Persons in the Trinity: 1-thanksgiving and praise to the FATHER; 2-the sacrificial memorial of CHRIST and his Body; 3-the presence of Christ by the power of his word and of his SPIRIT.

THANKSGIVING AND PRAISE TO THE FATHER

1359. "The Eucharist, the sacrament of our salvation, accomplished by Christ on the cross, is also a sacrifice of praise in thanksgiving for the work of creation. In the Eucharistic sacrifice the whole of creation, loved by God, is presented to the Father through the death and Resurrection of Christ. Through Christ the Church can offer the sacrifice of praise in thanksgiving for all that God has made good, beautiful, and just in creation and in humanity." In redeeming all men on Calvary, Christ offered to His Father all of mankind for entrance into heaven, since Christ opened to men the gates of heaven, which Adam had closed for all men by his sin. And since all earthly creation was made ultimately to aid man to get to heaven, and was cursed due to Adam, Christ lifted that curse and offered redeemed creation to the Father—and so do we at Mass.

1360. "The Eucharist is a sacrifice of thanksgiving to the Father, a blessing by which the Church expresses her gratitude to God for all his benefits, for all that he has accomplished through creation, redemption, and sanctification. Eucharist means first of all 'thanksgiving.' "

1361. "The Eucharist is also the sacrifice of praise by which the Church sings the glory of God in the name of all creation." The Father brought "everything together under Christ, as head, everything in the heavens and everything on earth"(Eph 1:10) "This sacrifice of praise is possible only through Christ: he unites the faithful to his person, to his praise, and to his intercession, so that the sacrifice of praise to the Father is offered THROUGH Christ and WITH him, to be accepted IN him."

THE SACRIFICIAL MEMORIAL OF CHRIST AND OF HIS BODY, THE CHURCH

1362. "The Eucharist is the memorial of Christ's Passover, the making present and the sacramental offering of his unique sacrifice, in the liturgy of the Church, which is his body. In all the Eucharistic Prayers we find after the words of institution a prayer called the "anamnesis" or memorial."

1363. "In the sense of Sacred Scripture the MEMORIAL is not merely the recollection of past events but the proclamation of the mighty works wrought by God for men. In the liturgical celebration of these events, they become in certain way present and real. This is how Israel understands its liberation from Egypt: every time Passover is celebrated, the Exodus events are made present to the memory of believers so that they may conform their lives to them."

1364. "In the New Testament, the memorial takes on new meaning. When the Church celebrates the Eucharist, she commemorates Christ's Passover, AND IT IS MADE PRESENT: the sacrifice Christ offered once for all remains ever present. 'As often as the sacrifice of the cross, by which Christ our Pasch has been sacrificed', is celebrated on the altar, the work of our redemption is carried out.' "

1365. "The sacrificial character of the Eucharist is manifest in the very words of institution: "This is my body which is given for you" and "This cup which is poured out for you is the New Covenant in my blood." The terms, "given up for you" and "poured out for you," in the original Aramaic and Greek texts are sacrificial terms, although they are not necessarily such in English. But, even in English we see the sacrificial character in the words, "poured out for many for the forgiveness of sins" and "this cup is the New Covenant in my blood." The Old Covenant was sealed with blood; and even in the Old Testament sacrifices were offered for the forgiveness of sins. "In the Eucharist Christ gives us the very body which he gave up for us on the cross, the very blood which he 'poured out for many for the forgiveness of sins." (Lk 22:19-20; Mt 26:28)

1366. The Eucharist is thus a sacrifice because it represents (makes present) the sacrifice of the cross, because it is its memorial (in the biblical and liturgical meaning, that is, it makes something from the past present in a certain and real manner), and because it applies its fruit." The Council of Trent [DS 1740] declared that at the Last Supper Christ left "to his beloved spouse the Church a visible sacrifice, as the nature of man demands, by which the bloody sacrifice, which he was to accomplish once for all on the cross, would be represented, its memory perpetuated until the end of the world, and its salutary power be applied to the forgiveness of the sins we daily commit."

In Heb 7:24 St. Paul says that Christ, "Because he remains for ever, can never lose his priesthood." Thus Christ continues to offer His one sacrifice, that of Calvary, in heaven in a passive and glorious manner, simply by remaining the Victim of Calvary. And at Mass, through the instrumentality of the priest, Christ consecrates the bread and wine , making Himself present as He is in heaven, and thus continuing to offer in a glorious manner His one sacrifice of the cross even here on earth till the end of time. The office of priest, which is given to a man when he receives the sacrament of Holy Orders, is simply a sharing in Christ's priesthood. As with Christ, death does not end the human priest's office.

✝ ✝ ✝

"You are a priest of the order of Melchizedek, and for ever."
(Ps 110:4)

The essence of the Mass is made crystal clear in **1367**: "The sacrifice of Christ and the sacrifice of the Eucharist are one single sacrifice: 'The victim is one and the same; the same now offers through the ministry of priests, who then offered himself on the cross; only the manner of offering is different.' 'In this divine sacrifice which is celebrated in the Mass, the same Christ who offered himself once in a bloody manner on the altar of the cross is contained and is offered in an unbloody manner.' " [DS 1743]

Christ offered but one sacrifice; and He offered it only once - BUT HE NEVER STOPPED OFFERING IT. He offered it beginning at the Last Supper; He continued offering it (not AGAIN, but CONTINUED to offer it) during His passion and death and while ascending into heaven, where He continues to offer it. At Mass he does not offer His sacrifice AGAIN, but is made present on the altar as He is in heaven, namely, still offering His one sacrifice of Calvary. The only difference in His offering on Calvary, in heaven, and at Mass is the MANNER in which he offers: on Calvary, in a bloody manner; in heaven and at Mass, in a glorious manner.

St. Paul in Heb 9:25-28 presents the doctrine this way: "He (Christ) does not have to offer himself again and again, like the high priest going into the sanctuary year after year with the blood that is not his own .... Instead of that, he has made his appearance once and for all, now at the end of the last age, to do away with sin by sacrificing himself. Since men only die once ... so Christ, too, offers himself only once." Since Christ offered His sacrifice "at the end of the last age," that is, in the last stage of salvation history, it need not be repeated, since it has the power to wipe out the sins of all men, because He offered in sacrifice His own divine blood, not that of animals.

When we say that Christ "continues" to offer His sacrifice, we do not understand that he continues to repeat the words of the Last Supper ("My body is given for you; my blood is poured out for you"). With those words he offered Himself ACTIVELY and thus put Himself in the permanent state of a Victim. He remains the glorious Victim PASSIVELY offering Himself in heaven and at Mass. (Similarly, at a wedding the bride and groom ACTIVELY put themselves in the permanent state of matrimony, in which they remain without repeating their vows.)

In items 1368 through 1372 the Catechism reminds us that, besides being the sacrifice of Christ, the Eucharist is also the sacrifice of the Church, the whole Church. We, the Church Militant, unite ourselves, our lives, work, suffering, and our prayer with Christ's offering, and thus they acquire a new value. We offer the Mass in union with the Church Triumphant in heaven, as well as for the Church Suffering in Purgatory. Thus, in the sacrifice of the Mass we not only join Christ offering His sacrifice of Calvary, but also offer to God the entire Church, all the redeemed, together with all His visible and invisible creation.

THE PRESENCE OF CHRIST BY THE POWER OF HIS WORD AND THE HOLY SPIRIT

1373. Rom 8:34: "Christ Jesus, who died, yes, who was raised from the dead, who is at the right hand of God, who indeed intercedes for us," "is present in many ways to his Church: in his word, in his Church's prayer, 'where two or three are gathered in my name' (Mt 18:20), in the poor, the sick, and the imprisoned (Mt 25:31-46), in the sacraments of which he is the author, in the sacrifice of the Mass, and in the person of the minister. But 'he is present....most ESPECIALLY IN THE EUCHARISTIC SPECIES.' "(Vat. C. II, SC 7)

1374. "The mode of Christ's presence under the Eucharistic species is unique. It raises the Eucharist above all the sacraments as 'the perfection of the spiritual life and the end to which all the sacraments tend.' (St. Thom. Aq. STh III,73,c.) In the most blessed sacrament of the Eucharist 'the body and blood, together with the soul and divinity, of our Lord Jesus Christ and, therefore, 'THE WHOLE CHRIST IS TRULY, REALLY, AND SUBSTANTIALLY CONTAINED.' (TRENT; D.S.1651) This presence is called 'real' - by which is not intended to exclude the other types of presence as if they could not be 'real' too, but because it is presence in the fullest sense: that is to say, it is a SUBSTANTIAL presence by which Christ, God and man, makes himself wholly and entirely present.' " (Paul VI, MF 39)

1375. "It is by the conversion [change] of the bread and wine into Christ's body and blood that Christ becomes present in this sacrament. The Church Fathers [as we have seen at some length] strongly affirmed the faith of the Church in the efficacy of the Word of Christ and the action of the Holy Spirit to bring about this conversion. Thus St. John Chrysostom declares: 'It is not man that causes the things offered to become the Body and Blood of Christ, but he who was crucified for us, Christ himself. The priest, in the role of Christ, pronounces these words, but their power and grace are God's. This is my body, he says. This word transforms the things offered.'

And St. Ambrose says about this conversion: 'Be convinced that this is not what nature has formed, but what the blessing has consecrated. The power of the blessing prevails over that of nature, because by the blessing nature itself is changed....Could not Christ's word, which can make from nothing what did not exist, change existing things into what they were not before? It is no less a feat to give things their original, nature than to change their nature.'"

1376 "The Council of Trent summarizes the Catholic faith by declaring: 'Because Christ our Redeemer said it was truly his body that he was offering under the species of bread, it has always been the conviction of the Church of God, and this holy Council now declares it again, that by the consecration of the bread and wine there takes place a change in the whole substance of the bread into the substance of the body of Christ our Lord and of the whole substance of the wine into the substance of his blood. This change the holy Catholic Church has fittingly and properly called transubstantiation." (D.S. 1642)

1377 "The Eucharistic presence of Christ begins at the moment of the consecration and endures as long as the Eucharistic species subsist. Christ is present whole and entire in each of the species and whole and entire in each of their parts, in such a way that the breaking of the bread does not divide Christ." (D.S. 1641) Since Christ is present in the manner that a substance is present, He is present whole and entire in each of their parts prior to any separation as well as after.

WORSHIP OF THE EUCHARIST

1378. 'In the liturgy of the Mass we express our faith in the real presence of Christ under the species of bread and wine by, among other ways, genuflecting or bowing deeply as a sign of adoration of the Lord. 'The Catholic Church has always offered and still offers to the sacrament of the Eucharist the cult of adoration, not only during Mass, but also outside of it, reserving the consecrated Hosts with the utmost care, exposing them to the solemn veneration of the faithful, and carrying them in procession.' " (Paul VI, MF 56)

1379. "The tabernacle was first intended for the reservation of the Eucharist in a worthy place, so that it could be brought to the sick and those absent, outside of Mass. As faith in the real presence of Christ in his Eucharist deepened, the Church became conscious of the meaning of silent adoration of the Lord present under the Eucharistic species. It is for this reason that the tabernacle should be located in an especially worthy place in the church, and should be constructed in such a way that it emphasizes and manifests the truth of the real presence of Christ in the Blessed Sacrament."

1380. "It is highly fitting that Christ should have wanted to remain present to the Church in this unique way. Since Christ was about to take his departure from his own in his visible form, he wanted to give us his sacramental presence; since he was about to offer himself on the cross to save us, he wanted us to have the memorial of the love with which he loved us 'to the end,' even to the giving of his life. In his Eucharistic presence he remains mysteriously in our midst as the one who loved us and gave himself up for us; and he remains under signs that express and communicate this love: 'The Church and the world have a great need for Eucharistic worship. Jesus awaits us in this sacrament of love. Let us not refuse the time to go to meet him in adoration, in contemplation full of faith and open to making amends for the serious offenses and crimes of the world. Let our adoration never cease.' "(John Paul II, Dominicae Cenae 3)

1381. "That in this sacrament are the true Body of Christ and his true Blood is something that 'cannot be apprehended by the senses,' says St. Thomas (STh III,75,1), 'but only by faith, which relies on divine authority.' For this reason, in a commentary on Luke 22:19 ('This is my body which is given for you.'), St. Cyril says: 'Do not doubt whether this is true, but rather receive the words of the Savior in faith, for since he is the truth, he cannot lie' "(cf. Paul VI,MF18).

† † †

> *Godhead here in hiding, whom I do adore*
> *Masked by these bare shadows, shape and nothing more,*
> *See, Lord, at thy service low lies here a heart*
> *Lost, all lost in wonder at the God thou art.*
>
> *Seeing, touching, tasting are in thee deceived;*
> *How says trusty hearing? that shall be believed;*
> *What God's Son has told me, take for truth I do;*
> *Truth himself speaks truly or there's nothing true.*
> *From: Adoro Te, by St. T. Aquinas;*
> *Tr. Gerard Manley Hopkins*

THE PASCHAL BANQUET

1382. "The Mass is at the same time, and inseparably, the sacrificial memorial in which the sacrifice of the cross is perpetuated, and the sacred banquet of communion with the Lord's body and blood. But the celebration of the Eucharistic sacrifice is wholly directed toward the intimate union of the faithful with Christ through communion. To receive communion is to receive Christ himself who has offered himself for us."

1383. "The altar, around which the Church is gathered in the celebration of the Eucharist, represents the two aspects of the same mystery: the altar of the sacrifice, and the table of the Lord. This is all the more so since the Christian altar is the symbol of Christ, as the victim offered for our reconciliation, and as food from heaven who is giving himself to us....The liturgy expresses this unity of sacrifice and communion in many prayers." [E.g. Euch. Prayer 1, after Consecration]

"TAKE THIS AND EAT IT, ALL OF YOU": HOLY COMMUNION

1384. "The Lord addresses an invitation to us, urging us to receive him in the sacrament of the Eucharist: 'Truly, I say to you, unless you eat the flesh of the Son of man and drink his blood, you have no life in you.' "

1385. "To respond to this invitation we must PREPARE OURSELVES for so great and so holy a moment. St. Paul urges us to examine our conscience: 'Whoever, therefore, eats the bread or drinks the cup of the Lord in an unworthy manner will be guilty of profaning the body and blood of the Lord. Let a man examine himself, and so eat of the bread and drink of the cup. For anyone who eats and drinks without discerning the body eats and drinks judgment upon himself.' (1 Cor 11:27-29) Anyone conscious of a grave sin must receive the sacrament of Reconciliation before coming to Communion."

1386. "Before so great a sacrament, the faithful can only echo humbly and with ardent faith the words of the Centurion: 'Lord, I am not worthy that you should enter under my roof, but only say the word and my soul will be healed.' And in the Divine Liturgy of St. John Chrysostom the faithful pray in the same spirit: 'O Son of God, bring me into communion today with your mystical supper. I shall not tell your enemies the secret [of your presence in the Host], nor kiss you with Judas' kiss. But like the good thief I cry, "Jesus, remember me when you come into your kingdom."

1387. "To prepare for worthy reception of this sacrament, the faithful should observe the fast required in their Church." Canon Law, n. 919, states: "One who is to receive the Most Holy Eucharist is to abstain from any food or drink, with the exception only of water and medicine, for at least the period of one hour before Holy Communion....Those who are advanced in age or who suffer from any infirmity, as well as those who take care of them, can receive the Most Holy Eucharist even if they have taken something during the previous hour."

"Bodily demeanor (gestures, clothing) ought to convey the respect, solemnity, and joy of this moment when Christ becomes our guest."

1388. "It is in keeping with the very meaning of the Eucharist that the faithful, if they have the required dispositions [not conscious of mortal sin, the proper fast, and a good intention], receive communion each time they participate in the Mass." Canon 917 states: "A person who has received the Most Holy Eucharist may receive it again on the same day only during the celebration of the Eucharist in which the person participates." The Canon makes an exception for those in danger of death: "Even if they have received Communion on the same day, those who are in danger of death are strongly urged to receive again."

"As the Second Vatican Council says: 'That more perfect form of participation in the Mass whereby the faithful, after the priest's communion, receive the Lord's Body from the same sacrifice, is warmly recommended.' " (SC 55)

1389. "The Church obliges the faithful 'to take part in the Divine Liturgy on Sundays and feast days' and, prepared by the sacrament of Reconciliation, to receive the Eucharist at least once a year, if possible during the Easter season. (Canon 920) But the Church strongly encourages the faithful to receive the Holy Eucharist on Sundays and feast days, or more often still, even daily."

1390. Since Christ is sacramentally present under each of the species, communion under the species of bread only makes it possible to receive all the fruit of Eucharistic grace. For pastoral reasons this manner of receiving communion has been legitimately established as the most common form in the Latin rite. But 'the sign of communion is more complete when given under both kinds, since in that form the sign of the Eucharistic meal appears more clearly.' (General Instruction of Roman Missal 240) This is the usual form of receiving communion in the Eastern rites."

† † †

O loving Lord Jesus Christ, with fear and trembling I approach the table of your most sweet banquet. I, a sinner, have no merits of my own to presume upon, but I trust in Your mercy and goodness.
[From a payer of St. Ambrose before Communion]

THE FRUITS OF HOLY COMMUNION

1391. "Holy Communion augments our union with Christ. The principal fruit of receiving the Eucharist in Holy Communion is an intimate union with Christ Jesus. Indeed, the Lord said: 'He who eats my flesh and drinks my blood abides in me, and I in him.' Life in Christ has its foundation in the Eucharistic banquet: 'As the living Father sent me, and I live because of the Father, so he who eats me will live because of me.' " (Jn 6:56-57)

"On the feasts of the Lord, when the faithful receive the Body of the Son, they proclaim to one another the Good News that the first fruits of life have been given, as when the angel said to Mary Magdalene, 'Christ is risen!' Now too are life and resurrection conferred on whoever receives Christ." (Fanqith, Syriac Office of Antioch) This is a reference to our

Lord's words in Jn 6:54: "Anyone who does eat my flesh and drink my blood has eternal life, and I shall raise him up on the last day."

1392. "What material food produces in our bodily life, Holy Communion wonderfully achieves in our spiritual life. Communion with the flesh of the risen Christ, a flesh 'given life and giving life through the Holy Spirit,' preserves, increases, and renews the life of grace received at Baptism. This growth in Christian life needs the nourishment of Eucharistic Communion, the bread for our pilgrimage until the moment of death, when it will be given to us as viaticum [food for the journey to heaven]."

1393. "Holy Communion separates us from sin. The body of Christ we receive in Holy Communion is 'given up for us', and the blood we drink 'shed for the many for the forgiveness of sins.' For this reason the Eucharist cannot unite us to Christ without at the same time cleansing us from past sins and preserving us from future sins: 'For as often as we eat this bread and drink the cup, we proclaim the death of the Lord. If we proclaim the Lord's death, we proclaim the forgiveness of sins. If, as often as his blood is poured out, it is poured for the forgiveness of sins, I should always receive it, so that it may always forgive my sins. Because I always sin, I should always have a remedy.' " (St. Ambrose)

When it states in item **1393** that one of the fruits of Holy Communion is that it cleanses us from past sins, obviously the reference is to venial sins, since anyone conscious of mortal sin must first receive the sacrament of Confession. And when it states that Communion preserves us from future sins, it must aid us in overcoming the evil effects of past sins, mortal and venial, such as the weakening of our will. Moreover, it is the common opinion among orthodox theologians, that if one is unwittingly in mortal sin but has attrition (sufficient sorrow for sin to receive absolution in Confession), that person receives forgiveness of mortal sin by receiving Holy Communion. If after making a good Confession, one remembers a mortal sin he forgot to confess, he may continue to receive Communion but must mention the forgotten mortal sin in his next sacramental Confession.

1394. "As bodily nourishment restores lost strength, so the Eucharist strengthens our charity, which tends to be weakened in daily life [through venial sin or moral imperfections due to a lack of moral generosity]; and this living charity wipes away venial sins. [Trent, DS 1638] By giving himself to us Christ revives our love and enables us to break our disordered attachments to creatures and root ourselves in him."

1395. "By the same charity that it enkindles in us, the Eucharist preserves us from future mortal sins. The more we share the life of Christ and progress in his friendship, the more difficult it is to break away from him by mortal sin. The Eucharist is not ordered to the forgiveness of mortal sins — that is proper to the sacrament of Reconciliation. The Eucharist is properly the sacrament of those who are in full communion with the Church.

† † †

St. Ambrose's prayer before Communion:
My heart and body are stained with many sins;
nor have I guarded well my mind and tongue.
Therefore, O loving God, O tremendous majesty,
wretched and surrounded with difficulties I return to you, the
fountain of mercy; I hasten to you to be cured;
I take refuge under your protection. You, whom I cannot face as my
Judge, I long to have as my Savior.

1396. "The unity of the Mystical Body: the Eucharist makes the Church. Those who receive the Eucharist are united more closely to Christ. Through it Christ unites them to all the faithful in one body-the Church. Communion renews, strengthens, and deepens this incorporation into the Church, already achieved by Baptism. In Baptism we have been called to form but one body [members of the Church, the mystical body of Christ]. The Eucharist fulfills this call: 'The cup of blessing which we bless, is it not a participation in the blood of Christ? The bread which we break, is it not a participation in the body of Christ? Because there is one bread, we who are many are one body, for we all partake of the one bread.' "(1 Cor 10:16-17)

1397. "The Eucharist commits us to the poor. To receive in truth the body and blood of Christ given up for us, we must recognize Christ in the poorest, his brethren." St. John Chrysostom says: "You have tasted the Blood of the Lord, yet you do not recognize your brother....You dishonor this table when you do not judge worthy of sharing your food someone judged worthy to take part in this meal....God freed you from all of your sins and invited you here, but you have not become more merciful."

1398. "The Eucharist and the unity of Christians. Before the greatness of this mystery St. Augustine exclaims, 'O sacrament of devotion! O sign of unity! O Bond of charity!' The more painful the experience of the divisions in the Church which break the common participation in the table of the Lord, the more urgent are our prayers to the Lord that the time of complete unity among all who believe in him may return."

Because the Eastern Orthodox Churches, by apostolic succession, have valid sacraments, Catholic ministers may administer to them the sacraments of Penance, Eucharist, and Anointing of the sick, if they ask for them on their own and are properly disposed. Since Protestant Churches lack a valid Eucharist and Holy Orders, their members may not receive the three mentioned sacraments except: in grave necessity, with the Bishop's approval, they cannot approach their own minister, ask for them on their own, manifest proper faith in them, and be properly disposed.

THE EUCHARIST — "PLEDGE OF THE GLORY TO COME"

1402. "In an ancient prayer the Church acclaims the mystery of the Eucharist: 'O sacred banquet in which Christ is received as food, the memory of his Passion is renewed, the soul is filled with grace and a pledge of the life to come is given to us.' If the Eucharist is the memorial of the Passover of the Lord Jesus, if by our communion at the altar we are filled 'with every heavenly blessing and grace', then the Eucharist is also an anticipation of the heavenly glory."

1403. "At the Last Supper the Lord himself directed his disciples' attention toward the fulfillment of the Passover in the kingdom of God: 'I tell you I shall not drink again of this fruit of the vine, until that day when I drink it new with you in my Father's kingdom.' (Mt 26:29) Whenever the Church celebrates the Eucharist she remembers this promise and turns her gaze 'to him who is to come.' In her prayer she calls for his coming: 'Marana tha!' 'Come, Lord Jesus!' (Rev 1:4; 22:20; 1Cor 16:22) 'May your grace come and this world pass away!' " (Didache 10,6)

1404. "The Church knows that the Lord comes even now in his Eucharist and that he is there in our midst. However, his presence is veiled. Therefore we celebrate the Eucharist 'awaiting the blessed hope and the coming of our Savior, Jesus Christ,' asking 'to share in your glory when every tear will be wiped away. On that day we shall see you, our God, as you are. We shall become like you and praise you for ever through Christ our Lord.' " (Eucharistic Prayer III)

1405. "There is no surer pledge or clearer sign of this great hope in the new heavens and new earth than the Eucharist. Every time this mystery is celebrated, 'the work of our redemption is carried on' and we 'break the one bread that provides the medicine of immortality, the antidote for death, and the food that makes us live for ever in Jesus Christ,' as St. Ignatius of Antioch says."

After presenting the Church's doctrine on the Eucharist, the Catechism of the Catholic Church, offers a brief summary of that doctrine in 14 items, each of which contains enough material for a meditation. We close our text by reprinting the items with their corresponding numbers.

1406. Jesus said: "I am the living bread that came down from heaven; if anyone eats of this bread, he will live for ever;...he who eats my flesh and drinks my blood has eternal life and...abides in me, and I in him." (Jn 6:51,54,56)

1407. The Eucharist is the heart and the summit of the Church's life, for in it Christ associates his Church and all her members with his sacrifice of praise and thanksgiving offered once for all on the cross to his Father; by this sacrifice he pours out the graces of salvation on his Body which is the Church.

1408. The Eucharistic celebration always includes: the proclamation of the Word of God; thanksgiving to God the Father for all his benefits, above all the gift of his Son; the consecration of bread and wine; and participation in the liturgical banquet by receiving the Lord's body and blood. These elements constitute one single act of worship.

1409. The Eucharist is the memorial of Christ's Passover, that is, of the work of salvation accomplished by the life, death, and resurrection of Christ, a work made present by the liturgical action.

1410. It is Christ himself, the eternal high priest of the New Covenant who, acting through the ministry of the priests, offers the Eucharistic sacrifice. And it is the same Christ, really present under the species of bread and wine, who is the offering of the Eucharistic sacrifice.

1411. Only validly ordained priests can preside at the Eucharist and consecrate the bread and wine so that they become the Body and Blood of the Lord.

1412. The essential signs of the Eucharistic sacrament are wheat bread and grape wine, on which the blessing of the Holy Spirit is invoked and the priest pronounces the words of consecration spoken by Jesus during the Last Supper: "This is my body which will be given up for you....This is the cup of my blood...."

1413. By the consecration the transubstantiation of the bread and wine into the Body and Blood of Christ is brought about. Under the consecrated species of bread and wine Christ himself, living and glorious, is present in a true, real, and substantial manner: his Body and his Blood, with his soul and his divinity (C. of Trent DS 1640; 1651).

1414. As sacrifice, the Eucharist is also offered in reparation for the sins of the living and the dead and to obtain spiritual or temporal benefits from God.

1415. Anyone who desires to receive Christ in Eucharistic communion must be in the state of grace. Anyone aware of having sinned mortally must not receive communion without having received absolution in the sacrament of penance.

1416. Communion with the Body and Blood of Christ increases the communicant's union with the Lord, forgives his venial sins, and preserves him from grave sins. Since receiving the sacrament strengthens the bonds of charity between the communicant and Christ, it also reinforces the unity of the Church as the Mystical Body of Christ.

1417. The Church warmly recommends that the faithful receive Holy Communion each time they participate in the celebration of the Eucharist; she obliges them to do so at last once a year.

1418. Because Christ himself is present in the sacrament of the altar, he is to be honored with the worship of adoration. "To visit the Blessed Sacrament is....a proof of gratitude, an expression of love, and a duty of adoration toward Christ our Lord" (Paul VI,MF 66).

1419. Having passed from this world to the Father, Christ gives us in the Eucharist the pledge of glory with him. Participation in the Holy Sacrifice identifies us with his Heart, sustains our strength along the pilgrimage of this life, makes us long for eternal life, and unites us even now to the Church in heaven, the Blessed Virgin Mary, and all the saints.

✝ ✝ ✝

PRAYER OF ST. AMBROSE BEFORE COMMUNION

I show you my wounds, O Lord;
before you I lay bare my shame.
I know my sins are many and great;
and I fear for them.
But I hope in your mercies,
which are innumerable.
Therefore, look on me with the eyes of your mercy,
Lord Jesus Christ, eternal King, God and Man,
who were crucified for me.
Hear me, who hope in You; have pity on me,
who am full of wretchedness and sin,
You who never stop the fountain of mercy from flowing.

Hail, saving Victim, Who was offered
on the gibbet of the cross for me and for all mankind,
when You washed away the sins of the whole world.
O Lord, be mindful of Your creature,
whom You redeemed with Your blood.
I am sorry for having sinned;
I wish to amend what I have done.
Therefore, most merciful Father,
take away all my sin and wickedness,
so that, purified in soul and body,
I may merit to partake worthily of the Holy of Holies.
Lord, grant that this offering of Your body and blood,
which, although unworthy, I intend to receive,
may be for the remission of my sins,
the perfect cleansing of my faults,
the banishing of bad thoughts,
the rebirth of good intentions,
the salutary performance of works pleasing to you,
and the firmest defense of body and soul
against the snares of my enemies. Amen.

✝ ✝ ✝

We close our meditations with the ejaculation:
Jesus in the Blessed Sacrament,
I believe in You, I hope in You, I love You.

[Translation by Roy J. Deferrari in The Sources of Catholic Dogma by B. Herder Book Co.; abbreviated subsequently as "Sources"]

[Quotes taken from VATICAN C. II, The Conciliar and PostC. Documents by Austin Flannery, O.P. Editor]

{Quotations from NCWC News Service; St. Paul Editions]